IRISH ANTIQUITY

CELTIC STUDIES

General Editor: Professor Alfred P. Smyth, University of Kent

Aubrey Gwynn, *The Irish Church in the 11th and 12th Centuries,*
edited by Gerard O'Brien

Louis Gougaud, *Christianity in Celtic Lands*

John Ryan, *Irish Monasticism*

James F. Kenney, *The Sources for the Early History of Ireland: Ecclesiastical*

Edmund Hogan, *Onomasticon Goedelicum*

Kenneth Jackson, *Language and History in Early Britain*

D.R. Howlett, *Liber Epistolarum Sancti Patricii Episcopi: The Book of Letters of
Saint Patrick the Bishop*

Donnchadh Ó Corráin, *Irish Antiquity*

FORTHCOMING

D.R. Howlett, *The Celtic Latin Tradition of Biblical Style*

IRISH ANTIQUITY

*Essays and Studies Presented to
Professor M.J. O'Kelly*

edited by

DONNCHADH Ó CORRÁIN

FOUR COURTS PRESS

This book is published by
FOUR COURTS PRESS
Kill Lane, Blackrock, County Dublin, Ireland

and in North America by
Four Courts Press
c/o International Specialized Book Services
5804 NE Hassalo Street, Portland, OR 97213

First published by Tower Books 1981
Reprinted 1994

A catalogue record for this book is
available from the British Library.

ISBN 1-85182-145-7 hbk
1-85182-174-0 pbk

Printed in Ireland by
Betaprint Ltd, Dublin

Foreword

The essays collected in this volume form a well deserved tribute to a scholar who, for a generation, has been a leader in archaeological studies in this country and a bold pioneer in many aspects of his discipline. It is a matter of pride and rejoicing for his friends and colleagues on the staff of University College, Cork, and outside, that his scholarly achievements should be signalized after so appropriate a fashion. The list of contributors alone is proof of the esteem in which he is held at home and abroad and of the honour he has brought to the College which he has so loyally and effectively served as a teacher and inspirer of research.

I have known Michael Joseph O'Kelly — who, for some reason unknown to me, is normally called Brian! — since we were fellow-students at University College, Cork, before World War Two; indeed, we have been colleagues on the staff of the College since his appointment as Professor of Archaeology in 1946. The volume and the variety of his achievements in archaeological studies and research during the past decades are ample proof of his skill and industry in fieldwork, of his unbounded enthusiasm, of his imaginative interpretative ability. He has built up a tremendous corpus of archaeological knowledge, and an outstanding reputation as a scholar of both national and international level.

But he has not neglected his teaching role as Professor of Archaeology in his alma mater. Here, the infectiousness of his enthusiasm and his well-recognised ability as a teacher have resulted in a phenomenal increase over the years in the size and activities of his Department at both undergraduate and postgraduate level. This, in itself, is an enormous tribute to his total dedication to his subject.

It is, therefore, with the greatest pleasure that I add my congratulations to Professor O'Kelly to those of his colleagues in this volume.

Tadhg Ó Ciardha
President
3 March 1981

Editorial Note

In 1978 an informal committee of friends and former students of Professor O'Kelly came together to plan a *Festschrift* in his honour to be published on the occasion of his sixty-fifth birthday. Invitations to contribute were sent out to archaeologists and other scholars and preliminary plans for the volume were drawn up. In March 1979 I was invited to act as editor — an invitation which I viewed with some alarm not least because I felt that as a mere medieval historian I was more than usually ill-equipped for the task. However, the views of the Committee eventually prevailed and if there are mistakes — and mistakes there must be — I can only plead in my defence the Old Irish saw *oscar cach i ceird araili*. Contributions came in slowly and so much yet remained to be done in the matter of planning and preparation that another year was required to see the work through the press. We can only hope that the wine is a little more mature for the delay.

In general we have followed the style of *Proceedings of the Prehistoric Society* and abbreviations and short titles, which should be self-explanatory, are generally in accord with BS 4148:1970 (= ASA Z.39-5.1963). There are minor inconsistencies from time to time but none, we hope, which will upset the reader.

In these days of inflation and rising costs the publication of academic books is very expensive and it was decided to open a public subscription to defray the costs, at least in part. As the *tabula gratulatoria* shows, the response of the public, individually and institutionally, at home and abroad, was magnificent. The Cork Historical and Archaeological Society (with which Professor O'Kelly has long been associated) made a substantial grant-in-aid and the Senate of the National University offered a generous subvention. To both we are profoundly grateful. We thank Ms Helen Moloney Davis, Ms Breda Long, Ms Catherine Power and Mr Frank Davis for editorial and bibliographical help; Mr Aidan Macdonald and Mr M.A. Monk who acted as advisers and most effective treasurers of the publication fund; Ms Veronica Fraser and Ms Charlotte Wiseman for patient and accurate typing and generous secretarial help; Ms Maura Collins and the typing pool, University College, Cork, who came to our aid in the hour of need; and the Librarian and his staff, University College, Cork, for essential facilities. Lastly, we wish to thank our printer and publisher, Mr Seán Daly of Tower Books of Cork, who bore patiently with all our troubles.

Donnchadh Ó Corráin

Contents

GENERAL ARCHAEOLOGY

ANCILLARY DISCIPLINES

PLATES
(Following page 352)

Introduction

E. Estyn Evans

The appearance of this volume of essays, offered to Professor Michael (Brian)[1] on his 66th birthday, happily coincides with the completion of his definitive report on Newgrange. *Si monumentum requiris, circumspice*. Professor O'Kelly will long be remembered as the excavator of Newgrange, which occupied him and his helpers for some fourteen years. To this mammoth task he brought not only his unique experience of excavation on a great variety of sites but also the personal qualities of one who pursues truth to the end and has always had the courage of his convictions. This independence of mind can perhaps partly be attributed to his Cork background: he has shown no inclination to accept blindly the orthodoxy of Dublin but has gone on his own nonconforming way. He has even dared to question the sacred tenet that Neolithic culture and the practice of agriculture were first brought to Ireland by megalith-building colonists from France, and by implication to cast doubt on the reality of that massive (prehistoric) French landing on the shores of Killala Bay.

I have long felt that Munster has an affinity with Ulster, Ireland's other peninsular end, in its attitude towards metropolitan Leinster, and indeed Brian has always taken a lively sympathetic fraternal interst in what was happening in Ulster, not least in archaeology.

But it would be quite wrong to think of Brian as a fanatical megalith-man: what strikes one about his published work is that it covers almost every period and aspect of Irish archaeology. His innate curiosity has never been satisfied with orthodox views or explanations: again and again he has put forward his own theories and submitted them to experimental test. His enterprise has been well illustrated and rewarded in his successful efforts to reconstruct ancient methods of smelting iron and in experiments conducted to investigate, and to put to the test gastronomically, the methods of operating the ancient Irish cooking-places (*fulachta fiadha*). When he has a problem to solve, whether in excavating or in the interpretation of an artifact, he displays the tenacity of an Irish terrier in sticking to it and pursuing it with relentless logic to the end of the trail.

His academic training was somewhat unorthodox. Born in Limerick, he obtained his secondary education at Rockwell College, Tipperary, before entering University College, Cork, as a student of engineering in 1934. After his first year, however, he

---

[1] It was intended, I have been told, that his Christian names should be Michael Joseph Brian, but Brian was accidentally omitted from the register. However, as they say in Belfast, 'Brian is all he ever gets'.

decided to train as an architect and became an articled pupil in the Cork office of
Henry Hill. His training in surveying and architectural drawing was to prove a great
advantage when he entered the Department of Archaeology in 1937. Moreover, his
subsidiary subjects for the Arts degree, while they included Irish, were appropriately environmental rather than literary. The combination of courses in geology,
geography and archaeology, together with his previous experience, admirably
equipped him for his life's work and gave him a unique place among Irish
archaeologists of his generation.

I first met him when I was external examiner in archaeology to the National
University from 1938 to 1941. Brian was awarded first class honours in his B.A.
degree in 1940. Professor Seán Ó Ríordáin was then engaged in his comprehensive
investigations of the storied sites around Lough Gur, and I paid successive visits to
the area in those years, when Brian was Seán's chief assistant. For many years
thereafter I kept in tough by visiting him on site at several of his excavations
elsewhere. I recall also that when I published my *Irish Heritage* in 1941 he promptly sent me sketches and photographs of several types of artifacts such as lobster pots
which he had observed in southwest Ireland. We have kept up a correspondence
over the years and I have never failed to receive courteous and illuminating replies
to any of my troublesome enquiries. I remember with gratitude the assistance he
gave the Northern Historic Monuments Branch in securing for publication, after
long delays, the text of Dr Van Giffen's report on the excavation of Ballynoe Stone
Circle in Co. Down.

The training of archaeologists in the National University at that time was essentially in Arts subjects and the emphasis was on the artifacts of Gaelic culture,
Christian and pre-Christian, so that field observers, surveyors and excavators were
in short supply. While Brian's interests embraced the traditional fields of Irish
archaeology, what set him apart was his primary training in science and his zeal for
testing hypotheses by experiment. It was a fortunate chance that he was available
when Seán Ó Ríordáin was looking for a surveyor when he was engaged on the excavation of the ring-fort at Garranes, Co. Cork, in the spring of 1937. Later that
year he began work at Lough Gur and it cannot be doubted that Seán's enthusiasm
found a ready convert to archaeology. The new recruit returned to University
College Cork in October. Lough Gur was an excellent proving-ground for field
study and excavation; and here Brian, using his skill with plane-table and pencil,
not only took charge of surveying and mapping but undertook the recording of
finds and practised his powers of observation and interpretation in excavation. My
recollections of those far-off days include not only lively discussions (the company
included Mr and Mrs John Hunt, who were then living at Lough Gur) but much
impromptu singing in which harmony was restored and in which Brian's fluty
tenor was conspicuous. He made friends wherever he went and was as much at ease
with fishermen and farmers as with parish priests and visiting pre-historians. I
remember that his digs were sometimes enlivened by the welcome appearance of

bottles of Spanish wine obtained from visiting trawlers and utilized refreshingly and instructively to demonstrate the reality and continuity of the Atlantic seaways.

A problem that exercised us in those days was that of the 'prepared floors' which Oliver Davies and I believed we has discovered underlying several of the megalithic cairns we had examined, most conspicuously at Browndod in Co. Antrim. We thought we could distinguish these floors, normally grey in colour, from natural layers of pre-cairn soil. My previous excavation experience had been mainly in Wiltshire, where I had not encountered the heavy leaching which often results from the percolation of water under the climatic conditions prevailing in Ireland and which produces podzols or grey earths which lose their colourful iron and manganese bases. While there may be many variable factors of site, soil composition and age to take into account, and while I would not entirely dismiss the 'prepared floor' as a ritual or functional feature, Brian convinced me that such sub-cairn layers could usually be explained by natural processes.

In 1941 he was able to put his training to the test by completing a survey of the antiquities in the barony of Small County, Co. Limerick, which won him the degree of MA with first class honours, and the award of the University's travelling Studentship in Archaeology. In the event, because of wartime restrictions, his travelling was done not on the continent but in Ireland, where he made friends among archaeologists in all parts of the country. He began work on the souterrain in Ireland with the intention of presenting a thesis for the PhD degree and amassed a great deal of material which he has generously mined in assisting other students of this intractable problem. Characteristically he could not be satisfied with his findings until he had carried out fieldwork in France which at that time was denied him. One hopes he will return to this challenging subject.

In 1942 he joined the staff of the Topographical and Archaeological Survey conducted by the Irish Tourist Association, and became Director of the survey in the following year, at the same time being responsible for preparing a new series of tourist guides. In 1944 his experience and interest in the practical aspects of archaeology were rewarded and expanded on his appointment as curator of the new Cork Public Museum, which he rapidly promoted as a centre of education and research in close association with the Archaeology Department at University College. In the following year he undertook his first major solo excavation on two ring-forts at Garryduff, Co. Cork, and the subsequent publication did much to establish his reputation. He spent the first part of 1946 in Britain and the Isle of Man, visiting and studying in all the leading museums and establishing contacts, which frequently developed into friendship, with most of the leaders in British archaeology.

In 1946, when Professor Ó Ríordáin moved to Dublin, he could have had no better successor in the Chair than Brian, who was so admirably equipped to build on the foundations already laid. In the following year he was elected a Fellow of the Society of Antiquaries of London, and in 1948 a Member of the Royal Irish

Academy. He became one of the most active and influential members of the National Monuments Advisory Council and was its patient, courteous and forceful Chairman from 1966 to 1970.

I have given example of the wide range of his interests and activities and must add a brief reference to some other significant work: on rock-art; on the coin-dated eleventh-century 'fort' of Beal Boru; on the techniques of fashioning and decorating that quaintly-named trio of treasures — the Cork Horns, the Bann Disc and the Petrie Crown; on the Moylough Belt Shrine; on the very early ring-fort at Carrigillihy; on house-types in ring-forts; on christian sites in Co. Kerry; on wedge-cairns and a solitary but significant 'horned cairn' (Shanballyedmond). I mention only the papers most familiar to me: what matters above all is the splendid ex ample he has set all his fellow archaeologists in publishing his findings fully and fearlessly. Twenty of his published papers were presented to the National University in 1963 and won him the degree of DLitt.

In all his work, whether at home or, whenever possible, in the field, he has been supported by the devotion and wisdom of his wife Claire, who was a fellow student of archaeology at Cork, who became his life partner in 1945, and whose name will be linked with his whenever Newgrange comes under discussion. Long may he continue to cast his cool but kindly Cork eye on problems of the Irish past.

TECHNIQUES
and
METHOD

Dendrochronology: the prospects for dating throughout Ireland

M.G.L. Baillie

INTRODUCTION

A fundamental question with regard to the dendrochronological dating of oak timbers in Ireland, must relate to the area of applicability of the Belfast oak chronology. Work has been in progress over the last decade on the construction of a 6,000 to 8,000 year tree-ring sequence, potentially one of the three longest in the world, drawing on material from an area approximately 50 km in radius centred on Lough Neagh. This work has been highly successful due to the availability of oak timbers from a large number of sources and from most ages. At the time of writing the chronology running back from the present to A.D. 1 is essentially complete while in the B.C. era chronologies cover the approximate periods 200 to 900 B.C., 1,000 to 4,000 B.C. and 4,000 to 5500 B.C. (Pilcher *et al*, 1977). Problems with the completion of this work will be alluded to below but are not the primary concern of this paper.

With an almost complete Belfast chronology available, what are the chances of being able to date oak timbers from say Athlone, Cork or Wexford? The simple answer is that it is impossible to predict. Dendrochronology is a highly empirical technique: all that the dendrochronologist can do is sample such timbers and attempt to date them against the Belfast, or other available chronologies. In practice the samples will either date clearly and easily or they will not. If they do not cross date this may be due to one of several factors. First and most important there may be sufficient 'climatic' (it is assumed that common climatic signal is responsible for cross matching between ring patterns) difference that trees from certain areas in the south and west of Ireland will exhibit little or no cross dating with the northern chronology. However, the possibility will also exist that any individual ring-pattern may not cross date because it is in some way aberrant, unusual, or distorted.

Until 1978 virtually the only Irish tree-ring work outside the north of Ireland had taken place using timbers from the extensive Dublin excavations (Baillie, 1973; 1977a). It was known that the Dublin master chronologies for the periods A.D. 855 to 1306 and 1357 to 1556 cross dated with Belfast and also with chronologies for Scotland and England (Baillie, 1978a). However, the Dublin and Belfast chronologies were far from identical and individual timbers from the excavations which dated clearly against the Dublin chronology frequently showed little or no agreement with that for Belfast (Baillie, 1978b).

This latter observation is an important one. A site chronology i.e. a master tree-ring chronology containing the information from a large number of trees, is a better reflection of the overall common signal to which the trees are responding than any individual ring-pattern. Therefore there is a greater likelihood of finding cross-agreement between master chronologies from two areas than between two individual ring-patterns from those areas. This is reasonable since the masters tend to iron out the 'noise' and enhance the common the matching-signal.

Where does this leave us with regard to the likelihood of successfully dating timbers from diverse parts of Ireland? Since 1978 two new lines of research have resulted in a better understanding of the relationship between ring-patterns from the northern and southern halves of Ireland. Both involved the comparison of ring-patterns and chronologies of similar age but from different areas. The motivation behind these studies was quite diverse, namely dendroclimatology and Dark Age dendrochronology. The former, which involved the construction of a number of modern oak chronologies, had its roots in the study of past climate. The latter which aimed at the exploitation of Early Christian timbers was founded on the failure of collecting, in the north of Ireland, to produce timbers which spanned the ninth century. Some of the lessons of this work and the results which have come from it are detailed below.

MODERN CHRONOLOGIES

There is a growing need and desire to know more about past climate. This is not simply academic but is part of a growing international recognition that climate can change and an awareness of how dependent the modern world is on the continuation of a relatively stable climatic regime. Thinking, until recently, reflected the attitude that year to year variations in weather were superimposed on an essentially constant and benign climatic regime. The growing awareness of the extremes which have taken place in the distant and in the recent past has produced a demand for some quantification of these past extremes. Equally important must be the fact that as man tampers with the natural balance of such substances as carbon dioxide and ozone, it is essential to know, as a control, what conditions were like before he started in order to separate his effects from those solely due to nature. Historical records are important in this respect but until recent times they were seldom written with climatology in mind. More obviously, observations from the days before instrumentation are without quantification: one might ask what does a good summer or a bad winter mean in real terms?

In the absence of good historical records on climate and in an effort to check those which do exist, there is an increasing move towards the exploitation of proxy data. In particular, there is currently a strong interest in tree-rings as records of past climate due to the tight temporal control which dendrochronology makes possible, the ability to study growth increments for specific years. In essence the science of dendrochronology has as one of its basic premises the implication that tree-rings record climate: 'two trees of a single species growing under the same conditions over the same period of years will exhibit recognisably similar patterns of wide and narrow rings'. The fact that dendrochronology works as a dating method suggests that this premise must be correct.

However, and this is where some workers have tended to go wrong in the past, the climatic signal which temperate trees record in their ring-widths is not a simple one. Wide rings do not necessarily occur in wet years nor are narrow rings associated with droughts. There is no direct correlation between ring-widths and rainfall or temperature and it is not possible to 'read' tree-rings in a simplistic manner. The fact that the recorded information is complex means that it will be some considerable time before realistic reconstructions of past climate become available from dendroclimatology but the first steps have to be taken. It was as part of an initial collection of Irish tree-ring data for dendroclimatology that modern oak chronologies were constructed for a spread of areas within Ireland.

Fig. 1 shows the seven sites for which chronologies have been constructed along with the area from which samples were collected during the establishment of the generalised Belfast chronology. Each of the new chronologies contains the averaged information from at least ten trees. For the purpose of comparison a common period, 1850 to 1969, was used. Each of the chronologies was compared with the published Belfast chronology (Baillie, 1977b) and the resultant *t* values are listed in Table 1. These values are a statistical measure of the degree of correlation between ring patterns and are calculated using a standard program CROS (Baillie and Pilcher, 1973).

TABLE 1

COMPARISON OF SITE CHRONOLOGIES WITH THE BELFAST CHRONOLOGY
FOR THE COMMON PERIOD 1850 TO 1969

SITE	COUNTY	t VALUE	SIGNIFICANT LEVEL
Ardara	Donegal	10.3	Extremely significant
Rostrevor	Down	6.0	Extremely significant
Glen of the Downs	Wicklow	2.9	Just significant
Enniscorthy	Wexford	4.8	Highly significant
Cappoquin	Waterford	2.9	Just significant
Killarney	Kerry	4.6	Highly significant
Lough Doon	Clare	7.4	Extremely significant

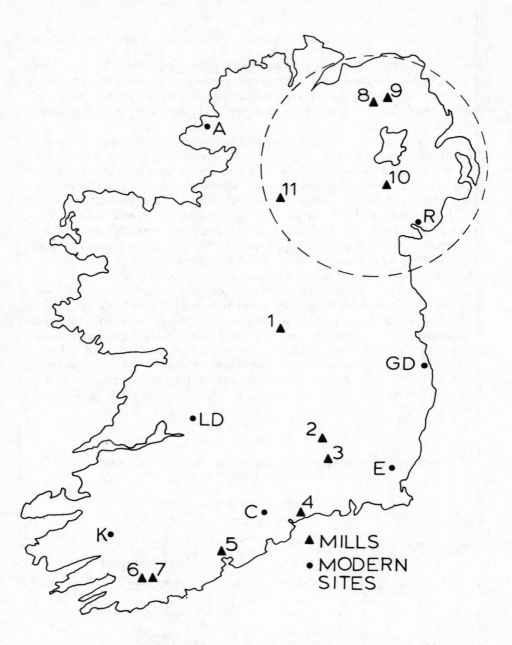

Fig 1: Ireland showing the sites of the modern oak chronologies: A, Ardara; R, Rostrevor; GD, Glen of the Downs; E, Enniscorthy; C, Cappoquin; K, Killarney; LD, Lough Doon. The horizontal mill sites are numbered as in Table 3 and the text. The dotted circle represents the area of sampling for the Belfast chronology.

As a guide, t values greater than 3.5 are expected when two ring-patterns cross match. This means that with the exception of the Glen of the Downs and Cappoquin chronologies, each of the other matches classes as highly significant or better and each of the chronologies would have been datable against the Belfast chronology even if their sampling dates had not been known.

To follow up this line of enquiry, the information contained in the seven site chronologies was combined into an overall Irish master chronology for the period 1850 to 1969. Each of the site chronologies was then compared with the Irish master in the same manner as above and for the same common period. The resultant t values are listed in Table 2 together with the comparison between the Belfast and Irish chronologies. There are several observations which can be made on these results. Obviously each of the chronologies shows extremely significant agreement with the Irish master chronology; however, it is clear that Glen of the Downs and Cappoquin show the least agreement. Since they are constituents of the Irish chronology and carry equal weight in its construction, it can be deduced that these two sites are recording the overall climatic signal least well. Whether this is due to purely geographical factors or some more localised site factors requires further study. This finding does help to explain why these two sites in particular showed the lowest significance levels when compared with the Belfast chronology above.

TABLE 2

EACH CONSTITUENT SITE CHRONOLOGY COMPARED WITH THE IRISH MASTER CHRONOLOGY FOR THE COMMON PERIOD 1850 TO 1969 AND FOR THE SUB-PERIODS 1850 TO 1909 AND 1910 TO 1969. THE CORRELATION WITH THE BELFAST CHRONOLOGY IS INCLUDED FOR COMPARISON.

SITE	t (1850 to 1969)	t (1850 to 1909)	t (1910 to 1969)
Belfast	9.2	6.4	6.5
Ardara	10.5	9.4	5.6
Rostrevor	12.4	7.2	10.4
Glen of the Downs	6.8	4.3	5.1
Enniscorthy	8.2	4.5	7.3
Cappoquin	7.8	5.1	5.6
Killarney	12.3	10.6	6.8
Lough Doon	11.6	8.4	7.8

The high level of agreement between the Irish and Belfast chronologies ($t = 9.2$) suggests that we are dealing with a generalised signal controlling tree growth in

Ireland. It could be suggested that site chronologies (where all of the samples come from a very small area, within a few hundred metres at most) tend to enhance the 'differences' due to localised site factors while the overall average signal remains similar. This is the only way one can explain the similarity between the Belfast chronology, with its northern sources, and the Irish master which should have a bias towards the more numerous southern sites. One implication of this might be that in the future, when sufficient information is available from a number of areas, it may be possible to construct a single 'average' chronology useful for dating within the whole of Ireland.

These observations tend to suggest a picture which may in fact be a little over-optimistic. The result of building these modern chronologies has been a slightly better understanding of the level of agreement existing between masters from different areas in recent times. Two points have to be stressed. Firstly, the level of agreement with any individual timber may not be anything like as good for reasons given above. Secondly, because there is agreement between for example the extreme SW and NE of Ireland in one (the modern) period does not mean that such agreement must be expected in other periods. Overall conditions can change in time. To illustrate this the cross-correlation of each site chronology with the overall Irish master was also carried out in two sections (a) for the period 1850 to 1909 and (b) for the period 1910 to 1969. Since the site chronologies contained only the information from identically the same trees in each period it is interesting to note the differences between the two sets of results in Table 2. Coming forward in time, two of the western sites, Ardara and Killarney, show a reduced agreement with the overall master while two of the eastern sites, Rostrevor and Enniscorthy, show an enhanced agreement, the others remaining broadly constant. The suggestion has to be, since the trees themselves can have changed very little, that some other, presumably climatic, factor has changed with time. This line of thinking introduces an imponderable into our considerations viz., even if it is possible to date diverse timbers against the Belfast chronology for some periods, there is no guarantee that the same will apply for all periods. Nonetheless, it is clear that a high level of agreement can obtain between master chronologies from diverse areas within Ireland.

DARK AGE CONSIDERATIONS

During the construction of the Belfast chronology it was observed that there were non-conformities in the availability of long-lived oaks in the north of Ireland and in the Dublin area. In particular the difficulty in finding trees whose ring-patterns spanned the fourteenth century threw light on a 'depletion/regeneration' phase centred on A.D. 1350 believed to be at least in part related to depopulation following the onset of the Black Death in 1349 (Baillie, 1977b; 1979a). While this gap in the tree-ring chronologies was subsequently bridged, the observation of a broadly similar tree-ring phenomenon centred on the ninth century (not necessarily with the same cause as the fourteenth century example) made it extremely difficult to consolidate the Belfast chronology to A.D. 1.

When extensive searching for suitable timbers to bridge the ninth century within Ireland had failed, it became inevitable that sources outside this area had to be considered. The construction of the modern site chronologies (above) had lent hope that suitable material from any part of Ireland might be of use in completing the chronology.

In outline, the state of Dark Age dendrochronology within the north of Ireland up to 1979 was as follows. A complete Belfast chronology ran back from the present to A.D. 919 (Baillie, 1977b) while a chronology for the Dublin area covered the period A.D. 855 to 1306 (Baillie, 1977a). Preceding these, a 907 year floating chronology derived solely from northern timbers spanned approximately the first eight or nine centuries A.D. This approximate placement in time was effected by a number of radiocarbon determinations for constituent timbers (Baillie, 1979b). In order to facilitate reference to this floating chronology, named the Teeshan-Drumard chronology after the two main constituent sites, an arbitrary ring was designated Teeshan Datum (TD) and each year of the floating chronology was designated plus or minus TD. In practice the 907 year chronology spanned the period TD – 490 to TD + 416.

An important finding in the late 1970s was that four horizontal mill sites from the north of Ireland, examined for tree-ring analysis, had all been constructed within a 150 year period (TD + 304 to TD + 448 ± 9). This latter date is beyond the range of the chronology due to the need to allow for missing sapwood with respect to the flume from Rossorry, Co. Fermanagh, the final existing growth ring of which was TD + 416. These mills at Drumard, Co. Londonderry, Rasharkin, Co. Antrim, Maghnavery, Co. Armagh and Rossorry had all been built between the eighth and tenth centuries A.D. This clustering of dates meant that all of the horizontal mills in the north of Ireland which were available for dendro-chronological dating fell within the narrow time span above. This suggested that the majority of horizontal mills in the north of Ireland must belong to this period since it is highly unlikely that such random site sampling could produce an exceptional grouping.

With this as a background it was possible to hypothesise that at least some other horizontal mills in Ireland must be broadly of this age range. If this were true then these sites, if they could be found, would represent an important source of oak timbers of the late first millennium, some of which might bridge the gap between the 907 year floating chronology and the precisely dated Dublin or Belfast chronologies. (This was before the appearance of radiocarbon dates for samples from six horizontal mills from Counties Kilkenny, Limerick, Sligo, Fermanagh (Rossorry above), Westmeath and Galway, all of which clustered between 1450 ± 60 and 1090 ± 70 b.p., i.e. 500 ± 60 to 860 ± 70 a.d. (Otlet and Walker,

1979). The samples had been submitted by Dr Lucas in 1974-5).

In 1979 a detailed list became available, compiled by the National Museum of Ireland, of all the horizontal mill sites known up to 1970. Apart from early finds, no longer extant, the list was made up of sites which had been found during extensive drainage operations in the 1950s and 1960s. In addition to this list, three further sites in Cork were brought to our attention by members of the Archaeology Department, University College, Cork. Here then was the opportunity to test two hypotheses. Firstly, could the timbers from horizontal mills from diverse parts of Ireland be dated against the Belfast chronologies and secondly, would the horizontal mills throughout Ireland conform to the tight dating of the northern examples? Equally important was the possibility of obtaining timbers which would allow consolidation of the floating 907 year chronology.

The results set out below deal with the dating of timbers from seven horizontal mills in the southern half of Ireland. No attempt is made to analyse or record the structure of these sites. That remains the province of the archaeologists who recorded details during their original examinations. This study is therefore independent of any considerations of typology (if indeed a typology exists). Each site has been treated equally in the sense that the ring-patterns of constituent timbers have been subjected to dendrochronological analysis of standard procedure. The ring-patterns and, where appropriate, site master chronologies have been cross dated both visually and statistically, using the Belfast CROS program (Baillie and Pilcher, 1973). An outline analysis of the statistics used is given in the appendix.

1. BALLYKILLEEN, CO. OFFALY (National Museum of Ireland (N.M.I.) 10)

This site was investigated by Lucas in 1953 (Lucas, 1955). The main timbers are preserved in a ditch some 100m east of the original site and were sampled in 1979.

Two trees were represented: Q.U.B. 3529 and 3530 with 153 and 172 rings respectively. Neither sample had sapwood although in the case of Q.U.B. 3530 it was clear that the outer existing ring represented the heartwood/sapwood boundary. In this case allowance for the missing sapwood allows the felling date to be estimated as 32 ± 9 years after the final heartwood ring (Baillie, 1974).

Both timbers were compared with the Teeshan/Drumard chronology (Baillie, 1975) and gave statistical values of $t = 5.9$ and $t = 6.3$ with their outer rings equivalent to TD + 90 and TD + 126 respectively. Allowing for missing sapwood on Q.U.B. 3530 the felling date of the timbers should lie in the range of TD + 158 ± 9.

Clearly Ballykilleen has been constructed considerably earlier (about 150 years) than the northern mills. The only observation which might be made in this context was the large size of Ballykilleen in comparison with the examples previously dated.

2. BRABSTOWN, CO. KILKENNY (N.M.I. 27)

This mill, originally discovered in 1964, is preserved as two side beams, an upright and a crosspiece in the bed of a stream at Brabstown. Samples from the side beams indicated that these were the two halves of a large oak, split and then partly squared. This effectively reduced the number of samples to three. The three samples cross dated with each other and with the Rossorry ring pattern. The side beam ring-pattern, Q.U.B. 3691, contained 292 rings without sapwood and cross dated with Rossorry (t = 5.6), Teeshan/Drumard (t = 3.1) and Maghnavery (t = 3.1) at the same position with its outer year at TD + 403. Allowing for missing sapwood a suggested felling date would be in the range TD + 435 ± 9, highly consistent with the estimate for Rossory above.

3. BALLYGEARDRA, CO. KILKENNY (N.M.I. 31)

This mill, originally investigated in 1965, survives as a weathered flume, Q.U.B. 3652, and a single oak beam. The flume produced a ring pattern of 150 years which cross dated with Brabstown Q.U.B. 3691 (t = 5.4) and with Rossory (t = 3.37) its outer heartwood ring being TD + 301 in each case. Allowing for sapwood the estimated felling date would be in the range TD + 333 ± 9. The beam is as yet undated.

4. BALLYDOWANE WEST, CO. WATERFORD (N.M.I. 42)

Discovered in 1970, this mill survives only as a morticed beam, Q.U.B. 3682, which had been deposited in a hedge some distance from the original findspot (local information). Its ring pattern of 221 rings cross dated with Brabstown Q.U.B. 3691 (t = 5.7) and with Rossory (t = 4.2) with its outer heartwood ring at TD + 331. Allowing for missing sapwood the felling date was in the range TD + 363 ± 9.

While the results are still tentative it is believed that this timber establishes a link between the Irish floating chronology and Hillam's London Tudor Street timbers which span A.D. 682 to 918; see below.

5. LITTLE ISLAND, CO. CORK (N.M.I. 55)

It is possible that this mill, which was uncovered and partially recorded during destruction in 1979, had been known previously as the N.M.I. list records the existence of a mill at Castlefreke District, Ahaglashin TD or Little Island TD in 1803 (Townsend 1810).

This mill or mills, as there is some evidence to suggest the presence of more than one flume, would appear to have exploited tidal changes rather than the more usual stream, river or spring. The amount of timber preserved at the site dwarfs most conventional horizontal mills which consist of a relatively simple side beam and cross piece 'underhouse', sometimes with a flume and occasionally with plank flooring. (A detailed report on the structure and possible function of this mill complex will be forthcoming from the principal investigators at University College, Cork). Dendrochronological aid was sought by Professor O'Kelly and his team in an attempt to answer two questions. Was the mill an Early Christian structure as suggested by O'Kelly and, if so, when was it built. Secondly, was it possible that more than one phase of mill building was represented by the complex of timbers recovered.

The advantages of dendrochronology in a situation of this kind are twofold. Firstly, it may be possible to establish an accurate date for the structure. If this can be done then a literature search can be initiated to see who or what may have occasioned the building. Secondly, since no opportunity had been afforded for careful excavation of the site it had been impossible to tell archaeologically if more than one phase was represented. Dendrochronological dating of the individual timbers offers a unique, independent method of establishing whether or not two phases of timbers exist.

In practise, the large number of timbers recovered from the Little Island site posed logistic problems. It was decided that a random sample of timbers from diverse parts of the site would be tackled in the first instance. If all of these turned out to belong to the one period it could safely be assumed that all of the timbers belonged basically to the one phase. If on the other hand any indication of different groupings was found then further sampling could be undertaken to elucidate this.

The timbers, all of which were oak, fell into three broad categories:
(a) a series of thick riven planks exhibiting long ring patterns;
(b) a series of essentially complete or partially squared tree trunks;
(c) pieces of flumes and unidentified capstan-like objects.
A selection of timbers from (a) and (b) were sampled. These timbers were very different in character: (a) tended to be long lived with sapwood whose rings were so narrow or compressed as to render them unmeasurable: (b) on the other hand were relatively young trees averaging little more than 100 years; and in each case the sapwood was complete out to the felling years. Each timber from group (a) cross dated and formed an overall chronology of 320 years without sapwood. The group (b) timbers yielded a chronology of 118 years. Visual and computer comparison showed that the (a) and (b) chronologies overlapped by 67 years giving a total chronology of 370 years. The tree ring evidence suggested that all of the trees had been felled at the one time and that the complex was a once off construction. The completed 370 year site chronology was compared with the Teeshan/Drumard chronology and cross dated with its outer year being TD + 152 ($t = 6.0$). Clearly the mill was a seventh-century structure.

6,7. KEELARAHEEN AND FARRANMAREEN, CO. CORK

The existence of these mills had been reported to the Archaeology Department, University College, Cork, during the 1970s and details had been recorded by members of the department. Both sites were finally destroyed in drainage operations in late 1979. Numerous timbers were available for sampling. During analysis it became clear that good cross dating existed between the ring-patterns from the two sites, to such a degree that from a dendrochronological viewpoint they were treated as a single unit for dating purposes. Unfortunately while several of the Keelaraheen samples retained their total sapwood none was observed on those from Farranmareen. So while it is possible to specify the felling year of the former timbers, in the case of Farranmareen an estimate for missing sapwood is required.

In practise a joint 174 year master chronology was constructed. This showed no agreement with the Little Island master above but subsequently cross dated with an Irish version of the Teeshan/Drumard chronology (on the strength of the findings with the modern chronologies above, a Dark Age chronology was constructed using all relevant material from Ireland) with its outer year at TD + 365 ($t = 4.56$). This was the felling date of the Keelaraheen timbers. The outermost heartwood ring of the samples from Farranmareen was two years earlier at TD + 363. Allowing for missing sapwood the Farranmareen timbers should have been felled in the range TD + 395 $\pm$ 9.

DISCUSSION

Two objectives were suggested at the onset of looking at horizontal mills from the southern half of Ireland. Firstly, could they be dated against available northern chronologies? Secondly, was the distribution of mills in time the same as in the northern group? Clearly the answer to the first question is yes. Sufficient examples could be cross-dated with the Teeshan/Drumard chronology (or with Rossorry, the most recent extension of that chronology) to allow a corpus of relative dates to be produced. Secondly, although two older mills have shown up, those at Ballykilleen and Little Island, it is clear that the majority of mills fall within the 150 year bracket from TD + 300 to TD + 450 already defined by the northern examples.

Now clearly the question of absolute date is important. So far, all these datings are relative to the floating Teeshan/Drumard chronology. It has been known for some time that this nine-century chronology must run from, at the earliest, 100 B.C. to A.D. 800 or, more likely, from around A.D. 1 to A.D. 900. This placement in time was solely on the basis of radiocarbon determinations and could in no way be relied upon for accurate dating.

Irish sites have consistently failed to yield timbers which would extend forward in time beyond TD + 416 to link the floating chronology with Dublin or Belfast. It was inevitable therefore that English Dark Age material would be considered for this elusive bridge. In England the earliest precisely dated timbers are from Tudor Street, London and span A.D. 682 to 918 (Hillam, personal communication). Clearly there must, on the basis of our placement of the Teeshan/Drumard chronology, be some overlap between the Irish floating chronology and the Tudor Street chronology. However no cross matching could be found with the northern timbers above. The broadening of the data base by the dating of the southern mills against the northern floating chronology appears to have yielded the link required. The most south-easterly site, Ballydowane West, shows significant agreement with Tudor Street and, if this placement is correct, specifies Teeshan Datum as A.D. 478.

It is the author's belief that this dating is correct and that the construction dates of the mills cited above are as listed in Table 3.

TABLE 3

THE FELLING DATES FOR TIMBERS USED IN THE CONSTRUCTION OF THE FOLLOWING HORIZONTAL MILLS ON THE ASSUMPTION THAT T.D. = 478. SITE NUMBERS AS IN FIG. 1 AND TEXT

Site	Relative Date of Outer Ring	A.D. Date
1. Ballykilleen	T.D. + 158 ± 9	636 ± 9
2. Brabstown	T.D. + 435 ± 9	914 ± 9
3. Ballygeardra	T.D. + 333 ± 9	811 ± 9
4. Ballydowane	T.D. + 363 ± 9	841 ± 9
5. Little Island	T.D. + 152	630
6. Keelaraheen	T.D. + 365	843
7. Farranmareen	T.D. + 395 ± 9	873 ± 9
8. Drumard	T.D. + 304	782
9. Rasharkin	T.D. + 344	822
10. Maghnavery	T.D. + 332 ± 9	810 ± 9
11. Rossorry	T.D. + 448 ± 9	926 ± 9

Figure 2 shows the relative placement of the ring patterns from the mills cited and a frequency diagram of the number of sites constructed per quarter century. It is clear that we are not dealing with a continuum of horizontal mill building. The majority of these sites belong to the early ninth century with more isolated phases in the second quarter of the seventh century and around A.D. 920 (the two latest dates for Rossory and Brabstown 913 ± 9 and 926 ± 9 hardly deserve the 50 year span dictated by the arbitrary division of the frequency diagram). It will be interesting to see how future examples reinforce or alter this distribution. The most surprising factor, both in this study and in the radiocarbon determinations obtained by Lucas above, is the absence of later examples. Where are the horizontal mills of the late tenth, eleventh and twelfth centuries and what of the later medieval period? Without labouring the point, it becomes apparent why these structures carry the label 'Danes' mills'. If not built by them, certainly these mills were being built in the main at a time when the Scandinavians were exerting an influence in Ireland.

From a dendrochronological viewpoint the value of this work has been in the accumulation of dated Dark Age material from outside Northern Ireland and in tying down the floating Teeshan/Drumard chronology. It is now possible to construct a tree-ring chronology for the southern half of Ireland for the period T.D. – 217 (the oldest end of the Little Island chronology) to T.D. + 403 (the youngest end of Brabstown), an Early Christian chronology of 621 years which spans A.D. 261 to 881. Since a Dublin area chronology is already published for the period A.D. 855 to 1306 it is reasonable to suggest that any long-lived oaks of the first millennium from anywhere in Ireland now stand a high probability of being precisely datable by dendrochronology. The opportunity which this offers for the resolution of at least some of the chronological problems of the Early Christian period must be considerable.

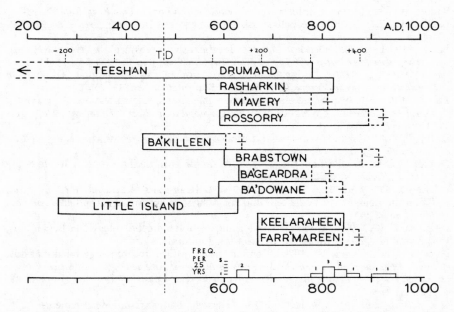

Fig 2: A block diagram of the position in time of the ring patterns of the timbers from the sites named. Error bars are present on those samples which lacked sapwood and where an allowance has been made. The histogram represents the number of sites constructed in each quarter century.

Finally, no mention has been made of the subject of prehistoric dating by dendrochronology. It is my opinion that the real value of dendrochronological dating lies in its compatability with historical documentation and hence in studies involving the last two millennia. At present there are few significant prehistoric sites in Ireland yielding suitable timbers for dendrochronological dating and, considering the now universal use of radiocarbon dating for the establishment of prehistoric chronology, it is likely that tree-ring dates for sites in that era would be over-refined. The real significance of the long north of Ireland chronologies lies in their contribution to the refinement of the radiocarbon calibration.

REFERENCES

Baillie, M.G.L., 1973. A dendrochronological study in Ireland, with references to the dating of medieval and post-medieval timbers. MS. Doctoral Dissertation, The Queen's University, Belfast.

Baillie, M.G.L., 1974. 'A tree-ring chronology for the dating of Irish post-medieval timbers', *Ulster Folklife* 20, 1-23.

Baillie, M.G.L., 1975. 'A horizontal mill of the eighth century A.D. at Drumard, Co. Derry', *Ulster J Archaeol ser 3* 38, 25-32.

Baillie, M.G.L., 1977a. 'Dublin medieval dendrochronology', *Tree-Ring Bull* 37, 13-20.

Baillie, M.G.L., 1977b. 'The Belfast oak chronology to A.D. 1001', *Tree-Ring Bull* 37, 1-12.

Baillie, M.G.L., 1978a. 'Dendrochronology for the Irish sea province'. *In* Peter Davey (ed), *Man and environment in the Isle of Man* (Brit Archaeol Rep Brit Ser 54), 25-37.

Baillie, M.G.L., 1978b. 'Dating of some ships' timbers from Woodquay, Dublin'. *In Dendrochronology in Europe* (Brit Archaeol Rep Internat Ser 51), 259-62.

Baillie, M.G.L., 1979a. 'Some observations on gaps in tree-ring chronologies'. *In Invited papers and abstracts of Symposium on Archaeological Sciences 4-7 January 1978*, 19-32. University of Bradford.

Baillie, M.G.L., 1979b. 'An interim statement on Irish dark age dendrochronology', *Ulster J Archaeol ser 3* 42 (forthcoming).

Baillie, M.G.L. and Pilcher, J.R., 1973. 'A simple cross-dating program for tree-ring research', *Tree-Ring Bull* 33, 7-14.

Eckstein, D. and Bauch, J., 1969. 'Beitrag zur Rationalisierung eines dendrochronologischen Verfahrens und zur Analyse seiner Aussagesicherheit'. *Forstwiss Zentbl* 38, 230-50.

Ferguson, C.W., 1970. 'Concepts and techniques of dendrochronology'. *In* Berger (ed), *Scientific Methods in Medieval Archaeology*. California.

Huber, B., and Giertz, V., 1970. 'Central European Dendrochronology for the Middle Ages'. *In* Berger (ed), *Scientific Methods in Medieval Archaeology*. California.

Lucas, A.T., 1955. 'Horizontal mill, Ballykilleen, Co. Offaly', *J Roy Soc Antiq Ir* 85, 100-13.

Otlet, R.L. and A.J. Walker, 1979. 'Harwell Radiocarbon Measurements 111', *Radiocarbon* 21, 358-83.

Pilcher, J.R., Hillam, J., Baillie, M.G.L., and Pearson, G.W. 'A long sub-fossil oak tree-ring chronology from the North of Ireland', *New Phytol* 79, 713-29.

Schove, D.J. and Lowther, A.W.G., 1957. 'Tree-Rings and Medieval Archaeology', *Medieval Archaeol* 1, 78-96.

Townsend, H., 1810. *Statistical Survey of the County of Cork*, 272-4. Dublin.

APPENDIX

This appendix was originally delivered as a paper entitled 'Objectivity in a Potentially Subjective Field' to the Cork Conference of the Irish Young Archaeologists' Association in December 1976.

The real importance of dendrochronology is that once a master chronology, for a species and a geographic area, is set up, almost all archaeological timbers of that species and from that area can be dated precisely. It is the calendrical precision of tree-ring dates which makes the eventual acceptance of dendrochronological dating so certain. No other method can at present rival the precision of dendrochronology nor is it likely that any other method developed in the future will be able to do so. At some future period we can look forward to the existence of a list of sites and levels whose calendar dates are known. The fact that this information will be available even for a few sites will inevitably make these sites the cornerstones of archaeological chronology.

Because of this it is absolutely essential that the master chronology for an area be precisely correct. It is not sufficient therefore that the cross-correlations between ring-patterns — the building blocks of a tree-ring chronology — be dependent solely on human judgement. There must be independent evidence of a statistical nature to back up the human eye. The information set out below is intended to show how simple yet powerful statistics can be applied to the field of tree-ring studies to reduce the possibility of errors in master chronologies.

CROSS-CORRELATION OF TREE-RING PATTERNS

Any dendrochronological study involves the establishment of cross-correlations between ring patterns. This is true in chronology extension, dating against floating or standard chronologies and comparison of standard chronologies from different areas. The method is based on a theoretical model which postulates that two trees, growing under the same conditions over the same period of time, should put on similar ring-patterns. A tree-ring pattern can be defined as a set of numbers corresponding to the widths of the successive rings, from the pith to the bark of a tree. This set of numbers constitutes a time series since oak, the species with which we are concerned, puts on one growth ring each year. When the successive ring widths are plotted against a scale in years, the resultant tree-ring curve presents itself to the eye as a random jagged curve. Superimposed upon the yearly fluctuations in ring width are trends towards wider or narrower rings, indicating respectively improving or deteriorating growth conditions. These trends can be long or short term and of varying intensity. Visual matching can be achieved in three ways: by observation of the patterns of wide and narrow rings in polished samples, by observing skeleton plots or by observing plots of ring-widths (Baillie, 1974).

Visual comparison of ring-width plots involves superimposing the two curves under study and shifting their relative positions until such time as significant agreement is obtained between them. In practice, the observer looks at significant features, such as wide or narrow rings, narrow bands, trends or signature patterns in one curve and attempts to duplicate them in the second curve. However, visual matching can be subjective. The ability of a trained observer to find sufficient similarities in two long curves to establish a cross-correlation is not a measurable quantity. Thus, it is essential, for consistent results, that some repeatable measure of the significance of a cross-correlation should be independently produced to substantiate each visual match.

STATISTICAL METHODS USED IN THE CROSS-CORRELATION OF TREE-RING CURVES

(i) NON-PARAMETRIC

Schove and Lowther (1957,80) drew attention to the subjective nature of visual matching of tree-ring curves and quoted a powerful non-parametric statistical method for checking visual agreement. This method involves calculating the percentage agreement or percentage parallel variation, between two ring curves. This is a measure of the number of years where the two ring curves under comparison show similar increases or decreases in ring-width. The expected percentage agreement for two random curves is 50% since for a long overlap there will be as many years agreeing as disagreeing. As with any statistical results the actual percentage agreement figures produced, in the random mis-matching of two ring curves, will follow a normal distribution. Thus percentage agreement figures for random curves are given by

$$\% A = 50 \pm (50/(n)^{1/2})$$

where n is the number of years under comparison and $50/(n)^{1/2}$ is one standard deviation (Huber and Giertz, 1970, 203).

At any mis-match position, the correlation between two tree-ring curves approximates closely to that between two random curves, and the percentage agreement figure will be distributed around 50%. Figures as far as three standard deviations from the mean are likely to occur about once in every thousand random matches. In order that an actual tree-ring cross-correlation should be significant, it should produce a percentage agreement figure greater than three standard deviations from the mean.

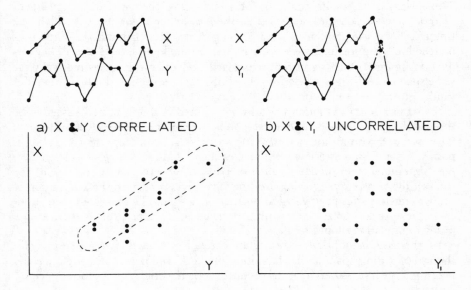

Fig 3: Two sets of tree-ring widths x and y: (a) in a match position where x plotted against y gives a linear distribution (perfect correlation would give a straight line); (b) with ring-pattern y moved one year to a non-correlation position where x plotted against y shows an essentially random distribution.

In practice, with computer availability, it is possible to slide one curve past the other, in increments of one year and calculate the percentage agreement at each point of overlap. All mis-match results should be distributed within three standard deviations of the mean; any value occurring outside these limits is highly significant. Eckstein and Bauch (1969) have published a computer program which calculates the % agreement figures and prints them together with their significance levels.

This method of establishing cross-correlations was used for some time at the inception of the Belfast project. The computer program used was written using basic principles before the publication of Eckstein and Bauch. However, it was found to be insensitive in many cases, especially with short overlaps. Further, the non-parametric nature of the percentage agreement method made it insensitive to changes in slope and overall profile. Its most serious drawback was the small tolerances between the percentages produced by actual agreements and those produced by chance where short overlaps were concerned. The technique is still used extensively in England and Germany.

(ii) PARAMETRIC

While significant results could be obtained using the percentage agreement method a more powerful statistical method was sought for use with Irish oak timbers. The basic problem is the matching of two sets of numbers. When mismatched these approximate to sets of random numbers and should present low correlation figures. When significantly matched, i.e. when the curves represent the same span of years, the correlations should be high, assuming the basic model of similar growth in similar conditions (Ferguson, 1970, 189).

If a set of points (x,y) shows a trend when plotted, x and y can be assumed to be correlated. Fig. 3a shows a high correlation between x and y in which an increase in x is associated with an increase in y and vice versa. In this case the correlation is positive. Increasing x associated with decreasing y would show negative correlation. Fig. 3b represents uncorrelated values of x and y. If we consider x and y to be the ring-widths of two trees growing over the same period then, on the assumption of similar growth patterns, in $year_i$, an increase in x_i should be associated with an increase in y_i or a decrease in x_i with a decrease in y_i. When this is true, a high positive correlation should result.

So, the basic assumptions of the dendrochronological method argue strongly for the use of a direct parametric correlation method. The degree of correlation between x and y is measured by r, the produce moment correlation coefficient. This is defined as:

$$r = \frac{\sum_i x_i y_i - N\bar{x}\bar{y}}{\sqrt{(\sum_i x_i^2 - N\bar{x}^2)(\sum_i y_i^2 - N\bar{y}^2)}}$$

where $\bar{x}$ and $\bar{y}$ are the mean of all the x and all the y values respectively. The term on the bottom line is the product of the standard deviations of all the x and y values. For r to be valid, the values of x and y should be evenly distributed about the means $\bar{x}$ and $\bar{y}$. Because of the overall trends towards wider or narrower rings, the simple mean of all the ring-widths in a tree-ring curve will not necessarily form a valid mean at any given point i.e. the curve may fluctuate from a simple mean value. In order to eliminate the possibility of decreased sensitivity when correlating tree-ring curves by this method, a running mean is used. In practice each ring-width in the primary data is converted to a percentage of the mean of five ring-widths: this reduces a ring-width curve to a percentage average curve about a mean value of 100%.

The correlation coefficient r can have values between -1 and $+1$. For perfect positive correlation r should equal 1, while correlation of two mis-matched curves should produce a value of r around zero. The value of r takes no account of the number of variables N. Thus if two curves are moved past one another and value of *r* calculated for each position of overlap (as above), the values of *r* are not immediately interpretable in terms of probability of concurrence.

In order to relate *r* values to probabilities the simple conversion to Students *t* is used, where

$$t = r\sqrt{N - 2} / \sqrt{1 - r^2}$$

the value *t* gives a measure of the probability of the observed value of r having arisen by chance in a sample N. In practice to ensure normality of the distribution of *t* values, the percentage average figures can be reduced to log values. Tables exist which relate the value of *t* to probability for any value of N.

Since most useful ring patterns contain 100 or more rings, the 0.1% significance level of *t* is $t = 3.5$ i.e. a value of this magnitude should arise by chance only once in over 1000 mis-matches. This is equivalent to the three standard deviation level for percentage agreement (above). In practise the background *t*-values fall between $t = 0.0$ and $t = 3.5$, correlations of ring patterns which grew over the same span of years normally produce *t* values between $t = 3.5$ and $t = 10.0$. No account is taken of negative correlations since dendrochronology by definition is dealing with positive similarities between ring patterns. A computer program which calculates *t* values for each position of overlap between two ring patterns is available and is now widely used (Baillie and Pilcher, 1973, 7-14).

Thus dendrochronologists have several lines of approach to extablishing crossmatches. The first and most powerful is the worker's own ability at visual matching and this can be backed up by the second, the use of statistical computer programs. It is advisable that the dendrochronologist should always have a final say in acceptance of cross-matches. It is a dangerous course to allow statistics to overrule human judgment. The routines outlined above are after all only mathematical approximations of the resolving power of the human eye and brain. Humans have had millions of years of evolutionary experience in pattern recognition and it would be impossible to program a computer to duplicate this experience adequately. The importance of the mathematical approximations lies in their independence.

There is however a third and very important back-up to visual matching and statistics which comes under the heading of replication. There are several levels of replication to aid the dendrochronologist. Firstly, there is the replication between the ring patterns of individual trees. This ensures that there are no problems with incorrect ring counts and, when masters are produced, reduces the 'noise' within individual ring patterns enhancing the climatic 'signal', the matching component. Secondly, there is replication between master chronologies. Each time a series of timbers is cross dated and a master produced this is matched against a standard chronology. This process allows the checking of the relevant portion of the standard chronology and, over a period of time, all portions of a standard chronology will be duplicated. In short, as the dendrochronologist dates timbers he replicates more and more of his work giving a continual cross-check. A third and increasingly important factor is that other workers, some in areas comparatively close at hand, will generate tree-ring chronologies which may well replicate existing chronologies. Recent evidence suggests that within Britain and Ireland as a whole, replication is to be expected at significant statistical levels (Baillie, 1978a). All chronologies will ultimately be checked by this means.

It is possible, in the light of the controls outlined above, to claim for dendrochronology the status of a science. This is so because the results produced by dendrochronology can obey the first law of science: they are capable of independent reproduction.

ACKNOWLEDGEMENTS

The author wishes to thank all of the various parties who have so generously supplied samples for study. In particular he acknowledges the important part played by Mr Victor Buckley in this research at all stages. The author would like to thank Dr Jon Pilcher who was instrumental in the collection of the modern data and Mrs Liz Francis for assistance with data processing. This work was carried out with the financial support of the Science Research Council who supported both the field work and the funding of research assistance.

Astronomical Alignment or Megalithic Muddle?

Ann Lynch

INTRODUCTION

Since the beginning of this century, numerous speculations and theories have been propounded regarding the possible astronomical significance of various archaeological monuments (for example, Lockyer, 1909; Boyle-Sommerville, 1922-23; Hawkins, 1966; Atkinson, 1974). The main contributor to this field in recent years has without doubt been Professor A. Thom (1954; 1964; 1966; 1967; 1971a; 1971b). On the basis of surveys of megalithic monuments throughout England, Scotland, Wales and Brittany, Thom concluded that their orientations were in fact astronomically significant and that the targets of orientation included the rising and setting of the sun at the equinoxes, the solstices and the quarter days, the rising and setting points of first magnitude stars (i.e. stars brighter than magnitude 1.5) and detailed motions of the moon. Reactions to these theories were varied and Thom's work in general was criticised on several points. The data on which the mathematical analyses were based were not considered sufficiently accurate because of the severe limitations imposed on accurate surveying by the removal, movement or re-erection of many of the standing stones. Thom's procedure regarding acceptance of foresights and backsights and even the direction in which to use an alignment was often considered dubious (Patrick and Butler, 1974). On astronomical grounds, several objections were raised concerning the practical difficulties in observing some of the more detailed stellar or lunar motions (e.g. the 9' perturbation) as claimed by Thom especially when considered within the limited technological context of Neolithic societies (Heggie, 1972).

As part of a general study of the stone alignments of SW Ireland (Ní Loingsigh, 1976), the following hypothesis was therefore tested: the centres of the stones of an alignment define a line which is orientated on an event of astronomical significance. The results of this test are outlined in this paper.

RESEARCH DESIGN

A brief outline shall be made of the basic definitions and assumptions inherently understood in this work, and the reader is referred to Ní Loingsigh (1976) for further details.

The definition of a stone alignment as accepted for this study is three or more standing stones, intervisible and in a straight line. A total of 37 such sites was located within the study area (i.e. W Cork and Kerry) and all were used for the subsequent analyses.

The alignment plans were drawn on the horizontal plane at ground level and each survey point was subsequently reduced by computer to (x,y) co-ordinates. By the simple process of averaging the x and y values, the centre of mass of a lamina, the shape of the base of the stone, was derived.

Since the term orientation implies a single and specific line pointing in some direction on the earth's surface, a least squares adjustment was used to find the line of best fit to the centre of the stones. Two criteria had to be met before such a line could be accepted as the line of orientation of a monument: (i) the horizontal distance errors (i.e. the distances of the centres of the stones from the proposed line) should not be significantly different from zero and (ii) in the event that the horizontal distance errors are not significantly different from zero, one should expect to find them normally distributed about some value close to zero. For each site, a Student's t test was applied to the horizontal distance errors and they were shown not to be significantly different from zero. The second criterion relates to the accuracy to which one can recover the direction of the original orientation line laid out before the monument itself was built. This accuracy is affected by three types of errors:

(a) errors involved in laying out the line originally and in laying large stones on this line so that their centres of mass defined it;

(b) the various errors introduced by settling etc. of the stones since the time of construction;

(c) errors involved in recording the sites.

The operation of the first two errors was accepted as random and the third error was shown to be negligible (the horizontal distance errors were normally distributed about a mean of -9 mm with a standard deviation of 17 cm). The accuracy to which the orientation of the monuments could be recovered was calculated at $1.791°$ (i.e. the mean horizontal distance error $\pm$ three times its standard deviation).

The azimuth of the line of orientation was derived by taking into account the local magnetic anomalies and also the secular magnetic variations (annual, seasonal and diurnal) for each site. Since each alignment is an open-ended structure, the azimuth in both directions was examined and it was seen that the alignments were consistently orientated NE/SW.

Finally, it is necessary to define what is meant by events of astronomical significance. The cosmological method of literate societies in antiquity has always been the recording, often over very long periods, of the occurrence of related phenomena with a view to deducing underlying cycles in the subsequent analysis of the observed data. It is assumed that this was the method used by the megalith-builders and that the simpler cycles of the sun and moon may have been observed. The turning points in the solar and lunar cycles, and their midpoint have therefore been accepted as significant astronomical events. These give a total of 14 possible 'targets' for orientation (i.e. seven points on the eastern and western horizons).

TABLE 1. EVENTS OF ASTRONOMICAL SIGNIFICANCE

EVENT (SOLAR)	DECLINATION	EVENT (LUNAR)	DECLINATION
Summer Solstice	+ 23.91°	S Limit of Major Lunar Standstill	− 29.95°
Winter Solstice	− 23.91°	N Limit of Major Lunar Standstill	+ 28.17°
Equinox	0°	S Limit of Minor Lunar Standstill	− 19.58°
		N Limit of Minor Lunar Standstill	+ 17.94°

The effects of parallax and changes in the obliquity of the ecliptic over the years have been taken into account for the lunar and solar declinations respectively.

When calculating the probability level at which the astronomical hypothesis operates, only solar and lunar orientations were taken into account since the declinations of these bodies have not changed appreciably in the past 5000 years while the stellar declinations vary greatly from century to century and not all in the same direction or at the same rate. Once the azimuths (in both directions) had been determined for each line of orientation, the declinations were then calculated. The angle of uncertainty (1.791°) already mentioned was taken into account in each case which means that for every site, two small angular spreads were obtained within which, if the monument was astronomically orientated, the declination of one of the astronomically significant 'targets' should occur. The probability level at which the hypothesis operates was then calculated from a version of Bernouilli's Theorem, a procedure commented upon by Heggie (1972).

RESULTS

Of the 37 sites examined, 23 had significant astronomical orientations and 21 of these 23 were significantly orientated in one direction only (13 being eastern orientations and the remaining 8 western).

The probability level at which this hypothesis operates is 0.00000089, that is to say that the chances of scoring 25 hits out of 37 sites by accident is one in a million. The astronomical hypothesis may therefore be accepted.

It is interesting to note that only one instance of an equinoctial orientation has been recorded, at Gneeves, Co. Cork. This is not surprising when one considers the amount of time and effort which would have been involved in counting the days

TABLE 2. INSTANCES OF SIGNIFICANT
ASTRONOMICAL ORIENTATION

SITE	ORIENTATION	SITE	ORIENTATION
Newcastle Co. Cork	Winter Solstice (W)	Glantane East Co. Cork	N Limit of Minor Lunar St. (E)
	Summer Solstice (E)	Rossnakilla Co. Cork	N Limit of Major Lunar St. (E)
Castlenalacht Co. Cork	S Limit of Minor Lunar St. (W)	Beenalaght Co. Cork	N Limit of Major Lunar St. (E)
	N Limit of Minor Lunar St. (E)	Garrane Co. Cork	S Limit of Major Lunar St. (W)
Cabragh Co. Cork	Winter Solstice (W)	Gneeves Co. Cork	Equinox
Dromdrasdil Co. Cork	Summer Solstice (E)	Dromteewakeen Co. Kerry	Summer Solstice (E)
Tullig Co. Cork	N Limit of Minor Lunar St. (E)	Kildrellig Co. Kerry	N Limit of Major Lunar St. (E)
Farranahineeny Co. Cork	N Limit of Major Lunar St. (E)	Eightercua Co. Kerry	Winter Solstice (W)
Monavaddra Co. Cork	Summer Solstice (E)	Doory Co. Kerry	S Limit of Major Lunar St. (W)
Kilcaskan Co. Cork	S Limit of Minor Lunar St. (W)	Cloonsharragh Co. Kerry	Summer Solstice (E)
Leitry Lower Co. Cork	Summer Solstice (W)	Ardamore Co. Kerry	Winter Solstice (W)
Cloonshear Beg Co. Cork	Summer Solstice (E)	Dromatouk Co. Kerry	Winter Solstice (W)
Dromcarra North Co. Cork	N Limit of Major Lunar St. (E)		

(W) indicates a western orientation
(E) indicates an eastern orientation

between the solstices in order to arrive at their mid-point. It is clear however from this study that the alignment-builders were aware of the more obvious events in the solar and lunar cycles and it was on these events that they orientated their monuments. These results are in remarkable agreement with those obtained by Barber (1972; 1973) for the recumbent stone circles of the same area. Such observations as those claimed here, would not have required any detailed scientific knowledge on the part of the alignment-builders and there is nothing at present to suggest an organised systematic study of the movements of celestial bodies during Neolithic/Bronze Age times in SW Ireland.

REFERENCES

Atkinson, R.J.C., 1974. 'Neolithic science and technology', *The Place of Astronomy in the Ancient World*, 123-33. London.

Barber, J., 1972. The stone circles of Cork and Kerry: a study. M.A. Thesis, University College, Cork.

Barber, J., 1973. 'The orientation of the recumbent stone circles of the south-west of Ireland', *J Kerry Archaeol Hist Soc* 6, 26-39.

Boyle-Sommerville, H., 1922-3. 'Instances of orientation in prehistoric monuments of the British Isles', *Archaeologia* 73.

Heggie, D., 1972. 'Megalithic lunar observatories: an astronomer's view', *Antiquity* 46, 43-8.

Lockyer, Sir N., 1909. *Stonehenge and Other British Stone Monuments Astronomically Considered*. London.

Ní Loingsigh, A., 1976. The stone alignments of Cork and Kerry. M.A. Thesis, University College, Cork.

Patrick, J. & Butler, C.J., 1974. 'On the interpretation of the Carnac menhirs and alignments by A. & A.S. Thom', *Ir Archaeol Res Forum* 1, 29-39.

Thom, A., 1954. 'The solar observatories of megalithic man', *J Brit Astron Ass* 6, 396-404.

Thom, A., 1964. 'Observatories in ancient Britain', *New Sci* 398, 17-19.

Thom, A., 1966. 'Megalithic astronomy: indications in standing stones', *Vistas in Astronomy* 7, 1-57.

Thom, A., 1967. *Megalithic Sites in Britain*, Oxford.

Thom, A., 1971a. *Megalithic Lunar Observatories*, Oxford.

Thom, A., 1971b. 'The astronomical significance of the large Carnac menhirs', *J Hist Astron* 2, 147-60.

Native Copper in North-East Ulster: A Contributory Factor in the Establishment of the Earliest Irish Metalworking?

B.G. Scott and P.J. Francis

During a long and productive career in Irish archaeology, Brian O'Kelly has been a leader in research on our earliest metalworking. For the study of ironworking, his experimental smelting represents some of the earliest European research in this important field; excavations at Ballyvourney in particular have given us invaluable information to use in building models of iron production in early Ireland. At the other end of the metallurgical time-scale, his continuing interest in the first non-ferrous metalworking, most recently expressed in a paper to the *Vth Atlantic Colloquium* (published in 1979), has provided us with careful collections of data and stimulating ideas. In many respects, perhaps O'Kelly's main contribution to Irish archaeology will be seen to have been the promotion of scientific study techniques, primarily by practical demonstration of the value of inter-disciplinary research in his own publications. We offer this paper, the result of collaboration between archaeologist and geologist, as some small tribute to a scholar who has striven to create conditions under which such collaboration might be possible on a regular basis.

1. INTRODUCTION

The problems surrounding the identification of the first users and producers of metals in Ireland admit of no easy solutions. Given the scarcity of helpful dating and associations among finds of our earliest cuprous artifacts this is hardly surprising; previous studies have paid only limited attention to broader questions relating to the ways in which knowledge of metal production and working might have been implanted here (*pace* Case and Coghlan, 1957; Case, 1966; ApSimon, 1969; Harbison, 1973, 1979; etc.). It is orthodox dogma that metallurgy is a foreign import into Ireland. Re-examination of the whole complex question as a case of 'foreign intervention' (i.e. 'invasion': cf. Waddell, 1978) *vs* 'indigenous ingenuity' seems to the writers too simplistic an alternative approach; many forces (not by any means always complementary) must have been in play for a long time between the later third and earlier second millennia B.C. before we can positively identify native Irish metallurgy proper (cf. Scott, 1979, 189n).

The recent Burgess-Shennan 'Beaker Cult Package Hypothesis' (Burgess and Shennan, 1976; cf. Scott, 1977a) highlights yet again the largely circumstantial nature of the evidence for Beaker involvement in the introduction here of non-ferrous metallurgy. Their model (see also Case, 1977; 1978) would remove from the scene 'Beaker itinerants' who have for too long haunted most previous thinking in Ireland on the stone/cuprous metal transition period. This hypothesis and the inadequacy of existing models nudge us towards reassessment; and it is unfortunate that one archaeologist has recently sought to encumber us with an anonymous new group of prospectors and metalworkers territorially connected with the builders of wedge-tombs (Harbison, 1979, 104). Substituting one nebulous influx of 'tinkers' for another is hardly a step forward. The core of the problem is the emergence of a vigorous, productive and confident copper-working tradition distinctly different from British Beaker-related metalworking (Burgess, 1979, 213) but with no obvious ancestry.

One of us (Scott, 1977b, 12; cf. Randsborg, 1979, 303) has suggested that, in view of the relatively unfavourable comparisons between the properties of a copper axe and one made of polished flint or stone and between the degree of effort required to manufacture each, immigrant metallurgical 'salesmen' would surely have faced severe marketing problems initially. Although metal trinkets are rare in the Irish Earlier Bronze Age, perhaps non-utilitarian (cf. Scott, 1979, 189n) applications may have been of much greater significance in Ireland than has previously been allowed. Finds of small ornaments made from limestone, steatite, quartz, rock crystal, jasper, black and green 'marble', serpentine and carnelian (list after Herity, 1974, 214f) from Irish passage graves reflect an interest, awaiting translation into metal, in the aesthetic value of rocks and minerals. But it is to be noted that, so far, no identification of even small pieces of copper minerals has been recorded from Stone Age contexts.[1]

Various workers (e.g. Case, 1969, 23; Burgess, 1979, 211f) have remarked on the blurring of technological boundaries between Late Neolithic 'Stone Age' and Earlier Bronze Age 'Copper Age'. We hope to demonstrate in this paper how even rare occurrences of native copper in Co. Antrim, an obviously important area technologically in prehistory, might have introduced non-metallurgists in that region to a wholly new substance, anticipating the arrival of true metallurgy by some considerable time. We will not suggest that exploitation of native copper resulted in indigenous discovery of true metallurgy (i.e. the deliberate conversion of friable 'stone' into malleable 'metal' via a liquid-state process). Since there are no artifacts from Ireland that could be identified with certainty as being made from native copper (either cold-worked or cast; cf. section 3), our model is obviously no more than speculative, and is to be viewed as only one tentative step towards continuing study of the stone/metal transition period.

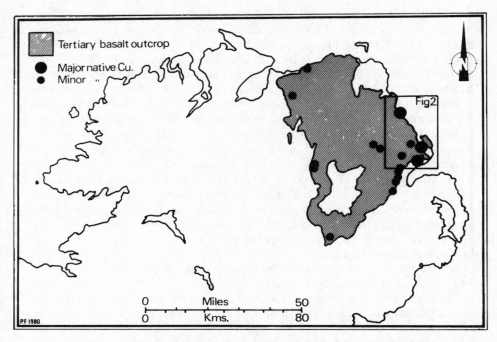

Fig 4: Distribution of known sources of native copper in Co. Antrim: major deposits indicate finds of masses over 2 gms; minor deposits indicate finds under 2 gms. The concentration at the margins of the basalts reflects recent quarrying activities and ease of access for sampling and not any geochemical zonation.

2. THE GEOLOGICAL SETTING

Native copper[2] has been recorded as a trace mineral in the basalts of Co. Antrim by several authorities (cf. Walker, 1959; Francis, 1972), and various specimens have been presented to the Ulster Museum and Queen's University Geology Departments from localities at Woodburn Glen, Magheramorne and Glenarm (fig 4). Walker (1959) recorded its occurrence in minute amounts accompanying zeolite minerals within a distinct zone of secondary hydrothermal mineralisation of the basalts which he termed the 'gmelinite' zone. Francis (1972), in specifically examining the occurrence of this copper, suggested that the unusual hydrothermal environment which gave rise to this gmelinite zone was also essential for the extraction by leaching of copper from the basalts themselves and for its recrystallisation in the native form. At this point, it will be useful to discuss, by way of explanation, some aspects of the late volcanic history of east Co. Antrim.

At the close of volcanism in Co. Antrim, heated water (similar to that which is often apparent at the surface as hot springs and geysers in modern volcanic regions)

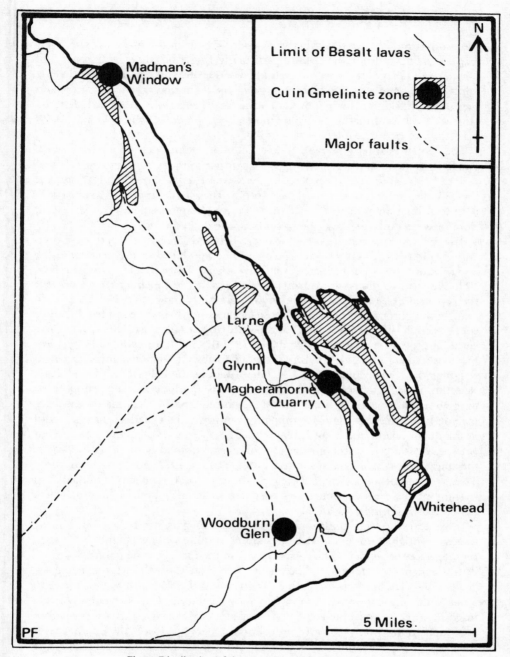

Fig 5: Distribution of the gmelinite zone in Co. Antrim.

Within the figure:

N

Limit of Basalt lavas

Cu in Gmelinite zone

Major faults

Madman's Window

Larne

Glynn

Magheramorne Quarry

Woodburn Glen

Whitehead

5 Miles

PF

was evolved and circulated within the lava pile. This hydrothermal water selectively leached elements from the basalt (particularly from the minerals feldspar and olivine) and redeposited new minerals known as zeolites in gas cavities and along joints. The type of zeolite evolved is largely dependent upon the temperature and pressure of dissolution and deposition. Since these generally increase with depth, a large-scale vertical zonation of zeolite minerals was produced which Walker (1959) has shown to be mappable.

The copper-bearing gmelinite zone (a suite of sodium-rich minerals of which gmelinite is the most distinctive: fig 5) is anomalous, however, due to the fact that while zeolite deposition was proceeding, a complex series of deep faults disrupted the lava pile in this eastern part of Co. Antrim. These faults appear to have permitted the infiltration of hydrothermal brine (derived from underlying salt deposits or from seawater) into the lava pile to produce the gmelinite zone.

The occurrence of native copper was once believed (Francis, 1972) to have been entirely limited by the extent to which these hydrothermal brines penetrated the lava pile, but subsequent research and fieldwork has shown that it occurs in at least 17 localities throughout Co. Antrim (fig 4). Outside the gmelinite zone, however, the copper is exceedingly scarce and crystals are never more than 2 mm across, so that for the purposes of this survey these localities need not be considered. Native copper within the gmelinite zone, and particularly at Magheramorne Quarry near Larne, is present in relatively large masses (Pl I-III) and more commonly than was previously thought. While the largest example known to date remains a specimen weighing 58.7 gms from Woodburn Glen (now in the collections of the Ulster Museum[3]), pieces weighing up to 35 gms have been found at Magheramorne, as have numerous smaller specimens. Most masses remain with their matrix attached, making more precise weight determinations difficult. This marked increase, both in the quantity and quality of native copper obtained at Magheramorne in recent years, is due largely to the greater ease of access afforded by the quarry owners; previously only occasional visits were feasible (Francis, 1972), not long-term study. This is important, for although the copper-bearing basalt is no longer worked, rain washing of the talus continually exposes new material, especially in areas where basalt debris is being excavated.

In general, the metal itself is not immediately recognisable in the field, but the associated bright turquoise malachite staining is quite striking, highlighting even minute traces of copper[4]. The copper occurs in the form of anhedral masses, dendritic filaments or wires and octahedral or cubic crystals, usually accompanying the zeolites and clay minerals which line gas cavities in the flow or flow unit tops and steam vents of the lowest lava flows (fig 6). Malachite staining, sometimes of very intense turquoise and blue coloration, may also occur on fracture surfaces within individual flints from the 'clay-with-flints' horizon (a fossil soil up to 2m in thickness which was formed by weathering before eruption on the chalk landscape and which is preserved below the lowest basalt flows: fig 6). Significant quantities of copper cannot be obtained from such flints, since the native metal only rarely remains, and even when it does, only usually as minute aborescent films.

Research into the nature and occurrence of native copper has centred on Magheramorne Quarry as this locality offers the largest exposure of unweathered basalt within the gmelinite zone. Appreciable quantities of copper in an exactly similar geological context have also been collected from quarry exposures in the area of Madman's Window, 1 km south of Glenarm. This latter area has been shown recently by our colleague Dr P. Woodman to have experienced extensive industrial activity in the Stone Age (Woodman pers. comm., 1980). Fieldwork undertaken in Woodburn Glen, near Carrickfergus, has met with little reward, despite the fact that it was from here that the largest known specimen of Antrim copper was recorded (see n. 3). The fact that the two localities from which appreciable quantities of native copper have been obtained (Magheramorne and Glenarm) are both quarry exposures reflects an obvious sampling bias towards fresh and easily accessible material, but study of two areas of natural basalt exposure in the vicinity of Madman's Window and at Glynn, near Larne, suggests a similar mode of occurrence of native copper throughout the entire gmelinite zone. These two areas were chosen to be representative of natural cliff exposures that occur at intervals along the whole of the east Antrim coast between Whitehead and Glenarm.

The most obvious difficulty arising at these natural exposures is that weathering and natural vegetation cover necessitate a much more concerted search for the small amounts of copper-bearing material present. In general, examination of the cliff

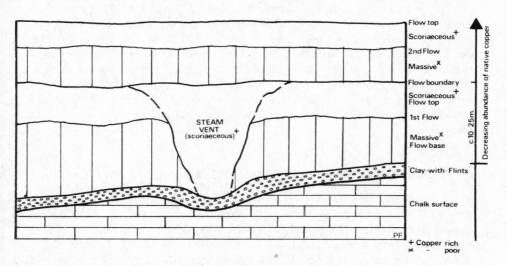

Fig 6: Schematic diagram of the stratigraphy of the lowest basalt flows in Co. Antrim.

face itself was unproductive, although to complicate matters, the largest specimen recovered so far from natural exposures (weighing approximately 12 gms) was found *in situ* at cliffs near Madman's Window. Smaller specimens proved to be most common amongst rock debris occurring as screes or as pebble beaches formed by natural weathering and consisting largely of mixed pebbles of chalk, flint and basalt. While the presence of copper minerals may be most easily detected on the fracture surfaces of flints exhibiting the characteristic bright red, orange or yellow coloration unique among Irish flint sources of the 'clay-with-flints' (see section 3), it is unfortunate that this horizon was not seen *in situ*, being comparatively soft and therefore prone to differential weathering. Whilst flints from this horizon which exhibit malachite pigmentation are *not* a source of metallic copper in Co. Antrim this form of bright staining is unique to copper compounds and could readily have been seen to be connected with similar corrosion products occurring on larger massses of native copper from the basalts themselves.

The only specimens of metallic copper encountered at natural exposures were collected from amygdales in basalt blocks or pebbles. Usually only minute traces were found, although a number of specimens weighing between 5 and 10 gms were collected. On the whole, however, native copper metal was collected relatively infrequently, and usually in quantities less than those found in quarry sections; although it did occur, it must be stressed that native copper is a very scarce mineral in Ireland (cf. n. 2), even in Co. Antrim. Nevertheless, in Co. Antrim, traces of copper (i.e. malachite staining of either zeolites or flints) are common; indeed, once such staining is noticed, it is our experience that it is difficult to escape its presence in what may be totally unrelated fieldwork! Samples weighing more than a few grams are rarely encountered and several of the larger masses obtained for this study came from freshly-exposed debris resulting from the turning over of the talus by a mechanical digger. But it must be borne in mind that planned collection, and that only on an occasional basis, has been in progress for less than a decade. Against this, continual exploitation of flint-bearing strata and weathered-out debris in copper-bearing areas lasted several millennia, and such a long period would surely have been adequate for observant generations to make observations and collect.

3. CO. ANTRIM NATIVE COPPER AND THE STONE-/METAL-USE TRANSITION

Of the various models proffered to explain the original circumstances leading (in the Old World) to the discovery of copper smelting, perhaps the most acceptable is that of observation, over a period, of reduction of minerals to globules of copper during firing (under reducing conditions) of painted ceramics (cf. Tylecote, 1976, 5). A relatively unexplored topic in Irish archaeology is the scope of prehistoric and early collection and use of minerals as pigments[5]. A variety of minerals are known to have been ground for pigments by prehistoric man in the Old World, particularly red iron ores. Our colleague Dr P. Woodman kindly informs us (pers. comm., 1980) that numerous fragments of red ochreous clay[6] were recovered from occupation debris during excavation of the Mesolithic habitation site at Mount Sandel, Co. Derry.

Although copper minerals occur throughout Ireland (cf. Scott, 1977b, 11, fig 3), the Co. Antrim native copper is of particular significance since it is in this region that we also have the most extensive stone, especially flint, resources in the country. And it is not unreasonable to suppose that industrial activity connected with lithic tool manufacture will have been most intense here (e.g., cf. Case, 1969, 11) from earliest times. That collection of flint in this region was not confined to the outcrops of flint in the chalk underlying the lowest basalt flows may be seen from the artifacts made from coloured flints unique to the 'clay-with-flints' horizon (section 2) or its weathered-out debris (Plate IV). If mineral pigments were prized and collected during the Irish Stone Age, our experience shows that they would have been easily located in Antrim in the course of systematic flint collection by the obviously intensely practical peoples of the time.

Preparation of stained zeolite minerals for use as pigments would have involved concentration by selection followed by crushing to powder. Obviously fragments of copper would not be powdered, but rather such treatment would have had the effect of demonstrating the malleability of copper. The scratching and abrading would also have clearly revealed the lustre and blush of fresh copper surfaces. On larger nuggets (from amygdales in the gmelinite zone; cf. Pl I-III), experiments with hammering and abrading would readily have shown that sample shapes could be made, also that such cold hammering soon hardened the metal by deformation of the crystal lattice to the point where it started to crack. Subjecting the new material to abrasion (i.e. treating it initially as a new type of 'stone') would not only have assisted with shaping but also significantly enhanced the appearance of the surface by removal of corrosion products.

Plate IV (arrowed specimen) shows a skeuomorph in native copper of a Neolithic leaf-shaped arrowhead made by the authors. Although modern metalworking hammers and a needle-file were used, there was no annealing and, since neither claims any skill in cold-working of metals, we expect that any advantage conferred by metal tools would be more than offset by the expertise of Stone Age workers in shaping by percussion and abrasion. The arrowhead weighs 1.1 gms and was made from a fragment removed from a sample being taken for analysis (see Appendix). If such tiny artifacts had been fashioned by Stone Age man in Co. Antrim, their chances of survival in a recognisable form seem small, being much more vulnerable to destruction by corrosion than the much more massive flat axes of the earliest Bronze Age (which, on average, weigh some 350-550 gms: Flanagan, 1979, 158n). The fact, however, remains that there is as yet no evidence for use of native copper in the Irish Stone Age (nor for the use of native gold). It could be suggested that such scarce material was kept among the living until the time when the establishment of true metallurgy prompted its melting down for casting. Also, it might be suggested (unkindly?) that since it is axiomatic that metals do not occur in the true Irish Stone Age, excavators of sites of this period could well have overlooked small, amorphous concentrations of copper corrosion products. While there would never have been sufficient native copper to have supported industries on the scale observed, say, amongst American Indians who exploited the native copper masses found around Lake Superior (e.g. Forbes, 1964, 2f) we might look to see if there is any evidence for the kind of occasional use seen in the Near East (e.g. Tylecote, 1976, 1f, and references therein).

Despite suggestions that native copper may be distinguished from smelted copper by its purity (e.g. Tylecote, 1962, 7; Ottaway, 1973) it is now abundantly clear that native copper can exhibit the same degree of impurity as copper produced from the purer ores (e.g. Coghlan, 1962, 61f; Tylecote, 1976, 1, and 2, table 1). Our own analyses of two samples of Co. Antrim copper support this view (see Appendix). Our colleague L.N.W. Flanagan in his own contribution to this volume (Flanagan, 1981) notes a group which included our earliest copper flat axes and whose compositions could not properly be distinguished from that of native copper: it is possible that at least some of the metal came from this source. However, such exploitation could only have accounted for a small proportion of axe production, and only as part of industrial activity of the earliest Bronze Age proper.

Although the Indians who exploited the Lake Superior native copper masses learnt to soften it by annealing, they did not melt or cast it. Despite the attractiveness of Thompson's vignette of petulance on the part of Stone Age users (Thompson, 1958), an open fire while softening by annealing would not be capable of reaching the melting point of copper, 1083°C, and forced draught would have been required. Melting and casting of copper are processes which form the second requirement for developed metallurgy, the first being the ability to reduce copper ores to metal deliberately. Thus, however widespread collection of native copper might have been in Co. Antrim in the Stone Age, this in itself would not have provided a technological bridge between stone-and copper-use.

Where Stone Age discovery of native copper in association with copper minerals could well have been important in the process of establishing metal-use in Ireland is in providing a first-rate demonstration of the connection between mineral (i.e. ore) and metal. If a group of Stone Age people in Co. Antrim were accustomed to collect copper minerals for use as pigments and to recover the larger masses of associated native copper, then introduction to smelting (from whatever source) would surely have met with quicker response than from those who had not previously encountered metals. We might envisage an initial period of collection, melting down and casting of native copper by people in the Co. Antrim region, followed quickly and replaced by smelting of copper ores. Thus, while in no way retreating from the view expressed (Scott, 1977b, 9) that indigenous Irish invention of smelting and melting of copper is an attractive but untenable hypothesis, we may yet see that acquaintance here with copper and its ore minerals is one way in which the development of indigenous copper production could have been accelerated.

Herity (1974, 126; cf. Herity and Eogan, 1977, 67) has noted the widespread occurrence of miniature pendants apparently imitating miners' mauls of the type known from the Early Bronze Age, but in firmly Stone Age settings. Use of copper by Stone Age peoples in Europe has been discussed by, amongst others, Ottaway (1973) and recently by Randsborg (1979). Although one could interpret the 'maul pendants' as imitating tools used to crush copper minerals for use as pigments in a metallurgical contexts, there existed a certain pool of knowledge of metals outside Ireland which predates the emergence of Earliest Bronze Age cultures. Ireland appears to have enjoyed extensive contacts with the outside world during the later Neolithic (as seen, for example, from some ceramics and in the widespread distribution of axes made from Tievebulliagh and Rathlin procellanite throughout the British Isles: Jope, 1952). With the east Antrim region being a focal area for industrial activity, is it not possible that it was contact with outsiders that was one source of introduction of knowledge of copper smelting via travellers from this area? With the Burgess-Shennan hypothesis making for a more static model of the 'Beaker phenomenon', we may at last be able to break away from the 'single source' (Beaker people, associates of wedge-tomb builders, etc.) explanation of how metallurgy came to be established in Ireland[7]. The role of the Co. Antrim native copper might then be seen as a source of background knowledge and experience of some properties of metals, paving the way for an easy understanding of the smelting, melting and casting processes. But even if diffusion of knowledge from this to other areas helped to stimulate indigenous uptake of metal production, it will only have been one among a number of stimuli coming from a variety of sources.

NOTES

1 We use the term 'Stone Age' here primarily in its technological sense, referring to that period when toolmaking was based on flint and stone, but when some trinkets or small copper tools might have been acquired and used without any knowledge of smelting.

2 Occurrences of native copper are not confined to Co. Antrim, having been recorded from a number of other localities (see Coghlan, 1962, 1964; Tylecote, 1962, 7f; and references therein: also, a specimen of native copper in the National Museum of Ireland is ascribed to Allihies, Co. Cork).

3 The Woodburn Glen specimen is unusual in various respects and for the following reasons: first, it was collected in 1900 'at a considerable depth below surface level . . .', but unfortunately no further informtion has been furnished that would more precisely indicate its provenance; second, if the specimen was found *in situ*, then it is most likely to have been collected at a quarry close to Woodburn village (OS 1" ref. J384895), but this quarry has now been filled in and no further traces of native copper were observed in exposures that remain; third, Woodburn Glen lies outside the gmelinite zone (fig 4) and, strictly speaking, if the proposed model for the deposition of the Antrim copper is correct, appreciable quantities of copper should not occur there. On this last point, however, Wodburn Glen lies on a major fault of similar trend to and in obvious association with the East Antrim fault zone and this is significant. It is quite possible that the gmelinite zone does occur in the glen, as present exposures of the lowest basalt flows are scant in areas close to the fault. Alternatively, the underlying Triassic salt deposits could conceivably have contributed to a localised zone of copper-forming hydrothermal brines. Further research is required in this area to provide a more definite explanation.

4 Also present is the mineral cuprite (a copper oxide) as a dark or black coating on the copper.

5 A few studies (e.g. Henry, 1974, 157f, and references therein) discuss the pigment types used in the (later 1st millennium A.D.) illumination of manuscripts. Unless knowledge of the mode of occurrence of mineral pigments and their use is shown to be imported technology and/or based on imported raw materials, we may assume a tradition of mineral pigment use, although how far back this could be traced is impossible to say in the light of present knowledge.
If the reduction of copper minerals used as pigments during firing of painted ceramics is accepted as the most reasonable mechanism whereby the principles of smelting could be observed and assimilated over a long period, then this also tells against any arguments for indigenous discovery of metallurgy here. Although some types of pottery were decorated, there is no evidence for painting of Irish Neolithic pottery.

6 This derives either from thin 'soil' or *tephra* horizons preserved between individual lava flows, or from lateritic soils of the upper or lower interbasaltic zones of the basalt series. It is to be noted that Mt Sandel lies within the source area of these ochreous pigments. Due to their friable nature they could not have endured natural transport without decomposition.

7 Obviously a model which sought to explain the establishment of metallurgy in Ireland as occurring as a result of channelling of knowledge through the inhabitants of one small area of Ireland would be unacceptable. We have not, for example, discussed the possibility that acquaintance with basic properties of metals could have been acquired in the Wicklow metalliferous region through discovery of nuggets of native gold. Beaker-associated involvement 'with metallurgy outside Ireland (whatever the nature of the Beaker phenomenon) as well as inside the country (e.g. O'Kelly and Shell, 1979), can hardly have failed to have contributed to the establishment and development of metallurgical knowledge and practise. Contacts between Ireland and Scandinavia (Case, 1969, 16f) in the Later Irish Neolithic at a time when copper artifacts were in circulation (Randsborg, 1979) are also to be taken into account. These and other factors, while outside the scope of this essay, require detailed individual attention.

APPENDIX

EXAMINATION OF TWO SPECIMENS OF CO. ANTRIM NATIVE COPPER

Two specimens of Co. Antrim native copper and their associated zeolite matrix were selected for examination and analysis.

(1) Native copper mass of approximately 30 gms (Pl Ia and III), in association with cuprite, natrolite (a fibrous zeolite) and malachite staining. No apparent crystal faces on exterior surface. Sectioned across maximum width (Plate III).

(2) Crystalline aggregate of native copper weighing approximately 15 gms, in association with cuprite, natrolite and malachite (not illustrated). Good octahedral faces visible on exterior. Sectioned as closely as possible to one of the three tetrad axes.

Following surface examination, the specimens were X-rayed to discover the precise outline of the metallic copper, mounted in plastic, hand sectioned and polished for qualitative XRF analysis and metallography. Examination of the unetched metal surface revealed internal growth of octahedral faces and cubic crystal habit. Etching with acidic iron (III) chloride solution revealed large polyhedral grains which gave microhardness values of $43.2 - 87.5H$.

Qualitative analysis by wavelength dispersive XRF of the specimen (1) copper in its matrix determined the presence of the following elements:

Na, Mg, Al, Si, S, K, Ca, Ti, Fe

Quantitative analysis of the copper in each specimen for five elements gave the following results:

TABLE 1

	Cu	Mg	Al	Ti	Fe
(1)	99.4	0.065	0.001	n.d.	0.41
(2)	98.9	0.35	0.018	n.d.	0.68

n.d. = not detected
all values given as %

The results of our examinations show that the Co. Antrim native copper may be compared in its composition and properties to specimens examined by other workers (e.g. Coghlan, 1951, 116-17, tables I-II; 1962, 64, table 1 and 65, table 2; Tylecote, 1962, 8, table 1; Selimkhanov, 1964, 68).

ACKNOWLEDGEMENTS

We are grateful to our colleagues L.N.W. Flanagan and P.C. Woodman for their helpful comments, and to R. Bunn, and R. Houston, Department of Industrial Science (N.I.) for the qualitative XRF analysis of specimen 1.

REFERENCES

ApSimon, A.M., 1969. 'The Earlier Bronze Age in the North of Ireland', *Ulster J Archaeol ser 3* **32**, 28-72.

Burgess, C., 1979. 'The background of early metalworking in Ireland and Britain'. *In* M.F. Ryan (ed), 207-14.

Burgess, C. and Shennan, S., 1976. 'The Beaker phenomenon: some suggestions'. *In* C. Burgess and R. Miket (ed), *Settlement and Economy in the Third and Second Millennia B.C.* (Brit Archael Rep **33**) 309-31. Oxford.

Case, H., 1967. 'Were Beaker people the first metallurgists in Ireland?', *Palaeohistoria* **12**, 141-77.

Case, H., 1969. 'Settlement patterns in the North Irish Neolithic', *Ulster J Archaeol ser 3* **32**, 3-27.

Case, H., 1977. 'The Beaker culture in Britain and Ireland'. *In* R. Mercer (ed), *Beakers in Britain and Europe* (Brit Archaeol Rep S **26**) 71-101.

Coghlan, H.H., 1951. *Notes on the Prehistoric Metallurgy of Copper and Bronze in the Old World,* Oxford.

Coghlan, H.H., 1962. 'A note upon native copper: its occurrence and properties', *Proc Prehist Soc* **28**, 58-67.

Flanagan, L.N.W., 1979. 'Industrial resources, production and distribution in earlier Bronze Age Ireland'. *In* M.F. Ryan (ed), 145-63.

Flanagan, L.N.W., 1981. 'Some aspects of the composition of Irish Earlier Bronze Age implements'. See below.

Forbes, R.J., 1964. *Studies in Ancient Technology*, IX. Leiden.

Francis, P.J., 1972. 'The occurrence of native copper in the tertiary basalts of Co. Antrim', *Ir Nat J* **17**(8), 274-6.

Harbison, P., 1973. 'The Earlier Bronze Age in Ireland', *J Roy Soc Antiq Ir* **103**, 93-152.

Harbison, P., 1979. 'Who were Ireland's first metallurgists?'. *In* M.F. Ryan (ed), 97-105.

Henry, F., 1974. *The Book of Kells,* 157f. London.

Herity, M., 1974. *Irish Passage Graves.* Dublin.

Herity, M. and Eogan, G., 1977. *Ireland in Prehistory.* London.

Jope, E.M., 1952. 'Porcellanite axes from factories in north-east Ireland', *Ulster J Archaeol ser 3* **15**, 31-55.

O'Kelly, M.J. and Shell, C.A., 1979. 'Stone objects and a bronze axe from Newgrange, Co. Meath'. *In* M.F. Ryan (ed), 127-44.

Ottaway, B., 1973. 'Earliest copper ornaments in Northern Europe', *Proc Prehist Soc* **39**.

Randsborg, K., 1979. 'Resource distribution and the function of copper in Early Neolithic Denmark'. In M.F. Ryan (ed), 303-18.

Ryan, M.F., 1979 (ed). *The Origins of Metallurgy in Atlantic Europe.* Dublin.

Scott, B.G., 1977a. 'Drink, drugs or dancing? Comments on the "Beaker Cult Package" hypothesis', *Ir Archaeol Res Forum* **4**, 29-34.

Scott, B.G., 1977b. 'Notes on the introduction of non-ferrous metal technology to Ireland', *Ir Archaeol Res Forum* **4**, 7-15.

Scott, B.G., 1979. 'The introduction of non-ferrous and ferrous metal technologies to Ireland: motives and mechanism'. *In* M.F. Ryan (ed), 189-204.

Selimkhanov, I.R., 1964. 'Was native copper used in Transcaucasia in Eneolithic times?', *Proc Prehist Soc* **30**, 66-74.

Thompson, F.C., 1958. 'The early metallurgy of copper and bronze', *Man* **58**, 1-7.

Tylecote, R.F., 1962. *Metallurgy in Archaeology*. London.

Tylecote, R.F., 1976. *A History of Metallurgy*. London.

Walker, F.P.L., 1959. 'The amygdale minerals in the Tertiary lavas of Ireland: II — the distribution of gmelinite'. *Min Mag* **32**, 202-17.

Waddell, J., 1978. 'The invasion hypothesis in Irish archaeology', *Antiquity* **52**, 121-28.

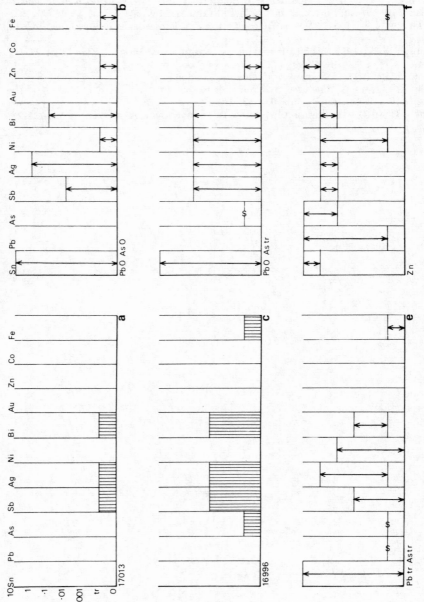

Fig 7: Composition of axes (analysis nos 17015 and 16996) and compositional ranges of metal groups.

Some Aspects of the Composition of Irish Earlier Bronze Age bronze implements

Laurence N.W. Flanagan

Brian O'Kelly has long been known for a particularly lively and active interest in the basic questions of archaeology, particularly of the 'how-exactly-was-it-done?' type. It is with mingled pleasure and regret that I offer the few thoughts below to his Festschrift — pleasure that I am in a position to contribute anything, regret that it is the inexorable passing of time that has made it appropriate for me to do so. (I am tempted to apologise that I have not, in fact, tried any of it out!).

In 1974 some 1,000 spectrographic analyses of Irish Earlier Bronze Age bronze implements were published (Junghans, Sangmeister and Schröder, 1974); this massive volume of information remains virtually untouched, probably, in the main, because of its sheer bulk.

One of the major difficulties in attempting to use these analyses is the lack of firm knowledge as to which of the elements listed are significant and at what quantities. While analyses of Irish copper sources have been published (Butler, 1963; Jackson, 1979) it is difficult satisfactorily to reconcile these with analyses of the bronze implements for two reasons: the elements sought by the analysts do not correspond and there is little, if any, certain knowledge of the precise manner in which elements in the ores behave in the conditions of smelting prevalent in the Irish Earlier Bronze Age.

Among the 1,000 analyses is a group containing no lead and no arsenic (the Pb0 As0 Group); another group contains no lead and no more than a trace of arsenic (the Pb0 Astr Group).

Looking first at the Pb0 As0 Group, represented by 29 analyses, we find that one of the metals looks very like pure copper (fig 7a)[1] (Junghans, Sangmeister and Schröder, 1974, No. 17013), containing no recorded alloying elements other than traces of antimony, silver and bismuth. The piece itself is an axe of Lough Ravel (sub-type Ballybeg) type (Harbison, 1969, no. 361, from Cloonmullin, Co. Roscommon), possibly one of the more likely objects to enjoy such a composition. While an axe of such simplistic content is interesting in its own right, without any clear (i.e. recorded) indication of alloying elements and apparently, on the face of it, most immediately suggesting an affinity with ores of Group C (Jackson, 1979), instanced by a bornite ore from near Ballydehob, Co.Cork, it is also important in

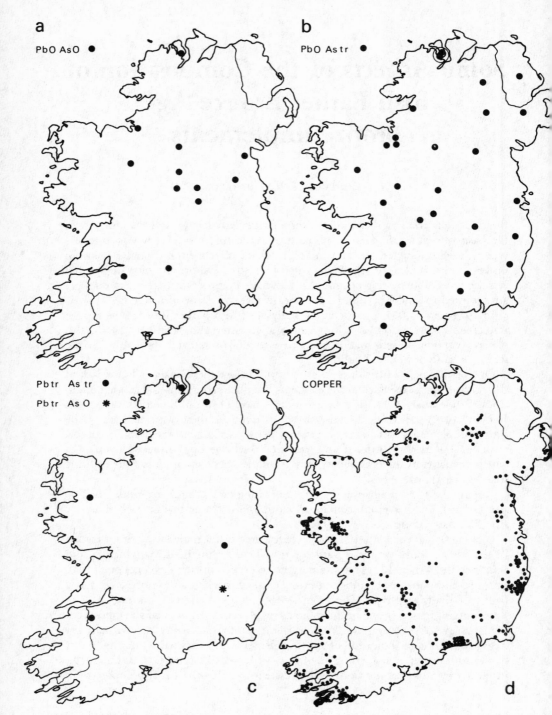

Fig 8: Distribution of objects of the four metal-groups discussed and of copper sources in Ireland.

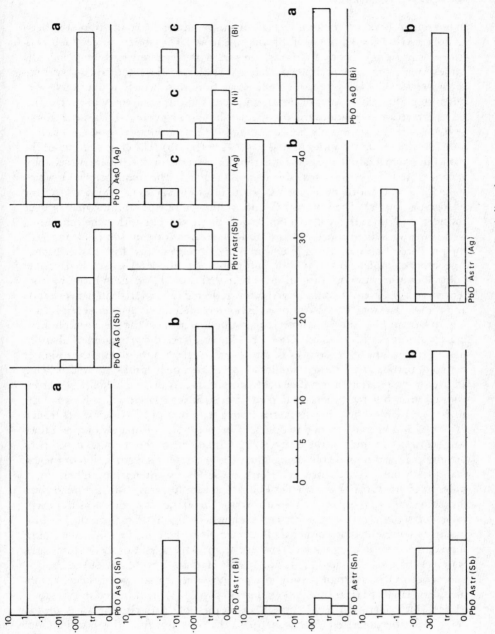

Fig 9:Incidence of selected single elements, at values indicated, in three of the metal-groups discussed.

suggesting a 'base' for the other metals of this group whose composition has been complicated by the addition of alloying elements. The objects represented constitute, surprisingly enough, a fairly cohesive typological series, the typologically earliest being the 'pure' copper axe referred to above. The recorded compositions show a remarkable consistency as well. Apart from iron, which in trace quantities seems to pollute all manner of metals and occurs in this group only in trace quantities, the greatest variations recorded are in the silver content, which varies from 0 to 0.43%; nickel varies only between 0 and 0.32%; antimony between 0 and ⟨ 0.005% while bismuth varies from 0 to 0.032% (fig 7b). The close confines of the group are remarkable. Even the distribution-pattern of the 12 for which provenances are recorded is remarkably compact (fig 8a). The frequencies with which some of the constituent elements occur at given values is indicated in the histograms (fig 9a). The PbO Astr Group, composed of 62 examples, may next be considered. While arsenic is notoriously volatile (to the extent that the continuing well-being of Earlier Bronze Age bronze-founders is a constant source of surprise[2], the presence of only a trace of arsenic in 6.2% of the analysed Irish Earlier Bronze Age bronze implements is a little surprising. At this level in smelted copper (alloyed or otherwise) it is difficult to believe that the wild variation in arsenic content of ores of Group A could be accurately reflected (i.e. a variation between 0.03 and ⟩15% (Jackson, 1979). Antimony is not recorded in all the analyses (it is lacking, in fact, in 11 of the 62 samples) suggesting that some of the metals might have greater affinities with Jackson's Group B. However since the geographical distribution of the groups of ore-sources is not dissimilar (fig 8d) premature ascription of metals to particular ore-sources would not necessarily be helpful — as well as being an over-interpretation of insufficient chemical data. Again one metal (fig 7c) contains no tin, while two others contain only traces. Silver is lacking in only two of the analyses available, and otherwise varies from a trace to 0.51%. Nickel varies from 0 to 0.14% and bismuth from 0 to 0.02%. Zinc occurs — fortunately only as a trace (see below) — in three of the analyses (fig 7d) and again the chemical confines of the group appear remarkably close. Again the geographical distribution of the 29 examples whose provenance is recorded (fig 8b) is interesting, albeit more widespread than that of the smaller PbO AsO group; it seems oddly excluded from the conventionally copper-rich south-west. The frequency with which variant values of some elements are present is shown in fig 9b. Typologically the implements represented are rather more diverse than those in the PbO AsO Group: they range from a Lough Ravel type axe from Doneraile, Co. Cork (Junghans, Sangmeister and Schröder, 1974, no. 16996; Harbison, 1969, no. 69) to daggers and rapiers. Of more than passing interest, however, is that two of the axes from the Glenalla Hoard (Harbison, 1969, nos 936 and 1583) are included in this group while a third (Harbison, 1969, no. 937) is in the PbO AsO Group. It has already been implicitly suggested (Flanagan, 1979) that two axes from this hoard are not only co-matrical but are of such similar compositions that they are almost certainly products not only of the same metal-source but are even likely to derive from the same 'mix' of founder's metal — even, perhaps, to have been poured from the same crucible[3], despite the presence of a trace of arsenic in one of the metals. It is now suggested, therefore, that the Glenalla Hoard may reveal a link with yet a further group of objects — a group of 9 analyses, whose composition is marked by traces only of both lead and arsenic — a Pbtr Astr Group. The comparative compositions of the Glenalla axes are shown in fig 10. The range of other trace elements in this group is well within those for the two groups already discussed (fig 7e) and the geographical distribution of the objects complies well with those of the other two groups (fig 8c), and continues to show an avoidance of the conventionally copper-rich areas of the south-west. By and large the avoidance of this area and Co. Antrim — the two areas in the country most densely populated by bronze axes of every type— is the strongest indication that these metals do form a special — and rather restricted — 'family'.

It is suggested, therefore, that these three metal groups (Pbo Aso, Pb0 Astr and Pb Tr As Tr) seem to form a consistent body, possibly emanating from an ore-source not in the south-west. It could be argued that the major 'family' of groups,

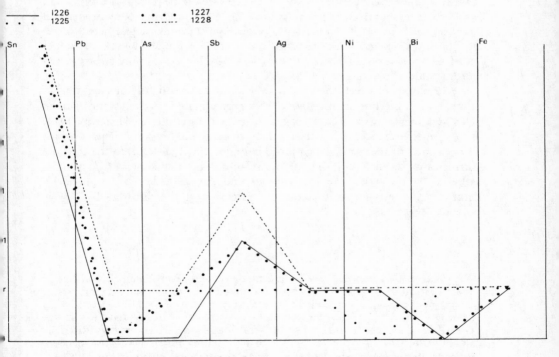

Fig 10: Comparative compositions of the four axes in the hoard from Glenalla, Co. Donegal.

to be called a PbO/tr AsO/tr family, could be expanded to include metals with more than mere traces of lead and arsenic; unfortunately it simply is not known at what levels trace-elements become significant and it would seem incautious to add more body to what is, after all, at this time no more than an hypothesis which seemed worth testing and seems to remain attractive after some admittedly not excessively rigorous testing, but within the limits of knowledge here and now. It is, perhaps, not too rash to add a group of metals containing a trace of lead and no arsenic — particularly since only one analysis of this group is recorded (Junghans, Sangmeister and Schröder, 1974, no. 16626) — a flat axe of Ballyvalley type (Harbison, 1969, no. 1008) from Tinriland, Co. Carlow. The metal, apart from the tin at 9.2% is remarkably pure with only traces of lead, antimony, silver, nickel and iron — suggesting that either the sources of both copper and tin were remarkably pure or that the extraction of metals was remarkably skilful. If this hypothesis does seem provisionally attractive it does, at least, reduce the daunting mass of unused analyses by slightly more than 10%.

At the other end of the tabulation of analytical results the zinc content is given. A further group of metals may be discerned with reference to the appearance in quantity of this element. While some 75 analyses show zinc present as a trace, and a few others at slightly higher levels (up to 0.72% (Junghans, Sangmeister and Schröder, 1974, no. 17407)) there is a positively breath-taking gap between this and the next lowest value recorded, at 4.4%, followed by 18 at values (undefinedly) in excess of 5%. In 10 instances these high zinc values are associated with lead values in excess of 5%. (fig 7f).

The 18 objects to which these analyses relate have one slightly unusual trait in common — all but one are unprovenanced; even among Irish prehistoric material such a high incidence of unprovenanced material is suspicious (cf. Flanagan, 1979, fig 1). The objects include 'flat axes', 'flanged axes' and 'daggers'. The 10 which can be related to the Harbison corpus (Harbison, 1969) all fall into the category described by him including the one provenanced object (Ballintoy, Co. Antrim, Harbison, 1969, 2002) as 'seeming spurious, and may be modern'. This provides a useful and interesting confirmation and extension of the discovery by Megaw (Burke & Megaw, 1966).

NOTES

1 The value-intervals used in these bar-graphs are those used in Waterbolk and Butler, 1965; a variant, evolved for more personally convenient recognition (and graphic presentation) of comparative composition-patterns (for a form of simplistic multi-variate analysis) is used to indicate the comparative compositions of the four axes in the Glenalla, Co. Donegal hoard, in fig. 10. While the value-intervals used by Waterbolk and Butler may have little or no significance in the ultimate ascription of Irish metals to Irish ore-sources (any more than the generalised 'statistical' groupings of Junghans, Sangmeister & Schröder) they have been used here since no better-based alternative has

presented itself or been presented. It is possible that a sophisticated computerised multi-variate analysis might ultimately produce an alternative or that more extensive analyses of smelted ores might do so. In the interim, however, we must make the best use of the evidence currently available and our means of interpreting it.

2 The temperature at which copper melts is 1083°C; the temperature at which arsenic sublimes, and therefore, produces (potentially) toxic volatiles, is below 100°C. It is probable that the major safety-factor in Irish Earlier Bronze Age bronze-foundries was their *al fresco* nature. However, the greater the amount of arsenic to volatilise out of the ores, the greater the hazard to the craftsmen involved, and the volatilisation of even 15% of the ore body would be a lot of arsenic — even out of doors.

3 The Glenalla Hoard (National Museum of Ireland, Dublin, Reg. Nos 1933: 1225, 1226, 1227 & 1228) is so important that it seems worthwhile to give the Stuttgart analyses in full, in addition to the graphic comparison in fig. 10:

		1225	1226	1227	1228
Harbison's no.		936	1582	1583	937
Analysis no.		16928	16930	16929	16927
Weight		662.5g	359.1g	318.36g	575.7g
	Sn	210	6	9.6	210
	Pb	0	0	0	tr
	As	tr	0	tr	tr
	Sb	tr	‹ 0.005	‹0.005	20.08
	Ag	tr	tr	tr	tr
	Ni	0	tr	tr	tr
	Bi	tr	0	0	tr
	Au	0	0	0	0
	Zn	0	0	0	0
	Co	0	0	0	0
	Fe	tr	+	+ +	+

One reason for the importance of the Glenalla Hoard is that it makes us start thinking about the size of Earlier Bronze Age crucibles: i.e. if nos 1226 and 1227 were poured from the same metal-mix in the same crucible then that crucible must have been capable of holding some 677.4g of bronze. This may seem a surprisingly large amount when it is recalled that average weights for bronze axes vary between 21.1g for 'ingots' to 536.9 for Killaha type (Flanagan, 1979, note 7). It should, however, be remembered also that the weight of one of the copper 'cakes' (presumably, in fact, a real ingot) that have been found in Irish Earlier Bronze Age contexts, in fact that from Knockasarnet, Co. Kerry, found with an axe of Killaha type (Harbison, 1969, no. 586) is 732.6g. Even more directly bearing on crucible size is the fact that at least 12 examples are known of one-piece Irish Earlier Bronze metal objects with weights in excess of 1,000 g (as well as one at

999.9g). In fact one object is known (a massive axe of Killaha type from Kilcrea Castle, Co. Cork (Harbison, 1969, 580) which weighs a remarkable 2212.6g — its casting would have consumed more than three ingots of Knockasarnet size. While it could be argued that a massive object like this would require the contents of successive crucibles its quality and size suggest that too many crucibles would have been ineffectual and that crucibles of the order of 750g capacity are likely to have used.

REFERENCES

Burke, J. and Megaw, J.V.S., 1966. 'British decorated axes: a footnote on fakes', *Proc Prehist Soc* **32**, 343.

Butler, J.R., 1963. 'A report on elements in Irish copper ores', *Ores and Metals*, Report of the Ancient Mining and Metallurgy Committee, Royal Anthropological Institute, **34**.

Flanagan, L.N.W., 1979. 'Industrial resources, production and distribution in Earlier Bronze Age Ireland'. *In* M.F. Ryan (ed), *The Origins of Metallurgy in Atlantic Europe, Proceedings of the Fifth Atlantic Colloquium, Dublin, 1978*, 145.

Jackson, J.S., 1979. 'Metallic ores in Irish Prehistory: copper and tin'. *In* M.F. Ryan (ed), *The Origins of Metallurgy in Atlantic Europe, Proceedings of the Fifth Atlantic Colloquium, Dublin, 1978*, 107.

Junghans, S., Sangmeister, E., and Schröder, M., 1974. *Kupfer und Bronze in der frühen Metallzeit Europas*. Berlin.

Harbison, P., 1969. *The Axes of the Earlier Bronze Age in Ireland*. Munich.

Waterbolk, H.T., and Butler, J.J., 1965. 'Comments on the use of metallurgical analysis in prehistoric studies', *Helenium* **5**, 227.

APPENDIX

In order to test the significance of the geographical distribution of this Pb0/tr As0/tr Metal Group the following statistics were extracted from the Harbison (1969 a & b) populations, where the populations for Cork and Kerry together with Antrim are compared with the total population for the whole of Ireland.

Class	Total	Cork Kerry	Antrim	% of Total
Axes (L. Ravel)	165	65	22	51.5%
Axes (Ballybeg)	48	21	2	47.9%
Axes ('Ingots')	21	2	5	33.3%
Axes (Killaha)	134	68	19	64.9%
Axes (Ballyvalley)	374	21	75	25.7%
Axes (Derryniggin)	118	6	19	21.2%
All axes	860	181	142	37.6%
Halberds (All types)	89	10	5	16.9%
Daggers (All types)	91	5	9	15.4%
All above	1040	196	156	33.8%
Pb0/tr As0/tr Metals	48	2	1	6.3%
Land (Sq. miles)	32598	4490	1190	17.4%

On the face of it, in terms of sheer area of land available, one might, from these figures expect, all things being equal, and if distributions were totally random, 17.4% of all archaeological objects to come from the parts now called 'Cork/Kerry together with Antrim'. Or, the matter of that, one might expect 51.5% of L. Ravel axes to come from these parts, or even 37.6% of all Harbison's axes. (In fact of the axes only of this composition only 2 out of 30 provenanced examples come from Cork/Kerry, together with Antrim, one of L. Ravel type, the other of Ballyvalley type).

While superficial interpretations such as these of the figures quoted above seem attractive it was decided to apply a χ^2 test to several relevant null hypotheses.

The first was that in terms of land area the distribution of all the EBA metalwork listed in tables above is proportionally evenly represented in the three areas Cork/Kerry; Antrim; Rest of Ireland. For this null hypothesis a value of $\chi^2 = 423$ with 2d.f. was obtained, representing a probability of $\langle\langle .1\%$, so that this null hypothesis is totally rejected.

The second was that in terms of land area the distribution of the Pb0/tr As0/tr group is proportionally evenly represented in the two areas Cork/Kerry + Antrim; Rest of Ireland. For this a value of $\chi^2 = 4.2$ with 1 d.f. was obtained, representing a probability of between 2½% and 5%. There are not, therefore, good grounds for rejecting this hypothesis.

The third null hypothesis was that the Pb0/tr As0/tr group has the same distributional trend in the three areas Cork/Kerry; Antrim; Rest of Ireland, as all the EBA metalwork listed in the tables above. For this a value of $\chi^2 = 16.4$ with 2d.f. was obtained representing a probability that the null hypothesis is correct of $\langle$ .1%; this hypothesis is therefore rejected.

The interpretation of these tests is reasonably straightforward: that EBA metalwork is by no means evenly distributed over the three areas Cork/Kerry, Antrim and the Rest of Ireland, but that metals of the Pb0/tr As0/tr group possibly are evenly represented in the two areas Cork/Kerry with Antrim and the rest of Ireland — in sharp contrast to the generality of EBA metalwork. It does seem justifiable, therefore, to regard the Pb0/tr As0/tr Metal Group as a significantly disparate entity.

I am grateful to Mr. R.B. Warner for performing the statistical calculations for me and for interpreting them for me.

REFERENCE

Harbison, P., 1969b. *The Daggers and the Halberds of the Early Bronze Age in Ireland*. Munich.

Dating Irish Glass Beads by Chemical Analysis

R. Warner and I.G. Meighan

INTRODUCTION

I am particularly happy to offer this note to M.J. O'Kelly not only because of his pioneering interest in the technical aspects of Irish archaeology but also because it was to his students in Cork that I first described this project. The spectral charts on which this short report is based were made, and the spectral lines identified, by I. Meighan on a Philips 1540 X-ray spectrometer. The technical details of this application will be described elsewhere but it should be noted that a non-destructive constraint prevented sample preparation, and consequently the calculation of element quantities, based on whole specimen irradiation and the measurement of scattered primary (anode) radiation as a measure of the area of the sample contributing secondary radiation may be unique in archaeological analysis. The calculation of quantities, the statistical treatment of the results and their archaeological interpretation were the work of R. Warner, who wrote this report and alone bears responsibility for any errors.

Glass beads are a major feature of the Irish archaeological assemblage from the middle of the first millennium B.C.(the middle of the Irish later Bronze Age) until the end of the first millennium A.D. (the end of the later Iron Age, more popularly called the Early Christian period). Their frequency, durability and often high degree of decoration and variability of shape allow the construction of a clear, consistent and well differentiated visual typology. This is particularly important in the case of cultures, such as the later Iron Age, in which a large part of the material assemblage, particularly that part most likely to occur in the excavation of a small settlement, was undifferentiated and simple, the object types continuing to be manufactured for very long periods without change, or in which the major part of the domestic assemblage was of material, such as wood or iron which only in exceptional circumstances escapes complete or severe deterioration. The potential value of beads therefore, in a basically coinless society, as a means of dating archaeological contexts is clear, diminished only by their chance of survival as heirlooms. In the absence, amongst the finds from most excavations, of artwork or fine metalwork (for stylistic dating), historic documentation, or large oak artifacts (for dendrochronological dating), and given the difficulties of interpreting radiocarbon dates, particularly on single-period sites, the glass bead offers great potential value as a chronological indicator.

There are, however, two serious drawbacks. One is that a large number, perhaps a majority, of the beads found in excavations, or other archaeological contexts, are not highly decorated or otherwise distinctive and cannot reliably be fitted into the visual typology. The other is that although a number of beads, or types, have been approximately dated, and a rough chronological framework can be given to the visual typology, this is not as sound nor as complete as one would like.

It was felt, therefore, that by analysing the beads and by treating the element quantities or ratios as traits, in precisely the same way as such visual traits as decoration or colour, we would increase the descriptive complexity of any bead by up to twenty or so extra characteristics. Hopefully, these extra descriptors, when subjected to various statistical processes, would produce groupings that would parallel the visual groupings, indicator elements that would distinguish the classes, and similarities that would show the connection between the various visually distinct groups. Hence we should be able to place the visually unclassifiable beads into, or into a clear relationship with, the visual or analytical classes and, in relative rather than absolute terms, put the chronological framework on a sounder basis. The main aim of the project was, therefore, to solve this particular typological problem. Clearly, however, the analysis has also produced a mass of purely technological information and although this will be alluded to here it will not be described in any detail. This typological application of chemical analysis has proved useful in the cases, for instance, of prehistoric gold (Hartmann, 1970) and of Continental early Bronze Age tools (Hodson, 1969). In both these cases the analytical results provided information for geographical as well as chronological groupings, and we expect this to be the case ultimately with the Irish beads.

THE VISUAL TYPOLOGY

The visual typology of Irish beads will be described in more detail elsewhere, with full justification for the claimed chronological framework. Here I will briefly describe only those classes used in the analysis. The dates given below are based on contextual and decorative considerations only and are therefore independent of the chemical work. For most of the types I will refer to conveniently illustrated examples from Garranes (Ó Ríordáin, 1942), Lagore (Hencken, 1950), Garryduff (O'Kelly, 1962) and Ballinderry 2 (Hencken, 1942). The beads from Clogher (a later Iron Age settlement) and Kiltierny (a series of earlier Iron Age graves) have not yet been published, but are well dated. I would add that most of the beads used in the analysis, although typical examples of the classes, are not from excavated sites, and are not contextually dated themselves. The class numbers used below are only for the convenience of this report and will not be used elsewhere.

The simple chronology I have used is as follows:—

earlier Iron Age = from the third century B.C. to the fourth century A.D.;

later Iron Age, first phase = from about the fifth to the eighth century A.D.;

later Iron Age, second phase = from the eighth to the twelfth century A.D.,

(the lack of beads from Ballinderry 1 (Hencken, 1936) might suggest a strong decrease in popularity after the tenth century, as we also find in the case of penannular brooches).

CLASS 1. DUMB-BELL.

These are almost always unpierced, being toggles rather than beads. Two date ranges are found which are difficult to allocate beads to visually. The beads vary considerably in colour, but not, apparently, in a chronologically useful fashion. For the earlier Iron Age we have an example from Kiltierny and two from Close ny chollagh, I.O.M. (Gelling, 1958). From the later Iron Age (probably the second phase) are examples from Lagore (no. 1471), Ballinderry 2 (no. 251) and Clogher. Five Class 1 beads were analysed.

CLASS 2. BLUE WITH SIMPLE WHITE SPIRALS.

2a, a large globular example (analysed), from Kiltierny, clearly belonged to Guido's class 6 (Oldbury type). This class, Continental and British early Iron Age, has several occurrences in Northern Ireland. Although the Kiltierny example is earlier Iron Age two others (2b) which were analysed, although similar, are not close enough to the Oldbury type to be sure of an earlier Iron Age date.

CLASS 3. BLUE GLOBULAR WITH YELLOW KNOBS.

The evidence of the Loughey find (Jope, 1960) suggests the earlier Iron Age. One was analysed.

CLASS 4. ZIG-ZAG ANNULAR BEADS.

Almost any colour of body will be found, usually very intense. The commonest type is 'black' (very dark blue) with a white paste zig-zag around the perimeter, usually not marvered into the surface (e.g. Garranes, no. 61). The evidence from Clogher, where several were found, suggests a date in phase 1 of the later Iron Age, perhaps just into phase 2. They are common in the Anglo-Saxon and Frankish world. Three were analysed.

CLASS 5. MOTTLED BEADS.

A usually blue body with haphazardly placed patches — marvered insets — of green, red, white and yellow. The date and distribution is as class 4, and at Clogher there is evidence of local manufacture in phase 1 of the later Iron Age (examples, Garranes, no. 61; Lagore, fig 68, D; Ballinderry 2, 440). Two were analysed.

CLASS 6. TRIPARTITE.

This wide group is heavily sub-divided, but shares a basic tripartite shape, and a blue body, either equal segments (e.g. Garryduff, no. 484) or a larger body with collars (e.g. Lagore, no. 65). Four plain tripartite beads (6a) were analysed. The class may be decorated (6b) with white multi-spirals (groups of interlocking spirals) flush or as knobs (e.g. Lagore, no. 125), and/or blue-white cables, often as the collars (e.g. Lagore nos. 65, 125). Three of these were analysed. 6c belong to the same class, but have other variations: two were analysed. Class 6 all belong to phase 2 of the later Iron Age.

CLASS 7. CABLED BLUE BRACELETS (e.g. Lagore, fig 70).

These are clearly allied to class 6, but unlike them the cables are usually marvered level with the surface of the bracelet. Later Iron Age, phase 2. Two were analysed.

CLASS 8. HERRINGBONE.

These beads were constructed of rings of two-coloured cables around a core, alternating in direction and finally moulded to form the bead. 8a, cables of yellow and 'clear' glass (e.g. Lagore, no. 984; Garryduff, no. 346). Although fine examples of this sub-class have been found in Irish earlier Iron Age contexts (Kiltierny and Dún Ailinne) there is no doubt that they are most common in the later Iron Age. The 4 rather crude examples analysed were of the latter date, probably the second phase. 8b, cables of blue and white glass, the same sort of cables as were used on the class 6 beads (e.g. Lagore no. 283; Ballinderry 2 no. 318). Phase 2 of the later Iron Age. One was analysed.

CLASS 9. CLEAR BODY WITH THREE LARGE YELLOW SPIRALS.

One Irish example, from Loughey (Jope and Wilson, 1957; Jope, 1960), clearly earlier Iron Age, an attribution in line with the date of the comparable British early Iron Age 'Meare class' (Guido's class 10). However the other Irish contexts (e.g. Garryduff no. 75; Lagore fig 67A) are certainly later Iron Age. One was analysed.

CLASS 10. STRIATED ANNULAR.

Guido (class 7) and Raftery (1972) consider these to belong to the British and Continental groups of 'swirl' beads. There is little evidence to the contrary, but the matter of date is open. One, blue and white, was analysed.

CLASS 11. SIMPLE.

As we have explained most sites have produced simple beads, usually of one colour or clear. These can be of any date; five (all undated) were analysed.

CLASS 12. BRAMBLE.

Not commonly found on excavations, but numerous in museum collections. This class of bead is of the size and surface appearance of a blackberry. Whatever the colour the body is always limpid. The few contexts (e.g. Lagore, fig 67B; and Lissue, unpublished) put the group into phase 2 of the later Iron Age. Four analysed.

THE CHEMICAL ANALYSIS

Twenty-one elements were recognised and measured in the 42 beads and bracelets analysed, and it was found that the elements could be divided into three groups: Group A, those elements showing discriminatory variation coinciding, in many cases, with the visual typological groupings but not correlating, usually, with such traits as colour (for instance antimony, arsenic and manganese); Group B, oxides present as intentional colourants or opacifiers, correlating to particular colours (such as cobalt, tin, lead and copper); and Group C, elements present in trace quantities and showing neither class discrimination nor colour correlation (such as barium and titanium). However, these groups were not clear-cut. In the translucent beads group B elements show good class discrimination, and in the opaque beads or paste decorations the group A elements (such as antimony) occasionally showed signs of colour correlation.

DISCRIMINATORS (fig 11)

It was suspected that multivariate statistical methods would be necessary in order to draw useful data from the analyses of the beads. This has been undertaken, but will not be described here. In fact the analyses proved to be substantially monothetic, the major variance being in the antimony. Further separation occurred within the manganese concentrations and on fig 11 the antimony and manganese oxide concentrations are shown for all the beads. It will be seen that the beads can be divided into several groups.

GROUP I (later Iron Age, phase 2).

It is evident that there is a typological division of the beads on fig 11 at the 0.6% antimony and 0.5% manganese levels. All the later Iron Age, phase 2 beads of classes 6, 7, 8 and 9 are below the manganese division and above that of the antimony, the antimony/manganese ratio being greater than 3. It will be seen that all the class 6 beads cluster tightly around 10% antimony, 0.4% manganese. With them in this tight cluster are one 8a bead, one 8b, one class 7 bracelet and one simple blue class 11 bead. A looser cluster, with lower antimony, contains three 8a beads, another class 7 bracelet, the class 9 bead and a class 1 dumb-bell. That these two clusters should be regarded as separate subgroups (1a for the higher antimony, 1b for the lower) is confirmed by the concentrations of the other discriminant elements (copper, iron, strontium). On fig 12 most of the elements are shown for the class 6a beads and the single class 11. The concentrations are so close that it is difficult to escape the conclusion that a single, presumably very large, glass batch was used for all of them. Two of the 6a beads were found on the same site (Teeshan crannóg, Co. Antrim). Curiously, despite the high antimony level of the group I beads, the opaque threads and knobs (found on several of them) and the opaque body glass of one of them are not likely to be antimonates (see below). For those beads where the body and decoration analyses can be compared the only elements in which concentrations differ markedly are those of the colourants (tin and lead). This strongly suggests that the same general mix was used for the translucent and opaque glasses and that the colourants were added to this (including the cobalt for blue — see below). Further, in a clear-yellow class 1 bead in this group the clear glass fitted the Ib group perfectly, but the yellow contained considerably less antimony (0.5%). This might represent the antimony level in the original glass, or cullet, the high antimony being added locally. The quite high level of colourants and opacifying agents, tin (0.4%), copper (1%), lead (1.4%) and iron (1.2%) should be noted in the translucent group I beads. Without much doubt were it not for the high antimony these would be opaque or semi-opaque and quite discoloured. It is surprising that the bead makers were aware of the value of antimony as a decolourant but unaware of its value as an opacifier.

GROUP II (Earlier Iron Age and Later Iron Age, phase 1).

This group lies, on fig 11, below the 0.6% antimony level, down to 0.1%, and above the 0.5% manganese level. The antimony/manganese ratio is less than 0.6. The group contains classes 2b, 3 and 10, which I have suggested are of earlier Iron Age date, and classes 4 and 5, which are certainly later Iron Age, phase 1. The group is not so clearly distinct, or consistent, on the other elements, and the typological differences between the earlier and later classes here are so great that it seems unlikely that they should be regarded as emanating from the same tradition. The high coloration of the classes 4 and 5 makes detailed consideration of their body glasses very difficult at present. I show below that both tin-oxide and calcium antimonate are used as the white opacifier in this group, with lead antimonate as the yellow opacifier. It could be that the antimony is present at anything above a

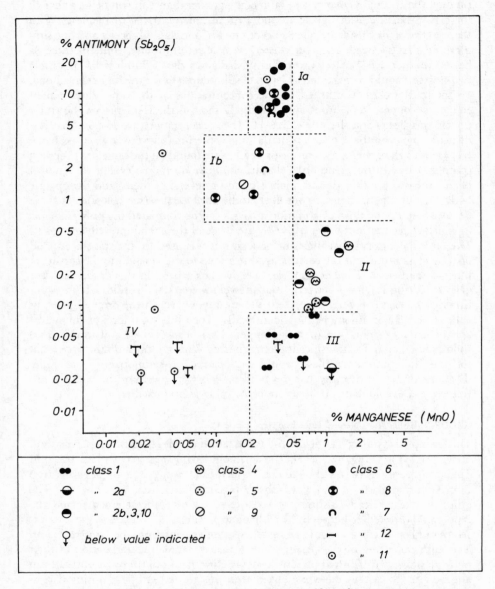

Fig 11: The percentage contents of antimony (as antimony pentoxide) and manganese (as manganese oxide) for all the beads and bracelets analysed.

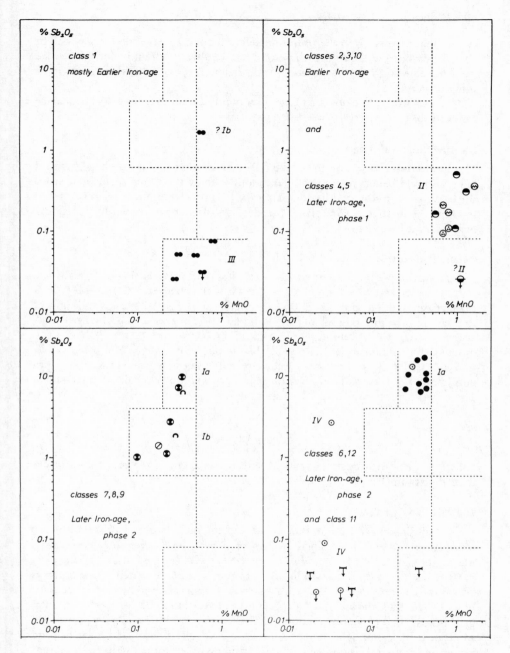

Fig 12: The percentage contents of antimony and manganese for the various classes, showing the chronological and typological separation into distinct analytical groups (I to IV). Symbols as on fig 11.

contaminant level only in the white and yellow decorative pastes and it may well be that the 2a bead in group III, whose trail has weathered out and which contained no detectable antimony in the body, really belongs to group II, which it fits in all other respects.

The lead level in the opaque glasses of group II usually exceeds 1%, but may be lower in the translucent (below 0.5%).

GROUP III (earlier Iron Age).

This group contains all but one of the class 1 beads, and the class 2a bead (which I believe should belong to group II). Antimony is below 0.1% and manganese spans the 0.5% level. In the translucent glasses the lead concentration is below 0.2% but reaches 5% in the opaque glasses, lead oxide often being necessary for aiding opacification by other oxides.

GROUP IV (later Iron Age, phase 2).

This group, whose translucent glass contains less than 0.1% antimony (usually less than the detectable limit of .02 — .04%) and between 0.01 and 0.06% manganese (with one outsider at 0.4%) contains all the class 12 beads and most of the class 11. The group is distinct on almost all the elements, and particularly in its arsenic (between 0.01 and 4.5%) and rubidium (between 0.02 and 0.2%). (The other classes contain little or undetectable amounts of either). It also has, in its translucent glass, less than 0.03% lead. One class 11 bead which on fig 11 falls into group I on its antimony level, in reality belongs to group IV on all other elements. The bead is opacified with yellow lead antimonate (see below).

COLORATION

I shall not deal with this matter in any great detail, giving my conclusions rather than the arguments.

TRANSLUCENT GLASS.

Amber and 'greenish' (due to iron) occur, but the main body colour is translucent blue (26 out of the 42 beads and bracelets, of all periods). In every blue bead cobalt was present (0.02 to 0.4%), and in no case was cobalt detected in a non-blue glass (0.01% was the lower detection limit). It can confidently be stated that cobalt was always the coloriser in the blue beads analysed. Copper showed no correlation with blue. I have, for some years, been applying a rule-of-thumb dating method to blue glass beads based on an observation that earlier Iron Age blue had a deep, rich hue when held up to sunlight, whereas the later Iron Age, phase 2, blue beads were watery and limpid. It is now clear that the richness of the former is due to 'pinking' by the high manganese (cf. Jope and Wilson, 1957), while the lower level of manganese in the later beads and the high level of decolorising antimony has resulted in their watery blue. A number of beads are 'clear' or contain 'clear' glass. In a 'clear' class 12 bead the expected arsenic white (see below) seems to have been decolorised by a highish level of manganese. In the case of the single group I, class 1, 'clear' bead the expected coloration has been decolorised by the 1% antimony present. Most of the other 'clear' glasses are actually slightly discoloured.

OPAQUE GLASS BODIES.

One red bead (class 4) was analysed and proved to contain 3% copper, 7% lead, 2% iron and a surprising 1% zinc. Some contamination of the spectrum by the white trail might account for the high tin (below) so cuprous oxide would seem to be the main colorant. The single opaque brown bead (class 4) contained very low copper, lead and tin and normal iron. Manganese (1.3%) and strontium (0.6%) were three times higher than expected, and with the .3% antimony as an opacifier may well explain the colour. A 'black' class 4 bead (really very dark opaque blue) was coloured by 0.04% cobalt, darkened by 5% iron (5 times normal) and opacified, perhaps, by the 0.1% antimony. An opaque green class 1 bead had 3.5% copper and 5% lead; we can hardly doubt cupric oxide. A late class 1 bead (group Ib, phase 2 of the later Iron Age) has lead tin oxide (tin was 3%, lead 10%) as the yellow colorant. A yellow class 11 (group IV) bead of the same general date contained no detectable tin but 5% lead and 2% antimony (causing it to appear to be in group I on fig 11). Lead antimonate is certainly the colorant here. Three opaque whitish beads (one early — class 1, two late — classes 11 and 12) were analysed. Neither antimony nor tin were present in more than trace quantities and the cause of the 'white' is not clear. In the case of the two large beads I suspect the arsenic (both were group IV), the very low level of manganese failing to clear it.

OPAQUE DECORATIVE GLASSES (pastes).

These are yellow or white in all the decorated beads analysed (except the class 5 whose colour complexity has defeated interpretation of the results). The decorative glass was usually in the form of a white or yellow thread. In the earlier Iron Age and the first phase of the later this was usually trailed onto the surface as a meander or zigzag, or a simple spiral. In the second phase of the later Iron Age we find the technique of trailing one to four white or yellow threads longitudinally down a glass rod (blue or 'clear' respectively). This was then twisted to form a two-coloured rope or cable, which could be wound around the bead, or the tip pressed onto the body and twisted off to leave a 'multi-spiral' decorative knob. Our coarse analytical method prevented separate analysis of these threads and other decorative features, but it was possible in some cases to analyse 'mostly body' and 'body and decoration' and compare the results. Hopefully microanalysis and X-ray diffraction analysis will give further information. It can, however, confidently be said that white decorative glass, present in all periods, is due to tin oxide in all except one bead (tin 2 to 7%). This is not to say that antimony, present in all the white trailed beads at a level above 0.1%, is not, in the form of calcium antimonate, an extra opacifier, but I have no evidence of this. One class 2b bead has only 0.14% tin, with no variation between thread and blue body, but has 1.5% antimony in the decorative portion (only 0.3% in the body). Calcium antimonate is clearly the opacifier in this single case. The class 2a bead, which contained no detectable antimony, had no surviving white trails, these having weathered out (this is not uncommon with the white and yellow decorative glasses, and will be exploited in future analyses).

The yellow decorative glass is associated with high (2-4%) lead in all cases and high (1-4%) tin in all those of group I. It would seem reasonable to assume that lead tin oxide is the colorant in these late yellow-decorated beads. The only yellow-decorated bead outside group I, the group II class 3 with yellow knobs, contained 3% lead, 0.5% tin and 0.5% antimony (in the combined body/paste analysis). Lead antimonate may well be the colorant in this case. (See Biek and Bayley, 1979, for a discussion on colorants, and references).

SOME CHRONOLOGICAL CONCLUSIONS

I have referred above to the discriminatory properties of antimony, manganese and arsenic. These are quite sufficient to show the dating potential of the analytical method. It may be uncertain, at this stage, whether the groups II and III are really separate and it seems unlikely that the earlier and later beads of group II would be separable on analytical grounds. But the three main blocks are quite reliable (I, II/III, IV). In the light of these analyses I shall make the following typological points.

CLASS 1.

Analysis seems to confirm the archaeological argument that these toggles can be early and late. Typological separation seems difficult so analytical separation should prove extremely useful.

CLASSES 2, 3, 10.

The class 2a bead is certainly earlier Iron Age, but I am not totally sure that the 2b, 3 and 10 beads were not slightly later. It will be argued elsewhere that the later Iron Age, phase 2, beads owed much of their decorative technique to, ultimately, the earlier Iron Age beads and it could be that these ones analysed fall in between, in the first phase of the later Iron Age. Their juxtaposition with the class 4 and 5 beads, certainly of the later date, might seem to support this. With regard to the class 10 bead, the comparable Continental 'swirl' beads, analysed elsewhere (Haevernick, 1960, table I: two-coloured 'ring-perlen'), gave quite different values in tin, antimony (usually none), iron, barium and strontium. It seems unlikely therefore that ours is an import. Similarly the 2a bead, which might well be regarded as an import, is much closer to the Irish beads on the discriminant elements than to the continental beads and bracelets.

CLASSES 4, 5.

These are closely allied in date and distribution, and despite their very different typological features, fall closely together in the analyses. This is further confirmation of the reliability and consistency of the method.

CLASSES 6,7,8.

These beads and bracelets, technologically and chronologically similar, are seen to group closely and consistently into group I.

CLASS 9.

We suggested above that, despite the evidence of the Loughey find and the British 'Meare' group, the Irish date for these beads should be the later Iron Age. The analytical position of our single example in group I confirms this, placing it in the later Iron Age.

CLASS 12.

Beads fall together (group IV), and are notable for their high arsenic and rubidium contents. In all respects they differ completely from all other groups.

CLASS 11.

It is these beads which were the main reason for the project, as they possess no distinctive visual characteristics with which to date them. The analyses provide just the evidence we hoped for, three of them falling into group IV on the antimony/manganese evidence (confirmed by the other constituents) and one joining the group when allowance is made for the fact that the antimony is an opacifier, not a decolorant. Finally one class 11 bead analysed fell squarely into group Ia.

These results are most satisfactory. I suggest three approaches, giving three levels of identification and of three levels complexity. The first is a fast X-ray fluorescent count of the antimony and manganese, without the use of standards, to give the ratio (fig 13), and a count of the arsenic simply to confirm its presence or absence. This will place the glass roughly into groups I, II/III or IV. The comparison with a

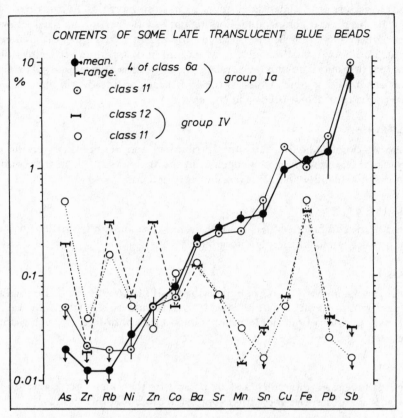

Fig 13: The percentage contents of four class 6a, one class 12 and two class 11 beads for 14 elements. All the beads are translucent blue. The separation of groups IV and I on most of the elements, and the fit of the class 11 beads, one to each group, will be noted.

standard to give real values for the antimony and manganese would give closer identification. Measurement of further elements would only be necessary when there was some ambiguity, or for confirmaton.

Finally, I should comment briefly on some technical implications. Sayre (1963) and Sayre and Smith (1967) suggest very strongly that antimonates were far commoner than tin or lead-tin oxides as the opacifier in the west before the fourteenth century A.D. Our evidence is certainly contrary to this for Ireland. Further they have found little evidence for the pronounced use of antimony as a decolorant in the west after the fourth century A.D., with perhaps a longer survival in the east. Our evidence shows a very heavy use of antimony in this capacity in Ireland after

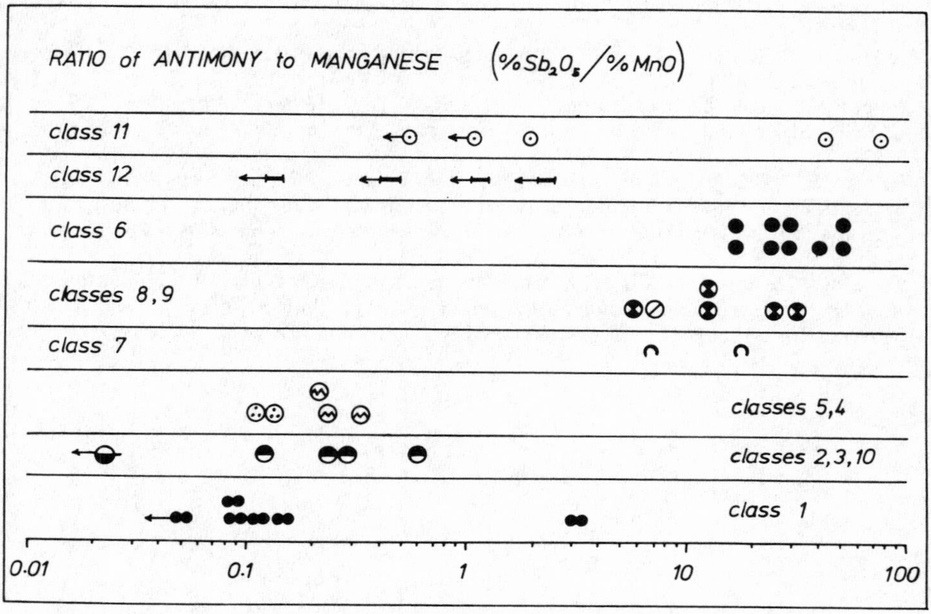

Fig 14: Ratio of antimony and manganese for all the specimens analysed. Symbols as on fig 11.

the seventh, or eighth, century A.D., the change from low antimony perhaps coinciding with the change from north Africa and the Mediterranean to Gaul as the origin of fine pottery and other goods (Warner, 1980). As workshops for Irish beads are discovered (Armagh for class 6, and Clogher for class 5, both unpublished) the many implications will be further explored.

REFERENCES

Biek, L., & Bayley, J., 1979. 'Glass and Other Vitreous Materials', *Archaeologia* 11, 1-25.

Gelling, P.S., 1958. 'Close ny chollagh, an Iron Age Fort at Scarlett, Isle of Man', *Proc Prehist Soc* 24, 85-100.

Guido, M., 1978. *The Glass Beads of the Prehistoric and Roman Periods in Britain and Ireland*. London.

Haevernick, T.E., 1960. *Die Glasarmringe und Ringperlen der Mittel-und Spätlatenezeit auf dem europäischen Festland*. Bonn.

Hartmann, A., 1970. *Prähistorische Goldfunde aus Europa*. Stuttgart.

Hencken, H., 1936. 'Ballinderry Crannog No. 1', *Proc Roy Ir Acad C* 43, 103-239.

Hencken, H., 1942. 'Ballinderry Crannog No. 2', *Proc Roy Ir Acad C* 47, 1-76.

Hencken, H., 1950. 'Lagore Crannog; an Irish Royal Residence . . .', *Proc Roy Ir Acad C* 53, 1-247.

Hodson, F.R., 1969. 'Searching for structure within multivariate data', *World Archaeol* **1**, 90-105.

Jope, E.M. & Wilson, B.C.S., 1957. 'A burial group of the 1st Century A.D. . .', *Ulster J Archaeol ser 3* **20**, 73.

Jope, E.M., 1960. 'The beads from . . . "Loughey" . . .', *Ulster J Archaeol ser 3*, **23**, 40.

O'Kelly, M.J., 1962. 'Two ring-forts at Garryduff, Co. Cork', *Proc Roy Ir Acad C* **63**, 17-124.

Raftery, B., 1972. 'Some late La Tène beads from Ireland', *J Roy Soc Antiq Ir* **102**, 14-18.

Sayre, E.V., 1963. 'The intentional use of antimony and manganese in ancient glasses'. *In* Matson, F.R. & Rindone, G.E. (ed), *Advances in Glass Technology*, 263-82. New York.

Sayre, E.V. & Smith, R.W., 1967. 'Some materials of glass manufacturing in antiquity'. *In* Levey, M. (ed), *Archaeological Chemistry*, 279-311. Philadelphia.

Warner, R.B., 1980. 'The Clogher Yellow Layer', *Medieval Ceramics* (in press).

A Short Study of the Botanical Zones on a Ringfort at Simonstown, Co. Meath, used as an aid to the recovery of archaeological features

Eamonn P. Kelly

In 1975 during the excavation of a ringfort at Simonstown, Co. Meath, a phenomenon was noted which, it appeared, could be used as an aid to the discovery of flattened archaeological sites and features. This phenomenon concerned the zoning of various types of vegetation on the site, in particular that of plants of the buttercup family, Ranunculaceae.

LOCATION AND SITING

The ringfort was sited at the western edge of the townland of Simonstown.[1] Here there was a low glacial ridge sloping away gradually from north-east to south-west. At the north-eastern end of the ridge there was a small glacial mound on which the ringfort was built. The ridge provided the only permanent dry-land approach to the site, the rest of the circumference of the mound being bordered by marshy ground (zone V).

The site was enclosed by an internal ditch (zone I), a main bank (zone II), a main ditch (zone III) and a counterscarp bank (zone IV) (fig 15). The defences took advantage of the topographical features and were at their greatest magnitude on the ridge. In this sector the height from the bottom of the main ditch to the top of the main bank was 2.50m. In the marshy ground there were no visible traces of the main ditch or the counterscarp bank (fig 15).

SOLID GEOLOGY AND GEOMORPHOLOGY[2]

The site is underlain by Lower Carboniferous limestones. The townland comprises a morainic area, an undulating terrain of glacial sand, gravel and boulder clay. Glaciation was from the north-west.

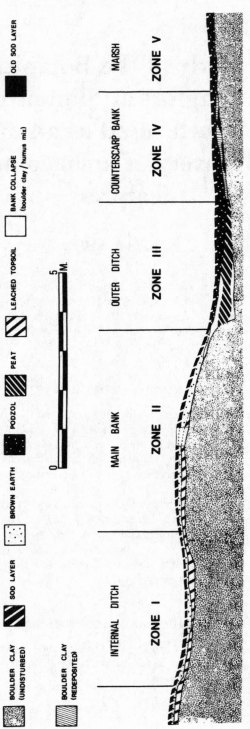

Fig 15.

BOULDER CLAY (UNDISTURBED)

BOULDER CLAY (REDEPOSITED)

SOD LAYER

BROWN EARTH

PODZOL

PEAT

LEACHED TOPSOIL

BANK COLLAPSE (boulder clay / humus mix)

OLD SOD LAYER

0   5 M.

INTERNAL DITCH   MAIN BANK   OUTER DITCH   COUNTERSCARP BANK   MARSH

ZONE I   ZONE II   ZONE III   ZONE IV   ZONE V

BOTANICAL ZONES

During the month of June when buttercups were growing in great profusion on the site the following observations were made:

1.   There was a marked absence of buttercups from the ditches of the ringfort (Pl V).
2.   At that point where the counterscarp bank adjoined the marsh (and apparently ended) its course was continued by a broad band of buttercups.
3.   The course of the main ditch was continued into the marshy area by a zone within which very few buttercups grew. This was all the more striking in view of the fact that buttercups were noticeably present in the marshy ground adjoining. Excavation subsequently revealed that the ditch and counterscarp bank continued into the marsh along the lines indicated by the distribution of the buttercups.
4.   Within the ringfort and on the ridge leading up to it, the buttercups grew in broad parallel strips. Excavation revealed that these strips coincided with lazy-bed ridges. Buttercups were almost completely absent from the intervening furrows. It was decided, on the basis of these observations, to compile a botanical cross-section of the relevant zones. This work was conducted by Mr Norman Allott, then studying botany at Trinity College, Dublin, and his findings are outlined as Appendix I.

Table 1 (see Appendix I) lists the species of grasses found in the various zones. Clear differences between these are immediately apparent. Although an overlap occurs, with the exception of zone IV each has species present which are exclusive to that zone. Creeping bent-grass (*Agrostis stolonifera L.*), which is present in zones III and V, is a grass of wet places and its absence from zone IV might suggest a reversion to drier conditions in that zone.

Table 2 (see Appendix I) lists the species of plants, other than grasses, identified in the zones. None was present in zone I. Zone II, which was the raised main bank of the ringfort, contained thirteen of the sixteen species identified. Twelve were exclusive to that zone.

This distribution is presumably principally due to the fact that rainwater would tend to drain off the bank into zones I and III, thereby leaving it drier for most of the year. The lower moisture levels would tend to limit grass growth in zone II, thus allowing the other plants to compete.

THE DISTRIBUTION OF PLANTS OF THE FAMILY RANUNCULACAE

Three species of buttercup were present in the sample. One of these, the Lesser Spearwort (*Ranunculus flammula*), was restricted to zone V. It is a marsh plant and it amounted to a sizeable proportion of the buttercups present in that zone.

In zone II the only species of buttercup present was the Meadow Buttercup (*Ranunculus acris*), which grew there in great abundance. In zone III *R. acris* was present in very small numbers. Also present, again in very small numbers, was the Creeping Buttercup (*Ranunculus repens*). Excavation revealed that both species of buttercup in this zone grew above a layer of soil which had slumped from the main bank (fig. 15). In zone IV *R. repens* became abundant and clearly indicated the course of the counterscarp bank. *R. acris* was present though rare.

In zone V, the marshy area, *R. flammula* was present in significant numbers. Proceeding outwards from zone IV into zone V, *R. repens* was rare at first, then increased in numbers. (In October 1975 when the site was bulldozed, it was observed that this increase in the numbers of *R. repens* coincided with a deposit of boulder clay upcast during the digging of a deep drain. The drain is recorded on the O.S. 6″ sheet[3]. It had been completely silted-up or backfilled by the time the botanical study was carried out. Neither was the upcast then observable).

The reason for the abundance of *R. repens* in zone IV was thought to be a lower moisture level caused by water draining off at the subsoil level into zones III and V.

Table 3, showing two soil properties of the various zones, was prepared to test this notion (Appendix I). Unfortunately, the moisture levels obtained were, for a number of reasons, unreliable. Only a 1% difference was noted between zones I and II. The samples were taken in mid-summer after a period of prolonged drought. If, for example, they had been taken after a period of rainfall, a much greater divergence of moisture levels between zones I and II would have been expected. One might have expected to have obtained a lower moisture level for zone IV than III. The contrary however was the case. This inconsistency may derive from the fact that for several weeks before the samples were taken series of deep cuttings were made in a number of sections of the outer ditch (zone III). These cuttings continually filled with water draining in from other parts of the ditch. This water was bailed out until the seepage ceased. At this stage the entire ditch had effectively been drained. The moisture level obtained for the zone (44.8) was, therefore, considerably lower than the figure one would have obtained had the sample been taken before excavation elsewhere in the ditch.

A reduction of the water-table in zone III is likely to have resulted in seepage across zone IV from the marsh (zone V). These factors would account for the higher figure obtained for zone IV than for zone III. Some significance might be attached to the lower figure obtained for zone IV than for zone V.

COMMENT

The results of the tests for moisture levels in the various zones were unreliable due firstly, to the draining of zone III and, secondly, to the way in which the water-tables of all the zones were affected by the very dry weather conditions of the time.

In any event it is highly unlikely that a test of the type undertaken would have yielded definitive results. The relative ranges of moisture levels in each zone over a long period of time would be the critical factor affecting the vegetation on the site. In order to determine what these ranges might be, regular tests would need to be undertaken in each zone over a period of at least one year. This was not feasible at Simonstown.

Whereas it is believed that the key to the zoning of the vegetation lies in the range of relative moisture levels in the various zones, it was not possible to verify this. If, as will be suggested, the sensitivity of *R. acris* and *R. repens* to subsoil drainage is of assistance to the recovery of archaeological sites by means of aerial photography then it may well be worthwhile conducting further more conclusive tests to prove this.

It is possible, though thought doubtful, that some other soil property was responsible for the abundance of buttercups in zones II and IV and their scarcity or absence from zones I and III.

Pollen cores were taken in the main ditch (zone III) at its deepest point where it crossed the ridge. A pollen core was also taken in the marsh, i.e. zone V (see Appendix II).

It was found that pollen was better preserved in zone III than in zone V. This suggests that zone III has been persistently waterlogged. Greater fluctuation between wet and dry conditions is indicated for zone V. This factor may further account for the presence of relatively greater numbers of *R. repens* in the latter zone than in the former.

DISCUSSION

The response of vegetation to the different soil conditions which result from disturbance on ancient settlement sites forms the basis for the recovery of such sites by means of aerial photography. The sensitivity of *R. acris* and *R. repens* to subsoil conditions which was indicated at Simonstown is a feature which has been observed by the writer at other locations also.

It is argued therefore that advantages might be gained from the employment of aerial survey techniques during the months of May to July when these plants are in season. Large areas of the country are covered by grasslands. Despite the fact that *R. repens* and *R. acris* are poisonous to livestock they have a wide distribution and commonly occur on grazing land. They have relatively large bright coloured flowers (*R. acris*, 1½-2½ cm across; *R. repens*, 2-3 cm across) and in season have a dense 'carpeting' effect. Growth patterns — for example, their absence from the ditch of a ploughed-out ringfort coupled with their presence elsewhere on a site — should make features easily observable from the air.

Field workers operating on the ground might also be advised to watch out for such growth patterns. I am informed[4] that the officers of the Archaeological Survey have on many occasions been assisted in surveying and interpreting sites by the occurrence of characteristic vegetation zones. For example, a filled up fosse at Slane More, Co. Westmeath, was detected because of the different vegetation found growing on it. The course of a removed bank forming part of a subrectangular feature at Kilgar, Co. Westmeath, and a possible entrance through it, were detected by similar means.

However, not all vegetation zones are easy to observe. For example, the zoning of the grasses at Simonstown (table 1), which so clearly reflected the nature of the defences, was by no means immediately apparent. Zoning of the more inconspicuous plants is only likely to become apparent as the result of a botanical study like that undertaken. It is my belief that the preparation of botanical cross-sections of sites is a technique which could find widespread application as an aid to surveying and interpreting field monuments. It could be of considerable assistance on sites where archaeological excavation is not intended.

NOTES

1 Par. Donaghmore; bar. Lower Navan; Co. Meath. O.S. 6″ sheet 25, 25 cm from W; 8.5 cm from N. Nat. grid ref. N857705. I wish to express my thanks to Tara Mines Ltd who generously financed the excavations.
2 Information supplied by Dr F.M. Synge and Dr R.R. Horne, Geological Survey of Ireland.
3 The feature is shown with a bridge across it on the revised 6″ sheet of 1955. It runs roughly from east to west immediately to the south of the ringfort.
4 Information supplied by Mr Joseph F. McCabe, Senior Archaeologist, Archaeological Survey, Office of Public Works. National Museum file IA/28/75.

APPENDIX I

A short botanical study of the flora of the different zones of a radial section of a ringfort at Simonstown, Co. Meath

By Norman Allott

TABLE 1. DISTRIBUTION OF GRASSES

Type	Zone I	Zone II	Zone III	Zone IV	Zone V
Phleum pratense	X				
Agrostis tenuis	X				
Poa trivialis	X				
Anthoxantum oderatum	X	X			
Holcus lanatus	X	X	X		
Dactylis glomerata		X			
Lolium perenne		X			
Cynosurus cristatus		X	X		
Juncus inflexus			X		
Juncus effusus			X		
Alopecurus geniculatus			X	X	X
Agrostis stolonifera			X		X
Deschampsia cespitosa					X

TABLE 2. DISTRIBUTION OF PLANTS OTHER THAN GRASSES

Type	Zone I	Zone II	Zone III	Zone IV	Zone V
Trifolium repens		X			
Trifolium pratense		X			
Lotus corniculatus		X			
Prunella vulgaris		X			
Cerastium fontanum		X			
Hypochoeris radicata		X			
Achillea millefolium		X			
Potentilla anserina		X			
Plantago lanceolata		X			
Oxalis acetosella		X			
Ulex europaeus		X			
Cirsium vulgare		X			
Irish pseudacorus				X	X
Ranunculus acris		X	X	X	
Ranunculus repens			X	X	X
Ranunculus flammula					X

TABLE 3. TWO SOIL PROPERTIES OF ZONES MARKED IN FIG 15

Soil Property	Zone I	Zone II	Zone III	Zone IV	Zone V
pH.	4.9	4.9	5.4	5.0	4.8
% Moisture (by weight)	21.5	20.5	44.8	63.4	66.1

Zone I. The flora of this zone consists more or less of grasses alone — in fact it is a typical grassland (pasture) flora.

Zone II. The flora here includes many other species besides the grasses — probably due to the fact that lower moisture levels limit grass growth thus allowing the other plants to compete successfully.

Zone III. This shows a change in flora marked by the presence of the moisture-loving species *Juncus inflexus, J. effusus* and *Alopecurus geniculatus*. The distinct rise in moisture level can be seen in table 3. *Ranunculus repens* and *R. acris* are present here though not in any great quantity.

Zone IV. Here *R. repens* becomes abundant. However the reason for this remains obscure. There does not seem to be any change in soil moisture or pH associated with this zone — I had thought that perhaps there would be a drop in soil moisture and perhaps a rise in pH. There is a change from pasture flora to marsh flora between zone III — zone IV — zone V. If the above were true it would have explained the slight reversion to pastureland in zone IV. The only thing I can suggest is that while there is not a significant difference in moisture level in summer (particularly after such a drought as we have had) there may well be in winter when the water table is higher, i.e. water would tend to run off zone IV at the subsoil level, into zone III and Zone V. Whether or not the change in flora (reflected in the distribution of the buttercup *R. repens*) can be correlated with any other soil property I do not know but I am doubtful.

Zone V. This is a typical marsh flora.

APPENDIX II

Pollen analysis on cores from Simonstown, Co. Meath

By Norman Allott

CORE FROM THE OUTER DITCH (zone III)

The core consists of a lower silty layer which passes into a mottled layer. In the mottled layer there are two occupation layers seen by flecks of carbon in the sediment. The fact that most of the sediment is secondarily deposited and contains very little pollen makes it meaningless to do a series of pollen counts up the core and construct a pollen diagram.

Eight samples were taken up the core and prepared for pollen counting. The only three worth counting were:—

Level 1. The lower silty layer, 117 cm below the surface.

Level 2. The lower occupation layer, 79 cm below the surface.

Level 3. The upper occupation layer, 64 cm below the surface.

The pollen counts give a clear picture of the vegetation surrounding the ringfort at the time. This is shown in table 4. All three counts show the vegetation to consist mainly of grasses and sedges with some weeds of agriculture. Tree pollen (hazel, birch and alder) is present but in very low quantities. The grass pollen, many grains of which are large, are not large enough to be cereal pollen grains. The largest grass pollen found measured 38mu; the smallest cereal pollens measure about 40mu. It is therefore unlikely that the sediment contains any cereal pollen.

I also washed samples of the sediment through sieves of various sizes and examined the fractions thus obtained. Samples were chosen from 117 cm, 79 cm and 64 cm again because of the increased likelihood of finding fossil material. Some small pieces of charcoal and rock were found.

CORE FROM THE MARSH (zone V)

Samples were taken at the following depths below the surface.

1. 58 cm. Silt/sand. No pollen.
2. 55 cm. Silt/sand. No pollen.
3. 46 cm. Silt/sand with some organic material. Flecks of iron oxide. Very little pollen.
4. Humus with some silt. A small amount of poorly preserved pollen. Mainly sedge type. Bryophyte and fern spores present.
5. 28 cm. Humus/silt. Very little, poorly preserved sedge and grass pollen.
6. 19 cm. Peat. A fair amount of pollen present but all poorly preserved. Mainly sedge type with a few grass pollen grains. I saw one liguleflorate (i.e. dandelion type) pollen grain. Bryophyte and fern spores were seen.
7. 10 cm. Brown top soil. No pollen.

The bottom 7 cm (58-51cm) consist of unsorted sand/silt mixture. Above this the core passes from sand/silt with some organic material through a humus layer which contains a small amount of silt to an upper peaty layer. The upper peaty layer is overlain by about 7 cm of brown top soil.

The fact that pollen is not well preserved anywhere in the core and the predominance of fern and moss spores (fern and moss spores are more resistant to decay than pollen) imply that reducing conditions did not prevail during deposition. The presence of humus (i.e. oxidized plant remains) also implies the absence of reducing conditions at intervals.

I conclude that this 'marsh' has been an area which has been subjected to fluctuations between wet periods and dry periods. When wet, deposition of organic matter would have taken place. When dry, the organic matter would have become oxidized.

FILL FROM PITS

I made preparations for pollen analysis from samples 490 (Sq. H6), 500 (Sq. I6) and 503 (Sq. I6). I could not find any pollen in any of the preparations.

TABLE 4. POLLEN PRESENT IN ZONE III

Type	% present		
	Level 1	Level 2	Level 3
Gramineae (grass)	60	32	32
Cyperaceae (sedge)	7	21	21
Compositae-tubuliflorae (daisy)	7	4	9
Compositae-linguliflorae (dandelion)	4	11	9
Ranunculus (buttercup)	6	-	8
Caryophyllaceae (carnation)	4	6	-
Cruciferae (wallflower)	2	40	5
Eu-Rumex (dock)	-	2	-
Ericaceae (heather)	-	10	1
Betula (birch)	1	-	-
Alnus (alder)	1	1	-
Corylus (hazel)	-	1	1
Bryophyte spores (mosses & liverworths)	1	2	2
Fern spores	2	5	10

An Old Stag from Lagore

Louise H. van Wijngaarden-Bakker

In the drawers 317/B/5 and 317/C/1 of the osteological collection at the Natural History division of the National Museum of Ireland are stored some of the animal remains that were recovered during the 1934-36 Harvard Archaeological Expedition campaigns at the site of Lagore crannóg in Co. Meath. The bones in these particular drawers form an almost complete postcranial skeleton of a red deer (*Cervus elaphus* L.) with some interesting characteristics which apparently led the excavators to depart from their usual custom of throwing away excavated animal remains and instead they were stored at the National Museum.

In drawer B/5 a label was found attached to a pelvis and bearing the heading 'Lagore 15/10/34 TT 15 Extreme SW corner extending into bank', while a label in C/1 reads 'belongs to deer with curious antlers'. The ground plan of the excavation shows that the SW corner of the excavated area of Lagore lies in the lake margin outside the palisades that surrounded the crannóg where most of the habitation refuse was dumped (Hencken, 1950). The skeleton cannot therefore be attributed to any one period and its dating cannot be made more precise than the general dating evidence for the crannóg habitation, i.e. between the seventh and tenth century A.D. With regard to the second label that accompanied the bones: a search through the Natural History division for the 'curious antlers' remained unsuccessful. No mention is made of the find in the original publication of the excavation (Hencken, 1950).

THE SKELETON

The skeleton such as it is present in the osteological collection is fairly complete. Most unfortunate is the already noted absence of the skull, while of the axial skeleton, some vertebrae and most of the ribs are missing. Most of the small bones of the appendicular skeleton, i.e. all the carpals and small tarsals and most of the phalanges are absent as also are three of the larger limb bones, one scapula, one pelvis and one femur.

A complete metrical analysis of the bones has not been undertaken. Only those measurements that are used by Pietschmann (1977) in her comparative study on the size of prehistoric red deer will be given here (table 1).

TABLE 1

MEASUREMENTS (IN MM) OF RED DEER SKELETON. DEFINITIONS
AND ABBREVIATIONS FOLLOW VON DEN DRIESCH (1976)

LM$_3$		30.9	31.0				
Scapula	SLC	37.6	-				
Humerus	Bd	56.2	56.2				
Radius	Bd	51.8	48.4				
Metacarpal	Bd	41.4	42.6				
Tibia	Bd	49.5	48.6				
Calcaneum	GL1	113.2	-				
Astragalus	GL	51.6	-				
Metatarsal	Bd	40.7	40.5				
Phalanx I	GL	52.7	53.2	53.8	54.2	55.0	56.8

The above measurements fall within the lower part of the variation range of European red deer measurements from the European continent and affirm the general east-west oriented size decrease of red deer (Pietschmann, 1977).

The mandibula shows severe attrition of the premolars and of the first molar (Pl VIa). The age of the animal can be estimated at *ca* 12-13 years, using the dental wear data of Mitchell and Youngson (1968). The two complete metacarpals (length 245 and 244 mm) and one metatarsal (275 mm) have been used to estimate the shoulderheight. Assuming that the animal in question was a male (as indicated by the 'curious antlers'), Godynicki's (1965) multiplication factors give a mean shoulderheight of 115 cm. Such a small height falls within the lower range of recent British red deer stags for which Southern (1964) gives a variation range of 105-140 cm. To the archaeozoologist the skeleton is especially interesting as it exhibits a healed injury in the scapula and several bones with well-marked pathological changes.

THE INJURY (Pl VIb, VIIa)

The left shoulderblade bears a more or less circular perforation with a diameter of ca 2-2½ cm. The rounded rim around the perforation indicates that the injury had healed and was therefore not the direct cause of death of the animal. Similar healed injuries were encountered on red deer scapulae from several mesolithic and early neolithic Danish sites (Noe-Nygaard, 1975). This suggests that although the weapons most likely to have been used were different (flint arrowheads or iron spearheads), the hunting technique of aiming at the heart and the big vessels just above it remained the same for nearly 7000 years. This observation is of course not surprising as the hunting technique is mainly governed by the body properties and proportions of the game animal rather than by the weapon that is used.

PALAEOPATHOLOGY (Pl VIIb,c; VIIIa,b)

Three consecutive thoracic vertebrae present a clear case of *spondylosis* (Pl VIIb). The bodies show many exostoses and the facets for the articulation with the ribs exhibit irregular and pitted surfaces. In the more extreme cases of spondylosis in domestic animals fusion of the bodies on their ventral side often takes place (van Wijngaarden-Bakker and Krauwer, 1979), but this has not been the case with the Lagore specimen. The articular head of a rib also has an irregular surface.

Pathological changes have also been found in the left hind leg of the animal where the distal epiphysis of the tibia and the articular part of the calcaneum present partly irregular articular surfaces with small exostoses around the borders (Pl VIIc). Even greater changes have been observed in the tarsal joint where *ankylosis* of the centrotarsal, first, second and third tarsals with the proximal metatarsal has taken place (Pl VIIIa,b). The proximal epiphyses of the right and left metacarpal also show some bony proliferations around the articular surface. All the above mentioned pathological changes point to a general degenerative condition known as *arthrosis*. This can be brought about by either old age or chronic overstress (van Wijngaarden-Bakker and Krauwer, 1979). In the case of the Lagore stag, which reached an age of *ca* 12-13 years, old age may account for the observed symptoms. Practically all known palaeopathological cases of arthritis/arthrosis are from domestic mammals and very little is known of its occurrence among wild mammals, mainly because very old animals are seldom encountered in archaeological bone assemblages.

The interesting combination of a healed injury with severe pathological changes is not so surprising if one imagines that the Lagore stag once managed to escape its hunters but did not succeed a second time when in old age it was riddled with arthrosis, and it was eventually brought to the royal residence of Lagore.

ACKNOWLEDGMENTS

The author wishes to thank Dr C.E. O'Riordan, Keeper of the Natural History division of the National Museum for permission to study the skeleton and Ann Lynch for the correction of the English text.

REFERENCES

Driesch, A. von den, 1976. *A guide to the measurement of animal bones from archaeological sites.* Peabody Museum Bulletin 1.

Godynicki, S., 1965. 'Determination of deer height on the basis of metacarpal and metatarsal bones', *Roczniki Wyzszej, Szkoły Rolniczej w Poznania, Posen* **25**, 39-51.

Hencken, H.O'N., 1950. 'Lagore crannóg: an Irish royal residence of the 7th to 10th centuries A.D.', *Proc Roy Ir Acad C* **53**, 1-247.

Mitchell, B. and R.W. Youngson, 1968. 'Teeth and age in Scottish Red Deer — a practical guide to the determination of age', *The Red Deer Commission Annual Report, 1968.*

Noe-Nygaard, N., 1975. 'Bone injuries caused by human weapons in Mesolithic Denmark'. *In* A.T. Clason (ed), *Archaeozoological Studies*, 151-9. North Holland Publishing Company, Amsterdam, Oxford.

Pietschmann, W., 1977. *Zur Grösse des Rothirsches (Cervus elaphus L.) in vor-und frühgeschichtlicher Zeit.* Diss. München.

Southern, H.N. (ed), 1964. *The handbook of British mammals.* Blackwell, Oxford.

Wijngaarden-Bakker, L.H. van and M. Krauwer, 1979. 'Animal palaeopathology. Some examples from the Netherlands', *Helinium* **19**, 37-53.

Concerning Chronology

Joseph Raftery

Brian O'Kelly is one of the few Irish archaeologists of our generation who has contributed massively to the development of our subject and this mainly by his devotion to a study of ancient technology. The work involved in this imaginative research was such that little time was available for his mind to shed its lustre on another aspect of archaeology, namely, chronology, which would undoubtedly have gained much from his attention. For this whole subject of time is important, indeed vital, to a proper understanding of the past and especially of those periods when circumstances should allow of close dating. Wrong dating, an unreliable system of chronology, confuse history, make contemporary things that can be divided by centuries and, in the last analysis, falsify grievously attempts to build up as complete a picture of life and living in the past as things preserved and interpreted will permit.

In thinking along such lines many questions occur to one. How reliably based is our present chronological system? Are we fully satisfied with it? Does it give us all the answers and as accurately as we would like them to be? Should the answers to such — and other similar — questions be negative, have we given any thought as to how a sound time-scale might be established and, once established, checked constantly for correctness and reliability?

In the tentative lines that follow I propose to confine myself to the period after the Birth of Christ, for it is here, I feel, that most imprecision exists. This is a time where a text-aided situation might be thought to be of help; but I would suggest that a questioning look at the chronology of the period in question, say, the first millennium A.D., will reveal serious uncertainty obscured largely by a satisfied acceptance by most of what friends and colleagues have written. Let us take as an example the eighth century A.D. This has become some sort of a miraculous cauldron into which every decorated metal object is dropped with relief, sometimes with reservations such as 'possibly' or 'probably' or 'most likely'; even occasionally doubt would seem to be removed by introducing the doubt of the double century, thus, '7th/8th century A.D.' or '8th/9th century A.D.'. Of course, what such phraseology means in absolute terms is anyone's guess but general satisfaction with the 'suggested dating' is the overall result. There are, however, exceptions to the general rule as demonstrated, for example, by Michael Ryan's studies of early historic pottery (Ryan, 1973) and by Barry Raftery's comments on Cahercommaun (Raftery, B., 1972).

We find, however, that once an object or a site has found its way in the original publication to the bottom, let us say, of our 8th century cauldron it acquires a new life with what purports to be an established date. Most subsequent publications, using the conclusions of the first one, take the tentative chronological supposition as factually demonstrated. In this I confess to have been as much at fault as the next one. One other common weakness to which I would refer is the sort of circular or chain argument: in this situation Site X is referred to a certain period or century. The next excavated site containing, in general, apparently similar material is dated by reference to the first, later sites by reference to the first and second and so on. It thus *appears* that we have established and can use with confidence a sound and well-based chronological framework. But if the first site happens to have been misdated by a century or more what is the final position? To answer the question just posed it is necessary to look briefly at selected portions of the archaeological record and, secondly, to devote some passing thought to what parades before us as history for, insofar as the period selected for our review — the first millennium A.D. — may be said to include material that could or should be text-aided, it is surely legitimate to try to test the validity of the historical record and to assess its value in placing in time sites and the objects associated with them.

Let us consider first of all one of the really important Irish excavated sites and introduce it by saying that Irish archaeology owes much to its excavator, Dr Hugh O'Neill Hencken of Harvard. Of him it may fairly be said that his excavations on a wide variety of sites here in the 1930s initiated for us the scientific approach to fieldwork. The site to which I would draw attention was investigated by Dr Hencken over three seasons, in 1934, 1935 and 1936, and was located at Lagore, Co. Meath. Here there was a large *crannóg* and the final report on the work was a model for its time and has come to be regarded as a sort of Bible for Early Christian archaeology in Ireland, as a definitive source constantly to be referred to, a yardstick against which other things and sites may properly be measured. This was and indeed still is, thought to be particularly true in regard to chronology.

And yet, when we look closely at the Lagore report (Hencken, 1950), we find conditions of uncertainty, doubt and even contradiction. On page 4 of this statement Hencken refers to a story the interpretation of which is that Lagore was occupied in 651 A.D., though he does not indicate the basis of this dating nor its reliability. On page 5 he says: 'All this implies that at least from 651 . . . the *crannóg* was a place of importance . . .'. He goes on to say: 'The next event of major importance in the history of the site occurred in 850 . . . when the 'island of Lagore' was burnt 'level with its floor' ' and this destruction was supposed by the excavator (p. 7) to indicate the end of the first phase of occupation of the site (Period I) and the beginning of refortification (Period II). What this burning 'level with its floor' was is certainly not at all clear from the archaeological record: there was absolutely no trace of any sort of the kind of conflagration referred to.

We thus would appear to have two important dates for Lagore — 651 and 850 — that is, assuming that the historical Lagore site is to be equated with that excavated and that the years quoted are reliable dates.

The earliest phase of occupation of the *crannóg* was divided into a Period Ia, defined as being 'represented by the body of the artificial island itself' and a Period Ib, a designation 'used to indicate the first occupation upon the island'(p.6). Of the dating of Period Ia the excavator writes (p. 6): 'Despite the fact that the site produced objects of Roman date and even some pre-Roman types, the period when the artificial island was made must be judged by the latest material included in the original foundation below the occupation layers'. This admirable view was, however, not adhered to for the latest period of occupation — Period III — when late mediaeval objects are dismissed 'since they can hardly be connected with the regular occupation of the *crannóg*', and this in spite of the fact that the occupation of some at least of the *crannógs* down at least to the seventeenth century is attested. The 'latest material' attributed to Period Ia comprises two objects — an iron sword and a piece of mounted gold wire filigree. Of the iron sword Dr Hencken writes that it 'has a broad longitudinal channel down the blade, a feature rare in these islands before the Viking Age, but a similar feature is seen on the Walthamstow sword of the 7th or less probably 8th century'. Insofar as we know virtually nothing about native post-La Tène swords in Ireland this statement is of doubtful value and the uncertain dating of the only English sword-parallel cited does not inspire confidence. Of the gold mount the excavator writes (p. 6): 'The gold ornament represents a borrowing from Anglo-Saxon metalwork which *most* authorities ascribe to the 7th century, but which Mr T.D. Kendrick puts earlier. Dr Henry ascribes such objects in Ireland to the 8th and 9th centuries' (italics mine). It should here be noted that in all the cases mentioned by Hencken opinions only are given; never once has factual proof as support for such opinions been forthcoming. The statement that the Lagore gold mount is 'a borrowing from Anglo-Saxon metalwork' is also suspect in that there is no proof whatever for it. Filigree work is very widespread in Europe in Late Antique and Migration times and especially in those areas of the mainland with which Ireland had close contacts in the centuries in question here.

It is clear from all this and from other statements in the Lagore report that the historical evidence, such as it is, is taken to provide the initial date for the site and that anything in the archaeological record likely to conflict with this tends to be explained away. The possibility that the first stages at Lagore could be as early, say, as late Roman times is barely allowed birth.

I devote perhaps more time to Lagore than, in such a brief paper, I should have done; but I justify this by the innumerable occasions since 1936 on which the views printed later have been used, almost as if they were Biblical utterances, to provide the dating for other sites excavated in the country and indeed sometimes outside it also. To quote an example, I refer to another of Dr Hencken's excellent excavations, that of the stone enclosure of Cahercommaun in Co. Clare. In reporting on that site in 1938 he writes: 'The dating of the fort to IX is suggested by the silver brooch of about 800 . . . This date is supported by the general similarity between the objects from Cahercommaun and from the recently excavated Lagore Crannog in County Meath, which on historical evidence was occupied from the latter part of VIII until IX' (Hencken, 1938). The author probably means that 'VIII' should read 'VII' and that 'IX' should read 'X'. Barry Raftery has dealt admirably with this dating for Cahercommaun and demonstrates with perspicacity that, in every case of groups of objects from the site discussed by the excavator, the date of such 'is seen to be influenced entirely by the date of the silver brooch' (Raftery, B., 1972). The Cahercommaun dating to about 800 A.D. is based entirely on the guessed date for the silver brooch; but we must not forget that, first of all, the figure of 800 A.D. for the brooch is one taken out of the air and, secondly, that its position in a souterrain inside the settlement area does not date even the souterrain in which it came to light. It must in any case be later than the period of construction of the fort.

What has here been written about Lagore and Cahercommaun could be expanded similarly by reference to report after report that has appeared since the publication of the two discussed above, but I will cite one further site only and the manner in which it has been dated. This was a house on Inishkea North, Co. Mayo. The excavator, Dr Françoise Henry, reports on the discovery at the hut of a tinned bronze brooch and a bronze handle resembling that of a Roman patera. These objects were used to date the site: 'It can be dated approximately to the late seventh century' (Henry, 1952). How this dating was arrived at gives us a very good idea as to the usual manner in which a chronology for the early historic period has been established. First of all, the brooch: 'It is not very easy to date this brooch accurately. It belongs to a type of zoomorphic brooch which is common from the end of the sixth century to the middle of the eighth' (Henry, 1952, 169). Dr Henry adduces no evidence in support of this statement and it will be no harm to point out here that Professor Haseloff (1979, 233) refers some at least of these brooches to the fifth century, a century before Dr Henry lets them begin. However, Dr Henry, in her Inishkea report, goes on to say that Mr Kilbride-Jones (1937, 435, No. 64) dates a similar brooch with millefiori to the late seventh century 'which *seems a quite reasonable* dating in view of its decoration' (italics mine). But Kilbride-Jones's ascription is itself open to question being largely unsupported by evidence of a convincing nature, so that when Dr Henry talks of the decoration of this brooch as 'reasonably' dating it to the late seventh century, she is not dealing with an established fact but rather with a feeling or a guess. Dr Henry refers to two further Irish brooches which are in the British Museum and which, she says, are similar to that from Inishkea. Of one of them she writes: 'Its terminals are decorated with interlacings of a type which *seems to belong to the eighth*' (italics mine). But she does not say why she so dates this interlacing nor does she provide any example of a properly dated eighth-century interlacing to support what can only be described as her opinion. She concludes this portion of her discussion with the statement: 'From these comparisons *it seems* that a date in the second half of the *seventh* century or the beginning of the *eighth* is most probable' (italics mine).

Having dealt with the brooch, Dr Henry (1952, 169) turns to the flat bronze handle and says of it: 'It is of a type very common in Roman pans and could be the handle of a bronze pan of sub-Roman type'. However, as there are the remains of two tiny rivet-holes on one edge of the specimen Dr Henry suggests 'that this is the handle of a bronze mirror' and then promptly forgets the first suggestion that it could have been a patera handle. After some discussion Dr Henry writes (p. 171): 'If the Inishkea handle belonged to a mirror the date of this early group [of Pictish stones, with which she brought it into comparison] would be easier to establish. The deposit on the roof of House A [in which the handle was found] being either exactly contemporary with the house itself or slightly later and *given the date of the brooch* found in the floor, the mirror (!) could only be of the late seventh or early eighth century, unless we consider it as an heirloom. Its presence in a seventh century hut suggests in any case that mirrors of that type were still in use, whatever their date of fabrication, in the seventh, in Ireland, and probably also in Scotland . . .'.

If we remove the *certainty* here expressed that the Inishkea handle belonged to a mirror and not to a Roman patera and if we similarly remove the proposed positive dating given for the brooch, we find that the whole case for a seventh or eighth century dating for the Inishkea site disintegrates.

At no stage has any real attempt been made by anybody to enquire as to whether any of the dates suggested for any of the sites or objects of the period under review has any real claim to credibility. And one of the interesting facts in all cases, known to those who have kept abreast of the literature, is the remarkable dependence on English parallels and the tacit assumption that the source of all Irish material is ultimately to be sought somewhere or somehow in an Anglo-Saxon context. For instance, in reading a recent study of the Roman coins and the material associated with them at New Grange (Carson and O'Kelly, 1977), one is forced to the conclusion that, in the minds of the writers, the only areas which existed in the early centuries of the first millennium A.D. were England, the giver, and Ireland, the receiver.

In addition to the attempts made by the many excavators of archaeological sites to assign dates to them — at any time and for any place no easy task — numberless treatises and comments have been written about the individual objects which from time to time are discovered in circumstances that preclude dating by association. It may be instructive to consider briefly the latest of such works, that by Professor Günther Haseloff (1979) and to select for comment a few of his statements. In the beginning he says (I translate freely): 'Irish art of the 5th and 6th centuries is represented especially on metal objects, particularly those associated with costume'. In this body of material he includes zoomorphic brooches, hand-pins and 'latchets' and says specifically that the brooches 'were taken over from Roman Britain at the beginning of the 5th century'.

In the remainder of his article Haseloff accepts the date he gives as established fact, though I am not aware of any single piece of evidence in favour of such dating. It must, to use the German word, be entirely *gefühlsmässig*: it is certainly subjective. The only dating evidence for this body of material of which I am aware — and this is tenuous in the extreme — is that *possibly* provided by two fragments from three-piece bronze horsebits which, at New Grange, Co. Meath, were found in a layer which produced Roman coins ranging in date from 81 A.D. to 385 A.D. (Carson and O'Kelly, 1977). If — and I would stress this word — the horsebit fragments are to be dated by the coins the latest date for them would be the second half of the fourth century. One of the fragments is part of a bit the type of which, as represented, perhaps, by the Attymon hoard, Co. Galway (National Museum of Ireland), is well-known in Ireland, not known outside the country and generally dated to late La Tène times. Now the ornament on the Attymon bits and 'pendants' bears thin scrolls and spirals roughly in what Kendrick and others used to refer to as the 'ultimate La Tène style'. This type of decoration, even to individual motives in the overall patterns, is reproduced on the Mullaghmast stone, on one at least of the 'latchets' and on some of the zoomorphic brooches and hand-pins. All this taken together would provide acceptable dating for a large body of decorated bronzes in Ireland and for an even larger body of undecorated domestic and other objects associated in some way with one or other of the presumed date specimens. The basis for such a chronology, that on which it all depends, remains the dating of the New Grange fragment and this I have already shown to be questionable. In other words, we are still in Ireland left without a date for the body of material to which Haseloff refers and it behoves us to search further for the sound chronological foundation. It may, of course, be argued that the ornamental devices referred to above occur also on hanging bowls found in England in Saxon graves of the late fifth and sixth centuries and also at the mid-seventh century site at Sutton Hoo but it would be most difficult to infer the dating of the Irish material from that of the British specimens. Was there a connection at all? If so, are the Irish objects earlier or later than or contemporary with the British ones? To these questions we cannot, as yet, give an objective and convincing answer.

As a final example of the difficulties facing Irish scholars I would point to some polished stone cones found with a burial at Knowth, Co. Meath. The excavator suggests (Eogan, 1966) a date in Viking times (ninth/tenth century) for these objects and this he bases on alleged parallels with objects from Birka Grave 986 (Arbman, 1943, 413, Taf. 150:2). Professor Eogan refers to stone objects from Professor O'Kelly's excavation of ring-forts at Garryduff, Co. Cork, and says of them that 'their shape *somewhat resembles* (italics mine) the "cone-shaped stones" ' (from Knowth) and later writes that 'further parallels *seem to be provided* (italics mine) by the conical gaming pieces at . . . Birka'. To this he appends a note, written after his paper had gone to press, to the effect that Dr Barry Raftery had identified a 'similarly-shaped object' in a sub-Roman context at the Iron Age hill-fort on

Freestone Hill, Co. Kilkenny (Raftery, B., 1969) and in later Knowth reports Dr
Eogan has accepted the new dating and applied it to the Knowth burial. However,
but for the fortunate piece of work at the Kilkenny site, we would have been left at
Knowth with a burial of ninth/tenth century date. The Freestone Hill cone is dated
by association with a fourth-century Roman coin. Once this dating is recognised
other things at Knowth, such as Burial 2, fall automatically into their proper place
in the Early Iron Age. Because of the existence of polished stone cones at Garryduff
it may be necessary to look again and critically at the date — seventh century —
assigned by the excavator.

I give this final example to indicate the difficulties which arise because of the
paucity of adequately dated archaeological material and because of the extremely
limited number of thoroughly-researched excavated sites.

To turn from the strictly archaeological, some passing reference must be made to
the historical side of our subject for, wherever it has been possible as for example
Lagore and Garranes, attempts have been made by using historical texts to identify
sites and to date them. Now this can of course be most satisfactory provided iden-
tifications can be established beyond question and that the dates supplied by or inferred from the texts are themselves unquestionable. But are these provisions met?
And here I must state that, not being a historian myself, I must depend not on my
own judgement but look carefully at the opinions expressed by some of the
foremost scholars in the field of early Irish history. For example, John V. Kelleher
(1963, 120) writes: '. . . the annals as we have them show clear evidence of extensive revision . . .' and he goes on to state that this revision was 'the source of that
traditional picture of the Irish polity which is stated as fact in all later medieval
documents that deal with the subject, and which was accepted almost without
question by Keating, by Roderic O'Flaherty, by Charles O'Conor in the eighteenth
century, by everybody in the nineteenth century, and though somewhat more
guardedly, by quite a few scholars in this century'. The 'Irish polity' referred to by
Professor Kelleher concerns the tradition of the position of the High King in
Ireland and he poses the very fair question: 'what and how good is the evidence
that supports the tradition?' He answers himself by saying that none of the
evidence is 'to be trusted very far' (p. 121) and goes on to the positive statement
that 'to appeal to the fact of tradition is a rather perilous means of substantiation'.
This I consider to be a comment of some significance because so many of our
modern scholars keep harping on the almost-sanctity of this undefined thing called
'tradition'.

Speaking of the annals, Professor Kelleher expresses his belief that every entry up
to about 590 is not reliable, that most of those up to 735 and even later are equally
suspect and that it will be a 'long time before we shall be able to say with confidence what is reliable and what has been tampered with or falsified'.

It is thus clear that, to Professor Kelleher's mind, the chronology of early historic
Ireland is a 'nagging uncertainty'. He is supported in his views for part of the

period, at least, by Professor D.A. Binchy who asks '. . . what value can we put on "tradition", that great mainstay of orthodox Patricians . . . when we find that within a period of two centuries it has so utterly distorted historical truth?' and who later states baldly: 'I do not believe that there is a single "genuine entry" throughout the whole of the fifth century' (Binchy, 1962, 66, 77). Binchy further indicates how, to the layman, confusion is engendered. In dealing with an Irish poem, wrongly, he says, attributed to Fiacc of Sletty, he indicates that 'on linguistic grounds I would assign [it] to the middle of the eighth century'. In a footnote he says that O'Rahilly would date the poem to *c.* 800 'which *to my mind* is too late' (italics mine). 'On the other hand MacNeill attributes it to Bishop Aed of Sletty († 700), which is too early'. Here, then, for the one poem and by three of our finest scholars we are given three different dates — before 700, *c.* 750 and *c.* 800 — and Professor F. Shaw may even add a fourth when he says that he regards the poem as a 'later interpolation'.

From the various critical comments published in recent years it would appear, first of all, that historians are beginning to question the validity of their sources and, secondly, that a chronological scheme for the material remains of the first millennium A.D. based on the annals and other native records must be looked at with severe reservation if not, indeed, with downright suspicion. In other words, 'text-aided' archaeology in Ireland is a very dubious commodity.

What, then, are we to say to the general uncertainty both in the archaeological as in the historical fields? It seems to me that the time has come when we, as archaeologists, must stand back from our subject and, with the objectivity of distance, try to achieve what will provide, if not an entirely true picture of the past, at least one that with some overpainting will lead in that direction. No longer must we be satisfied with the facile repetition of dates and dating groups based on the unsupported opinions or feelings of established scholars; no longer must the cauldron of the eighth century be the receptacle for every piece of ornamental Early Christian metalwork, including the latest discovery, the Derrynaflan hoard. Every date, every association must be examined fiercely to see whether the chronological position suggested is truly the right one: in other words, we must try to avoid dating objects and sites of, say, the fourth century A.D. to the ninth or tenth. For in this lies a complete, though unwitting, falsification of history.

To help us in this we must, of course, as we do, use whatever tools or aids may be available to us outside our own limited field. A sounder basis for our history, above all our social history, must be provided by our very competent historians and pollen analysis, radiocarbon methods, dendrochronology, thermoluminescence, geology, technology, osteology, statistics and many other means, will all contribute; but it would be a pity if the archaeologists of the future, dazzled by the light shed by the natural sciences, were to forget the men behind the things and the theories. In the last analysis, it is people who count, their history, their traditions and their aspirations.

90   *Joseph Raftery*

REFERENCES

Arbman, H. 1943. *Birka: I. Die Gräber*. Uppsala.

Binchy, D.A., 1962. 'Patrick and his biographers: ancient and modern', *Studia Hibernica* **2**, 7-173.

Carson, R.A.G. and O'Kelly, Claire, 1977. 'A catalogue of the Roman coins from Newgrange, Co. Meath and notes on the coins and related finds', *Proc Roy Ir Acad C* **77**, 35-55.

Eogan, George, 1968. 'Excavations at Knowth, Co. Meath, 1962-1965', *Proc Roy Ir Acad C* **66**, 299-382.

Haseloff, G., 1979. 'Irland' in H. Roth (ed), *Kunst der Völkerwanderungszeit*. Propyläen Kunstgeschichte, Supplement Band IV. Propyläen Verlag, Berlin.

Hencken, H., 1938. *Cahercommaun. A stone fort in County Clare*. Royal Society of Antiquaries of Ireland, Dublin.

Hencken, H., 1950. 'Lagore Crannog: an Irish royal residence of the 7th to 10th centuries A.D.', *Proc Roy Ir Acad C* **53**, 1-247.

Henry, F., 1952. 'A wooden hut on Inishkea North, Co. Mayo', *J Roy Soc Antiq Ir* **82**, 163-78.

Kelleher, John V., 1963. 'Early Irish history and pseudo-history', *Studia Hibernica* **3**, 113-27.

Kilbride-Jones, H.E., 1937. 'The evolution of the penannular brooches with zoomorphic terminals in Great Britain and Ireland', *Proc Roy Ir Acad C* **43**, 435.

Raftery, B., 1969. 'Freestone Hill, Co. Kilkenny: an Iron Age hillfort and Bronze Age cairn', *Proc Roy Ir Acad C* **68**, 1-108.

Raftery, B., 1972. 'Irish hill-forts'. In *The Iron Age in the Irish Sea Province* (Council for British Archaeology, Research Report 9), 51-3.

Ryan, Michael F., 1973. 'Native pottery in early historic Ireland', *Proc Roy Ir Acad C* **73**, 619-45.

GENERAL
ARCHAEOLOGY

The Post-Glacial Colonisation of Ireland: the Human Factors

Peter C. Woodman

One of the purposes of archaeology is to study man's attempts to adjust to his environment, manage and improve his means of survival and so forth. Yet we are usually confined to detailed analysis of the typology, chronology and economy associated with any prehistoric assemblage. Usually, it is assumed that the role of human societies is relatively passive when compared to the environmental factors which are thought to play a more dominant role in determining the direction and scope of man's activities. Most of these attitudes have a historical basis and so, in one sense, we are fortunate that studies of the Irish Mesolithic have not yet developed an unchallenged set of almost axiomatic attitudes. The purpose of the present study is to examine the problems of the post-glacial colonisation of Ireland in terms of its human problems rather than its typology or economy. These problems could be summarised as: (1) how and when did man come to Ireland; (2) what were the problems of this initial colonisation; (3) can the resultant industries be seen as a product of isolation and what are the mechanisms which have brought about this change.

HOW AND WHEN DID MAN COLONISE IRELAND?

Until recently conventional wisdom had dictated the date of 6,000 B.C. as that at which Ireland was colonised. This date was a product of the post-glacial geology of the shorelines of NE Ireland. Thus we must ask if our new date of colonisation, 7,000 B.C., could be a similar archaeological fiction. Within NW Europe it is possible to recognise a development from early industries containing what are often called simple non-geometric microliths. Industries of this type have not yet been found in Ireland. The earliest known industries in Ireland belong to a phase when the scalene triangle is the dominant microlith. With the exception of some southern French sites in the sauve-terrain such as Rouffignac (Rozoy, 1971) this type of industry dates, at its earliest, to some time just after 7,000 B.C. (Jacobi, 1976).

At the moment we have no non-geometric assemblages, not even undated ones, in the collections of our museums. Yet we must consider the possibility that such assemblages could exist. Gramsch (1973) has noted in Brandenburg and Mecklenburg that there is a gap between the industries of Zone III and those of the younger Pre-Boreal. He suggests that this is not a real absence of settlement but that, in the earliest phases of the post-glacial, water levels in lakes were significantly lower than today and therefore human settlement could be buried below more recent deposits. Similarly there is the evidence of a changing relative sea-level playing havoc with the coastal sites of the earlier half of the Mesolithic of Britain, Denmark and Holland.

In Ireland these two inter-related factors, a sea-level considerably below present levels (perhaps in excess of 40 metres in eustatic terms at the beginning of the post-glacial) and lower lake levels could contrive to create a misleading impression of the antiquity of human settlement in this island. If the coastal and estuarine sites are associated with shorelines which have either been buried below or eroded by the sea and if our lakes have silted up and, in the case of the centre of Ireland, been buried under massive peat bogs so that all evidence of the lake then disappears, as in the case of Lough Boora (Ryan, 1980), then we will be left with a very fragmentary record of the Irish Mesolithic. Our sample of sites can be biased still further by isostatic uplift in the NE of the island, an interesting geological phenomenon which inspired early research in the Mesolithic. This has been aggravated by the existence in the NE of flint, a raw material which could survive the vicissitudes of marine, lacustrine and riverine environments. Thus we are left with an historical bias towards the NE and a chronological bias towards the later part of the Mesolithic.

If we consider that the sites of hunter-gatherers are not scattered at random over the landscape but tend to cluster either at the nexus of several ecological niches or at a point where a food source can be best exploited, then many classic types of site location for the earliest Mesolithic will be precluded at the moment from easy or casual examination e.g. strategically placed lakeside and estuarine sites. Therefore only riverside locations might remain of the normal spectrum of sites. As has been shown by surface collection along the Louth rivers, sites in these locations need not necessarily be represented by massive concentrations of material as in the river Bann. Therefore outside very specific locations the river valleys may not have been exploited very extensively. The other problem is the question of exploitation of the uplands but this presents a more general problem rather than biasing evidence for the beginning of the Irish Mesolithic.

Before considering the point of origin for the Irish Mesolithic and the route taken to Ireland, it must be stated that it is assumed that man came to Ireland across a significant stretch of open water though the width of this channel is not known. It would be convenient to transport these people across a land-bridge and in fact it would solve many problems if this were true (see below) but, while there is little evidence for a post-glacial land-bridge, there is none for one which lasted a significant length of time into the post-glacial. We must assume therefore that there was an artificial means of transport.

If an attempt is made, on the basis of archaeological evidence, to asssess the possibility of sea transport we can only deal in generalities. Firstly, we do not know what type of craft would be available. We cannot state categorically whether dugouts or skin-covered boats were used. Similarly, there would appear to be no overall tendency towards adaptation to an open-sea economy nor colonisation in even the most favourable circumstances. Yet a certain type of environment would appear to encourage these trends.

The most striking example of a Mesolithic open-sea economy appears to be that found at Franchthi Cave (Jacobsen, 1973). Here during a rise in sea level there was an increase in the deep-sea fishing and, perhaps more significantly, Melian obsidian appeared in the upper part of the Mesolithic sequence. This site is set in a marine environment with a large bay in front and the Cyclades scattered across the adjacent part of the Aegean. Far-ranging voyages by boat will seem more possible when island-hopping can be used to develop skill and confidence.

Perhaps the best instance of island colonisation (leaving aside the contentious problem of when the island of America was colonised) must be the colonisation of the greater Australian land-mass. This would have required at some point an extensive sea journey of a greater magnitude than would be required to get to Ireland (Birdsell, 1977). It is to be noted that this colonisation seems to have taken place before the beginning of the Western European Upper Palaeolithic (Mulvaney, 1975), that is possibly by 40,000 B.C. Again this movement could be seen as beginning as an island-hopping exercise.

In spite of these impressive feats carried out at very early dates there is no certainty that these types of environments will *de rigueur* produce the necessary basis for an open-sea economy: in fact, the Oronsay shell middens, which occur in a classic archipelago, do not contain any clear pointers to extensive deep-water fishing (Mellars, personal communication) while the West Indies appear to have been colonised at a very slow rate and only Trinidad (the nearest to S America) was occupied significantly earlier than the rest, by 1,000 B.C. (Rouse, 1964). Although some pre-agricultural communities did reach islands such as Cuba the extreme end of the chain of colonisation, Jamaica and particularly the Bahamas (Sears & O'Sullivan, 1978), was colonised at a late date. The main problem here is that the Lesser Antilles are quite distant from Trinidad but again Rouse (1964) assumes that an island-hopping economy had developed first around Trinidad and other inshore islands and that hunter-gatherers based on this pushed out into the Antilles.

One point emerges from the study of island colonisation. There may be more likelihood of extensive sea crossing where offshore islands (and perhaps peninsulas) help to stimulate an economy which makes use of the resources of the sea and where long sea journeys with a perceived end became common. The corollary is that straight coastlines, where the marine productivity is also lower, are less likely to be the springboard for colonisation. This might explain the lack of Mesolithic colonisation of many of the Mediterranean islands.

The problem of a point of origin has been discussed in another paper (Woodman, 1978) which was written on the assumption that our earliest industries were the equivalent of the English Narrow Blade industries. If the possibility of an earlier occupation is admitted, then a crossing to Ireland from anywhere between Galloway and SW England must be a theoretical possibility (on typological grounds the Argyll/Antrim route still seems the least likely). There would appear to be several alternative routes: (a) Galloway/S Antrim-Down (b) Isle of Man/Co. Down-Co. Louth (c) Anglesey/Co. Dublin (d) S Wales-SW England/S Leinster.

If the colonisation was by boat then the width of the Irish Sea at various points is of importance. Here we are concerned with relative sea-level rather than absolute eustatic level; due to isostatic uplift in the extreme NE and the high relative sea-levels of Late Glacial times there has been less change in relative sea-levels in the N Antrim area than further south in the Irish Sea. Around 7,000 B.C. the sea-level (in eustatic terms) may have been about 20 metres below present day levels. However in areas of isostatic uplift the relative sea-level would have been up to 11 metres higher while in areas such as the North Sea, where the opposite action is still in progress, the relative sea-level was lower.

An examination of the contouring of the Irish Sea basin suggests that in many places around and before 7,000 B.C., particularly in the southern Irish Sea, a considerable area of the existing sea-floor would have been exposed (fig 16), perhaps just under 10 fathoms in the Isle of Man Basin and more than 10 fathoms farther south. Absolute distance across the remaining sea may be less important than perceived distance. Man will be more likely to cross to land which can be seen, therefore exposure of extensive flat areas of ground may not induce movement while high ground which can be seen will appear more attractive.

An extract of data on height/distance estimates in marine navigation provides a useful guide to perceived distance (Table I). From this it can be seen that the most southerly route is the least attractive. Garrard (1977) can only find evidence of dry land close to the Wexford coast and in Cardigan Bay; therefore, a slight diminution of the width of the channel, combined with an absence of high ground on either side, would make it the least likely route. At present route (d) is 45 miles across and twice that between areas of high ground. The shortest crossing on route (c) is just over 50 miles but mountains over 3,000 ft in Wicklow and Snowdonia are about 100 miles apart, just within range. In routes (a) and (b) we have shorter crossings within mountains: 3,000 ft in Cumbria, over 2,500 in the Mournes and Galloway, over 2,000 ft at Snaefall as well as hills over 1,500 ft in Antrim. In this area it is possible that there could have been bands whose territory abutted onto a shoreline of a substantially narrower sea with high ground behind and on the opposite shore. Therefore the area between the Isle of Man and Galloway seems to be closest to the ideal type of environment which might induce island colonisation. It has been suggested that the Isle of Man might almost have been a peninsula extending from the

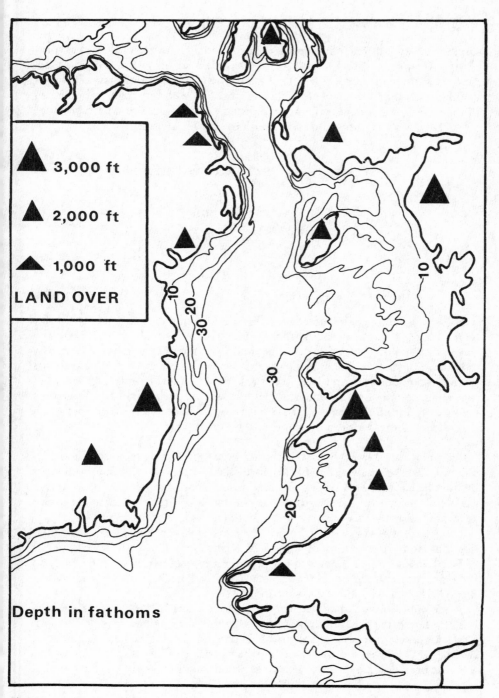

3,000 ft

2,000 ft

1,000 ft

LAND OVER

Depth in fathoms

Fig 16

Cumbrian coast. Although nothing as clear cut as the North Sea evidence has turned up (Kooijmans, 1971), Pantin (1978) has claimed to have found intertidal
deposits to the south east of the Isle of Man. Therefore with a substantially larger
island just off the Cumbrian and Galloway coast and with very high mountains in
all these areas, including Co. Down, the distances to Ireland would have been not
only relatively short but would have been perceptually shorter.

TABLE I

DISTANCE OF SEA-HORIZON FOR GIVEN HEIGHTS

HEIGHT	DISTANCE	HEIGHT	DISTANCE
1 ft	1.32 miles	250 ft	20.96 miles
10 ft	4.18 miles	500 ft	29.59 miles
25 ft	6.59 miles	1,000 ft	41.80 miles
50 ft	9.36 miles	2,000 ft	59.19 miles
100 ft	13.24 miles	3,000 ft	72.55 miles

There is of course at the moment no obvious progenitor for the Irish Mesolithic
on the Isle of Man, but as the coastlines have altered so radically, there is no reason
why Early Mesolithic material should be found and the Redkirk point hearths may
indicate settlement in Galloway. The extensive work carried out in Tasmania has
produced sites on the main island from the later part of that island's prehistory but
the earliest record of man comes from Hunter Island which would have been on a
peninsula protruding into the Bass Strait (Jones, 1977). Many other Tasmanian
coastal sites cluster suspiciously close to the period when the sea-level began to
stabilize.

On a more local level, Bonsall's (forthcoming 1981) study of Mesolithic settlement in the Esk Estuary also implies that coastal settlement is not random and that
the sites he has recovered belong to a very specific short chronological phase within
the Mesolithic when, due to a change in the course of the Esk, settlement in this
area could take advantage of a very productive estuarine environment.

Though we should not expect to find clear archaeological evidence of a colonisation route to Ireland, as most of the sites have been buried beneath the sea, the Isle
of Man/Galloway area appears to have the right type of coastal environment and
there are some parallels between the Manx site of Port St Mary and the Narrow
Blade Early Irish Mesolithic (Woodman, 1978).

When our minimum date for colonisation is considered, 7,000-6,800 B.C., then
it is of interest that it has been postulated that the first significant rise in the post-
glacial sea-levels took place at a slightly later date i.e. 6,700-6,500 B.C. (Huddart *et
al.*, 1977). This level, possibly caused by the balancing of isostatic and eustatic factors, has been noted by many others (e.g. Sissons and Brooks, 1973). Therefore, if

our earliest colonists did cross via areas which have been substantially altered by the rising relative sea-level, we can be certain on the basis of the dates from Mount Sandel that man had already reached Ireland before the significant rise in relative sea-level in the seventh millennium B.C.

THE ESTABLISHMENT OF A POPULATION

The major problem of the Irish Mesolithic is neither how these people first arrived in Ireland nor what range of economies may have developed but rather how they managed to survive the first few centuries of the initial phase of colonisation. Again, the archaeological precedence of the colonisation of the Sunda shelf (Australia and New Guinea) shows that it was possible for people with a primitive technology to build up from a tiny group to a massive viable population which, in the case of Australia, was hundreds of thousands.

The problems of island colonisation with little guarantee of either the ability to draw further on the human resources of the original population from which fission has taken place or of further waves of colonists present a potentially paradoxical situation. The larger the initial population the more problems there are in transportation while the smaller the initial population the more problems there are in ensuring the survival of the colonising group.

An *a priori* assumption has been made that the absence of the British Broad Blade industries in Cumbria and in the Lancashire/Cheshire Plain is in part due to the inundation of the contemporary coastal environments. Similarly all the early dates for the Narrow Blade industries of Northern England tend to come from the high ground. It is assumed that these coastal areas were occupied extensively. In fact, with various major river systems draining into two shallow-water bays these areas would have been exceptionally rich in food. Presumably the colonisation of Ireland was induced through the inundation of this low coastal plain.

As noted above the problem of colonisation is the balancing of the practicality of population movement against population size. Contemporary evidence takes two forms: computer simulation projects and recent historical colonisations. It has been suggested on the basis of a Monte-Carlo simulation project (in this instance for colonisation in Polynesia) that it might just be possible to colonise an area with six adults but an initial colonisation with the numbers of adults in double figures would be preferable (McArthur *et al.*, 1976). There have also been several cases of colonisation of small islands in the eighteenth and nineteenth centuries. These include the colonisation of Tristan da Cunha (Roberts, 1968) and Bass Strait Islands (Birdsell, 1957). Both these populations show remarkable increases; in fact Roberts notes specifically that in the first period after Tristan da Cunha was colonised the population increased dramatically due to the high fertility of the original colonists. Here the increase was limited by land area and population fluctuated around 250.

Similarly Birdsell notes that the Bass Islanders start with 21 adults and increase to 350 people within five elapsed generations. In this case the colonists lived the existence of hunter-gatherer communities.[1]

While there are instances of groups that function for much of the year as single extended families, many human societies appear to have a level of social organisation such as the local band. This has been noted in the field by Birdsell (1968) and Yengoyan (1968) and many others and it has also been suggested as a result of simulation projects by Wobst (1974). While a figure of 25 is often quoted for the size of a local band, perhaps more emphasis should be placed on the total range i.e. 15 to about 50. It is noteworthy that the upper limit approximates roughly to the number of people who took part in the initial colonisation of Tristan da Cunha and the Bass Strait Islands.

The near contemporary colonists may have avoided two of the problems which would have beset any primitive colonists. The first problem is transport. This could have significantly reduced the size of any group to the lower limit of a local band. While we know that water transport existed, can we suggest with justification that the Mesolithic of the Irish Sea boasted the equivalent of umiaks which Case (1969) has suggested were used in the Neolithic colonisation of Ireland? The second and related problem is that of population size. Schull (1972) has noted that if the population is very small there will be a tendency towards genetic sameness or homozygosity. If we have inherited diseases then these can become prevalent in a significant proportion of the population and can severely reduce the chance of the population's reproducing. Another problem of very small populations is that the normal male/female ratios cannot be guaranteed and so the ability of the group to reproduce may be reduced (Kunstadter, 1972).

Taking all these factors into consideration, we can suggest two possible alternatives for the post-glacial colonisation of Ireland: a colonising group of the size of a local band or a phase of colonisation during which time social and economic contacts were kept between the two main islands. While there are difficulties in visualising how man managed to reach Ireland, we do have the Australian and West Indian evidence that primitive hunter-gatherers have managed much more substantial sea-crossings.

The few archaeological indicators suggest that there is little reason to accept a concept of several waves of colonists. The local forms such as the needle points found at Mount Sandel, Co. Derry and Lough Boora, Co. Offaly, indicate not only earlier phases of as yet undiscovered settlement but have sufficient in common to show that both industries derive from a common stock. These needle points, apart from some in the Isle of Man, a later industry, are confined to Ireland. The development of a common form of Irish type fossil seems less likely in a context where separate groups of colonists had arrived from different points in Britain.

Ironically, the sea crossing to Ireland was a lesser problem than the establishment of a viable self-sufficient population. For reasons specified above it will be apparent that a single band does not in the long term constitute a viable population. In fact one must add the possible effects of a natural disaster either wiping out a proportion of a small breeding population or economic failure where there is no longer a social network for the band to fall back on. Wobst (1974, 1976) has concluded that for Palaeolithic and (by implication) Mesolithic peoples somewhere between 175 and 475 is required for a viable breeding population. Towards the bottom end of the range most marriage taboos would have to be sacrificed in order to keep the population levels up. This is particularly true if the population is as low as 100, while at the 500 level it makes no significant difference and so at the upper level complex kinship rules could be expected. However the implications of Schull's study of breeding populations (1972) are that genetic problems can only be avoided by the retention of the equivalent of kinship taboos.

Therefore one returns again to a delicate balance between numbers and marriage taboos. There is undoubtedly a potential to increase human population which is known as the founder effect (Birdsell, 1957; Fix, 1979). Therefore it would be possible to increase exponentially a small founder population so that within a few generations a viable population level would be reached. There are however at least two sources of drag on this exponential curve. Firstly Wobst's studies are based on life and fertility tables produced by Weiss (1973). These use an age range which does not match the few mortality curves of known Mesolithic populations. While the error could be partly caused by our inability to age skeletal remains correctly, the estimation of the archaeological record is of death by the lower thirties for females (bias in infants is to be expected and is excluded). Weiss's data suggests that 25% of the population was over 35 and that 20% of the births took place after this date. Therefore Wobst's studies may be optimistic in their estimates of the size of population required.

The second bias is more intangible. It has been assumed by many, such as Hayden (1972), that infanticide and birth spacing are a tool of a community regulating its population below the carrying capacity of the area. (This is more likely to be at a perceived social level of necessity rather than at a simple environmentally determined one). Howells (1976) has suggested that for many hunter-gatherers birth spacing might be a physiological phenomenon due to a lower level of fat reducing the level of fertility. It must be concluded that to achieve a viable population may not be at all a simple short process of a few generations.

The archaeological record can be examined for the answer to one important question. Is there evidence of continuity of occupation within the Irish Mesolithic? Mitchell (1976) has suggested that there is a gap within the Irish Mesolithic. When the number of sites dated is considered it is hardly surprising that there is a certain amount of clumping. In particular, there are only four sites from the Early Mesolithic and three of these probably belong to a phase when the Bann Estuary attracted intensive settlement in the Cutts area near Coleraine. All the C^{14} dates of any significance are listed in Table II.

TABLE II

RADIO CARBON DATES FOR THE IRISH MESOLITHIC UNTIL APPROXIMATELY 5,000 B.C.[2]

SITE	LAB. NO.	DATE
Mount Sandel Upper[3]	UB 912	6775 ± 115 b.c.
"	UB 913	6605 ± 70 b.c.
"	UB 951	6840 ± 185 b.c.
"	UB 952	7010 ± 70 b.c.
"	UB 2008	6490 ± 65 b.c.
"	UB 2007	6845 ± 135 b.c.
"	UB 2356	6815 ± 135 b.c.
"	UB 2357	7005 ± 185 b.c.
"	UB 2358	6845 ± 135 b.c.
"	UB 2359	5935 ± 120 b.c.
"	UB 2360	6720 ± 100 b.c.
"	UB 2361	6595 ± 165 b.c.
"	UB 2362	7040 ± 80 b.c.
Castle Roe	UB 2171	6805 ± 135 b.c.
"	UB 2172	6610 ± 75 b.c.
Mount Sandel Lower	UB 532	6420 ± 200 b.c.
Lough Boora	UB 2199	6525 ± 75 b.c.
"	UB 2200	6400 ± 75 b.c.
"	UB 2267	6500 ± 75 b.c.
"	UB 2268	7030 ± 350 b.c.
Toome	Y 95	5630 ± 110 b.c.
Cushendun (Lower Silts)	I 5134	5720 ± 140 b.c.
" "	UB 689	5445 ± 65 b.c.
Newferry: Site 3 (Zone Nine)	UB 888	6225 ± 145 b.c.
" " (Zone Nine)	UB 487	6240 ± 140 b.c.
" " (Zone Eight)	UB 641	5680 ± 195 b.c.
" " (Zone Seven)	UB 496	5535 ± 115 b.c.
" " (Zone Seven)	UB 517	5240 ± 110 b.c.
" " (Zone Seven)	UB 516	5005 ± 60 b.c.
" " (Zone Seven)	UB 887	5030 ± 115 b.c.
" " (Zone Seven)	UB 886	4935 ± 60 b.c.
" " (Zone Seven)	UB 637	6945 ± 125 b.c.

While these dates do tend to leave a gap on either side of 6,000 B.C., this is not as great as might appear at first sight. Two dates should be noted. From Newferry, Zone Nine, are two dates close to 6,000 B.C. and while only one flint flake was associated with this level, six stones were placed deliberately in the stone-free sand. These items may not provide much information about man's activities but they do indicate man's presence. Again the 5,900 B.C. dates from Mount Sandel came from the edge of the area of Mesolithic occupation and may not represent an aberrant date. Besides the chronological evidence, the main argument for continuity within the Irish Mesolithic is the simple fact that there is no parallel for the Later Mesolithic and so it is best explained as a local development. Therefore, in spite of the real typological dichotomy within the Irish Mesolithic, there is no real evidence that the population may have died out.

It can be assumed that there would be no environmental problem in establishing a viable population in Ireland; in fact if, as suggested elsewhere (Woodman, 1978), the range of .01 persons to .1 persons per square kilometre is taken, then the population of Ireland at this period would be between 800 and 8000 persons. A more practical comparison is that Tasmania, which was only marginally smaller, had a population of over 4000 people. If a slightly warmer climate is traded against land size (the former attribute may be very important in terms of food productivity (Jones, 1977)), it would be reasonable to assume that Ireland could have supported a population of several thousands. The major problem is whether the restricted insular resources of Ireland might have influenced the availability of food in the winter (Woodman, 1978). Therefore any attempt to estimate actual population levels must wait until more is known about the post-glacial native fauna and how it was exploited.

If it is accepted that availability of raw materials for the manufacture of stone tools does not present a problem, the two other major variables are those imposed by the slight changes in the topography of early post-glacial Ireland. The changing sea-level only reduced the land mass slightly, but most of the population would be clustered rather than evenly spread throughout the island and so the amount of coastline available and perhaps the number of major estuaries would be more important than slight reductions in land mass. With the concept of the use of the junction of ecological zones combined with their high marine productivity perhaps many of the major river estuaries of the south coast should be examined for evidence of settlement. The second factor is the development of the raised bogs which may have precluded settlement in certain areas (Woodman, 1978). These extensive bogs could have been established during the Mesolithic (Mitchell, 1976). While many did preclude human settlement, for example L. Boora (Ryan, 1980), others may have filled up at a much slower rate and could have been at a similar stage to Agerod Bog (Larsson, 1978) where extensive occupation took place at a time when this extension of the Ringsjo system was silting up. This can be a stage of high productivity (Maitland, 1979). The problem in Ireland is whether these lakes had resident fish populations or were visited by catadromous and anadromous fish. One cannot assume in early post glacial times the presence of freshwater fish in a lake system.

The population levels will therefore be conditioned by availability of land mammals as well as of fish. The population may cluster in areas where there is a wider spread of fish availability as a counter to the lean period which may occur in the winter and early spring. This must be combined with the size of estuary and the size of the associated river systems, as this will effect the size of the fish run. Thus Schalk (1977) has shown that the mean discharge of a river system is a reasonable indicator of its salmon population. An added problem with the smaller river systems is that the annual fluctuation in runs can lead to a reduction in numbers of salmon to a level at which they are virtually absent (Went, 1947). It is therefore interesting to contrast the potential of the E Antrim coast with that of the south coast of Ireland. As Went (1964) has noted, some of the rivers in the south and southeast are associated with runs of spring and summer salmon that make fish available throughout a large part of the year. This availability combined with numerous large estuaries would have made these areas extremely attractive, while parts of the Antrim coast, with their small rivers and more limited and almost concurrent runs of fish, may have only been exploited as part of a seasonal cycle. Therefore while there are many imponderables about the economic potential of Ireland, there is no ecological reason why a large population could not have survived in Ireland.

THE INSULARITY OF THE IRISH MESOLITHIC

In order to understand the reasons for the distinctive development of the Irish Mesolithic it is instructive to compare Ireland with the Isle of Man. There are at least three distinctive typological complexes within the Manx Mesolithic (Woodman, 1978a). Each has its own unique elements but in general the material can be compared to either the Irish or British Mesolithic. The distance from the Isle of Man to another land mass is not substantially less than two of the potential routes from Ireland to Scotland, yet its industries lack that exceptional difference which makes the Irish Later Mesolithic so distinctive.

The author has attempted to explain the development of the distinctive Later Irish Mesolithic in a relatively mechanistic fashion (Woodman, 1978): the explanation was that due to the uneven distribution of flint the human transportation of flint had been solved by the transportation of flint blades and that this had influenced the form of the implements. This could well be an explanation at a low level but it does not explain the fact that many other parts of these islands which lacked flint e.g. the Pennines (Jacobi, 1978) did not use the same system as that found in Ireland. The reason may lie in the development of an independent population which in the area most adjacent to Britain may not have had a fully developed marine economy. The rising relative sea level could have been a contributory factor but not the prime reason.

On the one hand there is no reason to believe that crossings from Antrim to Argyll were common, particularly if the coastal exploitation of E Antrim was not very intensive (the Glencloy project, Woodman, in preparation). In fact the presence of sea-bed flint pebbles on the west coast of Scotland suggests that even Antrim flint may not have been that much in demand in Scotland where the only known hoards are Neolithic (Callender, 1917). As a contrast there is evidence of contact outside Ireland in the similarity of the Manx heavy bladed tradition to the Irish Later Mesolithic. Ironically, the sea crossings here are longer than the Antrim/Argyll ones but here the preconditions for sea crossings may have existed in that the Strangford Lough area could be seen as an archipelago where sea transport was common. Therefore, while the Antrim coast presented a stark unyielding environment, there were areas where there is some archaeological evidence of some form of contact.

If distance in itself is not necessarily a barrier, then a more social explanation must be sought. The most tempting explanation would be linguistic but recent analyses do not support this. Cook found that northern Polynesians had no difficulty in understanding the Maoris from whom they had been separated for a millennium. In isolated populations the rate of linguistic change is very slow (J. Mallory, personal communication).

The most reasonable explanation appears to be based on the interrelationship between the levels of viable population and the process of self-identification of a community, a combination of biological and sociological factors. Price, in his examination of stylistic variations of the Mesolithic of the north European Plain (forthcoming) has suggested that the variation in the style of manufacture of certain implements and types may be correlated with the regional bands and that the areas within which the distinctive forms were found did in certain instances approach the expected size of a territory occupied by a band of the size suggested by Birdsell (1968).

Perhaps a distinction can be made between these minor distinctive traits which are found within the European Mesolithic and the more characteristic change which typifies the later Irish Mesolithic. Glynn Isacc (1972), when examining the short-term fluctuations in the African Acheulean within an apparent long-term lack of development, suggested that this could be best explained by the nature of the social organisation. His suggestion was that communities functioned within an open lattice which acted as an impediment to the transfer of innovative change and that there was therefore a tendency to return to a norm, thus creating an apparent, though not real, uniformity within the Acheulean.

This concept of organisation has been developed more explicitly by Wobst (1975, 1976) in his analysis of locational relationships in Palaeolithic societies. This he organises as a mating network which has much in common with locational networks used in geography. Price has suggested that the Mesolithic variations are caused by endogamous mating systems within this lattice and that these lead to the regional band or Birdsell's dialectical tribe (1968). Within this framework the concept of information-processing is implicit (Van der Leuuw, forthcoming). Thus at a simple level information will flow more easily within a mating network or tribe while there will be resistence to information exchange with other networks. Thus the radical typological alterations which David (1973) saw within the Noaillian as catastrophies to portions of a widely scattered sparse population can be seen as breakdowns of information-processing.

If we return to the question of mating networks then the choice is between the endogamous system or regional band and the exogamous system which will result in gradual changes or population clines. Even if the former model is accepted this does not usually result in the total isolation of a population, as often up to 20% of marriages are exogamous in primitive closely-knit societies. Therefore one can assume that any European mainland group is still held within a tenuous larger lattice which will, unconsciously of course, act as a damper on radical change.

Therefore the real distinction of the Irish Mesolithic may be that the links within this lattice have been so attenuated by distance and other factors that the damping effect has been removed. The important prerequisite for this is that a viable population was present in Ireland and that the tendency towards endogamy was more or less complete. Three types of island environment can be distinguished: those such as Ireland where large populations can be present; those at the other extreme such as Kangaroo Island, off Australia, where isolation by the sea appears to have caused the abandonment of the island as it was too small to support an independent population (Jones 1977); and, in between, islands such as the Isle of Man where there is evidence of periods of occupation which lasted long enough to allow distinctive implements to develop. Could it be that population levels on that island were so low that contact had to be kept with a nearby larger population or were there only disjointed short phases of occupation which did not allow sufficient time to develop a more distinctive 'Manx Industry'?

While this discussion may appear rather theoretical, it does relate to the archaeological realities of the Irish Mesolithic in two very important ways. Firstly, we can assume that the Mesolithic population of Ireland was sufficiently large to allow the development of regional bands. Therefore, typologically we should expect some stylistic variations rather than homogeneity. These will, of course, be at a minor level such as those discussed by Price. The second consideration bears on the nature of the insularity of the Irish Mesolithic. It would be unrealistic to suggest a total isolation of Ireland — in fact the Manx Broad Blade industries show that this is not so. However, if a series of 'introverted' social groupings did exist in Ireland then the need for outside contact is significantly reduced. Sahlins (1972) has shown that much primitive exchange is related to social needs such as rights of access, marital alliance, etc. Therefore, for reasons discussed above, excluding Antrim, it can be assumed that most coastal activity would have been within what Jones (1977) described as a marine envelope or area adjacent to the coast beyond which it was not usual to travel. Therefore contact across the Irish Sea is not by any means precluded but rather in terms of social organisation it is at too low a level to alter significantly the traditions of manufacture of stone artifacts which could be in part a product of an unconscious process of self-identification.

CONCLUSIONS

The purpose of this paper is to create a framework within which future work can be directed. Woodman (1978) has suggested two immediate goals for research within the Irish Mesolithic: the extent of occupation in Mesolithic Ireland and the nature of the economies which would have developed. A third objective could be the nature of the social organisation which developed in Ireland. It is possible to suggest a density of human population for the Mesolithic. An approximation of this sort for the Later Mesolithic could influence one's assessment of the inception of the Neolithic in Ireland. Was there, as Bender suggests (1978), a highly structural organisation for the Mesolithic?

Large complex social organisations could play havoc with simplistic interpretations of seasonal settlement. The examination of problems such as these requires not only a series of problem-oriented excavations but a testing of the most basic assumptions concerning the interpretation of settlements and the social and economic significance of artifact types.

There appears to be an archaeological form of the 'Hinsenberg Uncertainty Principle' which is that in attempting to answer a problem on one level several new problems are created on another. Yet, if prehistory is to escape from the twin talons of typology and chronology then perhaps the escape route must be through attempting to answer questions, such as those posed above, which are of themselves almost unanswerable. At the moment therefore our knowledge of the Irish Mesolithic could be summarized as follows: man successfully colonized Ireland in Early Post-Glacial times but no coherent picture of his economy or society has emerged.

NOTES

1 A distinction should be made between small populations living in a confined environment which would restrict the growth of the population, e.g. Tristan de Cunha or the Kaiadilt (Cawte, 1978) and small colonizing populations where there is a potential for growth. The natural disaster and psychological problems which can effect the former are not necessarily relevant to the latter.

2 All C14 dates are quoted as uncalibrated old half life. More information about the sites can be found in Woodman, 1978.

3 It was noted that several dates were excluded from previous lists. No intention of biasing the record was intended and all dates will be published in the final report. However, for completeness sake all other dates are given below.

    (a) UB 2205 Mount Sandel Upper 335 ± 70 B.C. This sample overlay a later palisade trench on the southern edge of the site.

    (b) UB 2041 Mount Sandel Lower 1235 ± 60 A.D. This date came from the ditch of Mount Sandel Fort.

    (c) UB 591 Mount Sandel Lower 5770 ± 525 B.C.

UB 592 – 5410 ± 695 B.C. and 4295 ± 90 B.C. These two dates were excluded because of their large standard deviations and because they could come from a disturbed context. UB 592 was dated twice. The first was a selected charcoal sample while the second was from a bulk sample and was fine particulate charcoal.

ACKNOWLEDGEMENTS

As this paper is dedicated to Professor O'Kelly I feel that it is only fitting to acknowledge the stimulus he has provided through numerous discussions on the nature of the Irish Mesolithic. Secondly, I should like to thank L.N.W. Flanagan for helpful criticism of the text and finally Dr J. Mallory and Capt. I. Lavery for advice on matters linguistic and navigational.

REFERENCES

Bender, B., 1978. 'Gatherer-hunter to farmer: a social perspective', *World Archaeol* 10(2), 204-22.

Birdsell, S.R., 1957. 'Some population problems involving Pleistocene man'. *In* K.B. Warren (ed), *Population Studies: animal ecology and demography*, 47-70. Cold Spring Harbor. Symposia on Quantitative Biology 22.

Birdsell, S.R., 1968. 'Some predictions for the Pleistocene based on equilibrium systems among recent hunter-gatherers'. *In* E.B. Lee and I. De Vore (ed), *Man the Hunter*, 229-40, 246. Chicago.

Birdsell, S.R., 1977. 'The recalibration of a paradigm for the first peopling of Greater Australia'. *In* J. Allen, J. Golson, R. Jones (ed), *Sunda and Sahul*, 113-68. London.

Bonsall, C., 1981. 'The coastal factor in the Mesolithic settlement of North West England'. *In* B. Gramsch (ed), *The Proc of the 2nd Mesolithic in Europe Symposium*, forthcoming. Potsdam.

Callander, J.G., 1917. 'A flint workshop on the hill of Skares', *Proc Soc Antiq Scot* **51**, 117-27.

Case, H., 1969. 'Settlement patterns in the North Irish Neolithic, *Ulster J Archaeol ser 3* **32**, 3-27.

Cawte, J., 1978. 'Gross stress in small islands: a study in micropsychiatry. *In* I.A. Brady, C.D. Laughlin (ed), *Extinction and survival in human populations*, 95-121. New York.

David, N., 1973. 'On Upper Palaeolithic society, ecology and technological change: the Noaillian case'. *In* C. Renfrew (ed), *The explanation of cultural change: models in prehistory*, 276-303. London.

Fix, A.G., 1979. 'Anthropological genetics of small populations', *Ann Rev Anthrop* **8**, 207-30.

Garrard, R.A., 1977. 'The sediments of the South Irish Sea and Nymphe Bank area of the Celtic Sea'. *In* C. Kidson and M.J. Tooley (ed), *The Quaternary History of the Irish Sea.* Liverpool.

Gramsch, B., 1973. 'Das Mesolithikum in Mecklenburg und Brandenburg — zeitliche Gliederung und Formengruppen'. *In* S. Kozlowski (ed), *The Mesolithic in Europe,* 209-35. Warsaw.

Hayden, B., 1972. 'Population control among hunter/gatherers', *World Archaeol* 4(2), 205-21.

Howell, N., 1976. 'Towards a uniformatarian theory of human paleodemography'. *In* R.H. Wand and K.M. Weiss (ed), *The demographic evolution of small populations,* 26-39. London.

Huddart, D.A., Tooley, M.J. and Carter, P.A., 1977. 'The coasts of N.W. England'. *In* C. Kidson and M.J. Tooley (ed), *The Quaternary History of the Irish Sea,* 119-54. Liverpool.

Isacc, G., 1972. 'Early phases of human behaviour: models in Lower Palaeolithic archaeology'. *In* D. Clarke (ed), *Models in Archaeology,* 167-200. London.

Jacobsen, H., 1973. 'Excavations in the Franchthi cave 1969-71, Part 1', *Hesperia* **42,** 45-88.

Jacobi, R., 1976. 'Britain inside and outside Mesolithic Europe', *Proc Prehist Soc* **42,** 67-84.

Jacobi, R., 1978. 'Northern England in the eighth millennium b.c.: an essay'. *In* P. Mellars (ed), *The Early Post Glacial Settlement of Northern Europe,* 295-332.

Jones, R., 1977. 'Man as an element of a continental fauna: the case of the sundering of the Bassian bridge'. *In* J. Allen, J. Golson, and R. Jones (ed), *Sunda and Sahul,* 17-86.

Kooijmans, 1971. 'Mesolithic bone and antler implements from the North Sea and from the Netherlands', *Berichten van de Rijksdienst voor het Oudheidkundig Bodemonderzoek* **20-1,** 27-73.

Kundstadter, P., 1972.'Demography, ecology, social structure, and settlement patterns'. *In* G.A. Harrison and A.J. Boyce (ed), *The structure of human populations,* 313-51. Oxford.

Larsson, L., 1978. *Agerod 1:B — Agerod 1:D. A study of Early Atlantic settlement in Scania.* Lund.

MacArthur, N., Saunders, I.W., Tweedie, R.L., 1976. 'Small population isolates: a micro-simulation study', *J Polynesian Soc* **85,** 307-26.

Maitland, P., 1979. *Synoptic Limnology.* Cambridge.

Mitchell, F., 1976. *The Irish Landscape.* London.

Mulvaney, J., 1975. *The Prehistory of Australia.* Ringwood.

Pantin, H.M., 1978. 'Quaternary sediments from the north-east Irish Sea: Isle of Man to Cumbria', *Bull Geolog Surv Great Britain.*

Price, T.D., 1981. 'Regional approaches to human adoption in the Mesolithic of the North European Plain'. *In* B. Gramsch (ed), *The Proc 2nd Mesolithic in Europe Symposium,* forthcoming. Potsdam.

Roberts, D.F., 1968. 'Genetic fitness in a colonizing human population', *Human Biology* **40,** 494-507.

Rouse, I., 1964. 'The prehistory of the West Indies', *Science* **144,** 499-514.

Rozoy,G.,1971. 'Tardenoisien et Sauveterrien', *Bull Soc Prehist Française* **68,** 345-74.

Ryan, M., 1980. 'An early Mesolithic site in the Irish Midlands', *Antiquity* **54,** 46-7.

Sahlins, M., 1972. *Stone Age economics.* London.

Sears, W.H. and O'Sullivan, S.O., 1978. 'Bahamas prehistory', *American Antiquity* **43,** 3-25.

Schalk, R.F., 1977. 'The structure of an anadromous fish resource'. *In* L. Binford (ed), *For theory building in archaeology*, 207-50. New York.

Schull, 1972. 'Genetic implications of population breeding structure'. *In* G.A. Harrison and A.J. Boyce (ed), *The structure of human populations*, 146-64. Oxford.

Sissons, J.B. and Brooks, C.L., 1971. 'Dating of Early Post-Glacial land and sea-level changes in the western Forth Valley', *Nature* (Phys Science) **234**, 124-7.

Weiss, K.M., 1973. 'Demographic models for anthropology', *Memoirs Soc American Archaeol* **27**.

Went, A.E.J., 1947. 'Salmon of the Kerry Blackwater', *Sci Proc Roy Dublin Soc* **24**, 179-88.

Went, A.E.J., 1964. 'Irish salmon — a review of investigations up to 1963'. *Sci Proc Roy Dublin Soc ser A* **1**, 365-412.

Wobst, H.M., 1974. 'Boundary conditions for Palaeolithic social systems: a simulation approach', *American Antiquity* **39**, 147-8.

Wobst, H.M., 1975. 'The demography of finite populations and the origins of the incest taboos', *Memoirs Soc American Archaeol* **30**, 75-81.

Wobst, H.M., 1976. 'Locational relationships in Palaeolithic society'. *In* R.H. Ward and K.M. Weiss, (ed) *The Demographic evolution of human populations*, 49-58. London.

Woodman, P.C., 1978. *The Mesolithic in Ireland* (Brit Archaeol Rep **58**). Oxford.

Woodman, P.C., 1978a. 'A re-appraisal of the Manx Mesolithic'. In *Man and Environment in the Isle of Man* (Brit Archaeol Rep **54**(1)), 119-40. Oxford.

Yengoyan, A.A., 1968. 'Demographic and ecological influences on Aboriginal Australian marriage sections'. *In* R.B. Lee and I. De Vore (ed), *Man the hunter*, 185-99. Chicago.

The Flint Javelin Heads
of Ireland

A.E.P. Collins

In the present state of archaeological research it may seem that the study of a single implement type needs some justification. I feel that the type in question, the leaf- or lozenge-shaped javelin head which frequently shares a combination of the methods of flaking and polishing in its manufacture, is intrinsically worth a study, especially since earlier writers have only afforded it incidental treatment. It must surely rank with the flint daggers and sickles of Great Britain as an outstanding piece of flint craftsmanship which in the best examples has hardly been equalled outside Denmark and predynastic Egypt. This alone, granted sufficient provenanced examples to give a distributional aspect to the study, would be justification enough. A further reason has been added by the discovery during the last fifty years of a significant number of examples in excavated contexts in both burial monuments and domestic sites.

Certain difficulties of method beset the study of these implements. One is to know where to draw the line between arrowheads and javelin heads; here, the purely arbitrary one of size has been chosen: implements over 5 cm long have been designated javelin heads. That this has some solid justification is borne out by a consideration of their thickness: most leaf and lozenge arrowheads are relatively thin in cross-section, while most javelin heads tend to be stout in the same dimension. Only a thin flint point could be accommodated in the cleft end of an arrow shaft, whereas a much stouter point could be fitted in the end of the thicker spear or javelin shaft. In the larger examples of javelin head the average maximum thickness is 8 mm.

It may be objected, even, that to call these larger leaf and lozenge points javelin heads is unwarranted by the evidence. There is little positive corroboration of their function as such. And yet if one measures the instances of arrow or javelin heads which still possess part of their wooden shafts or by reason of differential patination show a kind of 'ghost image' of the now vanished shaft it becomes clear that some of these by reason of the indicated diameter of their shafts should be designated javelins. The largest of three examples published by Knowles (1909, 280, fig 3) is a full 9 cm long. Many of the Irish javelin heads are much too large and heavy to have served as heads for any conceivable size of arrow, as shown in our fig 19. They are matched in general size and flaking technique by many ethnographic parallels. (Compare the larger American Indian projectile heads of pre-Columbian times

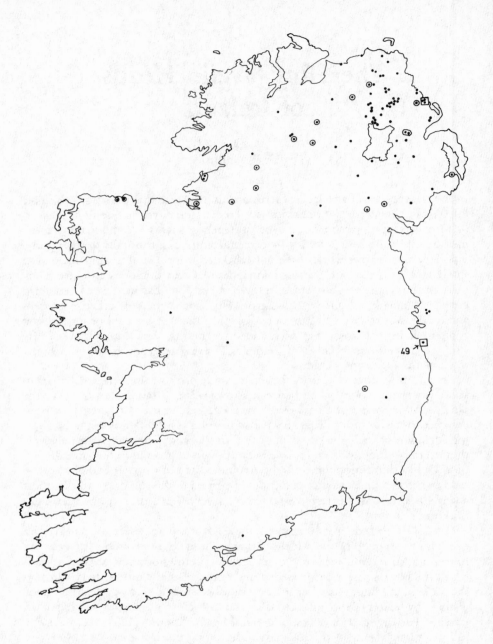

Fig 17: Distribution map of javelin heads. Note: ringed black dots indicate javelins in or under chambered tombs. Dots set in rectangles indicate javelins in domestic or industrial sites.

and, of course, the Australian aborigine spearheads of the last century, flaked from either porcelain telegraph insulators or from bottle-glass). The term javelin head rather than spearhead is preferred. The javelin is a throwing weapon, while the spear can serve equally as a thrusting weapon or pike. It seems more likely that the flint points would have been employed on relatively light shafts as projectiles.

Another point of method concerns the all too numerous unprovenanced examples. I have for the most part ignored these. Some can with confidence be attributed to a county (most to Co. Antrim) but the majority have no firmer indication of provenance than the known sphere of operations of a particular private collector. Occasional references will be made to individual examples where these exhibit technical points of interest.

TYPOLOGY AND TECHNOLOGY

Javelin heads range in length from the arbitrary minimum of 5 cm to a maximum of perhaps 25 cm in a broken unprovenanced example in the Ulster Museum, Belfast (reg. no. 1501). A selection representative of their forms is shown in fig 19. The forms can be classified (fig 18) into three main groups: (A), a leaf-shaped form with no obvious angles or shoulders; (B), a relatively broad lozenge form with distinct angles generally near the mid-point of the sides which may run straight, as shown, or may be slightly convex; (C), an elongated lozenge form with the shoulders much nearer the basal end than the point. In the last group the longer edges are frequently concave and the short edges between the shoulders and the base frequently, but not invariably, convex. In extreme form this convexity produces a generally rounded basal end (fig 19.61). In the schedule of provenanced examples (below) this ABC classification has added to it the letter *p* to denote that the example in question is polished.

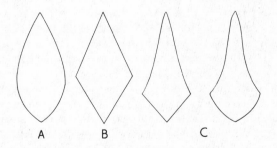

Fig 18: The main types classified.

A   B   C

The material used for javelins was almost invariably flint. Of the 147 listed examples all but three appear to be of flint. One of those from Dalkey Is., Co. Dublin, is of the black carboniferous chert frequently used for arrowheads and other small implements in the south and west of Ireland[1]. Fig 21.143, from Mountfield, Co. Tyrone, appears to be made from a black shale which has been dressed into shape by a gouging technique before being finally polished.

The larger javelin heads would perforce require to be made from large nodules of freshly extracted flint from the chalk of counties Down, Antrim or Londonderry. The small size of those from Dalkey Is., Co. Dublin, where a total of 21 complete examples ranged from 9 cm to 5 cm in length, with a mean length of just over 6.3 cm is a function of their makers' dependence on small flint pebbles from the local drift as raw material. That they stretched the available material to the limit is shown by the occurrence on many examples of small areas of cortex at each end of the implement, showing that the full length of the pebble was used.

In method of manufacture the bulk of the examples are clearly flake tools. Not only is their size within the limits possible by this technique but blank areas of the bulbar surface of the original flake are often left visible. This is especially note-worthy on nos. 10, 18, 35, 37 and 140 in the schedule. The curvature seen in edge view on such as nos. 135 and 139 is surely a product of the curve of the original flake which has not been removed by the subsequent secondary trimming. Yet it is doubtful whether the largest examples could have been made from flakes. Nos. 19 and 20, far more massive in cross-section than any of the others, are undoubted core tools. No. 20 in its outline reflects Form C of the javelins though no. 19 is closer in outline to a flint axe. Nevertheless, its thickness, seen in cross-section, is surely slighter than that of most axes. Both have been boldly worked by the removal of numerous broad and thin feather-edge flakes. No. 19 shows local grin-ding which has removed the main irregularities on each face. It is tempting to sug-gest that we have here two examples of the first blocking-out stage in the manufac-ture of the larger javelins. Similar blocking-out, combined with a very irregular outline is seen on a small example (fig 20.66) from Dalkey Is., indicating that this is an unfinished example.

The number of subsequent stages in the manufacture of javelin heads seems to have varied. That a neat and regular finish could be achieved by flaking alone is shown by a few examples of Form C, as for instance fig 19.38 (Lenagh, Co. An-trim) and fig 19.55 (Derrytagh North, Co. Armagh) and an even neater unillustrated example, no. 53 (Glenleslie, Co. Antrim). Similarly neat flaking is also seen on fig 19.13 (Ballyvaddy, Co. Antrim) and on a group of three from Lambay Is., Co. Dublin, of which one (fig 19.115) is illustrated. Naturally, cross-sections of these are of a general lozenge form, without the flattening of the central area of each face which polishing contributes. Polishing, where used, sometimes amounts to no more than the removal of a few major protuberances left by the previous flaking (e.g. fig 20.64 (Audleystown cairn)). Yet in a high proportion of cases polishing covers a very large part of each face and remains the final stage of manufacture. It is generally clearly identifiable by the soft blurred edge where it meets the previous flaking scars and by the fact that it is usually convex, curving down towards the edges of the implement, (e.g. fig 20.133 (Ballyglass court grave, Co. Mayo)). Occasionally a javelin head displays small local areas where edge flaking has been done after such polishing.

Complete edge flaking subsequent to the polishing is the normal technique for finishing the evolved Form C. Here the polishing frequently covered much of the centre of each face (e.g. fig 19.146 (Camaderry, Co. Wicklow) and fig 19.45 (Port Ballintrae, Co. Antrim)). The polished surface is usually remarkably flat or even concave. Scratch marks showing the direction of movement of the grinding rubber are frequent across the length of the implement, either at right-angles to the main axis of the implement or diagonal to it. Occasionally, especially on the largest examples, more than one direction of grinding has been employed. In all this group the final trimming of the edges and point of the javelin head has been carried out by pressure-flaking subsequent to the polishing, as is clearly shown by the way the flaking has bitten into the ground and polished surface. Here examples of Form C (e.g. fig 19.61 (Corlea, Co. Donegal)) show none of this post-grinding flaking. The typical cross-section of a javelin which has been polished and subsequently chipped shows a flat, parallel-sided central section which tapers steeply to the chipped edges.

An instructive unprovenanced example of Form C in the Sturge Collection, British Museum, shows extensive areas of polish in the centre of each face; the edges from basal end to shoulders were flaked before polishing, whereas the edges from shoulder to point were flaked after polishing, suggesting a re-sharpening of the functionally important point and its adjacent edges or perhaps the flaking down of a larger implement whose point had been broken.

The proportions of polished to flaked examples in each class are set out as follows:

A		B		C	
Unpolished	Polished	Unpolished	Polished	Unpolished	Polished
70	3 (4%)	15	15 (50%)	14	28 (67%)

The steady increase in percentage polished as one proceeds from A to C is striking. So, too, is the small proportion of A which shows any polish at all. The last is so small as to suggest that we are dealing with two distinct categories of implements in the leaf and lozenge types which may differ chronologically, culturally or functionally. Yet two points need to be borne in mind here: of the total of 68 unpolished examples of Form A, 54 are from domestic or industrial sites where they were made; many of these were broken before completion and it may be that they were originally destined for polishing, and further, examples found in Carlingford tombs have included all three types.

One may speculate as to the purpose of this extensive grinding and polishing of the javelin faces. That it produced a cross-section that was on average more regular and thinner than flaking alone could produce is true enough. Yet this was not invariably the case as is shown by the best of the purely flaked examples (e.g. No. 47 (Tehorny, Co. Antrim)) which, 13.5 cm long and 5.3 cm wide, has a maximum thickness of only 6 mm. A reason adduced elsewhere, as on the Gerzean knives of predynastic Egypt or on the finest of the Danish flint daggers — that it was a prerequisite for the regular serial flaking used for aesthetic reasons as a finish for these implements — does not apply to the Irish flint javelin heads. While the final edge trimming of the javelins is very neat and regular it differs little, if at all, from that by which the best unpolished examples have been finished; no regular 'fluting' or 'ripple' effect has been achieved. Another reason has been suggested for the similar pre-flaking polish on some Iberian flint dagger and halberd blades — the desire to imitate a metallic finish (Childe, 1957, 278). If this last suggestion should be accepted for the Irish Form C it might lend support to the suggestion that the concavo-convex profile recalls the outline of early types of bronze spearheads such as those from Arreton Down and Snow's Hill.

ASSOCIATIONS AND DATING

Until the 1930s no Irish flint javelin head had been found in the context of a modern excavation. One of Form C (fig 19.137) was accepted on somewhat dubious evidence as a find from the chamber of Listoghil, the largest of the Carrowmore group of round cairns (Knocknarea excepted) in Co. Sligo. It was assumed by Wood-Martin to be an implement found in the course of excavations in the early 19th century by R.C. Walker (Wood-Martin, 1888, 17, 114 and fig 94.11).

Over a dozen have been found in the last fifty years in excavations in Irish court-graves. They are listed as follows:

TOWNLAND NAME OF CAIRN	COUNTY	NUMBER IN SCHEDULE
Aghanaglack	Fermanagh	118
Annaghmare	Armagh	52
Audleystown	Down	64
Ballyglass	Mayo	133 & 134
Ballykeel	Armagh	53
Barnes Lower	Tyrone	138
Bavan	Donegal	60

TOWNLAND NAME OF CAIRN	COUNTY	NUMBER IN SCHEDULE
Behy	Mayo	Fragments
Clady Halliday	Tyrone	139
Creevykeel	Sligo	135 & 136
Kilnagarns	Leitrim	123 & 124
Tamnyrankin	Derry	131
Tully	Fermanagh	Fragment

Fig 20.119, a somewhat anomalous example with pronounced curvature visible in the edge view came from the main burial deposit in the inner of the two segments of the main gallery of Creevykeel 'lobster-claw' long cairn, Co. Sligo (Hencken, 1939, 80 and fig 6.15). A second (unillustrated) example (No. 120) with small areas of polish, generally comparable in size and outline with fig 20.139, though less angular, came from the same segment of the burial gallery, though from an Early Christian stratum where it was presumably derived from the megalithic stratum below (*op. cit.*, 84 and fig 8.5). Fig 20.131 shows a large blunt-pointed example from the main burial gallery of Tamnyrankin court-grave, Co. Derry. Fig 20.64 which has very small areas of polish on one face came from the outermost segment of the NE gallery of the dual court-grave of Audleystown, Co. Down (Collins, 1954, 28 and fig 9.1). Fig 20.118 came from the inner segment of the W gallery of the dual court-grave of Aghanaglack, Co. Fermanagh (Davies, 1939, 33, fig 3, and 37). Fig 20.122 came from packing between the portal stones of the gallery at Clady Halliday court-grave, Co. Tyrone (Davies and Radford, 1937, 85 and fig 2). Two unpolished leaf-shaped examples came from Bavan court-grave, Co. Donegal (Flanagan, 1966, figs 6C and 6J). Pieces were also found in Tully court-grave (Waterman, 1978 [1980]) and in the forecourt of Behy court-grave, Co. Mayo (De Valera and Ó Nualláin, 1964, 6). Fig 20.123 is the larger of two javelin heads from Kilnagarns Lower court-grave, Co. Leitrim (Corcoran, 1964, 189-90). The smaller, an unpolished example, is analogous in outline to our fig 20.64. From Ballyglass, Co. Mayo, come two javelins (fig 20.133 and .134), both excellent examples of their types. No. 20.133 of Form A shows almost complete pre-flaking polish. No. 20.134 is a shapely Form C with small areas of pre-flaking polish, both from the inner segment of the gallery. Fig 20.138 is a well flaked example of Form B , lacking polish, from the inner segment of the main gallery at Barnes Lower court-grave (Collins, 1966, fig 9.2). Fig 20.53 is a small but unusually stout example of Form C from the cist in the north end of the Ballykeel dolmen cairn, Co. Armagh[2] (Collins, 1965, fig 11.6). This shows a small area of post-flaking polish at the point of maximum thickness. Fig 20.52 is a well

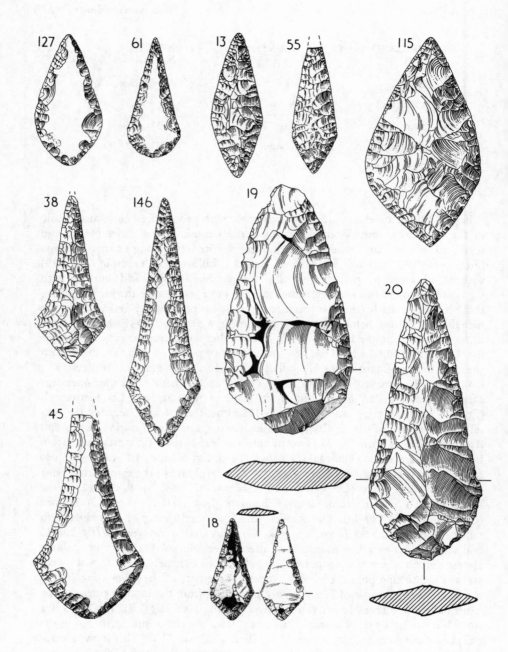

Fig 19: Provenanced but unexcavated javelin heads. Numbers are as in Schedule.

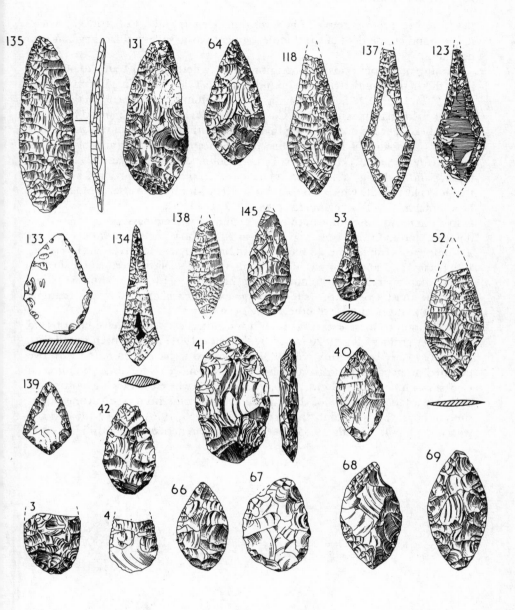

Fig 20: Excavated examples. Numbers are as in Schedule.

flaked and very thin example from Annaghmare court-grave, Co. Armagh, where it was found on the floor of the middle segment of the gallery; it lacks evidence of polishing.

Turning now from finds in long cairns we may note fig 20.41 and 20.42, both from the deposit underlying the round cairn on Lyles Hill, Co. Antrim (Evans, 1953, 51 and fig 20.27 and 20.22). Fig 20.145 is from a deposit beneath the round cairn of Baltinglass passage-grave, Co. Wicklow (Walshe, 1941, 230 and fig 6). In this connection it is worth recalling that heavily burnt fragments of two similar implements, probably of Form A, came from beneath the round cairn of passage-grave affinities at Knockmany, Co. Tyrone (Collins and Waterman, 1952, 29 and figs 3.1 and 3.2). Fig 21.143 is an anomalous example made from a black material that looks like lignite which was found with a bowl-form food vessel at Mountfield, near Omagh, Co. Tyrone (Abercromby, 1912, I, 143, 281).

In addition to these finds from burial monuments there have been others from domestic and industrial sites. Figs 20.66 to 20.69 show a selection from a total of 21 complete examples and 28 fragments from Dalkey Is., Co. Dublin (Liversage, 1968). Figs 20.3 and 20.4 are surface finds from a Neolithic occupation site adjacent to an opencast flint mining site on Ballygalley Hill, Co. Antrim (Collins, 1978). A third Co. Antrim site is Loughaveema, where a complete example (fig 20.40) and fragments of others have been found.

In addition to these excavated finds a few others are said to have been found with other artifacts. Fig 19.20 is said by Knowles (1903) to have been found with two others early last century. Fig 19.38 is also said to have been found with two polished stone axes beneath a rath that was removed in railway building at Cookstown Junction (Andrews, 1913, 97 and Pl 12, where the axes are illustrated). Probably a fair proportion of the stray finds have come from peat cutting operations in bogs; this is certainly the case with figs 19.55, 19.61, and 19.146 and also with no. 120. Of these fig 19.55 came from a known horizon in bogland just south

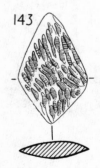

143

Fig 21: ?Lignite or shale javelin head
from Mountfield, Co. Tyrone.

of Lough Neagh and pollen analysis was carried out by Knud Jessen (1949, 117-8). Nos. 127 and 128 from Culbane, Co. Derry still have traces of the diatomite in which they were found adhering to them[3].

In the Irish court-graves it is fair to assume that the javelin heads with the other artifacts were in most cases intentional rather than accidental inclusions — in fact that they are true grave-goods — even if, as suggested by the burnt and damaged state of many of the objects, they were first cast on an external funeral pyre before being gathered up with the cremated bones and placed in the burial chambers. Since the weight of the evidence seems to favour the view that the court-graves were single rather than successive collective tombs (Collins, 1954, 33-4) we may regard the association of objects within them as valid and these other grave-goods may now be considered. Pottery of the plain carinated Lyles Hill type was an integral part of the burial deposits in most court-graves. It was associated with javelin heads at Audleystown, Barnes Lower, Clady Halliday, Clontygora Large, Creevykeel, and Tamnyrankin. At Annaghmare and Ballykeel the plain carinated bowls appeared to pre-date the main burial deposits where elaborately decorated Ballyalton bowls were the main ceramic content of the burial deposits. At Audleystown there was a Carrowkeel ware bowl as well as decorated Early Bronze Age wares at Clontygora Large. Associated flints included lozenge arrowheads at Audleystown and Clady Halliday and (probably associated) at Creevykeel; barbed-and-tanged arrowheads (in the next segment) at Aghanaglack; plano-convex knives at Audleystown, Barnes Lower and Tamnyrankin; hollow scrapers at Aghanaglack, Annaghmare, Clontygora Large and Creevykeel and convex scrapers at Audleystown and Creevykeel. In this list I have confined myself to objects found in the same segment of the burial gallery as the javelin head except at Tamnyrankin where the only information available in advance of the awaited full report refers to the whole of the main burial gallery.

In the round cairns both of Lyles Hill and of passage-grave type the finds of javelins have come not from burial chambers but from largely burnt strata full of artifacts and underlying the cairns themselves. Varying views have been expressed on the significance of these layers but first-hand experience at Knockiveagh cairn leads me to support the view of Professor Evans (1953, 10-13 and 66-7) with regard to Lyles Hill itself that these layers, for whatever reason, were deliberately placed as foundations on which the cairns should be built and that they are therefore closely linked both culturally and chronologically with the cairns themselves. This reasoning may well apply to passage-grave finds of javelins. Those from Baltinglass, fig 20.145 (Walshe, 1941, 228) and Knockmany are known to have come from sub-cairn deposits and the same may well also be true of Listoghil, Carrowmore (Wood-Martin, 1888) and the javelin head identified in a group of flint implements 'from the Cairns at Loughcrew' in the Kevin Collection in the National Museum, Dublin (Herity, 1974, 175-9). There is, however, one argument which may be used to support the contention that the Carrowmore and Loughcrew finds were actually part of the contents of burial chambers: early and mid-nineteenth-century chamber tomb 'excavations' seldom extended beyond removal of the contents of burial chambers and their approach passages.

In summary, therefore, we can say that Forms A, B, and C all with and without polish are represented in the chambered tombs. It is important to stress that at least 4 of the typologically sophisticated polished Form C with concavo-convex outline are represented in the chambered tombs. Polish on Forms A and B ranges from the vestigial at Audleystown to the almost complete at Ballyglass.

The evidence of association on domestic sites is unsatisfactory. The three broken javelin heads from Ballygalley Hill, Co. Antrim came from an area of thin soil on the headland where turf stripping revealed much worked flint and some sherds of Lyles Hill type. While there is every likelihood that they were chronologically and culturally homogeneous there is no proof that this is so. The implements found included horseshoe scrapers, a small lightly polished flint axe and leaf arrowheads as well as fragments of polished axes of porcellanite. Here, be it noted, javelin fragments were all of the unpolished simple Form A. The same holds for Dalkey Is., Co. Dublin. This site has been inhabited through most of the prehistoric and historic periods. Neolithic Sandhills-type pottery and English-type beakers of both A and B forms could equally well be associated with the 49 javelin heads all of which were of the unpolished Form A.

In terms of geological context the only examples worth considering are nos. 55, 127 and 128. No. 55 from a bog in Derrytagh North, Co. Armagh, was placed by Jessen at the junction of pollen zones VIIa and VIIb and in his opinion is synchronous with the main hearths and implement-bearing horizon in the Newferry, Co. Londonderry, diatomite in Movius' excavation of 1934 (Movius, 1936)[4]. Nos. 127 and 128 have been demonstrated to come from the diatomite, though there is no evidence of their horizon in that deposit which attains a thickness of 3 ft. And since more recent work by the former Nuffield Quaternary Research Unit (Queen's University, Belfast) on hearth sites in the diatomite opposite Movius' site has produced pollen evidence which conflicts with that of Jessen it would appear that the dating of the diatomite deposit in terms of forest history is open to question. The latest work at Newferry by Dr Peter Woodman (Woodman, 1977) has produced a consistent series of C^{14} dates for the diatomite.

DISTRIBUTION

The Irish distribution pattern for flint javelin heads is shown on fig 17. Its outstanding feature is the overwhelming concentration in the north-east corner of the country. Over 40 have come from Co. Antrim and the Co. Derry bank of the lower Bann, between Lough Neagh and the north coast. A variety of reasons can be advanced for this. The Bann itself and its valley have been of special significance to early man from Mesolithic times onwards: the river provided a corridor of access from the north coast to Lough Neagh and must have been at all times a paradise for fowlers and fishermen (the salmon fisheries at Coleraine were until recently the most valuable in the British Isles); large numbers of antiquities of all periods have been dredged from its bed, mainly concentrated at fording points; a strip of glacial sands and gravels on either side of the river must, too, have provided suitable light land for early agriculture. Since much of the flood-plain of the river has been dug over for diatomite and two major dredging operations have been carried out to improve both drainage and navigation, the chances of discovery of antiquities in modern times have been high. Other concentrations of flint javelin heads occur in the valleys of the Braid and the Main which unite southwest of Ballymena. These rivers flow through gently undulating land where glacial sands and gravels alternate with boggy lowland patches. Though less important than the Bann as through routes, these rivers and their valleys must have presented similar attractions to early settlers. The Braid valley which cuts east-west across the basalt plateau may well have been the route by which flint was brought from the sea cliffs of the eastern edge of the plateau to the Bann valley. Some finds in these valleys (e.g. nos. 14-17) must have come from dredging operations in the river beds though many are probably the result of peat cutting in the many bogs of the area. It is known, too, that Ballymena last century contained dealers who bought finds from the country folk for miles around (Joan Evans, 1943, 140). The provenance 'Ballymena' should be treated with reserve.

Many another Irish river valley, besides those of the Bann, Main and Braid possessed comparable attractions for fishermen, fowlers and early agriculturalists but few shared their proximity to chalk outcrops containing inexhaustible supplies of flint. These outcrops occur continuously around the east coast of Antrim where the plateau drops abruptly to the sea and less extensively to the west, along the western edge of the same plateau, from the neighbourhood of Slieve Gallion northwards. Such flint in large nodules was essential to the manufacture of large, finely finished implements like the javelins.

The distribution outside the Co. Antrim-Lower Bann area needs some explanation. In general, it is no exception to the distribution pattern of other types of post-Mesolithic flint implements. By far the majority even of small implements like arrowheads have come from the north-eastern area, too, reflecting the concentration of good flint in those parts. Yet where excavation of court-graves has been undertaken (as at Bavan, Creevykeel, Kilnagarns, Behy and Ballyglass), javelin heads have invariably been found in them. All that is needed to complete the picture is the discovery and excavation of Neolithic habitation sites. The court-grave connection is reinforced by the negative evidence at Lough Gur, Co. Limerick, a habitation site well to the south of the Carlingford-Connaught belt of court-graves and, equally to the south of the passage-grave belt from the Boyne to Carrowmore. At Lough Gur (Ó Ríordáin, 1954) no javelins occurred in the large assemblages of flint and chert implements.

This sparse distribution over the centre, west and south of Ireland may well be contrasted with Bronze Age distributions (cf. distribution maps, plates 9 and 12 in Raftery, 1951). The bulk of the bronzes mapped have probably come from peat cutting and the dredging of river beds and one imagines that flint javelin heads, if found, would be just as obvious artifacts as the bronzes, with as good a chance of finding their way into collections, public or private. One must therefore conclude that their absence from so much of Ireland is a very real one, little influenced by the chances of discovery and record in modern times. The more even distribution of bronze over the country presumably reflects an even coverage of the country by itinerant bronzes smith. Manufacture at or near the source of raw material seems to have been the rule with flint implements — understandable enough when one considers the relative bulks and weights of flint nodules and the finished products. The scarcity of flint javelin heads over most of Ireland would appear to imply that they figured little in long distance trade or folk movements. This is in striking contrast to the widespread trade in axes in fine-grained rocks in the British Isles or, say, the trade in implements of Grand Pressigny flint in western Europe.

EXTERNAL PARALLELS AND THEIR SIGNIFICANCE

In Britain, flint javelin heads are known in a variety of Neolithic contexts, though they seem almost invariably to be finished by flaking alone. The Scottish province of the court-grave culture would appear to be a likely region in which to search for flint javelin heads but they do not appear to be components of the tomb furniture there. Stray finds of one leaf arrowhead showing polish and a form A leaf javelin head lacking polish have been published from the Kintyre peninsula (Scott, 1969, 242).

It is to England that we must turn for most of the published examples. In domestic sites leaf-shaped points, presumably javelin heads, are known from the causewayed enclosures. Most, in fact, of the excavated examples of this type of monument have produced them. To such earlier discoveries at Windmill Hill, Whitehawk and Hembury may now be added the 1975 work at Orsett in Essex (Hedges and Buckley, 1978). Two other extensive settlement sites, Broome Heath in Norfolk (Wainwright, 1972) and Hurst Fen in Suffolk (Clark *et al*, 1960) have produced many, most of them being examples which have been broken in the course of manufacture; such, indeed, is the norm in all Neolithic occupation and industrial sites in Britain. To find finished and intact specimens one has to turn to the rare examples which accompanied barrow burials, such as the famous trio from the Winterbourne Stoke Down long barrow on Salisbury plain (Evans, 1897, 371). Other comparable examples have come from Neolithic round barrows on the Yorkshire Wolds. They include: Mortimer's no. 273 (Duggleby Howe); Towthorpe no. 18; and Huggate Wold no. 230 (Mortimer, 1905). These Yorkshire examples although they lack any trace of polish are superbly flaked. In one respect they differ from the majority of Irish javelins: they appear to be double-ended with almost equally sharp and narrow points at each end.

In attempting to trace parallels on the continent most of those who have discussed the Irish javelin heads have followed W. Bremer (1928, 17) in stressing links with Iberia. They (e.g. Raftery, 1951, 134) have used the flint javelin as one of a group of culture traits derivable from Iberia in Chalcolithic times to emphasize the importance of the Atlantic route in the movement of people and objects into Ireland.

It is true that in Iberia numerous large and generically leaf-shaped flint points have been found in the chambered tombs and settlement sites of southern Spain and Portugal. These have been illustrated and discussed at some length by the Leisners (Leisner, 1943, I, 465-8). While they agree that this group is related formally to the leaf and lozenge arrowheads, they tend to follow earlier writers in classing most of them as either dagger or halberd blades. One technical feature links them closely with our Irish javelins — the use of pre-flaking grinding and polishing on the faces, although this is commoner on the broad forms justifiably designated halberds. This to my mind constitutes the main strength of the Iberian argument, since the resemblances in outline are not close. It is in Portugal rather than in Spain that somewhat closer formal parallels are to be found, though here the unpolished simple, often elongated leaf form rather than the lozenge appears to predominate, for example, at Vila Nova de San Pedro (Jalhay and do Paço, 1945, 33-4 and plates 7-9). We thus have narrow forms which, however designated in the literature, could have functioned as javelin heads from passage graves at Los Millares. I have been unable to trace an Iberian example of the Irish Form C in its concavo-convex variant.

A feature found in both the broad 'halberd' blades and the narrow 'dagger' blades is the provision of hafting notches at either side near the basal end, even on a true narrow lozenge form (i.e. our Form C) from Los Millares (*ibid.*, Pl 9.120). One questions whether there has not been too great tendency to regard hafting notches as necessarily indicative of halberd or dagger function. A javelin function would seem more likely for the example last quoted.

The same problem arises in considering the large leaf-shaped blades found in the south French group of passage-graves (Arnal, 1953-4, figs 11.16, 11.17 and 12.7). Here, these relatively narrow leaf and lozenge blades are classed as dagger blades and admittedly the resemblances in general outline to the broad tanged W European copper dagger blades are very close. I would nevertheless submit that some of these could with equal justice be classed as javelin heads. Pre-flaking polish on one face only is commonly met with on these S French examples. It must not be forgotten, either, that quite large leaf- and lozenge-shaped arrowheads (some of them exceeding our minimum javelin length of 5 cm) are common surface finds in the S of France (Arnal, 1953-4, fig 26A) and are found, too, in the chambered tombs and burial caves of the Pyrenean region (e.g. Bosch-Gimpera, 1926, Pl 17 — with one from the Grotte de Bounias showing polish on the face, and Pl 19).

Further north in France no comparable examples are to be seen in the Breton megaliths, though there is one small leaf-shaped javelin head from the contemporary Camp de Lizo settlement site (Le Rouzic, 1934, 498-9).

In the present state of knowledge it looks as though relatively small (50-80 mm long) leaf-shaped and unpolished javelin heads are components of Early Neolithic cultures known from settlement sites like the English causewayed enclosures or the Ballygalley Hill and perhaps, too, the Dalkey Is. sites in Ireland. Such javelin heads, sometimes with varying degrees of either pre-flaking or post-flaking polish, as seen above, appear in the northern Irish long and round cairns of the Clyde-Carlingford culture and (in regular lozenge outline) in the Neolithic round barrows of E Yorkshire, perhaps contemporary with sites like Lyles Hill cairn. All these contexts, be it noted, are truly Neolithic in that they contain no hint either of metal or of a knowledge of metallurgy. The larger javelins, daggers and halberd blades with pre-flaking polish found in the Chalcolithic passage-graves of Los Millares and Palmella in Iberia and in the related S French passage-graves may well indicate that this technical device should be regarded as an imitation of smooth metallic surfaces. Yet this link with continental passage-graves is but weakly reflected in Ireland where the main link is with the largely contemporary but culturally distinct segmented galleries of the court-grave series of tombs.

NOTES

1 Identified by Dr J.W. Jackson, Keeper, Natural History Division, National Museum, Dublin. I am indebted to Dr Joseph Raftery for this information.

2 While Ballykeel long cairn is not a court-grave *sensu stricto*, tripod and portal dolmens set within long cairns are held to be developments from court-graves in long cairns.

3 Kindly verified by Drs J.H. Preston and R.E.H. Reid of the Geology Department, Queen's University, Belfast.

4 I am indebted to Professor A.G. Smith, Botany Department, University College, Cardiff, for the following account of this zonation: 'It is possible that Jessen's conclusion that the first javelin head lay at the transition between his zones VIIa and VIIb is correct; but the pollen diagram from Derrytagh no I is confused by local over-representation and it cannot be considered that the pollen-analytical evidence is incontrovertible'.

SCHEDULE OF IRISH JAVELIN HEADS

SPECIAL ABBREVIATIONS

Col. 4: *p* polished

Col. 6:
JCHAS	*Journal of the Cork Historical and Archaeological Society*
JGAHS	*Journal of the Galway Archaeological and Historical Society*
JRAI	*Journal of the Royal Anthropological Institute*
JRSAI	*Journal of the Royal Society of Antiquaries of Ireland*
PBNPS	*Proceedings of the Belfast Natural History and Philosophical Society*
PPS	*Proceedings of the Prehistoric Society*
PRIA	*Proceedings of the Royal Irish Academy* (C, unless otherwise stated).
PSAS	*Proceedings of the Society of Antiquaries of Scotland*
UJA	*Ulster Journal of Archaeology ser 3*
	For other short titles, see references below.

Col. 7:
ACM	Alnwick Castle Museum
AM	Ashmolean Museum, Oxford
BM	British Museum, London
CM	Cork Museum
CMAE	Cambridge Museum of Archaeology and Ethnology
NMD	National Museum of Ireland, Dublin
UMB	Ulster Museum, Belfast

NO	COUNTY	PROVENANCE	FORM	ASSOCIA-TIONS	REFEREN-CES	WHERE PRESER-VED
1	Antrim	Aghalee	B*p*			NMD 1884.25
2	Antrim	Ballybollen	C			UMB 572.1937
3-5	Antrim	Ballygalley Hill	A	Prob. assoc. with Lyles Hill pot & with flint mining	*UJA* 41	UMB
6	Antrim	Ballylummin Bog	B*p*			UMB (J.J. Wymer Coll.)
7,8	Antrim	Ballymacald-rack	A	Dooey's Cairn	*UJA* 1, fig 6	UMB
9	Antrim	Ballymena	C*p*			BM (Sturge Coll.)
10	Antrim	Ballymena	C*p*			CMAE 23.1082 C
11	Antrim	Ballymena	B*p*			CMAE 23.1082 C

NO	COUNTY	PROVENANCE	FORM	ASSOCIATIONS	REFERENCES	WHERE PRESERVED
12	Antrim	Ballyvaddy	C*p*			NMD 46.1918
13	Antrim	Ballyvaddy	B			UMB 572.1924 (Knowles Coll.)
14	Antrim	Braid river	C			UMB (Adams Coll.)
15	Antrim	Braid river	A			UMB 655.30 (Adams Coll.)
16	Antrim	Braid river	B*p*			UMB 655.30 (Adams Coll.)
17	Antrim	Braid river	B			UMB 655.30 (Adams Coll.)
18	Antrim	nr Broughshane	C*p*			UMB L42.1955 (Raphael Coll.)
19	Antrim	nr Broughshane	A*p*			UMB 573.1924 (Knowles Coll.)
20	Antrim	Carndoo nr Ballycastle	C	With 2 others *c* 1820	*JRAI* **33**, Pl 8.15	UMB 572.1924 (Knowles Coll.)
21	Antrim	Knocklayd	A			NMD 1959.221
22	Antrim	nr Carrick-fergus	B			UMB 649.30 (Adams Coll.)
23	Antrim	Clogh	C*p*		*JRAI* **33**, Pl 9.44	NMD 1918.38 (Knowles Coll.)
24	Antrim	Clough	C		*JRAI* **33**, Pl 11.42	
25	Antrim	Crumlin	A			NMD 1936.1452
26	Antrim	Drumnafivey	C		*UJA* **8**, 16-17	UMB 118.1945
27	Antrim	Dundrod	A			NMD 1897.644
28	Antrim	Dunteige	C	In court grave	*PRIA* **67**, 31	AM 3842.1886
29	Antrim	Dunteige	C	In court grave	*PRIA* **67**, 31	AM 3843.1886
30	Antrim	Glenhead	B			NMD 1931.256
31	Antrim	Glenaan	B*p*			NMD 1934.10730
32	Antrim	Glenleslie	C			UMB 571.1924 (Knowles Coll.)

NO	COUNTY	PROVENANCE	FORM	ASSOCIA-TIONS	REFEREN-CES	WHERE PRESER-VED
33	Antrim	Glenleslie	A			NMD 1927.390
34	Antrim	Gortconnie	B*p*			NMD 1934.10447
35	Antrim	Lough Guile	A			NMD 1934.2289
36	Antrim	Lough Guile	B			NMD 1934.2290
37	Antrim	Knocklayd	C*p*			UMB 316.1934
38	Antrim	Lenagh	C	With 2 stone axes	Andrews, 1913, pl 12	UMB 63.1936
39	Antrim	Lisburn	C			CMAE 23.1082A
40	Antrim	Loughaveema	A			UMB
41-3	Antrim	Lyles Hill	A	In burnt layer below cairn and in cairn	Evans, 1953, 51-4	UMB
44	Antrim	Magheraberry	A			Private Coll.
45	Antrim	Port Ballintrae	C*p*			UMB L30 1935
46	Antrim	Portglenone	B*p*			NMD 1885.283
47	Antrim	Tehorny	C*p*		*JRAI* 33, pl 11.47	UMB 570.1924 (Knowles Coll.)
48	Antrim	Toome	C*p*			UMB 668.1930 (Adams Coll.)
49	Antrim	Toome	C*p*			UMB 668.1930 (Adams Coll.)
50	Antrim	Toome	B*p*			UMB 668.1930 (Adams Coll.)
51	Antrim	Toome Bridge	B			UMB 752.36
52	Armagh	Annaghmare	C	In court grave	*UJA* **28**, 34	UMB
53	Armagh	Ballykeel	C*p*	In cist	*UJA* **28**, 64	UMB
54	Armagh	Clontygora	C	In court grave	*PBNPS* **1** (pt 2), 39	Armagh Mus
55	Armagh	Derrytagh N	C		*PRIA* **52**B, 117-8	NMD
56	Armagh	Tirgarve	C*p*		*UJA* **22**	UMB 76.1958
57	Cavan	L. Oughter	C*p*			UMB 580.3738

NO	COUNTY	PROVENANCE	FORM	ASSOCIA-TIONS	REFEREN-CES	WHERE PRESER-VED
58	Cork	Donickmore	B*p*		*JCHAS* **51** 61-2	CM
59	Donegal	Ardnasool	B*p*		*PRIA* **42**, 148	NMD
60	Donegal	Bavan	A	In court grave	*UJA* **29**, 26	NMD
61	Donegal	Corlea	C*p*			NMD P1951.114
62	Donegal	Maghera	B		*JRSAI* **63**, 97	
63	Donegal	Maghera S	A			UMB 313.1934 (D'Evelyn Coll.)
64	Down	Audleystown	B*p*	In court grave	*UJA* **17**, 28 fig 9.1	UMB
65	Down	Leitrim	C*p*		Evans, 1951, 91	UMB 78.1943
66-114	Dublin	Dalkey Is.	A	In occupation site	*PRIA* **66**, 2-222	NMD
115-117	Dublin	Lambay Is.	B		*PRIA* **38**, 240-6	NMD L.1947. 204-6
118	Fermanagh	Aghanaglack	C	In court grave	*JRSAI* **69** 33,37	UMB
119	Fermanagh	Tully	Frag.	In court grave	*UJA* **41**	Belfast, Archaeol. Survey
120	Galway	Kellysgrave	C*p*	13' deep in bog		NMD 1958.149
121	Galway	Killylean	C*p*	Deep in a bog	*JGAHS* **21** 99	
122	Kildare	Newtownhart-land	C*p*			NMD
123	Leitrim	Kilnagarns	B	In court grave	*JRSAI* **94** Fig 4.3	NMD
124	Leitrim	Kilnagarns	B	In court grave		NMD
125	Londonderry	Bellaghy × Castledawson	C*p*	In peat	*JRAI* **33**, Pl 11.45	UMB 569.1924 (Knowles Coll.)
126	Londonderry	Castlerock	C*p*			UMB 3571 12.20 (Grainger Coll.)
127	Londonderry	Culbane	B*p*	In diatomite		UMB 64.1936
128	Londonderry	Culbane	B*p*	In diatomite		UMB 744.1936

NO	COUNTY	PROVENANCE	FORM	ASSOCIA-TIONS	REFEREN-CES	WHERE PRESER-VED
129	Londonderry	Dungiven	B*p*			NMD P185
130	Londonderry	Maghrabann	C*p*			AM 1927.4572 (Evans Coll.)
131	Londonderry	Tamnyrankin	A	In court grave		UMB
132	Mayo	Behy	Frag.	In court grave	De Val-era & Ó Nualláin, 1964,6	NMD
133	Mayo	Ballyglass	B*p*	In court grave	*JRSAI* **102**	
134	Monaghan	Kilmore W	B*p*			NMD 1947.233
135	Sligo	Creevykeel	A	In court grave	*JRSAI* **69**, 80 fig 6.15	NMD
136	Sligo	Creevykeel	A*p*	In court grave	Ib. fig 8.5	NMD
137	Sligo	Carrowmore (Listoghil)	C*p*	In chamber (?)	Wood-Martin, 1888, 17	ACM
138	Tyrone	Barnes Lower	B	In court grave	*UJA* **29**, 67-8	UMB
139	Tyrone	Clady Halliday	B*p*	In court grave	*PBNPS* **1**, 85	UMB
140	Tyrone	Cookstown	B		BM *Stone Age Guide* Pl 9.4	BM
141	Tyrone	Is. MacHugh	C*p*	On island shore	Davies, 1950. Fig 17.507	UMB
142	Tyrone	Is. MacHugh	A*p*	In 'Bronze Age' level	Ib. Fig 14.F37	UMB
143	Tyrone	Mountfield	B*p*	With bowl food-vessel	Abercro-mby, *BAP* (1) 143, 281	NMD
144	Tyrone	Pomeroy	C*p*		BM *Stone Age Gui-de* (1926) Pl 9.6	BM
145	Wicklow	Baltinglass	A	Below passage grave cairn	*PRIA* **46** 230, fig 6	NMD

NO	COUNTY	PROVENANCE	FORM	ASSOCIA-TIONS	REFEREN-CES	WHERE PRESER-VED
146	Wicklow	Camaderry	Cp	Deep in peat	PRIA 42 60	NMD 1931.74
147	Wicklow	Knockananna	B		PRIA 42, 61	

ACKNOWLEDGEMENTS

Mr B.R.S. Megaw, formerly of the School of Scottish Studies, Edinburgh University, has most generously placed at my disposal the material that he collected in the 1930s for a paper on Irish flint javelins. I owe thanks also to many past and present museum curators: to Dr A.T. Lucas and Dr Joseph Raftery of the National Museum of Ireland, Dublin; to Mr W.A. Seaby, Mr Laurence Flanagan and Dr Peter Woodman of the Ulster Museum, Belfast; and to the late Mr T.G.F. Paterson and Mr D.R.M. Weatherup of the Armagh County Museum. Generous financial assistance by the Gulbenkian Foundation made possible in 1961 a study tour of Portuguese and southern Spanish museums. In the course of the trip local scholars including Dr Concepcion Fernandez-Chicarro Y de Dios, Professor Carriazo of Seville and Colonel do Paço gave generously of their time and knowledge.

REFERENCES

Abercromby, J., 1912. *The Bronze Age pottery of Great Britain and Ireland*. Oxford.

Andrews, E., 1913. *Ulster Folklore*. London.

Arnal, J., 1953-4. 'Presentacion de dolmenes y staciones del Departmento de Herault', *Ampurias* 15-16, 67-108.

Bremer, W., 1928. *Ireland's place in Prehistoric and Early Historic Europe*. Dublin.

Childe, V.G., 1957. *The Dawn of European Civilisation*. London.

Collins, A.E.P., 1954. 'The excavation of a double horned cairn at Audleystown, Co. Down', *Ulster J Archaeol ser 3* 17, 7-56.

Collins, A.E.P., 1965. 'Ballykeel dolmen and cairn' *Ulster J Archaeol ser 3* 28, 47-70.

Collins, A.E.P., 1966. 'Barnes Lower court cairn, Co. Tyrone', *Ulster J Archaeol ser 3* 29, 43-75.

Collins, A.E.P., 1978. 'Excavations on Ballygalley Hill, County Antrim', *Ulster J Archaeol ser 3* 41, 15-32.

Collins, A.E.P. and Waterman, D.M., 1952. 'Knockmany chambered grave, Co. Tyrone', *Ulster J Archaeol ser 3* 15, 26-30.

Corcoran, J.X.W.P., 1964. 'Excavation of two chambered graves at Kilnagarns Lower, Co. Leitrim', *J Roy Soc Antiq Ir* 94, 177-98.

Davies, O., 1939. 'Excavation of a horned cairn at Aghanaglack, Co. Fermanagh', *J Roy Soc Antiq Ir* 69, 21-38.

Davies, O., 1950. *Excavations at Island McHugh*. Supplement to *Proc Belfast Nat Hist Phil Soc*.

Davies, O. and Radford, C.A.R., 1937. 'Excavation of the horned cairn of Clady Halliday', *Proc Belfast Nat Hist Phil Soc* 1, 76-85.

De Valera, R. and Ó Nualláin, S., 1964. *Survey of the Megalithic Tombs of Ireland: Co. Mayo*. Stationery Office, Dublin.

Evans, E.E., 1951. *Mourne Country*. Dundalk.

Evans, E.E., 1953. *Lyles Hill: a Late Neolithic Site in County Antrim* (Archaeol Res Publ 2), Stationery Office. Belfast.

Evans, Joan, 1943. *Time and Chance*. Longmans, London.

Evans, Sir John, 1897. *Ancient Stone Implements of Great Britain*. Longmans Green, London.

Flanagan, L.N.W. and Flanagan, D.E., 1966. 'The excavation of a court cairn at Bavan, Co. Donegal', *Ulster J Archaeol ser 3* **29**, 16-38.

Hedges, J. and Buckley, D., 1978. 'Excavations at a Neolithic causewayed enclosure at Orsett, Essex, 1975', *Proc Prehist Soc* **44**, 219-308.

Hencken, H. O'N., 1939. 'A long cairn at Creevykeel, Co. Sligo', *J Roy Soc Antiq Ir* **69**, 53-98.

Herity, M., 1974. *Irish Passage Graves*. Dublin.

Jalhay, E. and do Paço, A., 1945. *El Castro de Vilanova de San Pedro*. Madrid.

Jessen, K., 1949. 'Studies in Late Quaternary deposits and flora history of Ireland', *Proc Roy Ir Acad B* **52**, 85-290.

Knowles, W.J., 1903. 'Irish flint arrow- and spear-heads'. *J Roy Anthrop Inst* **33**, 44-56.

Knowles, W.J., 1909. 'On the mounting of leaf-shaped arrowheads of Flint', *Proc Soc Antiq Scot* **43**, 278-83;

Leisner, G. and Leisner, V., 1943. *Die Megalithgräber der iberischen Halbinsel*. Erste Teil: Der Suden. Berlin.

Mortimer, J.R., 1905. *Forty Years' Researches in British and Saxon Burial Mounds of East Yorkshire*. London.

Movius, H.L., 1936. 'A Neolithic site on the River Bann' *Proc Roy Ir Acad C* **43**, 17-40.

Ó Nualláin, S., 1972. 'A Neolithic house at Ballyglass, near Ballycastle, Co. Mayo', *J Roy Soc Antiq Ir* **102**, 49-57.

Ó Ríordáin, S.P., 1954. 'Lough Gur Excavations: Neolithic and Bronze Age houses on Knockadoon', *Proc Roy Ir Acad C* **56**, 279-459.

Raftery, J., 1951. *Prehistoric Ireland*. London.

Scott, J.G., 1969. 'The Neolithic period in Kintyre, Argyll'. *In* T.G.E. Powell (ed), *Megalithic Enquiries in the West of Britain*. University Press, Liverpool.

Wainwright, G.J., 1972. 'The excavation of a Neolithic settlement on Broome Heath, Ditchingham, Norfolk, England', *Proc Prehist Soc* **38**, 1-97.

Walshe, P.T., 1941. 'The excavation of a burial cairn on Baltinglass Hill, Co. Wicklow', *Proc Roy Ir Acad C* **46**, 221-36.

Waterman, D.M., 1965. 'The court cairn at Annaghmare, Co. Armagh', *Ulster J Archaeol ser 3* **28**, 3-46.

Waterman, D.M., 1978. 'The excavation of a court cairn at Tully, County Fermanagh', *Ulster J Archaeol ser 3* **41**, 3-14.

Wood-Martin, W.G., 1888. *The Rude Stone Monuments of Ireland (Co. Sligo and the Island of Achill)*. London.

Poulawack, Co. Clare: the Affinities of the Central Burial Structure

Michael Ryan

In 1935, Hencken published the report on his excavations at the multiple cist (or cemetery) cairn of Poulawack. Before excavation the round cairn measured 20.75 m N-S and 21.25m E-W. Under it were found two concentric kerbs or revetments, an outer one of slabs set on edge 13.40m in diameter N-S and 14.5m E-W. Ten graves were found, most of them within the revetments. The cairn material, which had consisted in the main of limestone flags, had been carefully laid and it was evident from a change in the orientation of the stones that a considerable part of the upper levels of the cairn had been disturbed in the course of a secondary intrusion of a number of cist-graves — Nos 2 and 3 in Hencken's system (1935, 199-202). A third grave, No. 4, was also inserted after the primary phase of building (Hencken, 1935, 202). The excavator's plan of the site is reproduced here as fig 22.

Of the primary¹ burial structures uncovered Nos 1,5,6,7 and 8 with 8A, one, no. 5, was a regular, rectangular short cist (Waddell, 1970) while the others show a greater or lesser degree of irregularity in their plans and sections. Of the secondary structures, Nos 2 and 4 are fairly regular. It is however to Graves 8 with 8A that this offering is mainly devoted. Hencken's plan and section of this structure are reproduced here as fig 23.

These two graves together formed a single burial structure and occupied the 'very centre of the mound and were obviously the principal burials' (Hencken, 1935, 206). The structure may be described as a pair of irregular paved, conjoint cists made of vertical slabs, some set in fissures in the underlying limestone, others bedded on OGL. The two graves lacked the packing of small stones used to consolidate the other cists on the site; instead, a series of propping-slabs — 49 in all — were placed on edge, leaning inwards to support them. In addition, further slabs had been laid horizontally on the capstones of the cists. The cist containing grave 8 measured internally 70 cm long, 40 cm wide and 75-85 cm deep; that containing 8A was 95 cm long, 40-50 cm wide and 90 cm deep. In the former were found some scattered bones, a boar's tusk, a hollow scraper of flint and two indeterminate sherds of pottery; in the latter were the unburned, disarticulated remains of an infant, a young adult female and a middle-aged male and female (Hencken, 1935, 208-9). Most of the bones were found in 8A but a few occurred in 8 perhaps as a result of rodent activity. Hencken suggested that the individuals buried in 8A had previously been interred elsewhere perhaps to await the construction of a suitable tomb.

At the time of publication and indeed for many years afterwards no obvious, clear parallels to the Central graves suggested themselves. Clearly the excavations had revealed a small, sealed tomb erected probably for only one rite of interment, the principal features of which were that it was:

(i)   centrally placed in a small, round, carefully built cairn;
(ii) irregular in plan;
(iii) supported by a multiplicity of leaning propping-slabs;
(iv) sealed by multiple capstone roofing;
(v)   paved;
(vi) and contained a small number of unburnt burials.

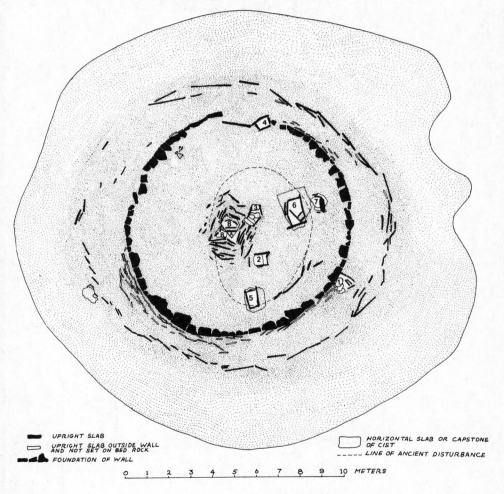

Fig 22: Poulawack: general plan (after Hencken)

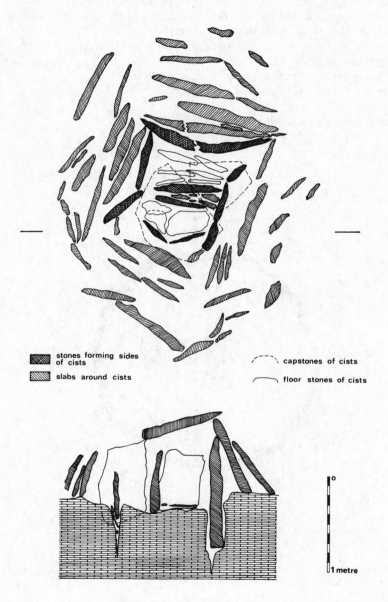

stones forming sides
of cists

slabs around cists

capstones of cists

floor stones of cists

Fig 23: Poulawack: graves 8 and 8a (after Hencken).

Fig 24: Linkardstown Cists: plans and sections:
A. Baunogensraid (after B. Raftery);
B. Jerpoint West
C. Linkardstown (I am grateful to Dr J. Raftery
for his permission to reproduce this
unpublished plan);
D. Ballintruermore (after J. Raftery);
E. Drimnagh (after Kilbride-Jones).

Grave 6 and 6A, an irregular double compartmented cist built 55 cm above bedrock but still in the primary cairn, produced a sherd of Beaker pottery thus suggesting that the period of the original construction and use of the monument belonged somewhere in the later Neolithic or the beginning of the Earlier Bronze Age.

Subsequent discoveries (Raftery J., 1944 and 1974; Ryan, 1973; Raftery B., 1974; Wallace, 1977) combined with a re-assessment of old finds (Herity, 1970; Herity and Eogan, 1977; Ryan, 1972) have made it clear that a type of burial monument with a remarkably consistent morphology existed in Late Neolithic Ireland to which the term Linkardstown Cists has been applied (Ryan, 1972) after the classic site of that name reported on by J. Raftery (1944).

Seven of these sites (Appendix) have been excavated in modern times — since Kilbride-Jones's (1939) work at Drimnagh — and three probable examples were published in the 19th century (Cloghmanta Hill, Co. Kilkenny, Knockmaree, Phoenix Park, Co. Dublin and Cuffsborough, Co. Laois — see Appendix for references). A number of other, possibly related, sites investigated in the past are included with suitable comment in the appended list. The consistently occurring traits of Linkardstown Cists are:

(i)   the central placement of a large sealed polygonal cist in a small round mound, often carefully constructed, frequently kerbed, sometimes with internal revetments;

(ii) the cist (fig 24) is frequently paved, either irregularly polygonal or roughly rectangular in plan, built often with inwardly inclined sidestones, usually roofed by multiple overlapping capstones, sometimes propped by additional leaning flags;

(iii) the cists are always constructed on the original surface under the mounds and not set into pits below it;

(iv) half of the well-documented Linkardstown Cists have produced evidence of the burial of two or more individuals (portions of a third skeleton were present at Knockmaree) usually unburned and usually articulated. At Jerpoint West, Co. Kilkenny, one of two burials in the cist was a cremation. The remaining monuments contained single, unburnt, adult males. Partial disarticulation of the remains was noted in four instances, and less certainly in a fifth — Norrismount, Co. Wexford.

(v)   The range of grave goods is limited and shows a remarkable degree of consistency — highly decorated Neolithic bowls, plain 'Western' Neolithic pottery, polished bone pins or toggles, a flint arrowhead, a jet ornament of uncertain character, a polished stone axehead and a necklace of *Nerita Littoralis* shells are the most noteworthy finds.

It is the contention of the writer that in most morphological respects the cairn at Poulawack, planned as it was around the complex central burial structure, merits inclusion in the Linkardstown group, a suggestion first made at a time when it was

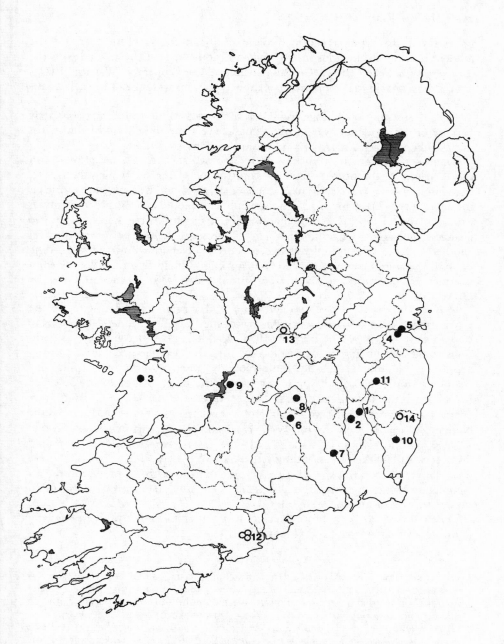

Fig 25: Linkardstown Cists location map: open symbol denotes possible examples (numbers as in appendix).

believed that that type was confined to the south-eastern part of the country.[2] The re-identification of old finds in Co. Kilkenny and Co. Laois, combined with the discovery of a Linkardstown Cist at Ardcroney, Co. Tipperary (Wallace, 1977) clearly show that burial monuments of this type were widespread in their occurrence.

The full distributional range (fig 25) is so far impossible to indicate accurately because of the accidental way in which most have come to light and because it is not usually possible to classify round tumuli without excavation.

Poulawack is a Cemetery Cairn — grave 5, a regular short cist, and graves 6, 6A and 7 belong to the primary phase of construction at the site while other graves were inserted later. It is clearly an example of a type of burial arrangement which is common in the Earlier Bronze Age in Ireland. This should not obscure its affinities with the Linkardstown Cists, the mounds of five of which were used, and, in two instances, enlarged to accommodate later interments. It may be regarded as yet another instance of continuity between the later Neolithic and the succeeding period. The use of conjoint cists at Poulawack links it clearly to the double compartmented examples of the Earlier Bronze Age recently documented by Glover (1974).

It is not the place to enter here into a discussion of the origins of the Linkardstown Cists amongst which Poulawack may now be included. It appears to some (Ryan, 1972, 1973; Raftery B., 1974; Waddell, 1978) that indigenous traditions could account for the appearance of the type. Passage grave links are suggested by the round carefully built mounds, internal revetments, polygonal chambers which fall within the lower part of the range of size of the so-called 'B-dolmens' and other structures of that tradition.[3] Others, arguing from grave goods, have suggested that we should look elsewhere to points as far distant as the Nordic area (Herity and Eogan, 1977, 111), and the Iberian Peninsula (Savory, 1978, 6; Kilbride-Jones, 1939, 205-7, 215). Whatever view we adopt, few would disagree with Hencken's concluding remark about Poulawack: 'It may not be too imaginative to see in this special regard for the remains of the dead, and in the accumulation of burials around the central ones some survival of the megalithic tradition which was so strongly rooted in Co. Clare'.

This tradition has been illuminated for us by Brian O'Kelly's work especially at Moneen, Baurnadomeeny and Newgrange.

NOTES

1 The term 'primary' is used here to denote structures erected on OGL before the cairn was raised and evidently an intrinsic part of the planning of the monument. Where it is clear from the context that other structures were erected in undisturbed parts of the cairn and thus completed during the main process of construction, then the term is applicable also.

2 Kinahan (1879, 69) describes a strange structure in Co. Mayo which he regarded as a clochán and which shares some of the constructional features of Linkardstown Cists, especially additional propping side slabs. In plan it resembles somewhat certain small passage graves. The date and context of the monument are a puzzle.

3 E.g. Herity (1975, 218-9), An. 2 (Lemnabeg), An. 3 (Clegnagh), An. 10 (Cloghs).

APPENDIX

LINKARDSTOWN CISTS

TOWNLAND	COUNTY	REFERENCE	NOTES
1. Baunogenasraid	Carlow	Raftery B., 1974	A round, kerbed tumulus covered a polygonal dolmen-like structure (internal dimensions 1.45 m × Im) built on OGL and placed slightly off centre. It contained the unburnt, disarticulated bones of a single adult male accompanied by a highly decorated, round-bottomed pot, a perforated, lignite toggle and a bone point. A Food Vessel and other secondary burials occurred in a later build-up of the mound.
2. Linkardstown	Carlow	Raftery J., 1944	A polygonal cist (2 m × 2.30 m) was covered by a round kerbed mound ca. 25 m in diameter. The cist walls were supported by external propping slabs — two of the wall slabs being bedded into OGL the rest merely resting on it. The structure was roofed by two capstones. The grave contained the unburned remains of an adult male accompanied by sherds of, perhaps, five vessels including one highly decorated example with a 'T' rim, a sherd of plain 'Western Neolithic' and a polished stone axehead.
3. Poulawack	Clare	Hencken, 1935.	This paper.
4. Drimnagh	Dublin	Kilbride-Jones, 1939.	A primary mound with a great deal of sod incorported in the make up and an oval central cairn-core, ca. 22m in diameter and ca. 3 m high — a great deal of charred timber occurred near its surface — covered an irregular, polygonal cist with one open side and two capstones. The sidestones of the cist were irregularly aligned but set so as to maintain a constant depth of ca. 38 cm. The max. width of the cist was 1.02m. In the grave was the unburnt skeleton of an adult male, partly flexed and accompanied by a highly decorated, ribbed and lugged, round-bottomed bowl, pierced for suspension. The mound was considerably enlarged, surrounded by a ditch and used for burial in the E.B.A.

TOWNLAND	COUNTY	REFERENCE	NOTES
5. Knockmaree (Phoenix Park, Dublin)	Dublin	Wilde, 1857, 180-3. Herity in Herity and Eogan, 1976, 84 & 82, fig 26, 1.	An oblong cist formed of 7 slabs lay at the centre of a mound 120 ft in diameter, 15 ft high. It contained two male skeletons and the tops of the femora of another, a necklace of *Nerita Littoralis* shells, a barbell bone toggle and a plano-convex flint knife. A contemporary MS. drawing recently published by Herity reveals the presence of lean-to propping slabs and a cairn core. 4 Food Vessel burials in cists were secondary in the mound.
6. Cloghmanta Hill	Kilkenny	Graves, 1851.	*Probable example*: A cairn 70 ft in diameter covered a massive central cist. The E side of the cist consisted of 4 massive slabs 'piled one on the other', the W side was similar in construction. The Northern extremity was built up with smaller stones '. . . piled against it without any order or regularity'. The south end was closed by a large slab, placed on edge and rather inclining inwards. The cist was about 6 ft (ca. 2m) long 4 ft 6 inches (ca. I.50m) wide and 3 ft. 6 inches (ca. 1m) deep. It had been roofed by two large limestone flags measuring 5 ft × 4 ft (ca. 1.60m × 1.30m). The fill of the cist contained two skeletons, heads to the south. A secondary Urn or Food Vessel burial in a cist was found in the cairn.
7. Jerpoint West	Kilkenny	Ryan, 1973.	A circular tumulus 24m in diameter with a cairn-core covered an approximately central polygonal cist (2.14m long × 1.87m wide × 1.19m deep). The cist had outer propping-slabs, three capstones and a cobbled floor. It contained the unburned skeleton of a young adult male, a cremation, sherds of a decorated shouldered bowl, sherds of plain 'Western Neolithic' ware, a bone pin and a fragment of a leaf-arrowhead of flint. The bones of a child, perhaps a prehistoric secondary burial, came from the mound.

(142)

TOWNLAND	COUNTY	REFERENCE	NOTES
8. Cuffsborough	Laois	Graves, 1850.	*Probable example*: A (?) corbelled, beehive-shaped chamber, 5 ft (ca. 1.60m) in diameter, under a tumulus. The corbelling sprang from orthostats about 3½ ft (ca. 1.15m) in height. Inside were the remains of two skeletons lying confusedly.
9. Ardcrony	Tipperary	Wallace, 1977	A denuded tumulus, originally 33m in diameter with an exposed surviving cairn-core about 20m in diameter and 2.5m in height. A massive, central, polygonal cist was covered with a large capstone (1.9m long × 1.73m wide × 51cm thick). The sidestones are inclined inwards at an angle of ca. 60°. The floor of the cist was paved and measured 1.75m × 1.40m The mouth of the structure was 1.48 m × 93 cm. It was 69 cm deep. Two unburned skeletons, partly disturbed before excavation, lay on the floor. Between them were sherds of a round-bottomed, highly decorated Neolithic bowl.
10. Norrismount	Wexford	Lucas, 1950	A round mound ca. 35m in diameter and originally ca. 3m in height covered a central cairn-core and cist. The cist was rectangular, built of four inwardly inclined slabs. It measured internally 1.60m × 50 cm at the floor and 1.26m × 35 cm at the mouth. It was 65 cm deep. Each sidestone had on top an oversailing slab which further reduced the dimensions of the mouth by 10 cm The capstone measured 1.25m × 80 cm × 10 cm thick. In the cist were the unburned bones of a young adult male — whether crouched or extended is uncertain — accompanied by sherds of a decorated round-bottomed bowl.
11. Ballintruer-more	Wicklow	Raftery, 1973	A tumulus 32m in diameter with internal kerbed sod-mound and cairn-core, covered a complex polygonal central cist with inclined sidestones and external propping-slabs. The floor level dimensions of the cist were 95 cm × 73 cm On

the floor were a flagstone and a layer of fine sand. On the stone and sand were the disarticulated remains of an adult male accompanied by a decorated, round-bottomed bowl.

POSSIBLE EXAMPLES

12. Ballyvourisheen (3 sites)	Cork	Anon, 1913, 188-9. Borlase, 1897, 14-15	A large mound 80 ft in diameter, composed of alternative layers of earth and stone about a foot in thickness. In the centre was a huge capstone ca.6m square, 45 cm thick covering a large stone chest about 2.50m square. A quantity of bones considered to be the remains of about 20 skeletons was removed from it. A small stone secondary cist in the same mound contained two skeletons. Two adjacent mounds were also levelled and contained similar structures covered with large stones, and containing 2 skeletons each. The covering stones of all the structures 'were considerably sloped'.
13. Clonaslee	Laois	Harris, 1739, 148-9 (I am grateful to Mr John Feahan for this reference).	Discovered in 1735 under a low, kerbed tumulus was a massive cist with lozenge shaped capstone, 8 ft (ca. 2.60m) long and 5 ft 4 inches (ca. 1.70m) broad. It was apparently oblong — with one corner sealed by a subsidiary slab. The sidestones were described as 5 ft 7 inches (ca. 1.75m) long and 4 ft (ca. 1.30m) broad. The cist contained the 'skeleton of a middle sized man, the head placed westward, the feet to the east'.
14. Cummer	Wexford	Kinahan, 1888, 156	A cist opened in or about 1877 was full of 'ashy clay'. It contained an 'urn', which was broken on finding. The 'urn' appeared from the fragments to have been about 12 inches in internal rim diameter and about 9 inches high. 'It was of a different shape and differently ornamented from any of the urns in the Academy collection, its greatest peculiarity being the flat lip, about two inches wide, around the mouth'. The lip feature suggests comparison with vessels well known from Linkardstown Cists — this is the only justification for including it here.

TOWNLAND	COUNTY	REFERENCE	NOTES

ADDITIONAL NOTE

| Morenane | Limerick | File Nat. Museum and Raftery B., 1974, 304n | *Rejected*. Included as a Linkardstown cist by B. Raftery. A five-sided cist just over 1m long contained a crouched unburned skeleton. It has none of the characteristics of the Linkardstown type and is almost certainly to be regarded as a slightly unusual E.B.A. short cist. |

REFERENCES

Anon, 1913. 'Antiquarian remains and historic spots around Cloyne', *J Cork Hist Archaeol Soc* 19, 181-92.

Borlase, W.C., 1897. *The Dolmens of Ireland,* I. London.

Glover, W., 1974. 'Segmented cist grave in Kinkit townland, Co. Tyrone', *J Roy Soc Antiq Ir* 105-6, 150-5.

Graves, J., 1851. 'Observations on the excavation of a cairn at Cloghmanty Hill', *J Roy Soc Antiq Ir* 1, 289-94.

Graves, J., 1853. In 'Proceedings', *J Roy Soc Antiq Ir* 2, 358.

Harris, W., 1739. *The Whole Works of Sir James Ware concerning Ireland Revised and Improved in three volumes,* II, 148-9. Dublin.

Hencken, H. O'N., 1935. 'A cairn at Poulawack, Co. Clare', *J Roy Soc Antiq Ir* 95, 191-222.

Herity, M., 1970. *In* Jan Filip (ed), *Actes du VIIᵉ Congrès International des Sciences Prehistoriques et Protohistoriques.* Prague.

Herity, M., 1975. *Irish Passage Graves.* Dublin.

Herity, M. & Eogan, G., 1977. *Ireland in Prehistory.* London.

Kilbride-Jones, H.E., 1939. 'The excavation of a composite tumulus at Drimnagh, Co. Dublin', *J Roy Soc Antiq Ir* 69, 130-220.

Kinahan, G.H., 1879. 'New (?) type of Clochaun . . . .' *Proc Roy Ir Acad* 15, 69-70.

Kinahan, G.H., 1887. 'Sepulchral and other prehistoric relics, Counties of Wicklow and Wexford', *Proc Roy Ir Acad* 16, 152-9.

Lucas, A.T., 1950. 'Neolithic burial at Norrismount, Co. Wexford'. *J Roy Soc Antiq Ir* 80, 155-7.

Piggott, S., 1954. *Neolithic Cultures of the British Isles*, Cambridge.

Raftery, B., 1974. 'A prehistoric burial mound at Baunogenasraid, Co. Carlow', *Proc Roy Ir Acad C* 74, 277-312.

Raftery, J., 1944. 'A Neolithic burial in Co. Carlow', *J Roy Soc Antiq Ir* 74, 61-2.

Raftery, J., 1974. 'A Neolithic burial mound at Ballintruermore, Co. Wicklow', *J Roy Soc Antiq Ir* 103-4, 214-19.

Ryan, M., 1972. 'Some burial monuments of the later Neolithic', *Carloviana* 2, 18-21.

Ryan, M., 1973. 'The excavation of a Neolithic burial mound at Jerpoint West, Co. Kilkenny', *Proc Roy Ir Acad C* 73, 107-27.

Savory, H.N., 1978. 'Some Iberian influences on the Copper Age pottery of the Irish Channel area', *Univ Valladolid Bol del Seminario de Estudios de Arte y Arqueologia* 44, 5-13.

Waddell, J., 1970. 'Irish Bronze Age cists: a survey', *J Roy Soc Antiq Ir* **100**, 1-139.

Waddell, J., 1978. 'The invasion hypothesis in Irish prehistory', *Antiquity* **52**, 121-8.

Wallace, P.F., 1977. 'A prehistoric burial cairn at Ardcroney, Nenagh, Co. Tipperary', *N Munster Antiq J* **19**,3-20.

Wilde, W., 1857. *A Descriptive Catalogue of the Antiquities of Stone, Earthen and Vegetable Materials in the Museum of the Royal Irish Academy*. Dublin.

Gold Discs of the Irish Late Bronze Age

George Eogan

Only two definite finds of gold discs are known from the Irish Late Bronze Age and these belong to the Dowris Phase (*c.* 8th century and later). Their decoration and mode of manufacture links them to other Dowris Phase gold objects, especially the gorgets. Their makers may have had some knowledge of continental Later Bronze Age discs but in particular they reflect the inventive skills of native goldsmiths.

INTRODUCTION

From the beginning of the metal age discs were one of the types that were made in the new medium. The earliest examples were current during the Hungarian Copper Age (the Bodrogkerstur Culture) and before the end of the Neolithic discs of copper were in use in Denmark (Driehaus, 1960, 166; Butler, 1963, 168-9). But gold discs were also used from an early date as the Stollhoff find from Austria shows (cf. Makkay, 1976, 286). During the Bronze Age gold discs were becoming popular in parts of Europe. In the east by the Hajdúsámson horizon of the Carpathian area they were relatively common as their occurrence in hoards such as Ostrovul Mare and Ţufalau (Cófalva) show (Mozsolics, 1965, 50, 54).

The first recorded find of a gold disc in Ireland was made near Ballyshannon towards the end of the 17th century (Case, 1977, 30-1) and since MacAdam's paper of 1856 discs have been recognised in Ireland as a type. Six years later Wilde published the seven specimens then in the collection of the Royal Irish Academy and he termed them 'circular gold plates' (Wilde, 1862, 82-3). By 1920 when Armstrong published the first edition of his *Gold Catalogue* the number had risen to fifteen and he was able to add in press a description of a new find from Lattoon, Co. Cavan (Armstrong, 1933 (2nd edition), 35-7, 84-5, 47-9).

For the Early Bronze Age Ireland was one of the main areas where gold discs were used: at least twenty examples have survived whereas Britain has only about four finds (Case, 1977). In contrast to this, the Late Bronze Age is poor in finds. Nevertheless, I hope that this study of them will interest Professor O'Kelly, especially in view of his own contributions to the study of early metalworking.

DESCRIPTION

CO. CAVAN (fig 26.5)   LATTOON

This is a thin sheet of gold with all-over decoration. The central motif consists of a low boss surrounded by multiple concentric circles. In the space between the second and third circle out from the boss there is a row of raised dots. The central area is enclosed by a herring-bone pattern with a medial line and faint ridges on the outside. A similar pattern occurs along the edge. At one point a transverse band links up these two patterns. This band consists of a central ladder pattern with a band of hatched lozenges and triangles on each side. This design interrupts the three main decorative bands. The decoration of the inner and outer bands is similar. The main motif is a small boss surrounded by multiple concentric circles (eighteen in the inner, sixteen in the outer). Each is separated from the other by hatched triangles. As a result each circular motif is within a hexagonal compartment. These bands are bordered by two or three lines concentric to them and between these is a band of hatched triangles. The method of manufacture is difficult to determine. Faint repoussée work does occur but chasing also appears to have been employed after first marking out the motifs with a compass.

> Diameter   120.5 mm   N.M.I. 1920:28
> Weight   3 dwt., 20 gr.

This disc is part of a hoard which was found in a bog in June 1919 (fig 26). The other objects, also of gold, are two penannular bracelets with solid body of rounded cross-section and solid evenly expanded terminals (N.M.I. 1920:26-7) and two 'dress-fasteners' (N.M.I. 1920:24-5).
Principal reference: Armstrong, 1933, 47-9, fig 17.

CO. WEXFORD   Nr. ENNISCORTHY

1. (Pl IX) This disc has three components, a face-plate, a back-plate and an edging. The plates are decorated, repoussée could be the technique used but it is possible that the sheet could have been pressed into a die. The face-plate is more highly decorated than the back-plate. The central motif consists of a conical boss surrounded by fourteen concentric ridges of similar size. Between this and the edge there are two bands the principal motif in each being a conical boss surrounded by concentric circles; three or four in the inner band, five or six in the outer. There are eleven such motifs in the inner band and seventeen in the outer. Each is separated from its neighbour by an X-shaped design. This places the boss and circle motif in a compartment which is usually hexagonal in shape. There are two enclosing ridges on the inside of the inner band, on the outside of the outer and in between both. The back-plate is decorated by twenty kite-shaped areas each being outlined by a double ridge. There is a roughly circular hole in the centre. This has jagged edges

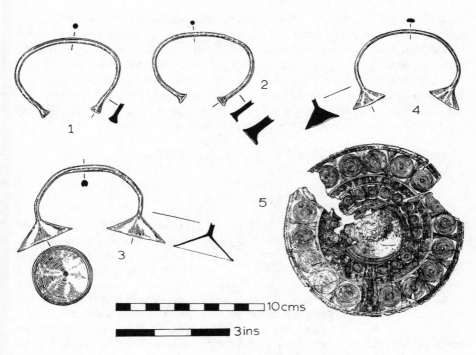

Fig 26: The Lattoon hoard. Drawing courtesy N.M.I.

and it measures around 33 mm across. Both plates are gripped along the edge by a C-sectioned binding strip.

D. 117 mm   M.M. New York 47.100.14
Weight 1.213 oz. troy, 37.75 gr.

2.   (Pl X) Structurally and decoratively this disc is similar to no. 1. The face-plate has a slight convexity but its scheme of decoration is similar to no. 1. On the back-plate the decoration differs slightly. It consists of twenty-seven lozenge- and twenty-seven kite-shaped areas which are framed by ridges. The central circular hole is around 39 mm in diameter.

D. 121-124 mm   N.M.I. IA/L/1963:2
Weight 1.214 oz. troy, 37.75 gr.

3-4.   These two discs were melted down soon after discovery but according to Ousley the four discs were 'exactly alike'.
    The four discs were found in October 1795 by a man ploughing. They were sold

to a silversmith in Enniscorthy, a Mr Gurly, who melted two down. He 'sent the other two for sale to the Earl of Charlemont', who was the first President of the Royal Irish Academy. It is not known if they were acquired by Charlemont and their subsequent history is unknown until recent times. One of the discs (no. 2) was acquired by Trinity College, Dublin, but at what date has not been recorded, and the other (no. 1) was in the possession of the Grogan family of Johnstown Castle, Co. Wexford. The contents of the castle were sold in 1944 and shortly after that the disc was acquired by the Metropolitan Museum, New York.

Principal references: Eogan, 1975, 23-4; Ousley, 1797, 31-4.

DISCUSSION

The discs from Lattoon and Enniscorthy are the only two definite finds of the Irish Late Bronze Age. A gold disc was part of the collection of miscellaneous gold objects, some of which were certainly fakes, allegedly found in the neighbourhood of Strangford Lough, Co. Down (Macalister, 1914). This material no longer exists but the disc was described as being slightly concavo-convex, 72 mm (2⅞ inches) in diameter and weighing 10 dwt, 16 grs. It was decorated with bands of concentric circles and zig-zags. At one point the edge is notched and there are four holes in a row across the disc. The object was 'roughly and carelessly made, there are distinct traces of three different attempts at ornamenting it'. It is, therefore, likely that this is not a genuine piece. There is a bronze or copper disc from Ireland in the British Museum (British Museum, 1920, 110, fig 117, reg. no. 54.7-14.100). It is 70 mm in diameter and has two lateral projections and a hole in the centre. This is surrounded by concentric circles. There is a band of radial ornament on the outside and beyond this there are ten motifs consisting of a dot surrounded by five grooves. Triangular ornament fills a band along the edge. There is no evidence for gold foil covering. The object in the 'South of Ireland' hoard, gold on a copper or bronze backing (Eogan, 1967, 56-7, Pl 6 c-d; 1974, 87, 114, Pl 3b), has the remains of a projection in the centre. It is more likely that this is the head of a disc-headed pin with bent stem like those from the Ballytegan hoard, Co. Laois (Raftery, 1971, 87, Pl 18b). There are also two gold discs in the Arboe/Killycolp(y), Co. Tyrone, hoard (Raftery, 1970, 172; 1971, Pl 20:6-7, reproduction of a 19th century illustration by George de Noyer which lacks a scale). One of the discs, that with the dot and multiple concentric ornament, cannot be traced but the examination of the other disc was facilitated through the good offices of the National Museum of Ireland. This disc is decorated with bossed ridges which surround a central depression. It measures 27 mm across and it is, therefore, much smaller than the Lattoon and Enniscorthy discs. Furthermore, there is slight evidence for a flange on one side. It appears that this disc was attached to a backing. It is therefore more likely that it, and the other example, were foil coverings from the heads of disc-headed pins.

The Enniscorthy discs are much more stable than the Lattoon discs and they differ also in structure and in the technique of ornamentation. They were made from thicker gold and they consist of bound double sheets. The ornament is in relief and was applied by the repoussé technique or die stamping. In contrast, the Lattoon disc is a very thin sheet of gold and chasing or incision were the principal techniques used in applying the ornament. But the discs from both find-places have a number of decorative features in common. The comparison applies to the disposition of the ornament as well as to the motifs, especially the boss and circle motif and the location of these in hexagonal compartments, and the occurrence of ridges. In broader terms the decorative scheme is similar to that which is found on some other gold objects, mainly from north Munster, which date from the final phase (Dowris Phase) of the Late Bronze Age. This is especially so with regard to gorget terminals (Armstrong, 1933, 13-14, 57-8; Raftery, 1967, 62-3; Powell, 1973), the boxes (Armstrong, 1933, 40, 88-9) and possible bowl (Armstrong, 1933, 89, no. 376) and also the other items already mentioned such as the heads of disc-pins and the bullae from the Bog of Allen and from the Arboe/Killycolp(y) hoard (Armstrong, 1933, 92, no 400; 1922, 133, find-place not given). In addition the technique of manufacture of the Enniscorthy discs is close to gorget terminals not only in the use of the double sheets but also the C-sectioned edge binding occurs on the Shannongrove gorget terminals (Powell, 1973, Pl 26 right) and also on the 'lock-rings' (Eogan, 1969, 105).

The dating is straightforward. The association of the disc with bracelets and 'dress-fasteners' at Lattoon places that hoard in the Dowris Phase. As the decoration on the Enniscorthy discs is close, these must be contemporary. By comparing the ornament, the technique of manufacture and the structure, one can widen the comparisons especially to the gorgets which are one of the outstanding types of the Dowris Phase (Eogan, 1964, 306).

As already pointed out, discs made from gold and other metals were used in different regions of Europe from the beginning of the 'Bronze' Age, Ireland being one of the leading areas of production (above). But as the discs of the Irish Later Bronze Age are quite different especially in ornamentation from those of the Early Bronze Age, they cannot be descended from them. Furthermore, all the Irish Early Bronze Age discs belong to the beginning of that period and so the chronological gap is much too long to span. The Later Bronze Age discs must then be considered as a new element that emerged at the end of the Bronze Age but the reason for this is not easy to explain. Gräslund (1967, 63-4) has compared the Lattoon disc on the grounds of its concentric ornament and more especially its radial 'interrupting' band, to shields from Nuragi, Sardinia, but in the absence of corroborating evidence for contacts between the Sardinian area and the west of Europe this view cannot be proven.

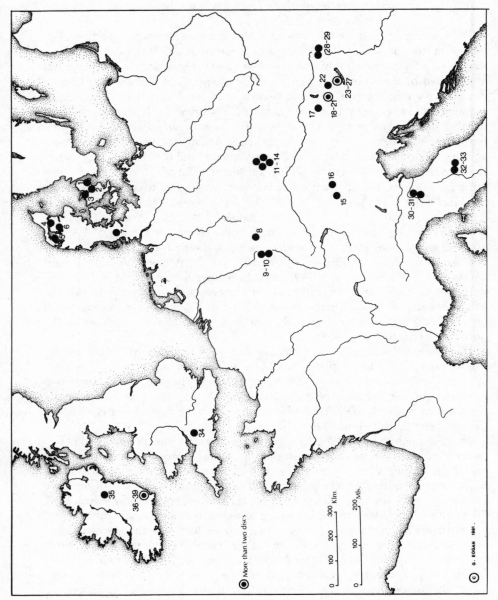

Fig 27: Provisional distribution of gold discs of the European Later Bronze Age.

In the matter of the continental evidence, not only were gold discs known in Early Bronze Age Europe but they were also used during its later stages and perhaps the tradition of gold-disc manufacture continued on the continent if not in Ireland. Up to forty gold discs dating from the later phases of the Bronze Age are known from Europe (below). These usually consist of gold foil over a bronze or copper backing. All-over decoration is a feature. The multiple concentric circle is a leading motif but ridges, bosses, bands of short transverse lines, cord decoration and zig-zags also occur. The largest examples occur in Denmark where the Jaegersborg disc is 35 cm in diameter. The Bohemian group averages 10 cm in diameter, those from Gualdo Tadino 13 cm, the Irish pieces 12 cm, the Balaton-Neusiedler group 4-6 cm, Borgo Panigale 3.3 and 5 cm respectively with the smallest example, that from Mühlau being only 2.8 cm in diameter. The use of discs was confined to certain areas (fig 27). The Danish area has a concentration and so does the west Hungarian/south-east Austrian area principally in the general region of Lake Balaton-Neusiedler See. There is a scatter of discs over Bohemia, southern Germany, western Austria and central Italy. In order to study fully the origins and contexts of discs of the Later Bronze Age it would be necessary to evaluate discs in other media such as bronze and horn. Account should also be taken of the wide range of other decorated objects, not only metal but also pottery, bone and other materials. However, even when one confines a review to the gold discs and bears in mind the limitations outlined, it is nevertheless possible to come to some conclusions.

No gold discs have been found in early contexts in the north of Europe. However, the disc from Moordorf in the East Frisian area of Lower Saxony (Jacob-Friesen, 1931; Menghin, 1977, 106, Abb. 64) is generally considered earlier than the main group. This is largely based on style but there are other differences. Moordorf is smaller (14.5 cm), it was found in a bog and it is outside the main area of distribution. But it also has features in common with some of the Later Bronze Age discs. Its side tabs can be compared to those on the Trundholm disc and Trundholm (and some contemporary discs) has a band of decoration consisting of short radial lines. It may be noted that the bronze disc from an unrecorded find-place in Ireland, already referred to, also has two side tabs and amongst its decorative motifs are zig-zags or triangles and a band of short radial lines but the dot-and-multiple circle motifs clearly place the Irish piece in a Later Bronze Age context. Furthermore, the absence of what can be considered as immediate forerunners for the main group in the Nordic area could be an argument for considering the Moordorf disc as part of that group. While one cannot be certain about the precise date of the Moordorf piece, however, the general composition of its decoration suggests an earlier Bronze Age date.

Concerning the Balaton-Neusiedler See groups, this was indeed an area where gold discs were previously worn but this was back in the Copper Age (Bóna, 1963-4, 34-7); Makkay, 1976, 286-9) and as such too early to be relevant as was the case in Ireland. During the Hajdúsámson phase of the Transylvania/north-east Hungarian Bronze Age (roughly equivalent to Reinecke A2) gold discs were common and there are at least eight find-places which produced between them over a hundred discs. Practically all were parts of hoards (Mozsolics, 1965-6, 28-34).

There is a group of gold discs from the Pilsen area of Bohemia. These came from graves which date to late Tumulus times, Bronze Age C2 (Čujanová-Jílková, 1975; 1970, 52-3, 62-3, 85-6, 123-4; see below). The burial rite at Nová Huť was cremation; the others had inhumed remains but very little survived. However, from the nature of the grave goods Čujanová-Jílková concludes that they were the graves of males. The disc from Sedlec Hůrka has running spirals surrounding bosses, Milínov-Javor and Nová Huť have triple concentric circles surrounding bosses and a meandering line curving around them. The two former are domed; the latter is flat. Zelené has concentric ornament. All have ridges but the ornamentation on the Zelené disc makes it the more elaborately decorated. It is damaged but may have been flat. This ornamentation recalls that occurring on the gold discs, but more especially on other metal objects of the Hadjúsámson horizon of the Carpathian area. On this evidence Čujanová-Jílková (1975, 121) considers that the Bohemian discs have their forerunners in the discs of the Hadjúsámson horizon. This raises the question as to whether the Bohemian group represented the end of an old series or the beginning of a new series. In fact it may be both. The disc from Zelené could be considered an early version, leading up to the characteristic Later Bronze Age type as represented at Mühlau at a slightly later date. The disc from Volders close by could be Early Urnfield in view of the form of the associated urn. The Goldbach (Germany) disc should date from the same time. The Italian discs are of equivalent date, Bietti Sestieri (1973, 389) has dated Gualdo Tadino to the Proto-Villanovan culture, c. 12th century B.C. Ság-Berg, with its solid-hilted sword and other objects may be Late Urnfield (Mozsolics, 1950, 40-1). Velemszentvid, and possibly the other discs in the Balaton-Neusiedler area may equally well be late (cf. Patek, 1968, for the Urnfield Period in Transdanubia). The Danish discs came into existence within Period II (cf. Althin, 1945, 188-96; Jørgensen, 1975, 99-101) and could, therefore, have been as early as the Bohemian group but relationships, if any, between the two groups are not clear. Despite the fact that the west Austrian discs are later than the Bohemian ones and that the Balaton-Neusiedler group, or at least some of the discs forming it, are later still the genealogy of the Later Bronze Age discs is not clear-cut. The concept of a pan-European gold disc emerging through a series of typological developments in one area is unproven. The Danish discs might have emerged as a result of local development; after all that area had splendid decorated bronzes, such as belt-plates, during Period II. The covering of bronze objects, for instance belt-hooks, with gold foil was also a technological advance that took place during Period II. Indeed, if a slightly modified belt-plate was covered with gold leaf a disc would ensue and in this connection it may be remarked that one of the zones of decoration on the Trundholm disc consists of a running band enclosing the tangential spirals just as is found on some belt-plates, for instance an example from a burial at Sonnerup, Kregine, Zealand (Aner and Kersten, 1973, 72-4, Taf. 39:228E). But the bronze belt-plates have been exclusively found in female graves while the gold discs from graves were associated with males. Furthermore, the technique of elaborate gold-working has a longer tradition in east-central Europe, especially in the Carpathian region and it may be the case that the north of Europe received stimulus from that area, as Kersten (1935, 93) suggested. While the Danish discs have been found in Period II contexts it is difficult to know if they were in use from the beginning of that period. The Trundholm wagon suggests a date towards its end and Thrane (1962a, 114) has pointed out that the decoration on the Jaegersborg disc can be compared to that on the Østermarie bronze vessel which he would date to Period II-III transition. At that time, changes were taking place in the Bronze Age of Denmark. In decoration, concentric circles, rows of bosses and star-shaped motifs were becoming common. Technologically the manufacture of bronze vessels by chasing seems to have been practiced and new types of such vessels emerged. Most of these events can be attributed to stimulation from outside (Thrane, 1962a).

In the matter of the last use of gold discs, the Bohemian, south German and west Austrian discs came from graves. In the north of Europe the discs also came from graves or were associated with a wagon model; the lone English disc also came from a grave. But in the west, east and south peripheries, Ireland, the Balaton-Neusiedler See area and Italy, the discs form parts of hoards. They were, therefore, of sufficient importance to be placed in a grave or deposited with other objects. Their original use is unknown although the view has often been advanced that they were sun-symbols, possibly used on ceremonial occasions. On the grave evidence they can be considered as objects that were worn or used by males. The Trundholm disc was mounted on a waggon model so it must have served as some part of a cult. It may also be noted that a four-spoked wheel, like the Trundholm wheels, was deposited about mid-point on a skeleton in a grave at Storehøj, Ribe, Denmark (Thrane, 1962b). The Lattoon example is so frail that it must have had a backing, possibly bronze or copper like so many of the continental discs. The Enniscorthy discs are more substantial and the hole in the back-plate indicates that they were mounted. In connection with the Rothengrub find, Pittioni (1952) has suggested that the discs could have formed a central point on a leather belt with eighteen triple disc plaques arranged on both sides. The Milínov-Javor disc was directly associated with four gold bands and Zelené with one band. Čujanová-Jílková (1975, 88) thought that these bands might have been parts of a belt. While the skeleton in the Milínov-Javor grave has not been preserved it has, nevertheless, been inferred that the disc and bands were in the area of the head. The Sedlec Hůrka disc was in the western end of the grave and consequently at either the head or the foot of the burial. Perhaps some of the discs were worn as head ornaments. The Danish discs from Jaegersborg, Gug, Karlstrup and seemingly Tødsø were in the middle of the grave, a location occupied in other approximately contemporary graves by a bronze belt-plate. In addition Jaegersborg had strips of leather and a belt-hook, and a belt-hook was also found in the Mühlau grave. However, the evidence so far available is not sufficient to enable one to say if the discs were worn on the person and if so where. Neither has their precise function been established. Nevertheless, it is interesting to note that a number of graves and hoards containing discs had several other items. For instance, the Velemszentvid hoard is a spectacular assemblage of gold ornaments. This evidence, and the fact that most of the Danish discs came from coffin burials, indicates that those males were buried with considerable pomp and ceremony. The reason for this may have been that during life they had access to wealth and possibly power, temporal or spiritual. If one assumes that the discs were the possessions of individuals, they may only have been worn on special occasions as symbols of rank and as indications of wealth. Or perhaps their function was non-secular and they were part of the accoutrements of cult or religious activities.

The origin of the Irish pieces is no clearer than that of the continental ones. Apart from a possible example from a grave at Lansdown Links, Somerset (British Museum, 1920, 89-90), discs of Later Bronze Age date are not known from Britain. The Lansdown piece, gold on a bronze backing, is in fragments but it does appear, among other motifs, to have a star-shaped pattern. As Butler (1963, 174) has remarked this can be compared to the design on the gold disc from Jaegersborg, Denmark, which can be assigned to Period II. The Irish pieces are later in date, hardly earlier than the 8th century and by then, apart possibly from western Hungary, gold discs had gone out of fashion. There is no definite evidence of contact between Ireland and the Austro-Hungarian area during Urnfield times and so inspiration could hardly have come from the latter source but there was contact between Ireland and the Danish-north German region. The best evidence for that is provided by the thick penannular bracelet from Gahlstorf near Bremen which is an Irish type (Hawkes and Clarke, 1963, 195-210). There are also Irish Later Bronze Age types, disc-headed pins for instance, that appear to have a background in that region (Eogan, 1974). But if gold discs were not current in the north into Period IV then that area too must be excluded as a source of origin or inspiration. Perhaps the Irish discs are a product of native ingenuity. The period during which they were current was a time of development and innovation by Irish goldsmiths. The presence of boxes which lack external forerunners and also gorgets and 'lock-rings' clearly shows this. If there was external stimulus it may be that discs and gorgets reflect the idea of wearing such ornaments but at a later date than the currency of neck ornaments and discs in northern Europe.

PROVISIONAL LIST OF LATER BRONZE AGE GOLD DISCS (fig 27)

DENMARK: No .1. *Jaegersborg*, Zealand (Aner and Kersten, 1973, 147-8, no. 417, Taf. 88; Broholm, 1943, 45, Grave 191. N.M.D. 2576178). Burial in a wooden coffin which was found in 1863. In addition to the disc, which had a bronze backing, the grave goods consisted of a tanged sword, a bronze belt-hook, four bronze conical knobs ('tutuli'), a palstave, a bronze socketed chisel, a bronze awl, a pottery vessel and pieces of leather. Near the disc there was a yellow mass covered by seaweed. The disc was in the middle of the grave with the sword, belt-hook and knobs under it. The pieces of leather lay on top of the disc. No. 2. *Karlstrup*, Zealand (Aner and Kersten, 1973, 185-6, Abb. 114, Taf. 109). This burial (Grave Q) contained the remains of two men, skeletons A and B, in a wooden coffin. Skeleton A had the following objects, bronze unless otherwise stated: a tanged sword, a scabbard of leather and wood, knife, tweezers, razor, a fishing hook and line, two fibulae, two knobs, a double button, a flint strike-a-light and a small piece of sheet gold. This piece is decorated with concentric circles, parallel ridges and transverse band. The sheet is thicker than that of the other discs but its context and place in the grave, in the middle of the skeleton, suggests that it may be part of a gold disc (N.M.D.B 16450). No. 3. *Trundholm*, Zealand (Aner and Kersten, 1976, 63, no. 867, Pl 138-40, N.M.D. B7703). Found on the edge of a bog in 1902 when the area was being ploughed for the first time. The double-faced disc was mounted on a six-wheeled waggon model. No. 4. *Gug*, Sønder Tranders, Jutland (Broholm, 1943, 74, Grave 607. N.M.D. B7058-9). Burial that contained the disc and rapier. The disc was in the centre of the grave. No. 5. *Tødsø*, Jutland (Broholm, 1943, 72, Grave 578, N.M.D. B9576-81). Burial with the disc and remains of a bronze backing, a solid-hilted sword, a wooden scabbard, a dagger and two fibulae. The disc, which was in fragments, lay above the sword and dagger and these were around the centre of the grave. No. 6. *Lille Sjørup* (Kongehøj), Flejsborg, Jutland (Broholm, 1943, 74, Grave 600. N.M.D. 22079-80). Disc and sword.

All the Danish discs, except Trundholm, were in burials in wooden coffins but apart from Karlstrup the remains had decayed. However, the presence of weapons in these graves indicates that they, too, were those of males. The discs had a bronze backing.

In addition to the above references see Althin, 1945, 193-6 and Jørgensen, 1975, 80, 99-101.

GERMANY: No. 7. *Glüsing*, Schleswig-Holstein (Jacob-Friesen, 1931, 36; Kersten, 1935, 93, 161, no. 284; Struve, 1971, 56, Museum für Vor- und Frühgeschichte Berlin: Im 2153, lost during the war of 1939-45). Seemingly from a male burial and associated with a solid-hilted sword, seemingly a dagger blade and two palstaves. No. 8. *Goldbach*, Kr. Aschaffenburg (Hartmann, 1970, 106, Taf. 27, Au 1334; Peschenck, 1958, Taf. 37:12, Mainsfränkischen Museum, Würzburg, L 2162). From a cremation grave (no. 2) that also had an urn, two other pottery vessels and parts of bronze bracelets. Nos 9-10. *Worms* (Behrens, 1927; Mozsolics, 1950, 16-17; Städtisches Museum, Sammlung Nassauischer Altertümer,

Wiesbaden: 5353). The two discs were found in the vineyards north of the Liebfraukirche and no other details are available.

CZECHOSLOVAKIA: In western Bohemia in the region of the city of Pilsen there are a number of barrows of the Tumulus culture. Four inhumation graves, which may have contained the remains of males, produced gold discs.

No. 11. *Milínov-Javor* (Plzeň-jih), Mound 5, grave A (Čujanová-Jílková, 1975, 75-6, 88, Abb. 6, 7 and 9, bottom left for plan of mound; see also id., 1970, 52, Abb. 48-9, 116:5. Západočeské Muzeum, Pilsen, 1444). Grave A was divided into two compartments. The burial in the northern compartment may have been an inhumation. The grave-goods were in two groups. The northern group (in the area of the head?) consisted of a gold disc, four rectangular gold bands, parts of a spiral ring or rings, pin with disc head and ribbed stem and two penannular bracelets. The southern group consisted of four ribbed 'finger' rings, two penannular bracelets, four pottery vessels and stone pebbles.

No. 12. *Nová Huť* (Plzeň-sever), Mound 3/1909 (Čujanová-Jílková, 1975, 76, 92, Abb. 11; 1970, 62-3, Abb. 30. Západočeské Muzeum, Pilsen, 8626). This cremation grave contained, in different places, a gold disc, a narrow gold band, four gold spiral finger rings with double body, two bronze bracelets with broadish body and double spiral ends, two pins with flat evenly-expanded head, two stems of pins, tweezers, razor, palstave, leaf-shaped spearhead and pottery vessel.

The disc, the gold band, the two spiral-ended bracelets and one of the pins were in direct association in the grave, but position not recorded.

No. 13. *Sedlec-Hůrka* (Plzeň-jih), Mound 39, grave 3 (Čujanová-Jílková, 1975, 76-7, Abb. 3:C, 4; 1970, 85-6, Abb. 116:11; 58:1. Západočeské Muzeum, Pilsen, 8623). An inhumation, grave goods consisted of a gold disc, five rectangular gold plaques, six gold spiral rings with double body, pin with evenly expanded and stepped head, flange-hilted sword, ten bronze barbed-and-tanged arrowheads and two pottery vessels. The disc was in the western end of the grave.

No. 14. *Zelené* (Plzeň-jih), Mound 30 (Čujanová-Jílková, 1975, 78, 96, Abb. 17, 18, 19A; 1970, 123-4, Abb. 97A-98. Západočeské Muzeum, Pilsen, 8620). There were three groups of grave goods, southern, middle and northern, and these may represent different burials. The southern group of grave goods, which was associated with an inhumation, consisted of a gold disc, four rectangular bands of gold, two bracelets with ribbed body that tapers to the terminals, three penannular bracelets, an armring of double bars wrapped with wire, a gold coiled bracelet with double body, two pieces of wire, a dagger, two pins with flat evenly-expanded head and ribbing on parts of stem, part of stem of pin, eight pottery vessels, three glass beads, an amber bead and two stones, The grave-goods were grouped fairly close together and the disc was between the two gold bands. Their position suggests that if there was an extended skeleton the disc might have been around the middle.

It may also be noted that there is a hoard from Čehovice u Prostejova in Moravia about fifty miles north-east of Brno. This consisted of gold wires and seven gold discs, 4-6 cm in diameter, and decorated with dot-and-circle ornament. It is not possible to date this hoard accurately (Čujanová-Jílková, 1975, 122).

No 15. *Mühlau* (von Merhart, 1930; Mozsolics, 1950, 16, Sammlung des Ferdinandeums, Innsbruck: 10400). A cremation grave that contained, in addition to the disc which had a bronze backing, gold spiral-twisted wires, pottery vessels, perhaps as many as fourteen, and the following bronze objects — fibulae of Peschiera type, two stick pins with vase-shaped heads, a plain and a twisted bracelet, a belt-hook, a model of a bird, five hollowed bosses, ninety-five to a hundred small bosses, a small stand, a clapper, a handle of a jar, a bronze object of uncertain use and three glass beads. No 16. *Volders* (Kasseroler, 1959, 148, fig on p. 226, private collection). In a cremation grave that also contained a bronze finger ring, fragments of molten bronze, a pottery urn and a bowl. No 17. *Rothengrub* (Pittioni, 1952, Naturhistorisches Museum, Vienna: 72474). Hoard containing the following gold objects: a disc (bronze with gold leaf), a 'pectoral' made from fine gold wires twisted around a bronze or copper wire, eighteen plaques in the form of three conjoined penannular discs and nearly all decorated with multiple concentric circles, three coiled rings made from double wires that are twisted in place, pieces of fine gold wire.

HUNGARY: Nos 18-21. *Velemszentvid* (Mozsolics, 1950, 8, Taf. 2. Szombathely Museum). Hoard of gold objects consisting of four gold discs and twelve fragments of discs, a diadem, twenty-six spiral-twisted wires and other fragments. The discs had a bronze backing. No 22. *Ság-Berg* (Mozsolics, 1950, 11, Taf. 4:2, Sammlung Lázár, Celldömölk). Hoard consisting of the disc, diadem, a flange-hilted sword, a solid-hilted sword, a scabbard for each, three winged axes, five socketed axes and nine broken axe pieces, two awls, eleven sickles and three broken sickles, twenty penannular bracelets, eleven broken pieces of bracelets, two knives and part of a knife, spiral ring, plain ring and a broken ring, pieces of spearheads, two hundred bronze knobs, two hundred and thirty-three bronze rings, seven hundred and eighty-eight bone beads, 30 kg of bronze cake and broken pieces. Nos 23-27a. *Felsözsid* (Tompa, 1928, 204-7, 344-5; Mozsolics, 1950, 14-15, Taf. 7, National Museum of Hungary, Budapest: 30.1927). Hoard of four discs, fourteen wire objects, possibly neck ornaments, and a ball of wire. Nos 28-9. *Óbuda* (Mozsolics, 1950, 14, Abb. 7. Naturhistorisches Museum, Vienna: 51299). Hoard consisting of gold ornaments — two discs and a coiled spiral-twisted wire.

ITALY: Nos 30-1. *Borgo Panigale*, Bologna, Emilia (Bietti Sestieri, 1973, 417, footnote 43; Von Hase, 1975, 108-11, Taf. 14 bottom. Museo Civile, Bologna: 1756.7). The two gold discs were found in September 1950 during the excavation of a Late Bronze Age occupation site at S. Agneses. The occupation layer contained other objects such as pottery vessels, a pottery animal-headed terminal and two pottery animal figures. Nos 32-3. *Gualdo Tadino*, Umbria (Bietti Sestieri, 1973, 389, fig 2; Von Hase, 1975, 101-4 and footnote 9. Museo Preistorico dell' Italia Centrale, Perugia). Hoard consisting of two gold discs and the following bronze objects — four violin-bow fibulae, three pins, four disc heads, two spiral rings, ten fragmentary spiral rings, a belt-hook (?), stud, fifteen needles, tweezers, socketed chisel with leaf-shaped blade, rod chisel, longish object with perforated ends and a dagger with perforated tang. There were also four biconical amber buttons, a disc-shaped amber bead, three perforated dogs' teeth, two bone buttons and parts of one or two bone combs. The hoard, which was found in 1937, may have been in a pottery vessel.

ENGLAND: No 34. *Lansdown Links*, Somerset (British Museum, 1920, 89-90, B.M. 1906:10-11). A cremation burial that had a disc with a copper backing and sherds of two pottery vessels. Only fragments of the gold leaf and its backing survive. It is, therefore, difficult to be certain about the exact nature of the decorative scheme.

IRELAND: No 35. *Lattoon*. Nos 36-9. *Enniscorthy*. Both hoards. Present paper.

ACKNOWLEDGEMENTS

I wish to thank the Keeper of Irish Antiquities, National Museum of Ireland (Mr Michael Ryan) and Dr Helmut Nickel, Metropolitan Museum, New York, for permission to examine and publish discs in their collections. For permission to examine comparative material in the Naturhistorisches Museum, Vienna, I am most grateful to Dr Fritz Eckart Barth and in the National Museum of Hungary to Dr Tibor Kemenczei. I am grateful to the authorities of the National Museum of Denmark for facilities to study the Danish discs and especially to Dr David Liversage and Dr Poul Otto Nielsen of the First Department for their help. For information about particular problems of continental discs I wish to record my thanks to Professor Dr Albrecht Jockenhövel, Institute of Archaeology, University of Frankfurt-am-Main, Professor Dr Walter Torbrügge, Institute of Archaeology, University of Regensburg and Professor Dr C. Eibner and Miss Susanne Klemm, Institute of Archaeology, University of Vienna, Dr Henrik Thrane, Odense Museum, Denmark, Dr Klaus Randsborg, Institute of Archaeology, Copenhagen University, and Mr David Ridgeway, Department of Archaeology, University of Edinburgh. The map (fig 27) was prepared by Mr John Aboud. For checking and typing the manuscript thanks are due to Miss Veronica Meenan, Secretary, Department of Archaeology, University College, Dublin. For making financial contributions to the cost of continental travel I am grateful to University College, Dublin.

REFERENCES

Althin, Carl-Axel, 1945. *Studien zu den Bronzezeitlichen Felszeichnungen von Skåne*. Lund/Copenhagen.

Aner, Ekkehard and Kersten, Karl, 1973. *Die Funde der älteren Bronzezeit des nordischen Kreises in Dänemark, Schleswig-Holstein und Niedersachsen. Band I. Frederiksborg und Københavns Amt.* Copenhagen and Neumünster.

Aner, Ekkehard and Kersten, Karl, 1976. *Die Funde der älteren Bronzezeit des nordischen Kreises in Dänemark, Schleswig-Holstein und Niedersachsen.* Band II. *Holbaek, Sorø und Praestø Amter.* Copenhagen and Neumünster.

Armstrong, E.C.R., 1922. 'Notes on some Irish gold ornaments', *J Roy Soc Antiq Ir* 52, 133-42.

Armstrong, E.C.R., 1933. *Catalogue of Irish Gold Ornaments in the Collection of the Royal Irish Academy.* Dublin.

Behrens, G., 1927. *Bilderheft zur Vor- und Frühgeschichte Rheinhessens. I. Die Vorrömische Zeit.* Mainz.

Bietti Sestieri, A.M., 1973. 'The metal industry of continental Italy, 13th to the 11th century B.C., and its connections with the Aegean', *Proc Prehist Soc* 39, 383-424.

Bóna, István, 1963-4. 'The peoples of southern origin of the Early Bronze Age in Hungary I-II', *Alba Regia* 4/5, 17-63.

British Museum, 1920. *A Guide to the Antiquities of the Bronze Age in the Department of British and Medieval Antiquities.* London.

Broholm, H.C., 1943-9. *Danmarks Bronzealder*, 4 vols. Copenhagen. Vol. I 1943; II 1944; III 1946; IV 1949.

Brøndsted, Johannes, 1939. *Danmarks Oldtid: II, Bronzealdern.* Copenhagen.

Butler, J.J., 1963. 'Bronze Age connections across the North Sea', *Palaeohist* 9, 1-286.

Case, Humphrey, 1977. 'An early accession to the Ashmolean Museum', *In* Vladimir Markotic (ed), *Ancient Europe and the Mediterranean*, Warminster.

Čujanová-Jílková, Eva, 1970. *Mittelbronzezeitliche Hügelgräberfelder in Westböhmen.* Prague.

Čujanová-Jílková, Eva, 1975. 'Zlaté předmety v hrobech českofalcké mohylové kultury (Gegenstände aus Gold in Gräbern der böhmisch-oberpfälzichen Hügelgräberkultur)', *Památky Archeologické* 66, 74-132 (German summary 126-30).

Driehaus, J., 1960. *Die Althemer Gruppe und das Jungneolithikum in Mitteleuropa.* Mainz.

Eogan, George, 1964. 'The Later Bronze Age in Ireland in the light of recent research', *Proc Prehist Soc* 30, 268-351.

Eogan, George, 1967. 'The Mull ("South of Ireland") hoard', *Antiquity* 41, 56-8.

Eogan, George, 1969. ' "Lock-rings" of the Late Bronze Age', *Proc Roy Ir Acad C* 67, 93-148.

Eogan, George, 1974. 'Pins of the Irish Late Bronze Age', *J Roy Soc Antiq Ir* 104, 74-119.

Eogan, George, 1975. 'An eighteenth-century find of four late Bronze Age gold discs near Enniscorthy, County Wexford', *Metropolitan Museum J* (New York) 10, 23-34.

Gräslünd, Bo., 1967. 'The Herzsprung shield type and its origin', *Acta Archaeol* (Copenhagen) 38, 59-71.

Hartmann, Axel, 1970. *Prähistorische Goldfunde aus Europa.* Berlin.

Hawkes, C.F.C. and Clarke, R.R., 1963. 'Gahlstorf and Caister-on-Sea: two finds of Late Bronze Age Irish gold', 193-250. *In* I. Ll. Foster and Leslie Alcock (ed), *Culture and Environment: Essays in Honour of Sir Cyril Fox.* London.

Jacob-Friesen, K.H., 1931. 'Die Goldscheibe von Moordorf bei Aurich mit ihren Britischen und nordischen Parallelen', *Jahrbuch für Prähistoriche und Ethnographische Kunst*, 25-44.

Jørgensen, Mogens S., 1975. *Guld fra Nordvestsjaelland.* Holbaek.

Kasseroler, Alfons, 1959. *Das Urnenfeld von Volders*. Innsbruck.

Kersten, Karl, 1935. *Zur älteren nordischen Bronzezeit*. Neumünster.

MacAdam, R., 1856. 'Gold disks found in Ireland', *Ulster J Archaeol Ser 1* **4**, 164-8.

Macalister, R.A.S., 1914. 'On a Hoard of remarkable Gold Objects recently found in Ireland', *Proc Roy Ir Acad C* **32**, 176-87.

Makkay, János, 1976. 'Problems concerning Copper Age chronology in the Carpathian Basin', *Acta Archaeol* (Budapest) **28**, 251-300.

Menghin, Wilfried, 1977. *Magisches Gold: Kultgerät der Späten Bronzezeit*. Germanisches Nationalmuseum, Nürnberg.

Mozsolics, Amália, 1950. *Der Goldfund von Velem-Szentvid*. Praehistorica I, Basel.

Mozsolics, Amália, 1965-6. 'Goldfunde des Depotfundhorizontes von Hajdúsámson', 46-7 *Bericht der Römisch-Germanischen Kommission*, 1-76.

Ousley, Ralph, 1797. 'Account of four circular plates of gold found in Ireland', *Trans Roy Ir Acad* **6**, 31-3.

Patek, Erzsébet, 1968. *Die Urnenfelderkultur in Transdanubien*. Budapest.

Pescheck, Christian, 1958. *Katalog Würzburg I. Die Funde von der Steinzeit bis zur Urnenfelderzeit im Mainfränkischen Museum*. Materialhefte zur Bayer. Vorgeschichte xii.

Pittioni, Richard, 1952. 'Der Goldfund von Rothengrub (N-Ö) und seine wirtschaftsgeschichtliche Verankerung', *Archaeol Austriaca* **11**, 89-99.

Powell, T.G.E., 1973. 'The Sintra Collar and the Shannongrove Gorget: aspects of Late Bronze Age goldwork in the west of Europe', *N Munster Antiq J* **16**, 3-13.

Raftery, J., 1967. 'The Gorteenreagh hoard', 61-71. *In* Etienne Rynne (ed), *North Munster Studies*. Limerick.

Raftery, J., 1970. 'Two gold hoards from Co. Tyrone', *J Roy Soc Antiq Ir* **100**, 169-74.

Raftery, J., 1971. 'A Bronze Age hoard from Ballytegan, Co. Laois', *J Roy Soc Antiq Ir* **101**, 85-100.

Schranil, Josef, 1928. *Die Vorgeschichte Böhmens und Mährens*. Berlin/Leipzig.

Struve, Karl W., 1971. *Die Bronzezeit, Periode I und II (In* V. Pauls (ed), *Geschichte Schleswig-Holsteins*). Neumünster.

Thrane, Henrik, 1962a. 'The earliest bronze vessels in Denmark's Bronze Age', *Acta Archaeol* (Copenhagen) **33**, 109-63.

Thrane, Henrik, 1962b. 'Hjulgraven fra Storehøj ved Tobøl i Ribe Amt (The Wheel-grave from Storehøj)', *Kuml*, 5-37.

Tompa, Ference, 1928. 'Ujabb szerzemének a Nemzeti Múzeum öskori gyütjeményében. I. A hangospusztai lelet. II. A felsözsidi lelet (Neue Erwerbungen der praehistorischen Abteilung der Nationalmuseums. I. Der Goldfund von Hagospusta. II. Der Goldfund von Felsö-Zsid)', *Archaeol Ertesitö* **42**, 202-7, 344-5.

Von Hase, Frederich-Wilhelm, 1975. 'Zur problematik der frühesten Goldfund in Mittelitalien', *Hamburger Beiträge zur Archäol* **5**, 99-182.

Von Merhart, Gero, 1930. 'Urnengrab mit Peschierafibel aus Nordtirol', *Schumacher-Festschrift*, 116-21 (reprinted: *In* Gero von Merhart, 1969. *Halstatt und Italien* (ed. Georg Kossack), 7-15. Mainz).

Wilde, W.R., 1862. *Catalogue of the Antiquities of Gold in the Museum of the Royal Irish Academy*. Dubin.

The Antique Order of the Dead: Cemeteries and Continuity in Bronze Age Ireland

John Waddell

One of the earliest accounts of the discovery of an Irish Bronze Age cemetery was communicated to the Dublin Philosophical Society in June 1685, by Dr Allen Mullen, celebrated author of *An Anatomical Account of the Elephant accidentally burnt in Dublin* . . . and other works (Hoppen, 1970, 37, 156). One of his correspondents, Anthony Irby, had reported a discovery made near Duntryleague, Co. Limerick:

Capt. Massy laid his commands upon me to give you this following account concerning some urns that were found upon his lands of Dontrilegue, which was thus: upon the 6th of June 1682 some of his Irish tenants were digging a ditch about a small garden plot and as they were at work they found several stones standing up square and a broad stone upon the top, under which they saw a red urn or pitcher with a small round stone upon the top of it (one of which, with some fragments of urns and a few bones, he has sent you), and in the said urn they found ashes and earth which was blackish, and some small pieces of bones which had been burned. There was fifteen of these in number, which stood all in a row about three foot deep in the earth, some of which held, as was supposed, a pottle, some a quart, and some small ones a pint. Some of them had creases round about them, and some were plain, but by the negligence and ignorance of the workmen were all broken. A piece of an urn was brought me by my brother Massy, which was very red and fresh. Capt. Massy and I went the next morning to the place, where we found a great deal of the ashes and pieces of burned bones, and I unhappily standing against the wind, a very nasty stench struck me, which I think occasioned an illness which seized me that day. Since that, Capt. Massy several times made trial by digging about that place to see if he could find any more of them, but he only found a heap of stones and a broad flat stone or two underneath, and under them ashes and pieces of burned bones without any urns, and particularly yesterday he found one of them and I saw it myself.

This report, which concludes with the ascription of the graves to either the heathen Romans, the Danes, or the natives of the country, is clearly an imperfect account of a flat cemetery comprising one, if not two, cist graves, and several urn burials.

In the three centuries since the Duntryleague discovery, over 130 Bronze Age cemeteries containing three or more graves have been found and, regrettably, the great majority of them have been documented with no greater precision. The first scientifically excavated cemeteries were examined in the 1930s by the Archaeological Mission of the Harvard Irish Survey: Hencken and Movius excavated the cemetery mound on Knockast, Co. Westmeath, in 1932, and another example in Poulawack, Co. Clare, two years later (Hencken and Movius, 1934, 1935). A portal tomb and Bronze Age cemetery were excavated by Evans in Aghnaskeagh, Co. Louth, in 1934 (Evans, 1935) and, more or less at the same time, S.P. Ó Ríordáin examined a small flat cemetery at Cush, Co. Limerick (Ó Ríordáin, 1940), but since then — and excluding several rescue excavations — surprisingly few cemeteries have been excavated and published. One noteworthy example, however, is the cemetery cairn in Moneen townland, Co. Cork, which was excavated by Professor M.J. O'Kelly, with customary skill, in 1948 (O'Kelly, 1952). The remarkable sequence of ritual and funerary events observed there are pertinent both to any consideration of Bronze Age burial practices and to any discussion of cultural continuity in the prehistoric past.

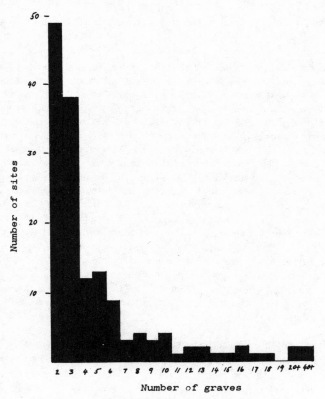

Fig 28: Number of graves in Bronze Age cemeteries.

I have suggested that a Bronze Age cemetery may be defined by the occurrence of three or more individual graves related by contiguity or by content or both (Waddell, 1970). For Flanagan, however, a cemetery may contain as few as two graves (Flanagan, 1976). My suggestion of a minimum of three graves was prompted by something more than a vague recollection of Oscar Wilde's assertion that 'three is company and two none'. Even allowing for the possibility that some sites which have produced two burials may yet yield more (as Flanagan found at

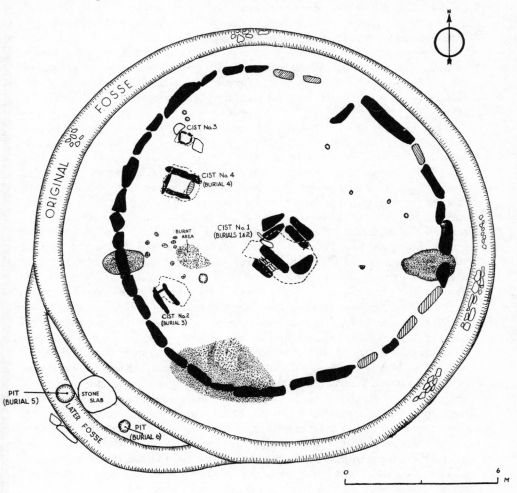

Fig 29: Moneen, Co. Cork, cemetery cairn (after O'Kelly).

Cloghskelt, Co. Down) and mindful of the grossly unsatisfactory nature of the archaeological record, when the number of sites with a minimum of two graves is
plotted in a histogram (fig 28), there does appear to be a numerical difference of
some significance between sites with only a few graves and those with a greater
number. Surprisingly, the major distinction appears to occur between sites with
three and sites with four burials. Of 150 sites plotted, 58% have two to three
graves, 32% have four to ten graves and 10% have contained eleven or more.
Clearly it would be a profitless task to argue the merits of two, three, or even four
graves as the diagnostic minimum in a cemetery. Of greater interest is the question
why some sites contain a mere two or three graves, and others received additional
burials to become more extensive cemeteries. Given the very scanty information
available about such sites and the paucity of excavated examples, it is not surprising
that this question cannot be satisfactorily answered at present. However, it is worth
examining the evidence for cultural continuity which some of these cemeteries
afford.

While O'Kelly inclined towards the view that the four cist graves at Moneen
were constructed at one and the same time and J. Raftery (1960) concluded that the
burials in the small cemetery mound in Corrower, Co. Mayo, were all contemporary, there is also evidence that some cemeteries were used, if intermittently,
over a period of time. This too was the case at Moneen where O'Kelly discovered
that the cemetery cairn had been placed within a Neolithic ring-ditch (fig 29), four
graves being found in the cairn and two clearly later graves being found outside its
kerb on the south-west. The central cist was of megalithic proportions and the
primary burial comprised the unburnt remains of two persons, a male and possibly
a female; these were considerably disturbed by the later insertion of the cremated
remains of a young person. Three small cists in the western half of the cairn were
thought to be contemporary with the central grave for all were covered by cairn
material. However, variations in orientation indicate the possibility (as O'Kelly
noted) that some interval of time may have elapsed between the construction of
some of the cists before all were finally incorporated in the cairn. Of the smaller
cists, one (cist no. 2) contained the poorly preserved unburnt remains perhaps of
an adult male, a second (cist no. 4) contained the disarticulated unburnt remains
of two adults and a child, and a third cist (cist no. 3) was empty; there were no
grave goods. A pit (burial no. 5), outside the kerb, contained a cremation and
fragments of at least one bowl, possibly of the tripartite type, with characteristic
comb-impressed and false-relief ornament. This burial was disturbed by the dig-
gers of a section of ditch which enclosed an encrusted urn burial (burial no. 6); the
most remarkable feature of this final burial was the fact that the arc of ditch within
which the urn was placed was added to the pre-cairn ring ditch, eloquent testimony
of the duration of the importance of the Neolithic sacred circle.

The sequence of funerary events at Moneen is of particular interest not only
because it illustrated some of the complexities of Bronze Age burial ritual but also

because the stratigraphical relationship of two burials and the accompanying pottery was determined. There is evidence from several other cemeteries, including Grange, Co. Roscommon, and Edmondstown, Co. Dublin, that pottery of the Vase Tradition was deposited later than pottery of the Bowl Tradition (Waddell, 1976). A similar sequence occurred at Fourknocks I, Co. Meath: the mound of a passage tomb, with an added secondary mantle of clay, contained eight Bronze Age burials; in one instance, an inverted vase urn burial had disturbed a cist containing an unburnt burial and a bowl (Hartnett, 1957). On the south-east of the Lyles Hill, Co. Antrim, cairn, an encrusted urn burial had disturbed a cremation accompanied by a bowl (Evans, 1953). The disturbance of an earlier burial by a later one is recorded in other cemetery mounds too; perhaps not surprisingly, it has rarely been noted in flat cemeteries but then it is true that the great majority of these have been examined under rescue conditions or in a piecemeal fashion — the fourteen graves of the Keenoge, Co. Meath, flat cemetery, for example (briefly described in Waddell, 1970, 127), were discovered in the course of digging for sand in an esker over a seven-year period. A succession of burials has been recorded at Baunogenasraid, Co. Carlow, where a cremation overlay and disturbed an unburnt, possibly crouched, burial (B. Raftery, 1974). At Poulawack, Co. Clare, Hencken and Movius (1935) believed four cists to be contemporary, they being incorporated in the cairn during its construction; these cists, in which one burial was a cremation and the others unburnt, were earlier than three other cists, one containing a cremation, the others unburnt bones, which had been inserted into the cairn itself. Finally, at Knockast, Co. Westmeath, two, possibly three, burials disturbed others, and it was suggested that this mound may have served several succeeding generations (Hencken and Movius, 1934).

A pattern of successive individual burials would be quite in keeping with the belief that these various cemeteries belonged to the one family group, to an extended family, or to one small community. Too few studies have been made of the limited skeletal material to allow fruitful discussion of this point. In the Poulawack cairn, the ratio of five males to four females, with ten individuals of indeterminate sex all below fourteen years of age, was thought to be 'fairly normal' by Movius (Hencken and Movius, 1935, 222). However, a surprisingly large number of young adults, from twenty-one to thirty-five years of age, were buried at Knockast, and at Fourknocks I, of eight Bronze Age graves, no less than four contained the remains of children, the identifiable bones representing five childen and three adults. More often than not, the remains of children appear to be under-represented, as in Britain (Petersen, 1972), and their corpses may often have been more casually disposed of. Finally, it is worth recalling that Movius, in his examination of the Knockast bones, considered the cremated remains to be of a physical type different to the few unburnt individuals (Hencken and Movius, 1934, 283). Thus it seems possible that social and other factors may, on occasion, have dictated who was to be given formal burial and not all members of a particular family or community may

have been entitled to this privilege. Nevertheless, the archaeological evidence indicates that the assumption that some of these cemeteries reflect a measure of social
or cultural continuity is not unreasonable. On rare occasions cemeteries contain
pottery of just the one tradition; the Corrower cemetery mound and, possibly, the
small flat cemetery of three crouched skeletons — one accompanied by a bowl — in
Halverstown townland, Co. Kildare (Raftery, 1940), can be attributed to the Bowl
Tradition. The small flat cemetery in Clonshannon, Co. Wicklow (Mahr and Price,
1932) and, probably, Letterkeen, Co. Mayo (S.P. Ó Ríordáin and MacDermott,
1952), for example, can be assigned to the Vase Tradition. Cemeteries such as these
appear to support the individuality of these traditions but, as is well known, the
great majority of cemeteries with pottery have produced a mixture of types, most
commonly (in about 66% of cases) a mixture of vessels of just the Bowl and Vase
Traditions. If one accepts my claim (Waddell, 1976) that these, the two major
ceramic traditions of the Irish early Bronze Age, are related in so far as they each
seem to have broadly similar, if differently proportioned, mixed origins, and since
the Vase Tradition apparently superseded the Bowl Tradition, then even such a
diverse range of pottery types as bowl, vase, vase urn and encrusted urn, may still
be indicative of essential continuity.

It would be wrong to imagine, however, that funerary continuity necessarily implies the regular use of a cemetery for individual burials in a continuous sequence
from generation to generation. The evidence from sites such as Moneen and
Poulawack implies that several cist graves may have been constructed at one and
the same time. As in Britain (Petersen, 1972), mounds such as these may have been
built or remodelled in several stages, with one or more burials coinciding with
various events in the history of the monument. The occurrence of disarticulated
burials (as in cist no. 4 at Moneen) suggests the possibility that some bodies were
temporarily buried or stored elsewhere, or even ceremonially exposed, before being
accorded final burial. Interesting evidence for the practice of exposure to the
elements comes from a beaker burial at Bredon Hill, Worcestershire (Thomas,
1967) where a barrow covered a rock-cut grave which, along with two beakers, contained the skeleton of an adult male and to which the body of an adult female had
been added later. Inside the female skull were found the shells of a carnivorous
species of snail *Oxychilus* (which could not live for long in anaerobic conditions)
and the regurgitated food pellet of a bird of prey, perhaps a kite or a buzzard. It
seemed that the female corpse had possibly been partly dismembered and then exposed for sufficiently long to allow snails and birds of prey to be attracted to it.

The question whether or not these cemeteries were used for successive burial by
the one community or family group is an important one. If this was invariably the
case, the numerically small size of so many examples suggests they could only have
served, at most, a fraction of one or two generations. Perhaps after two or three
burials some groups sought a new site in the general locality or even further afield.
Another intriguing possibility is, of course, that we are wrong to name all these

sites 'cemeteries' and equally wrong to expect always to find evidence of successive communal use therein. It is possible that, unlike the cemeteries of today, that some of these prehistoric sites were not solely or even primarily funerary. The variety of pottery types, particularly in some of the smaller cemeteries, is quite puzzling. True, pottery of both the Bowl and Vase Traditions may indicate a general cultural unity but what is the significance of the occurrence of pottery of the Collared Urn and Cordoned Urn Traditions? The Harristown, Co. Waterford, cemetery (Hawkes, 1941), for example, yielded a bowl and three cordoned urns and a small flat cemetery in Ballymacaldrack, Co. Antrim (Tomb and Davies, 1938; 1941) contained five graves and the pottery comprised a vase, a vase urn and three collared urns. It is conceivable that sites such as these were intended more to serve the living than the dead; if the various burials are coeval, could it be that different communities with different pottery and burial traditions contributed just one or two burials and pottery vessels in one or more communal ceremonies with some magico-religious, social or political significance? Some such purpose, to placate the other world, to strengthen relationships between communities, or to demarcate territories, would explain not merely the relatively small number of burials but also their variety. In short, it seems possible that the range of sites which we choose to call cemeteries may, in fact, have had diverse roles in Bronze Age society.

As already mentioned, the excavation of Moneen revealed that the cairn had been built within a Neolithic ring ditch which enclosed an area just over 15 m. in diameter containing pits with fragments of Neolithic pottery, stake-holes, charcoal spreads, a burnt area and part of a human skull. Clearly this monument was of considerable importance to the later practitioners of funerary rites on the site. Several areas of burnt earth, and pits containing charcoal and animal bones, were also found beneath the Knockast cairn, as well as some sherds of Neolithic pottery from on, or very close to, the pre-barrow surface (Hencken and Movius, 1934, 247, 253 and section D-C). Ritual sites such as these are surely related to Neolithic Goodland type sites such as Goodland itself and Langford Lodge, Co. Antrim (Waterman, 1963) where, Case (1973) suggests, practices took place which included the deposition of settlement debris in pits as part of sympathetic magic rituals. Goodland sites occur beneath the cemetery mounds at Dun Ruadh, Co. Tyrone, and Lyles Hill, Co. Antrim (Case, 1969, 15).

Other Neolithic monuments have also been reused as Bronze Age cemeteries. At several sites a Neolithic mound had been enlarged to contain the later burials. This was so at the Fourknocks I passage tomb mentioned above and at the Mound of the Hostages, Tara (De Valera, 1965). Seven secondary graves were found in a passage tomb mound in Harristown, Co. Waterford (Hawkes, 1941) but it is uncertain whether or not the primary mound was enlarged to protect some of these burials. This may have been the case, however, at Aghnaskeagh (Cairn A), Co. Louth, where six secondary cists were found in cairn material to the west and south-west of a portal tomb (Evans, 1935). The mound of the Linkardstown type grave

Baunogenasraid, Co. Carlow, was considerably enlarged to contain at least ten secondary burials, one accompanied by a bowl (B. Raftery, 1974). A similar sequence of events was revealed at Drimnagh, Co. Dublin (Kilbride-Jones, 1939). The central grave in the Poulawack cairn is similar in several respects to Linkardstown type graves (Ryan, 1972, 1973) and here, as perhaps in the small cemetery mound in the Phoenix Park, Dublin (Wilde, 1857, 180), a Neolithic grave may have formed the focus for the later cemetery. Other Neolithic monuments with later, Bronze Age, cemeteries include Fourknocks II, Co. Meath (Hartnett, 1971) and the Kilmashogue wedge tomb in Co. Dublin (Kilbride-Jones, 1954).

These instances of the deliberate re-use of Neolithic sites, both Goodland sites and burial mounds, clearly indicate a little more than just a desire to use a convenient ready-made tumulus. It is true that there are striking differences in the apparent purpose of a Goodland site and of the grave and pottery of a Linkardstown type burial on the one hand, and the grave types and pottery types of the cemeteries on the other. Furthermore, at Baunogenasraid, for example, the Bronze Age bowl differed not just in form and ornament but also in fabric and grit from the late Neolithic vessel and the difference suggests entirely different pottery traditions (B. Raftery, 1974, 311). ApSimon (1969, 57) thought there was little continuity between the tomb builders and the later users of the site at the Mound of the Hostages because of the apparently ruthless disturbance of the original burials in the passage tomb. It is also a puzzling fact that, at the moment, no flat cemetery has yielded evidence of Neolithic activity (and flat cemeteries do not appear to differ greatly from cemetery mounds in either variety of burial rite or pottery type). Caution is obviously necessary in considering claims for either continuity or discontinuity, particularly in the absence of an absolute chronology. However, having briefly reviewed the evidence from a dozen cemetery mounds, all examined in the last half century, and remembering in particular, the discovery of the arc of ditch at Moneen and the ritual continuity it implies, the possibility of some cultural continuity must be admitted. The future excavation of Bronze Age cemeteries will no doubt help to determine more precisely the nature of this continuum and the degree of influence of various Neolithic traditions on the innovations in pottery and burial rite which are such a conspicuous feature of the second millennium B.C. These innovations may obscure a fundamental continuity of tradition briefly glimpsed at sites such as Moneen. Clearly these cemeteries and those Bronze Age members of what Francis Thompson has called 'the antique order of the dead' deserve our most careful study. Considerable progress has been made in this century and, no longer, I hope, would the plunderers of a prehistoric grave be encouraged (as by one 18th century west of Ireland landowner) with the observation that 'the person buried there was not a Christian, but a heathen, which being d--d, it was no sin to dig up his bones' (Wilde, 1871, 150). In the past a great deal of valuable archaeological information has been irretrievably lost but, as the excavation of Moneen demonstrates, our remaining Bronze Age cemeteries will amply repay careful scrutiny.

ACKNOWLEDGEMENT

I am very grateful to Dr K.T. Hoppen, The University of Hull, for kindly providing me with details of Mullen's communication to the Dublin Philosophical Society.

REFERENCES

ApSimon, A., 1969. 'The Earlier Bronze Age in the north of Ireland', *Ulster J Archaeol ser 3* **32**, 28-72.

Case, H., 1969. 'Settlement-patterns in the north Irish Neolithic', *Ulster J Archaeol ser 3* **32**, 3-27.

Case, H., 1973. 'A ritual site in north-east Ireland'. *In* G. Daniel and P. Kjaerum (ed), *Megalithic Graves and Ritual. Papers presented at the III Atlantic Colloquium, Moesgard 1969*. Jutland Archaeol Soc Publ XI, 173-96.

De Valera, R., 1965. 'Excavation of the Mound of the Hostages', Supplementary note appended to Ó Ríordáin, S.P., *Tara, the Monuments on the Hill*, 26-7. Dundalk.

Evans, E.E., 1935. 'Excavations at Aghnaskeagh, Co. Lough, Cairn A', *Co Louth Archaeol J* **8**, 234-55.

Evans, E.E., 1953. *Lyles Hill: A Late Neolithic Site in County Antrim*. Belfast.

Flanagan, L.N.W., 1976. 'The composition of Irish Bronze Age cemeteries', *Ir Archaeol Res Forum* **3**, 7-20.

Hartnett, P.J., 1957. 'Excavation of a passage grave at Fourknocks, County Meath', *Proc Roy Ir Acad C* **58**, 197-277.

Hartnett, P.J., 1971. 'The excavation of two tumuli at Fourknocks (Sites II and III), Co. Meath', *Proc Roy Ir Acad C* **71**, 35-89.

Hawkes, J., 1941. 'Excavation of a megalithic tomb at Harristown, Co. Waterford', *J Roy Soc Antiq Ir* **71**, 130-47.

Hencken, H. and Movius, H., 1934. 'The cemetery cairn of Knockast', *Proc Roy Ir Acad C* **41**, 232-84.

Hencken, H. and Movius, H., 1935. 'A cairn at Poulawack, Count Clare', *J Roy Soc Antiq Ir* **65**, 191-222.

Hoppen, K.T., 1970. *The Common Scientist in the Seventeenth Century. A Study of the Dublin Philosophical Society 1683-1708*. London.

Kilbride-Jones, H.E., 1939. 'The excavation of a composite tumulus at Drimnagh, Co. Dublin', *J Roy Soc Antiq Ir* **69**, 190-220.

Kilbride-Jones, H.E., 1954. 'The excavation of an unrecorded megalithic tomb on Kilmashogue Mountain, Co. Dublin', *Proc Roy Ir Acad C* **56**, 461-79.

Mahr, A. and Price, L., 1932.'Excavation of urn burials at Clonshannon, Imaal, Co. Wicklow', *J Roy Soc Antiq Ir* **62**, 75-90.

O'Kelly, M.J., 1952. 'Excavation of a cairn at Moneen, Co. Cork', *Proc Roy Ir Acad C* **54**, 121-59.

Ó Ríordáin, S.P., 1940. 'Excavations at Cush, Co. Limerick', *Proc Roy Ir Acad C* **45**, 83-181.

Ó Ríordáin, S.P. and MacDermott, M., 1952. 'The excavation of a ringfort at Letterkeen, Co. Mayo', *Proc Roy Ir Acad C* **54**, 89-119.

Peterson, F., 1972. 'Traditions of multiple burial in Later Neolithic and Early Bronze Age England', *Archaeol J* **129**, 22-55.

Raftery, B., 1974. 'A prehistoric burial mound at Baunogenasraid, Co. Carlow', *Proc Roy Ir Acad C* **74**, 277-312.

Raftery, J., 1940. 'Bronze Age burials at Halverstown, Co. Kildare', *J Roy Soc Antiq Ir* **70**, 57-61.

Raftery, J., 1960. 'A Bronze Age tumulus at Corrower, Co. Mayo', *Proc Roy Irish Acad C* **61**, 79-93.

Ryan, M., 1972. 'Some burial monuments of the Later Neolithic', *Carloviana* **21**, 18-21.

Ryan, M., 1973. 'The excavation of a Neolithic burial mound at Jerpoint West, Co. Kilkenny', *Proc Roy Ir Acad C* **73**, 107-27.

Thomas, N., 1967. 'A double Beaker burial on Bredon Hill, Worcs.', *Trans Birmingham Archaeol Soc* **82**, 58-76.

Tomb, J.J. and Davies, O., 1938. 'Urns from Ballymacaldrack', *Ulster J Archaeol ser 3* **1**, 219-21.

Tomb, J.J. and Davies, O., 1941. 'Further urns from Ballymacaldrack', *Ulster J Archaeol ser 3* **4**, 63-6.

Waddell, J., 1970. 'Irish Bronze Age cists: a survey', *J Roy Soc Antiq Ir* **100**, 91-139.

Waddell, J., 1976. 'Cultural interaction in the Insular Early Bronze Age: some ceramic evidence'. *In* S.J. De Laet (ed), *Acculturation and Continuity in Atlantic Europe . . . Papers presented at the IV Atlantic Colloquium, Ghent 1975*. Dissertationes Archaeologicae Gandensis XVI, 284-95.

Waterman, D., 1963. 'A Neolithic and Dark Age site at Langford Lodge, Co. Antrim', *Ulster J Archaeol ser 3* **26**, 43-54.

Wilde, W.R., 1857. *A Descriptive Catalogue of the Antiquities of Stone, Earthen and Vegetable Materials in the Museum of the Royal Irish Academy*. Dublin.

Wilde, W.R., 1871. 'Memoir of Gabriel Beranger, and his Labours in the Cause of Irish Art, Literature, and Antiquities from 1760 to 1780', *J Roy Soc Antiq Ir* **11**, 121-52.

Iron Age Burials in Ireland

Barry Raftery

INTRODUCTION

Discussion of the origins of Iron Age influences in Ireland has, up to comparatively recently, concentrated largely on the surviving metalwork of the period and, overwhelmingly, the argument has been dominated by considerations of typology and style. Using this evidence, population movements into the country of various forms and of various orders of magnitude have been postulated; but, at the same time, the concept of basic ethnic stability within the country has derived support from the essentially indigenous nature of the majority of native metal artifacts.

The issue has been vigorously debated and such is the inadequacy and the ambiguity of the artifactual evidence that totally opposing views have quite legitimately been held. The question of the mechanics of cultural change has always been an issue in a consideration of Irish prehistory, but in the last millennium B.C. — a period of major cultural, economic and social change, when those forces which we refer to as 'Celtic' were beginning to take their distinctive form — the question of the mechanics of change becomes especially critical.

The burial record of the Irish Iron Age has scarcely entered the debate. This is not, perhaps, surprising for relevant sites are few and dating evidence is frequently distressingly vague. In the writer's view, however, it seems that the funerary evidence, limited though it still is, is not unimportant in a consideration of cultural developments in late prehistoric Ireland, so that it seems worthwhile to offer here a brief, summary outline of the burial practices of Iron Age Ireland.

LATER BRONZE AGE BURIALS IN IRELAND

Our understanding of the role of Iron Age burial customs in the context of the change from a Bronze Age to an Iron Age society in Ireland is complicated by our basic ignorance of the nature of the burial rites practised during the later Bronze Age. Thus, since we have so little knowledge of how the dead were disposed of during this period, we are scarcely in a position to determine with any degree of certainty the extent to which the burial traditions evident during the Iron Age reflect either innovation or continuity from earlier times.

The matter is not entirely hopeless, however, since there are now several burial sites from Ireland for which a date within the later Bronze Age can be suggested. Of these, perhaps the most important is the burial complex recently uncovered by

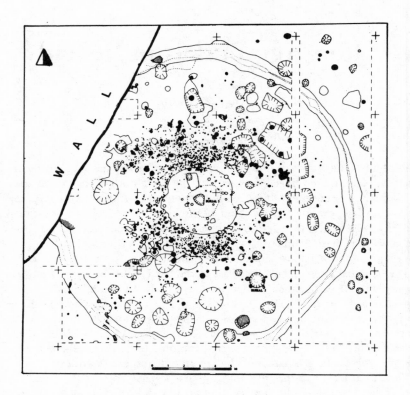

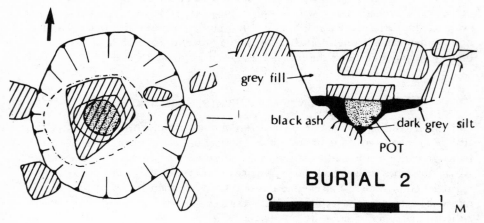

grey fill

black ash   dark grey silt

POT

BURIAL 2

0   1
                                        M

Fig 30: Rathgall, Co. Wicklow. Late Bronze Age burial complex. Detail of burial 2
(Scale: 35 cm in all figures).

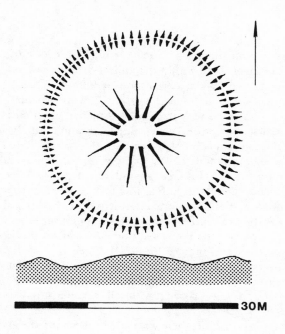

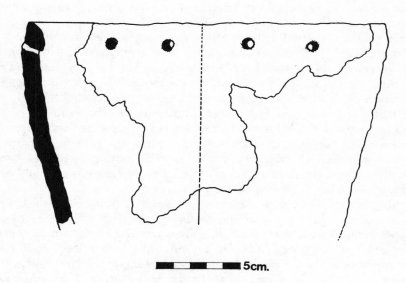

Fig 31: Mullaghmore, Co. Down. Ringbarrow and examples of coarse vessel with rim perforations.

the present writer during the excavation of a hillfort at Rathgall, Co. Wicklow (Raftery, B., 1973). Here, both within the hillfort defences and on the slopes outside, extensive areas of settlement were uncovered dating broadly to the first half of the last millennium B.C. Associated with this activity was the funerary monument (fig 30). This consisted of a shallow, V-sectioned ditch enclosing a circular area some 16m in diameter, within which three cremation burials were found. An unaccompanied deposit had been placed in a small, central, stone-lined pit which was excavated through soil reddened by fire, possibly of the funeral pyre. A large number of stake-holes were clustered around this deposit. A second cremation comprised the remains of a child, buried in a matrix of black, sooty material in a small pit to the north-east of the central interment. The third burial within the circular enclosure was the most interesting. In this instance the ashes of the deceased were contained in a coarse, flat-bottomed pottery vessel which stood upright in a carefully dug, funnel-shaped pit (fig 30; Pl XI). Black sooty material, mixed with tiny flecks of burnt bone, was packed tightly around the urn. A flat slab was placed directly upon the rim of the vessel and this slab was covered by a second, somewhat larger, stone which in turn was covered with soil. The burnt remains were those of an adult and child.

As well as the three burial pits there were other pits within the enclosure. One of these contained a fragment of the blade of a leaf-shaped sword of bronze, an incomplete socketed bronze spearhead and a chisel or graving tool of metal, possibly but not certainly of bronze. At all levels of the enclosing ditch coarse potsherds were found and from it also came two beads of amber.

The burial site at Rathgall calls strongly to mind ringbarrow A at Mullaghmore, Co. Down (Mogey, 1949; Mogey *et al.*, 1956). The monument was some 30 m in overall diameter and comprised a low circular mound with enclosing fosse and external bank (fig 31). Centrally placed within the mound was a cremation deposit accompanied by sherds of coarse pottery and a single blue glass bead. The bones represented those of at least four people. Immediately to the south-east of the mound and within a roughly rectangular setting of four standing stones, a second cremation was encountered; this was contained within an upright pot, the fabric of which was identical with that of the pottery from the central burial. The bones within the urn were those of an adult male and the burnt remains of a child were found scattered in the immediate vicinity of the urn.

The date of these Mullaghmore burials has never been firmly established. Tentative suggestions of a date in the centuries around the birth of Christ have been put forward on the basis of the bead allegedly associated with the central deposit (Mogey, *et al.*, 1956, 19; Jope, 1960, 40) but the bead is neither closely datable nor is it even positively linked with the burial (Mogey, *et al.*, 1956). The possibility of an earlier date for the Co. Down burial monument, within the Bronze Age, was however put forward by Ó Ríordáin (1954, 357).

The association of coarse pottery with cremation and in particular the use of a pot in an upright position as a container for the ashes, is an important factor linking Rathgall and Mullaghmore. At both sites pottery of closely similar type was found and the presence at both of rims with pin-prick perforations (fig 31) — a detail by no means widespread amongst the so called 'flat-rimmed' wares of later prehistoric Ireland — strengthens further the notion of cultural and chronological overlap between the two burial monuments. It may be, therefore, that the interments at Mullaghmore belong to the earlier rather than the later part of the last millennium B.C.

The only other Irish burial site for which a date in the later Bronze Age is possible is that at Lugg, Co. Dublin (Kilbride-Jones, 1950). This enigmatic site consisted of a circular bank-and-ditch enclosure of ringfort type (though lacking, it seems, any obvious entrance gap) within which there were numerous postholes, an area of habitation and a low central mound which covered two cremation burials in pits. A considerable quantity of coarse pottery, apparently representing bucket-shaped containers, came to light, but their association with the various structural remains on the site is not clear. Some sherds were found in the mound 'near the burials' but not, it seems, directly linked with them.

On the basis of the pottery the excavator placed Lugg unhesitatingly in the 'Early Iron Age' but on such evidence chronological precision is not, in fact, possible. A date in the later Bronze Age could equally be argued for the Co. Dublin monument but the presence of thumb-nail scrapers and a leaf-shaped arrowhead of flint along with a polished stone axe-head (Kilbride-Jones, 1950, 327) may point to the existence at Lugg of a far earlier chronological horizon to which the burials may belong.

Our knowledge of burial customs in immediately pre-Iron Age Ireland is thus limited. As far as we can say at the moment, cremation alone was practised. The remains were placed simply in pits or contained within coarse pots placed upright. The concept of an enclosing ditch and of ring barrow construction (if Mullaghmore is accepted as early) was in existence.

But what of the thousands of later Bronze Age burials which must have taken place over the centuries and of which we have no knowledge? It may be that these still await discovery but this is unlikely. A more plausible suggestion is that the dead were widely disposed of in a manner which left no trace in the archaeological record, such as exposing the corpse on an open air scaffold or dispersing of the ashes of the dead in rivers or lakes. A simpler solution is that the dead were cremated and interred without gravegoods in pits, thus rendering them, under normal circumstances, archaeologically undatable.

IRON AGE BURIALS IN IRELAND

Iron Age burials in Ireland may be described under two broad headings, those

(after Macalister, 1916–17. No scale given. Overall D 15.30M)

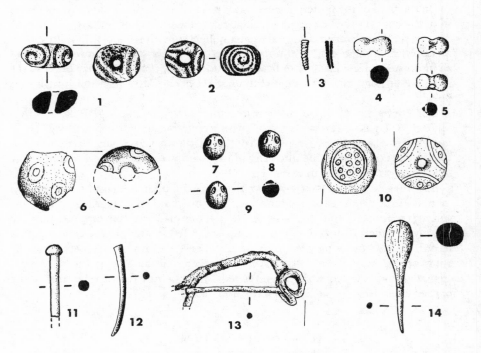

Fig 32: Grannagh, Co. Galway. Ringbarrow and selection of finds. 1-4, 6, 10 — glass; 5, 7-9, 11, 12, 14 — bone; 13 — bronze. Scale 1/1.

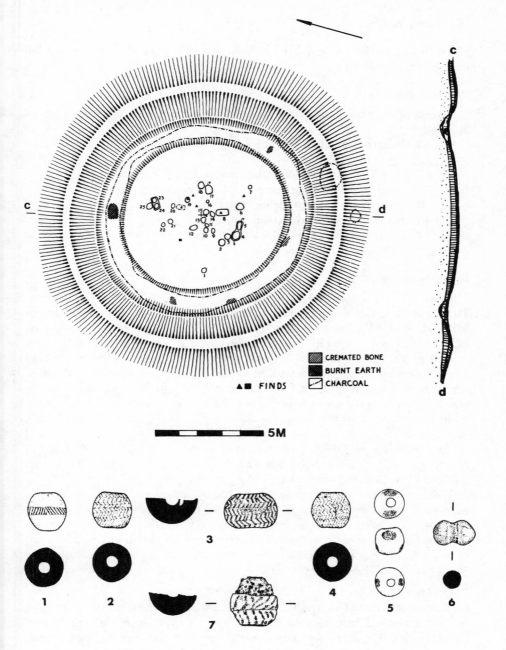

CREMATED BONE
BURNT EARTH
CHARCOAL

▲■ FINDS

5M

Fig 33: Carrowjames, Co. Mayo. Ringbarrow and selection of finds.
1-5 — glass; 6 — bone. Scale 1/1.

which are likely to be native and those which are clearly intrusive. The majority fall into the first category.

NATIVE BURIALS

For ease of description the native Irish burials are divided into four main groups as follows:
  I. Burials primarily associated with an earthen monument
     (a) Ringbarrow
     (b) Simple mounds with or without enclosing ditch
     (c) Embanked enclosures without any covering mound
  II. Secondary burials in earlier burial mounds
  III. Simple unprotected cremations in pits
  IV. Inhumations, protected or unprotected, deposited either singly or grouped in cemeteries

Ia. RINGBARROWS

1. Grannagh, Co. Galway (fig 32).

The site consisted of a circular mound of earth enclosed by a fosse with external bank. The overall diameter was some 15.30m. The central mound was just over 5m in diameter and 61 cm high. It was described by Macalister as of earth with a core of stones. Macalister's early investigations were confined to the central mound where no formal burials were found. However, the cremated remains of three individuals were found under the surface of the soil 'strewn in handfuls on the ground'. The bones of an ox were found deeper in the mound and almost at the bottom were fragments of two rather colourless glass beads and the upper portion of a small bone pin.

More recently (1969) the Grannagh monument was re-excavated by Professor E. Rynne, University College, Galway. The results of the excavation are not yet published but Professor Rynne has kindly given the writer permission to refer to the site in advance of the definitive report. The latest work at Grannagh revealed a number of cremation deposits in the fosse and this excavation produced an interesting range of artifacts, some associated with burials, some not. Included amongst the finds were three fragmentary bronze fibulae, beads of glass and bone, bone pins and some miscellaneous objects of iron.

Macalister, 1916-17.

2. Oranbeg, Co. Galway.

Ringbarrow similar to Grannagh and situated a short distance from it. During the as yet unpublished excavation by Professor Rynne (to whom thanks are extended for permission to refer to the site) a number of cremation deposits were found. Gravegoods included beads of glass and bone (fig 30) as well as a number of miscellaneous objects of bronze.

3. Carrowjames, Co. Mayo (fig 33).
A total of ten burial mounds originally existed in an area of low lying, now somewhat marshy, land. They covered an area roughly 180m by 110m and were dispersed in two groups, one of three mounds (Carrowjames I) the other (Carrowjames II) including the remaining seven. The two groups were about 90m apart.

Tumuli 1 to 7 were of Early/Middle Bronze Age date and the date of Tumulus 9 was uncertain. Tumulus 8, however, was of certain Iron Age construction. It was the largest monument in the cemetery and consisted of a circular mound with enclosing fosse and external bank. Its overall diameter was 15.50m. The mound was 7.30m in diameter and 21 cm high. There were 25 burials in this tumulus. Each comprised a simple cremation in a pit. Nine of the 25 contained gravegoods. These included beads of glass and bone as well as some miscellaneous objects of bronze.

Raftery, J., 1938-9; 1940-1.

Ib. **SIMPLE MOUNDS, WITH OR WITHOUT ENCLOSING FOSSE**

4. Carbury Hill, Co. Kildare, Site C (fig 34).
The highest of three hilltop monuments. It consisted of a circular mound of earth some 8.23m in diameter and 91 cm high. There was no fosse. A single cremation deposit was found east of centre under the mound in a hollow in the bedrock. There were no gravegoods.

Willmot, 1938.

5. Cush, Co. Limerick (fig 35).
Three circular mounds of earth were located close together in the immediate vicinity of an interesting complex of ringforts and related field boundaries. Tumulus I was of Early/Middle Bronze Age date and differed in form and construction from Tumuli II and III which were probably of Iron Age date. Each was about 2m high and consisted of a circular mound with enclosing fosse. The diameter of Tumulus II was 13.70m, that of Tumulus III was 16.46m. On the old ground level under the mound of Tumulus II a circular area of charcoal mixed with fragments of human bone was encountered. This was interpreted as the site of the funeral pyre. At the centre of this layer was a small pit containing cremated human bones and an ornamented bone plaque which had been cracked and warped by heat. Under the mound of Tumulus III an area of bones and charcoal similar to that just described was found together with the remains of a cremation burial. Recent disturbance had, it seems, disturbed the burial deposit.

Ó Ríordáin, 1930, 133-9, 154-6.

6. Dunadry, Co. Antrim.
This was a burial mound destroyed in the last century. A brief and unsatisfactory

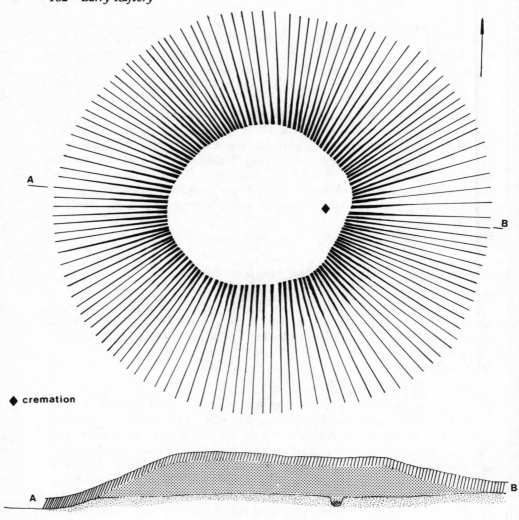

◆ cremation

Fig 34: Carbury Hill, Co. Kildare, Site A.

account of the site describes the tumulus as 'exceedingly large'. It seems that an extended inhumation in a cist may have existed in the mound. This appears to have
been accompanied by the two fragmentary bracelets of glass and jet which are
preserved in the National Museum. A 'stone urn' said to have handles and a 'brass

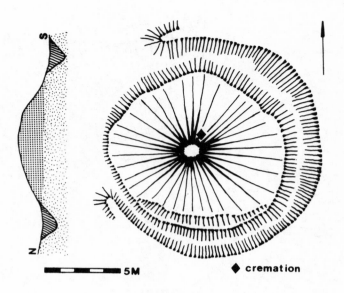

Fig 35: Cush, Co. Limerick. Tumulus and bone plaque. Scale 1/1.

top' is also referred to as well as a glass urn, but this last is considered by Macalister to be a mistaken reference to the glass ring. The ring of lignite is stated to have been on the head. No trace of the 'urn' or the 'glass vessel' survives.
Macalister, 1928, 202-3.

7. Seskin, Co. Kilkenny.
Like Dunadry, this site was destroyed in the last century without adequate scientific record. It appears to have been a tumulus slightly over 9m in diameter and 1.50m to 1.80m high. When the mound was being reduced to the level of the surrounding land a heap of irregularly placed stones was found within it. Under the stones there were two bronze pins and an iron shears. No human bones were recognised though 'about a dozen bones, said to resemble those of young goats' came to light.

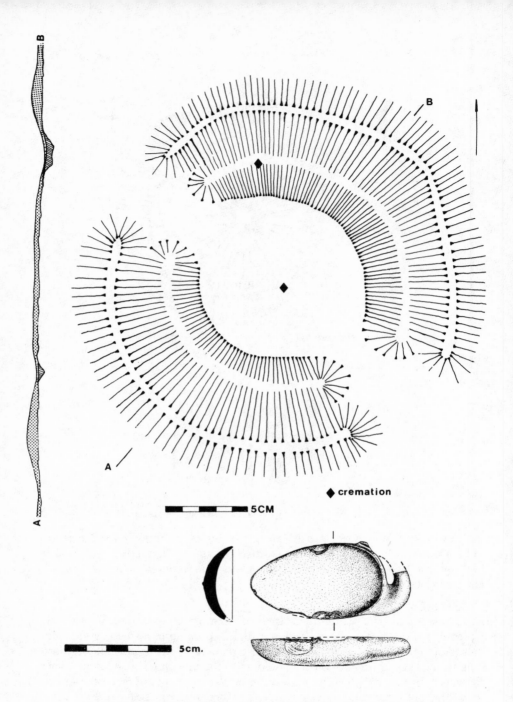

B

B

A

A

◆ cremation

5CM

5cm.

Fig 36: Carbury Hill, Co. Kildare, Site C. Embanked burial site and jet spoon.

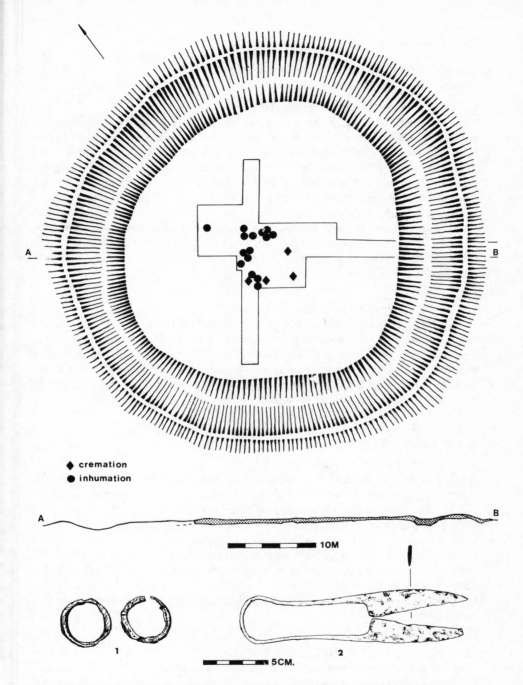

♦ cremation
● inhumation

Fig 37: Carbury Hill, Co. Kildare, Site B. Embanked burial site and finds (both iron).

The whereabouts of the finds are now unknown.
Graves, 1849, 32; Macalister, 1928, 203.

8. Pollacorragune, Co. Galway, Mound II.
The monument was situated on a glacial ridge some 210m south-east of an earlier burial monument, Mound I (see below, no 14). It was extremely ill-defined before excavation but appears to have been a low, circular mound about 90 cm high and 7.80m in diameter. The possibility that the 'tumulus' is entirely of natural origin is however suggested in the somewhat unclear sections reproduced in the published account. Apart from a quantity of animal bones (all probably recent) four extended inhumations were uncovered. All observed the same precise orientation (head to the north-west) and all were unprotected. Indeterminate fragments of iron accompanied two of the skeletons. In one instance, the fragments were near the right elbow; in the other example, there were iron fragments close to the head and near the middle of the chest.
Riley, 1936, 45-8.

9. Rath of the Synods, Tara, Co. Meath.
Ó Ríordáin's excavation of this site remains unpublished so that the date of the earthen mound incorporated within the ramparts of the triple banked ringfort is uncertain. The brief note in Ó Ríordáin's guide to Tara states that the mound at the west (of the Rath of the Synods) — a burial mound with skeletal and burnt burials — had three building phases, in the third of which it was brought within the outer bank of the general enclosure'.
Ó Ríordáin, 1971, 26.

Ic. EMBANKED ENCLOSURES WITHOUT COVERING MOUND

10. Carbury Hill, Co. Kildare, Site A (fig 36).
An internally-ditched rampart, breached by entrance gaps and corresponding causeways in the north-west and south-east, formed a circular enclosure 25.90m in overall diameter. The bank averaged 4.80m in width and was 61 cm high. A single, unaccompanied cremation deposit was found in the silt of the ditch. Centrally-placed within the enclosure was a second cremation in a pit. A fused fragment of blue glass came from this. A number of other objects came from the site but their relationship to the primary monument is not stated. These included some worked flints, an unfinished stone spindle whorl, a jet spoon, an iron file, two potsherds of indeterminate type (probably medieval or recent) and the tip of a horn or antler.
Willmot, 1938, 130-5.

11. Carbury Hill, Co. Kildare, Site B (fig 37).
This was similar in construction to Site A and some 183m west of it. The overall diameter of the enclosure was 51m and a single gap in the east may be an original

opening. Within the enclosure four cremations and fifteen inhumations were un-covered. Two of the cremations appear to have been disturbed by inhumations. None of the inhumations was protected by a cist. All were extended, with the head generally to the south-west or west. That the site was used as a cemetery over a period of time was shown by the fact that four of the inhumations were disturbed by other inhumations. One of the cremations contained a pair of iron rings and a pin-shaped fragment of the same metal. An iron shears accompanied one of the in-humations. Scattered finds from the site included flint flakes, a circular stone disc, a medieval potsherd and a corroded knob-ended fragment of bronze. Willmot, 1938, 135-140.

The possibility that Carbury Hill Site A dates within the Iron Age has given rise to the suggestion that a similar, double-entranced enclosure at the Curragh, Co. Kildare (Site 4) might also be so dated (Ó Ríordáin, 1950; fig 38). At this site a central inhumation, so positioned as to suggest the possibility of burial alive, seem-ed to indicate ritual rather than primarily sepulchral intent. A bronze spiral finger ring uncertainly stratified there leaves the possibility of Iron Age dating open but clearly a date far earlier than this for the Curragh monument (and indeed Carbury Hill Site A) is equally likely.

II. SECONDARY BURIALS IN EARLIER BURIAL MOUNDS

12. Kiltierney, Co. Fermanagh.
Here there was a circular mound *c.* 19.50m in diameter and 2.10m high surround-ed at some distance by a bank with internal fosse. Some stones, apparently associated with the mound, bear cup marks and traces of Passage-Grave-type orna-ment. A number of secondary cremation deposits in pits was uncovered during the recent (1969), as yet unpublished, excavation of the site. The writer is indebted to L.N.W. Flanagan, Keeper of Antiquities, Ulster Museum, Belfast, for permission to include Kiltierney in the present work. A bronze safety-pin brooch and four glass beads came from the site (fig 39) though not all, it seems, from the same burial.

13. Carrowbeg North, Co. Galway.
At this site two burial mounds of the Early/Middle Bronze Age occurred and one of these (Tumulus I) had been reused as a burial place during the Iron Age. The primary monument consisted of a hexagonal cairn some 12.50m in diameter sur-rounded by a roughly flat-bottomed ditch. Four secondary inhumations were in-serted into the fill of the ditch around its northern sector. Three were extended, one partially flexed. Orientation varied from north-west to south-west. There were no cists. The flexed burial (that of a female) was accompanied by twelve bone beads in the area of one ankle and by a bronze, locket-like object (fig 40), which rested in the vicinity of the right shoulder. Traces of woven cloth adhered to the back of this object. Willmot, 1939.

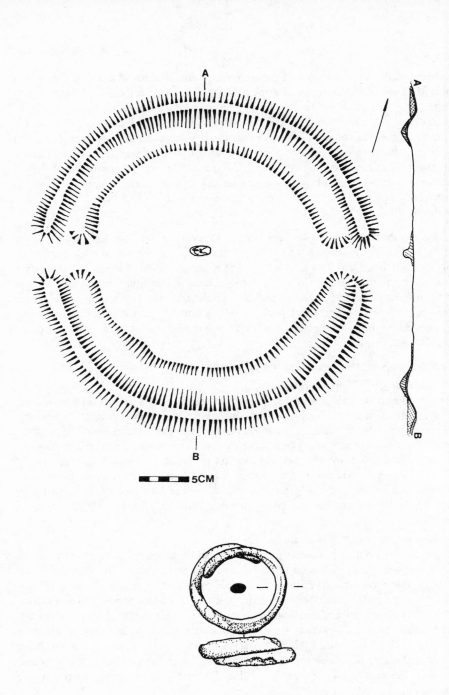

Fig 38: The Curragh, Co. Kildare, Site 4. Embanked burial site and bronze ring. Scale 1/1.

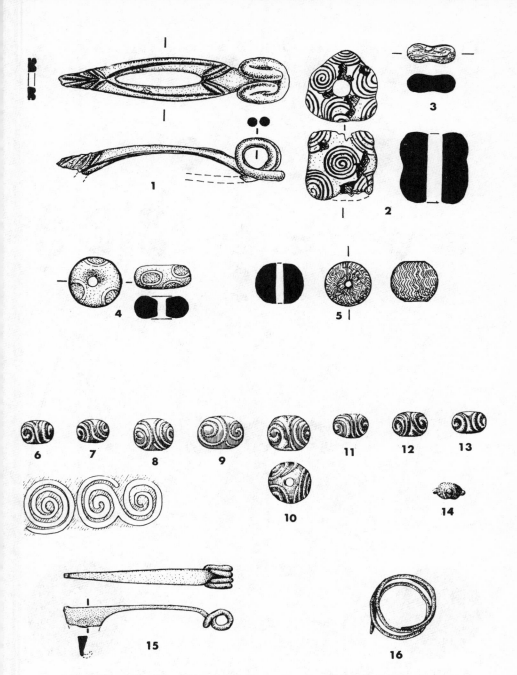

Fig 39: Finds from cremation burials. Nos. 1-5, Kiltierney, Co. Fermanagh. Nos. 6-16, 'Loughey', Co. Down. Nos. 1, 15, 16 — bronze. The rest glass. Scale 1/1. (Bow of no. 15 slightly restored).

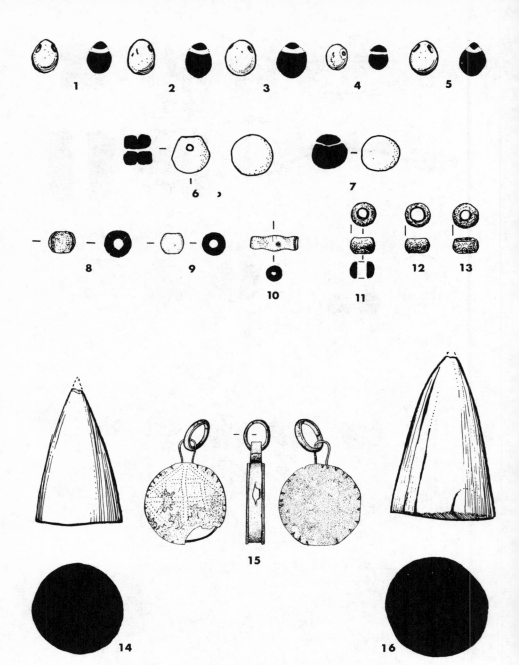

Fig 40: Knowth, Co. Meath — nos. 1-5, 14, 16; Newgrange, Co. Meath — nos. 6, 7; Carrowbeg, Co. Galway, nos. 8-10, 15; Oranbeg, Co. Galway, nos. 11-13. Nos. 1-13 — bone; nos. 14, 16 — stone; no. 15 — bronze. Scale 1/1.

14. Pollacorragune, Co. Galway, Mound I.

This mound, known as Carnfanny, was raised initially during the Early/Middle Bronze Age. It was situated on the summit of a natural rise in an esker ridge and was circular in plan, 7.50m in diameter and about 1.50m high. The primary interment consisted of an inverted cinerary urn covering a cremation and a bronze razor. Near the surface of the mound, just below the sod, animal bone fragments and scatters of charcoal were found and not far from these seven tiny, blue glass beads were recovered. No formal burial associated with the beads was found but it is possible that they had accompanied a destroyed secondary burial.

Riley, 1936, 48 and fig 4.

III. SIMPLE CREMATIONS IN PITS

15. The Long Stone, Cullen, Co. Tipperary.

Recent, as yet unpublished, excavations at this site have revealed a long sequence of prehistoric activity, both sepulchral and habitational, from Neolithic times onwards. A number of simple pits with cremation deposits, several accompanied by bone beads, belong to the latest phase of burial activity here. The excavator suggests the possibility of a date within the Iron Age for them. Information by courtesy of Mr Peter Danaher, Office of Public Works, Dublin.

IV. INHUMATIONS, PROTECTED OR UNPROTECTED, DEPOSITED EITHER SINGLY OR GROUPED IN CEMETERIES

Burials of Type IV are of frequent occurrence throughout Ireland but in most cases clear dating evidence is absent. When gravegoods are not present chronology is essentially a matter for speculation and the possibility of dating within the Early Bronze Age (Waddell, 1970, 94), the Iron Age (Raftery, J., 1941; Rynne, 1974) and the Viking period (Warner, 1976, 288, n. 43a) has variously been put forward. The practice of extended inhumation in long stone cists and often in cemeteries was undoubtedly carried on in the Iron Age but that it was not exclusively confined to this period is now hardly in doubt. Only those burials for which a date within the Iron Age is reasonably probable are included here.

16. Turoe, Co. Galway.

Within the ringfort enclosure a disturbed inhumation, extended and originally in a long stone cist, was discovered. The skeleton was orientated with the skull to the west. The interment was assigned by the excavator to his Period 4, the latest phase of Iron Age activity on the site. An earlier cremation burial from Turoe recorded by Knox cannot be reliably dated.

Raftery, J., 1944, 28-30.

17. Hawk Hill, Co. Kildare.

Twelve skeletons were found in a sandhill from which a glass bead of Late La Tène

type was recovered. It is possible that the bead was associated with one of the burials.
Raftery, B., 1972.

18. Bettystown, Co. Meath.
A number of inhumations, some unprotected, some in pits, have recently (1980) been found together at this site. Position and orientation varied and it seems clear that the cemetery was used over a period of time. One of the inhumations was accompanied by a number of metal objects including two iron penannular brooches. I am indebted to Mr E.P. Kelly, National Museum, for permission to refer to this find.

19, Knowth, Co. Meath.
Excavations in the immediate vicinity of the great Knowth Passage Grave have to date unearthed a total of twenty-seven inhumation burials. Of these twenty-three were unprotected, the remaining four (not yet published, information by courtesy of Professor G. Eogan, University College, Dublin) consisted of extended skeletons in long stone cists. Of the twenty published interments several were in a disturbed and fragmentary state so that their original position could not be determined. The majority of the skeletons were, however, in a flexed position: two appear to have been extended. Four were found in the chamber or passage areas of the smaller 'satellite' tombs. There was little evidence of consistency in the orientation of the bodies though, of the fourteen instances where this feature could be observed, nine had the head to the north-west, west or south-west. One interment was of particular interest. This was the double burial of two adult males who appear to have been decapitated before burial. Eight of the twenty published burials were accompanied by gravegoods. Several of the recently discovered unprotected burials were also accompanied by gravegoods. The material from the graves consisted mainly of glass and bone beads, bronze rings, bone dice and other gaming pieces (fig 40). Eogan, 1968, 365-73; 1974, 68-87.

20. Newgrange, Co. Meath.
Four bone beads and a bone ring are recorded as having been found in a grave at Newgrange (fig 40). It is possible, because of the similarity between some of the Newgrange beads and examples from Knowth and Grannagh, that the alleged grave was of Iron Age date.
Flanagan, 1960, 61-2.

21. Rath of the Synods, Tara, Co. Meath.
Ó Ríordáin notes that within the enclosure formed by the ramparts of the Rath five unburnt bodies were found which had been 'placed there some time before the final desertion of the site'.
Ó Ríordáin, 1971, 26.

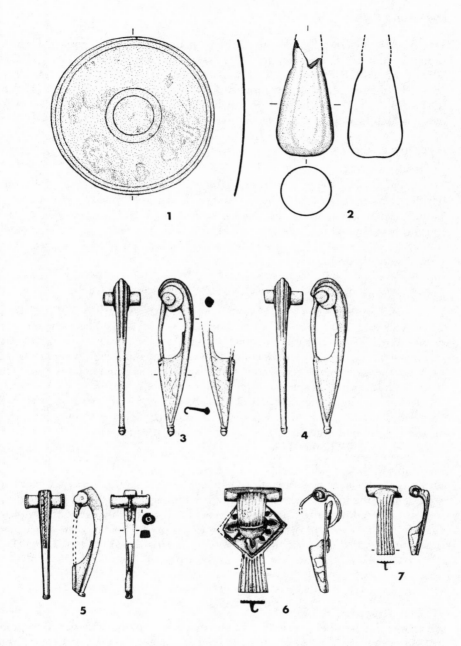

Fig 41: Roman material in Irish graves. Stoneyford, Co. Kilkenny — nos. 1, 2; Lambay, Co. Dublin
— nos. 3-5. No. 2 — glass; the rest bronze. Scale ½.

A date in the immediately pre-Christian period has been suggested for un-protected inhumation cemeteries at Kiltale, Co. Meath, Ballybrickoge, Co. Westmeath and Ballinlough, Co. Laois (Rynne, 1974; 1972-3; 1974-5). The possibility that extended inhumations in long stone cists at Gortcargy, Co. Cavan (Ó Ríordáin, 1967) and Farganstown/Ballymacon, Co. Meath (Kelly, 1979) may date to the Iron Age has also been mooted.

INTRUSIVE BURIALS

22. 'Loughey', Co. Down.
This burial was discovered some time before 1856 and neither the exact find spot nor the precise details of its nature are known. It consisted, in all probability, of a simple cremation deposit in a pit. Associated with the burial were 150 glass beads, finger rings of bronze (fig 39), glass bracelets, a safety pin fibula and other bronzes (fig 39). A number of objects from the grave, including, possibly, a coin, were lost immediately after discovery.
Jope and Wilson, 1957; Jope, 1960, 40.

23. Lambay, Co. Dublin.
An unspecified number of burials was discovered on the western side of the island while work was being carried out on the harbour in 1927. The cemetery was destroyed before scientific examination took place. At least two burials existed, one of a female, the other of a warrior complete with sword and shield. It seems that in each case the burials consisted of crouched inhumations interred in pits which were 'filled with fine sand'. An extensive range of gravegoods, apart from the weapons, was recovered. These included five Roman brooches (fig 41), an iron mirror, a bronze beaded torc, rings, bracelets and numerous fragments of sheet bronze, two of which could be reconstructed to form decorative plaques.
Macalister, 1928-9; Rynne, 1976.

24. Stoneyford, Co. Kilkenny.
This is the only burial of genuinely Roman type from Ireland. Discovered in either 1832 or 1852 the interment is said to have been found 'in a rath and protected by stones. . .' The human remains were cremated and were contained within a glass cinerary urn (now lost). A small glass bottle (cosmetic holder?) and a circular bronze mirror used as a cover for the glass urn, accompanied the burial (fig 41).
   Such details of the burial as exist are preserved in Royal Irish Academy MS 24 E 34.
Ó Ríordáin, 1947, 82; Bateson, 1973, 72-3; Warner, 1976, 274.

25. Bray Head, Co. Wicklow.
An unspecified number of extended inhumations in long stone cists was discovered in 1835 during the levelling of a bank of sand on the north side of Bray Head. The graves are said to have been laid out regularly on an east-west axis. Each skeleton

seems to have been accompanied by one or two Roman coins placed on or beside the breast. The coins have been attributed to Trajan (97-117 A.D.) and Hadrian (117-138 A.D.).

Bateson, 1973, 45 and references; Warner, 1976, 275, 279, 288.

CHRONOLOGY

It is already evident from the preceding brief descriptive list that there are many problems associated with the dating of native Iron Age burials. There are even doubts as to whether some examples tentatively listed here do in fact belong to the period under review. In some cases, however, the surviving gravegoods do give a clue as to the broad dating range of the various types and it is possible to reach a number of general conclusions regarding the dating of Iron Age burials in Ireland. All the objects considered below have been described and discussed at some length by the writer in two forthcoming works[1] so that dating evidence for them is reviewed here in summary form only.

Beads, bracelets and brooches of varying type — those items related to personal adornment — are the objects which occur most frequently in Irish Iron Age burials. The iron shears from Carbury Hill (and Seskin ?) are also likely to have been for personal use. Several burials have also produced objects associated with gaming activities.

The study of glass beads in Ireland is as yet in its infancy and individual specimens are rarely of themselves susceptible of close dating. A number of distinctive types for which a measure of chronological precision is possible do, however, stand out and several of these are recorded from burials. Grannagh, for instance, has produced two beads with inlaid spiral decoration of Guido's so-called 'Mearespiral' family (fig 32:1,2; 1978, 79-81) and her dating for them in the centuries spanning the birth of Christ is given support by the presence of similar beads in the 'Loughey' burial (fig 39:6-13; see below) which also contained a Nauheimer-derivative brooch (fig 39:15) and other material fitting comfortably within these chronological limits. That the type in Ireland might date slightly after rather than slightly before the birth of Christ (*pace* Raleigh Radford, in Bersu, 1977, 63n; 85n) and as, indeed, suggested by Jope and Wilson (1957) is perhaps indicated by the tiny segmented bead of blue glass from Grannagh (fig 32:3) for which a sub-Roman background seems appropriate (Guido, 1978, 91-3, fig 37:1) and by the apparent use of Roman bottle glass in the manufacture of two of the colourless beads from the same site (Guido, 1978, 69, 167). A glass dumb bell bead from Grannagh (fig 32:4) does not conflict with such a chronological context and calls to mind the presence of similar beads from other Irish burials (see below). The existence of glass dumb bell beads at Lough Crew, Co. Meath, where numerous decorated bone flakes of probable first century A.D. date were found (Herity,

1974, 237 and fig 139, 33-5) should also not be forgotten. The fragmentary bronze fibulae from Grannagh (fig 32:13) are essentially, it seems, of late La Tène construction but the significance of this for Ireland in terms of absolute chronology is not certain.

A cautionary note should be sounded with respect to the dating of the Grannagh material, for one of the beads from the site, that with dot-filled circular inlays (fig 32:10) has its closest parallels in examples from an Early La Tène royal burial at Reinheim in Germany (Keller, 1965, Taf. 26a). A comparable date is, however, hardly possible for the Grannagh monument.

The fine fibula from Kiltierney (fig 39.1) is rather more amenable to dating considerations than are the Grannagh fragments. The trumpet curves and the openwork bow of this brooch clearly place it in the same artistic and technical milieu as the native openwork brooches of 'Navan' type. For these a date shortly after the beginning of our era can be argued (Jope, 1961-2, 34-7; Raftery, B., 1982, forthcoming) and the Kiltierney specimen cannot be far removed from them in time. The presence at Kiltierney of a bead of Guido's 'Oldbury' type (fig 39:2; 1978, 53-7) and of a glass dumb bell bead (fig 39:3) does not conflict with the concept of a date for the Co. Fermanagh cremations either shortly before or shortly after the birth of Christ.

A third bead recorded from Kiltierney, that with inlaid bands of herringbone decoration (fig 39:5), is important; for, if it may be taken to be contemporary with the other material from the site, it provides the best clue to the dating of the Carrowjames 8 tumulus where two such beads were found in one of the cremations along with several others of less distinctive form (fig 33:2;4). A dumb bell bead of bone from Carrowjames (fig 33:6; not included in the excavation report) calls to mind a similar bone bead from Lough Crew (Herity, 1974, 237) and links Carrowjames again with Grannagh, Kiltierney and Knowth (information by courtesy of Professor Eogan), all of which produced glass dumb bell beads. None of the other objects from Carrowjames is as yet closely datable.

Excepting the possibility that the Late La Tène ring bead from Hawk Hill, Co. Kildare, was associated with one of the inhumations recorded from the site, there is little else to be said about the remaining beads from the native Irish burials. Tiny blue glass beads from Grannagh, Oranbeg, Knowth and Pollacorragune may suggest some sort of chronological overlap between the burials in question but only future scientific study of these objects can reveal what their cultural or dating significance may be.

In addition to the glass beads, the Knowth inhumation complex produced a number of other objects which may have some bearing on the dating of the burials there. A date for the bone dice from that site in the early centuries A.D. is likely (Clarke, 1970; Carson and O'Kelly, 1977, 51 and Pl VIIa) and the two polished stone cones from another inhumation at Knowth (fig 40:14,16) are closely parallel-ed at two sites in Ireland — Freestone Hill, Co. Kilkenny, and the Rath of the

Synods, Tara, Co. Meath (Raftery, B., 1969, 79-82) — for which a similar early-centuries-A.D. dating may also be postulated.

Grannagh, Knowth and Newgrange are linked by the presence in each of them of sub-pear-shaped bone beads with V-perforations and several other sites (Oranbeg, Carrowbeg North and Cullen) have yielded bone beads with cylindrical perforations (fig 40). It is not yet clear to what extent such simple items may be used as chronological indicators. At Carrowbeg North the beads were accompanied by a bronze 'locket', so far without parallel (fig 40:15). This object, in its form, may reflect influences from late Roman seal-boxes — though it clearly served a function quite different from that of the Roman objects. The simple decoration on the 'locket' is reminiscent of the uninspired, mass-produced ornament found, for instance, on late, provincial Roman bracelets (Raftery, B., 1969, 62-5) and the Carrowbeg North specimen may be contemporary with their period of manufacture.

The existence at Knowth of several objects associated with gaming calls to mind the decorated bone plaque from Cush, Co. Limerick, for which such a function is likely (fig 35). Within Ireland the only comparable bone specimen is a stray find (now in the National Museum) from Mentrim Lough, Co. Meath. Happily, however, compass-drawn decoration present on the Cush specimen is repeated precisely on several of the bone flakes from the Passage Grave at Lough Crew earlier referred to and there can thus be little doubt that the date of these flakes centres on the first Christian century (Raftery, B., 1982, forthcoming).

The finds from Carbury Hill are not closely datable. The association of an iron shears (fig 37:2 with one of the inhumations at Site B is interesting but the custom of placing such objects with burials has a long antiquity in Europe from the Iron Age through the Roman period and into later times. The shears from the site and the iron rings from one of the primary cremations there (fig 37:1) at least establish a post-Bronze Age dating. Sites A and C at Carbury are even more insecurely dated. There was no dating evidence for Site C and no gravegoods are recorded from Site A. The handled jet spoon from the latter monument (fig 36) may, however, be compared to handled silver communion spoons of late Roman Europe (Milojčic, 1968) and the specimen in question may be an Irish version of the type. It could thus date in the second quarter of the first Christian millennium, a date which might have some bearing on the date of construction of the Carbury Hill monument. It must be admitted, however, that such flimsy evidence is a poor base for chronological argument so that the date of Site A (and indeed Site C) is best left open. Notwithstanding the presence of a spiral finger ring of bronze (fig 38) at the Curragh Site 4 (an embanked enclosure closely similar in form to Carbury Hill Site A) the same reservations regarding its date must also be expressed (Ó Ríordáin, 1950b).

Reference has earlier been made to the uncertainty regarding the dating of the long stone cist as a type in Ireland. This form of interment could have been in use over a long period of time here but some of the graves are undoubtedly of Iron Age date. The iron brooches accompanying one of the inhumations recently discovered at Bettystown, Co. Meath, seem to be of a sub-Roman type of the early centuries A.D. and at Turoe, Co. Galway, the long stone cist burial was related to the latest Iron Age phase on the site. Long stone cist burials at Bray Head (see below) can hardly date other than to the second century A.D.

The dating of unprotected, unaccompanied inhumation cemeteries is, if anything, even more uncertain than that of long stone cists. Rynne's suggestion adverted to above that some at least may belong to the very end of the pagan Iron Age is plausible but this remains to be more positively demonstrated.

The four burial sites from Ireland which may be regarded as the likely last resting places of foreigners are more readily placed in their cultural and chronological contexts than is the case with the native burials. The 'Loughey' cremation has been discussed at length by Jope and Wilson (1957) and a south English origin has been convincingly argued for it. A date in the first century A.D. is probable though a somewhat earlier more directly Continental background has been suggested by one commentator (Raleigh Radford, in Bersu, 1977, 63n, 85n).

Even more clearly of English origin are the Lambay interments, though in this instance it is the north rather than the south of England which seems to have been the homeland of the people buried at the Co. Dublin site. A date around or just after the middle of the first Christian century is hardly in doubt for the interments and it may well be, as both Rynne (1976, 242) and Warner (1976, 279) argued, that the presence of north English (Brigantian ?) settlers at Lambay results from the politically troubled times of the later first century in Britain.

Stoneyford is, of course, remarkable, for here, in the south of Ireland, is a classic Roman burial probably of second century date. The Bray Head interments are not so obviously Roman but the presence of early second-century coins accompanying each corpse represents a standard Roman custom. The coins were to pay the fee of Charon, the ferryman of the River Styx, but a point of difference between the Bray burials and the Roman ones proper is that in the latter the coin was usually placed in the mouth of the dead, thus allowing the hands of the traveller to the next world to be free to feed cakes to the two heads of the dog Cerberus, guardian of the underworld (Toynbee, 1971, 44, 49; Wacher, 1978, 245-6).

DISCUSSION

The first point which emerges when burials of recognisably Iron Age date in Ireland are considered as a group — apart from their very scarcity — is that there is no single burial form which may be regarded as diagnostically Iron Age. Ringbarrows with low central mounds may yet emerge as a common Iron Age burial type but such monuments have a long antiquity in this country (Ó Ríordáin and de Valera, 1979, 141-2) so that on superficial examination alone they are undatable.

It is, however, the paucity of burials dating to the pagan Iron Age here which is so striking. It is evident from the foregoing chronological discussion that none of the burials considered can be dated earlier than the first century B.C. and even this date can in most cases be questioned. The majority, if not indeed all, belong after, rather than before the birth of Christ. There are thus no burials in Ireland which can be dated as early as the earliest of the La Tène metalwork. Our failure to recognise in the archaeological record burials contemporary with the earliest Iron Age influences in the country is however of potential importance, for this failure reflects precisely the situation confronting us in the preceding Late Bronze Age. Obviously people died and were buried in the later Bronze Age just as they were in the Early Iron Age. Could it be that those unknown aspects of the burial ritual which prevent us from identifying the standard mode of burial in later Bronze Age Ireland continue without change into the succeeding iron-using phase? May it thus be that the paucity of evidence of burial can be taken as indicating a strong element of cultural continuity throughout the whole of the last millennium B.C.? The scarcity of burials would thus, in a sense, become a 'negative type fossil' of the period.

The meagre burial evidence which we possess does not contradict such a hypothesis. As suggested at the outset of this enquiry, cremation in simple pits (sometimes in containers) was practised in the later Bronze Age (possibly exclusively) and the ringbarrow was probably also in use. As far as we can tell the earliest of the burials of the pagan Iron Age are those associated with ringbarrows and mounds of varying types and the rite practised was exclusively cremation. The relationship of the inhumation to the mound at Dunadry is unknown and there are strong grounds for viewing the Pollacorragune II mound with its four extended inhumations as being of natural, rather than artificial origin. A distinction seems thus to emerge between the cremations and the inhumations of Iron Age Ireland. The former are almost always associated with above-ground monuments of varying type, the latter seem in general to lack artificial covering monuments. When inhumations occur in mounds they are usually secondary. In the only firm instance where cremation and inhumation occur together on the same site (Carbury Hill, Site B; relationship of cremation and inhumation at the Rath of the Synods unknown) cremation was shown to be the earlier.

It is possible, therefore, that in the admittedly inadequate burial record we can detect more than a hint of population stability throughout Ireland in the last pre-Christian millennium. This may perhaps be inferred both from the continued absence of recognisable burials over almost the entire millennium and from the use, when Iron Age burials first become recognisable, of long-established indigenous methods of interment. The gravegoods themselves are also almost entirely of native manufacture. A few of the beads may be foreign but there is otherwise nothing in these Irish Iron Age cremation burials which reflects even to a slight degree the presence of intrusive population groups.

The cremation deposit from 'Loughey', Co. Down, stands apart from the rest of the Irish cremations discussed above for this, as earlier stated, argues for a foreign element. The strength or extent of this element is, of course, quite unknown and there is no reason to believe that burials such as that at 'Loughey' had any influence on the development of Irish Iron Age funerary practices.

As indicated above, the inhumation burials seem to represent a sepulchral tradition distinct from that of the cremations and there are grounds for believing that cremation was gradually replaced by inhumation in the early centuries of our era. Some overlap with cremation burials is evident in the gravegoods but it is probable that inhumation, unassociated with any form of mound, had become the exclusive burial method in Ireland by the third or fourth century A.D. Such a change in burial customs need not reflect any radical change in population here nor need it necessarily be related to Christian beliefs. A more plausible explanation for the change in Irish burial customs is to see in it influence from the Roman world where, during the reign of Hadrian in the second century A.D., the exclusive rite of cremation was gradually replaced by inhumation and this, by the middle of the third century, had become universal within the Empire (Toynbee, 1971, 40; Collingwood and Richmond, 1969, 166).

There is a not inconsiderable body of evidence for the presence in Ireland of strong Roman influence during the very centuries when such changes in the burial rite were taking place outside and in the burial record itself there is evidence for the actual presence here of alien intruders from the Roman world. The so-called Brigantians inhumed at Lambay were strongly Romanised in their material culture and at Bray Head it seems reasonable to accept that a community of provincial Roman immigrants is represented by the interments. The iron brooches at Bettystown, too, in all probability reflect influence from the Roman world (and it is not impossible that an intrusive element is here also indicated). Above all else, however, a Roman presence in Ireland is indicated by the cremation burial at Stoneyford in Co. Kilkenny. Warner's suggestion, that the presence of such fragile material as a glass cinerary urn demonstrates a stable and permanent Roman settlement at the intersection of trade routes in the south of Ireland, must be taken seriously (1976, 274) especially so since the burial is likely to be that of a Roman lady. At Knowth, though no Roman objects came from the burials, Roman potsherds and bronzes of Roman types were recovered during the excavation of the secular settlement there (Eogan, 1968, 375, fig 38:14) and it may be that these are contemporary with the burials. At the Rath of the Synods, where inhumation burials were unearthed, there was considerable evidence for Roman influence, in all probability contemporary with the interments (Ó Ríordáin, 1971, 26).

It seems evident, therefore, that in the inhumation burials of the early centuries A.D. a strong Roman connection is detectable and it may be more than mere coincidence that the apparently strongly eastern bias in their distribution (fig 42)

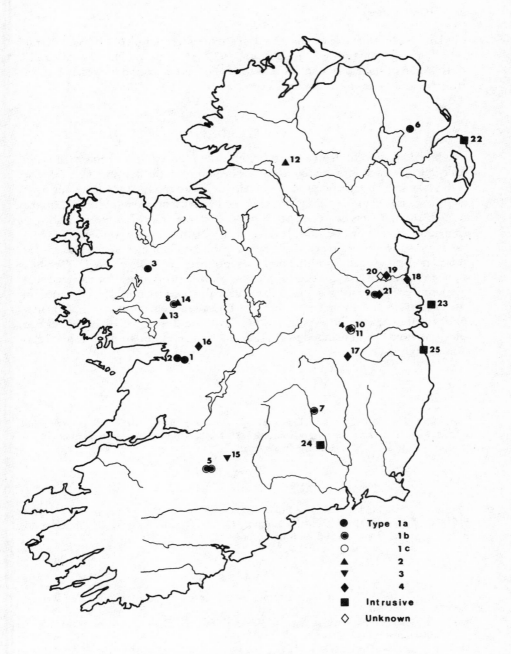

Type 1a
1b
1c
2
3
4
Intrusive
Unknown

Fig 42: Distribution map, Iron Age burials in Ireland.

overlaps to a considerable extent with the eastern concentration of first/second century Roman imports to Ireland (Bateson, 1973, 35, Map 4). The eastern coastal distribution of three of the intrusive burials emphasises too the importance of the Irish Sea as a routeway in the early centuries A.D.

CONCLUSIONS

The burial record of Iron Age Ireland offers little support for the concept of large-scale folk intrusions into the country at the beginning of the iron-using period. The earliest datable burials appear to be cremations in earthen mounds of various types and these, as well as the gravegoods associated with them, are indigenous. Limited though the numbers are there are hints that future research will establish that cremation burials in barrows, especially ringbarrows, may yet emerge as a predominantly western type. The absence of burial monuments of exotic type at this period is noticeable and the non-existence here of the distinctively Yorkshire square-ditched barrows is especially relevant (Stead, 1979) in view of repeated suggestions that Yorkshire was one of the principal sources of Iron Age influences in the country. A small number of intrusive Roman or Romano-British burial complexes of the early centuries A.D. has been noted and it may be that influence at this time from the Romanised world caused a change in burial ritual from cremation to inhumation.

NOTE

1 *A Catalogue of Irish Iron Age Antiquities*, forthcoming, Royal Irish Academy; *The Irish Iron Age, Problems of Origin, Development and Chronology*, forthcoming 1982, Moreland and Co., Bad Bramstedt, Germany.

ACKNOWLEDGEMENTS

I am deeply indebted to Professor Etienne Rynne, Professor George Eogan, Mr L.N.W. Flanagan, Mr Peter Danaher and Mr Eamon P. Kelly for generously giving permission to include material from their unpublished excavations in the present work.

REFERENCES

Bateson, J.D., 1973. 'Roman material from Ireland: a re-consideration', *Proc Roy Ir Acad C* 73, 21-97.
Bersu, G., 1977. *Three Iron Age Round Houses in the Isle of Man*. The Manx Museum and National Trust.
Carson, R.A.G. and O'Kelly, C., 1977. 'A catalogue of the Roman coins from Newgrange, Co. Meath, and notes on the coins and related finds', *Proc Roy Ir Acad C* 77, 35-55.

Clarke, D.V., 1970. 'Bone dice and the Scottish Iron Age', *Proc Prehist Soc* 36, 214-232.

Collingwood, R.G. and Richmond, I., 1969. *The Archaeology of Roman Britain*. London.

Eogan, G., 1968. 'Excavations at Knowth, Co. Meath, 1962-5', *Proc Roy Ir Acad C* 66, 299-400.

Eogan, G., 1974. 'Report on the excavation of some passage graves, unprotected inhumation burials and a settlement site at Knowth, Co. Meath', *Proc Roy Ir Acad C* 74, 11-112.

Flanagan, L.N.W., 1960. 'Bone beads and ring from Newgrange, Co. Meath', *Ulster J Archaeol ser 3,* 23, 61-2.

Graves, Rev. J., 1849. 'Implements and ornaments', *J Roy Soc Antiq Ir* 1, 31-2.

Guido, M., 1978. *The Glass Beads of the Prehistoric and Roman Periods in Britain and Ireland* (Reports of the Research Committee of the Society of Antiquaries of London, No. 35). London.

Herity, M., 1974. *Irish Passage Graves*. Dublin.

Jope, E.M., 1960. 'The beads from the First Century A.D. burial at "Loughey" near Donaghadee: supplementary note', *Ulster J Archaeol ser 3* 23, 40.

Jope, E.M., 1961-2. 'Iron Age brooches in Ireland: a summary', *Ulster J Archaeol ser 3* 24-5, 25-38.

Jope, E.M. and Wilson, B.C.S., 1957. 'A burial group of the First Century A.D. from "Loughey" near Donaghadee', *Ulster J Archaeol ser 3* 20, 73-94.

Keller, J., 1965. *Das Keltische Fürstengrab von Reinheim*. Mainz.

Kelly, E.P., 1977 [1979]. 'A burial at Farganstown and Ballymacon, Co. Meath' *Ríocht na Midhe* 6, 65-7.

Kilbride-Jones, H.E., 1950. 'The excavation of a composite Early Iron Age monument with "Henge" features at Lugg, Co. Dublin', *Proc Roy Ir Acad C* 53, 311-32.

Macalister, R.A.S., 1916-17. 'A report on some excavations recently conducted in Co. Galway', *Proc Roy Ir Acad C* 33, 505-10.

Macalister, R.A.S., 1928. *The Archaeology of Ireland*. London.

Macalister, R.A.S., 1928-9. 'On some antiquities discovered upon Lambay Island', *Proc Roy Ir Acad C* 38, 240-6.

Milojčic, V., 1968. 'Zu den spätkaiserzeitlichen und merowingischen Silberlöffeln', *Ber Röm-Germ Komm* 49, 111-52.

Mogey, J.M., 1949. 'Preliminary report on excavations in Mullaghmore townland, Co. Down', *Ulster J Archaeol ser 3* 12, 82-8.

Mogey, J.M., Thompson, G.B. and Proudfoot, V.B., 1956. 'Excavation of two ring-barrows in Mullaghmore townland, Co. Down', *Ulster J Archaeol ser 3* 19, 11-28.

Ó Ríordáin, S.P., 1940. 'Excavations at Cush, Co. Limerick', *Proc Roy Ir Acad C* 45, 83-181.

Ó Ríordáin, S.P., 1947. 'Roman material in Ireland', *Proc Roy Ir Acad C* 51, 35-82.

Ó Ríordáin, S.P., 1950. 'Excavation of some earthworks on the Curragh, Co. Kildare', *Proc Roy Ir Acad C* 53, 249-77.

Ó Ríordáin, S.P., 1954. 'Lough Gur Excavations: Neolithic and Bronze Age houses at Knockadoon', *Proc Roy Ir Acad C* 56, 297-459.

Ó Ríordáin, S.P., 1971. *Tara, the Monuments on the Hill* (rev. ed.). Dundalk.

Ó Ríordáin, A.B., 1967. 'A prehistoric burial site at Gortnacargy, Co. Cavan', *J Roy Soc Antiq* 97, 61-74.

Ó Ríordáin, S.P. and de Valera, R., 1971. *Antiquities of the Irish Countryside* (rev. ed.). London.

Raftery, B., 1969. 'Freestone Hill: an Iron Age hillfort and Bronze Age cairn', *Proc Roy Ir Acad C* 68, 1-108.

Raftery, B., 1972. 'Some Late La Tène glass beads from Ireland', *J Roy Soc Antiq Ir* **102**, 14-18.
Raftery, B., 1973. 'Rathgall: a Late Bronze Age burial in Ireland', *Antiquity* **47**, 293-5.
Raftery, B., 1982 (forthcoming). *The Irish Iron Age: Problems of Origin, Development and Chronology*. Bad Bramstedt.
Raftery, J., 1938-9. 'The tumulus cemetery of Carrowjames, Co. Mayo, Part I', *J Galway Archaeol Hist Soc* **18**, 157-67.
Raftery, J., 1940-1. 'The tumulus cemetery of Carrowjames, Co. Mayo, Part II, Carrowjames II', *J Galway Archaeol Hist Soc* **19**, 16-88.
Raftery, J., 1941. 'Long stone cists of the Early Iron Age', *Proc Roy Ir Acad C* **46**, 299-315.
Raftery, J., 1944. 'The Turoe stone and the rath of Feerwore', *J Roy Soc Antiq Ir* **74**, 23-52.
Riley, F.T., 1936. 'Excavations in the townland of Pollacorragune, Tuam, Co. Galway', *J Galway Archaeol Hist Soc* **17**, 44-64.
Rynne, E., 1972-3. 'Ancient burials near Coolatore, Co. Westmeath', *J Old Athlone Soc* **1**, 184.
Rynne, E., 1974. 'Excavations at "Madden's Hill", Kiltale, Co. Meath', *Proc Roy Ir Acad C* **74**, 267-75.
Rynne, E., 1974-5. 'Ancient burials at Ballinlough, Co. Laois', *J Kildare Archaeol Soc* **15**, 430-3.
Rynne, E., 1976. 'The La Tène and Roman finds from Lambay, Co. Dublin: a re-assessment', *Proc Roy Ir Acad C* **76**, 231-44.
Stead, I.M., 1979. *The Arras Culture*. York.
Toynbee, J.M.C., 1971. *Death and Burial in the Roman World*. London.
Wacher, J., 1978. *Roman Britain*. London.
Waddell, J., 1970. 'Irish Bronze Age cists: a survey', *J Roy Soc Antiq Ir* **100**, 91-139.
Warner, R.B., 1976. 'Some observations on the context and importation of exotic material in Ireland, from the first century B.C. to the second century A.D.', *Proc Roy Ir Acad C* **76**, 267-92.
Willmot, G.F., 1938. 'Three burial sites at Carbury, Co. Kildare', *J Roy Soc Antiq Ir* **68**, 130-42.
Willmot, G.F., 1938-9. 'Two Bronze Age burials at Carrowbeg North, Belclare, Co. Galway', *J Galway Archaeol Hist Soc* **18**, 121-40.

Celtic Problems In The
Irish Iron Age

Séamas Caulfield

Ireland likewise constitutes a problem of its own as far as the Celtic migrations are concerned. The Irish Celts differed from the remainder of the recorded Celtic world in that they spoke a language which is designated Q-Celtic by philologists. Apart from slight traces of so-called Q-Celtic forms in Spain and Gaul in place-names and inscriptions, this branch of the language is only represented in Ireland from whence it was introduced into Scotland at the end of the fourth century A.D. and into Man. Whether this stems direct from a Hallstatt rather than a La Tène context is impossible to demonstrate; if it was the descendants of the Yorkshire Parisi who settled in Ulster in the first century B.C. and introduced their particular pastoralist traditions and heroic ideals, one may wonder why their P-Celtic speech did not gain ascendancy over the predominant, possibly more archaic Q-Celtic dialect. When literature begins their language is Gaelic (Ross, 1974, 41).

This paragraph encapsulates the problem of trying to reconcile the archaeological and linguistic evidence for the celticisation of Ireland. The continental Celts are well known from both their depiction in sculpture and literature by the classical writers and from the rich artifactual remains they have left in the archaeological record. The Celts in Ireland are equally well known from their place-names, their language, their sagas and their archaeological remains. But while the sagas and the archaeology bear close comparison with the continental Celts the language and place-names whilst Celtic are of the more archaic Q-Celtic branch of the Celtic languages.

Faced with this dilemma, many archaeologists have refused to become involved in the Celtic question in Ireland while others have opted for a very much earlier introduction of the language. Dr. J. Raftery (1972, 5) for instance takes the view that 'if a Celtic language were ever introduced into Ireland this (the Iron Age) is the very last period during which one would expect it to have been introduced'. The simplistic view of a Beaker invasion current up to a decade ago seemed to offer an agency for the celticisation of these islands earlier than the recognisably Celtic Iron Age. It should be acknowledged that the question and the suggested answers to this problem are mainly archaeological since linguists cannot normally offer suggestions for periods fifteen hundred years or more before their earliest sources. Myles Dillon acknowledges this situation in *The Celtic Realms*: 'Archaeology has made great strides in recent years and it is difficult for an outsider to form a personal judgement. It becomes a matter of choosing one's authority. At present in our opinion either view is tenable and we confess to preferring the early date.' (Dillon and Chadwick 1972, 4-5). Ironically Dillon's modesty and caution have not been taken into account by more recent writers who quote Dillon as an authority for the early introduction of Celtic in pre-Iron Age times (Waddell, 1978, 127).

The great difficulty in reconciling the archaeological and linguistic evidence in Ireland has arisen from the concept of the Irish Iron Age as being a homogeneous population marked by intrusive Iron Age forms of La Tène type. Dr J. Raftery for instance equates the Irish Early Iron Age and La Tène in the final centuries B.C.: 'This used to be called a La Tène culture, in modern times simply Early Iron Age culture or civilisation' (Raftery, J., 1972, 3). Apart however from the linguistic difficulties, this notion that Irish Iron Age equals Irish La Tène is unacceptable archaeologically. With a homogeneous La Tène Iron Age the half of Ireland south of a line from Galway to Dublin either remains in a retarded Late Bronze Age for the millennium after its demise abroad or else the southern half of the country is deserted at this time. The former view is untenable in the light of Eogan's (Herity and Eogan, 1977) work on the Late Bronze Age which shows that there is no evidence of a very late survival. The second interpretation, that of a deserted Munster, does not warrant consideration. A further problem with equating the Irish Iron Age with the Irish La Tène is that as one emerges into the second half of the first millennium A.D. the material culture shows little influence of a preceding La Tène Age.

Recently the writer published a paper identifying a new Iron Age artifact in Ireland, the Beehive quern, and showed that this object was an integral part of the La Tène corpus of material in this island (Caulfield, 1977). The implications of the common distribution, art, origin abroad and sub-types in Ireland were discussed, and a radical new interpretation of the Irish Iron Age was proposed. The La Tène element, including the Beehive querns confined to the northern half of the country and divorced from the settlement sites such as ringforts and crannógs, was identified as merely one element in a heterogeneous Iron Age. What is more, the La Tène element within the Iron Age was recognised as being ephemeral while the southern non-La Tène Age survived to form the basis of early historic Celtic Ireland. This is a view which is shared by Dr Barry Raftery who also recognised from his work on hillforts a division within the Irish Iron Age with the La Tène element now being assigned a much less important role than previously (Raftery, B., 1976, 197). At the end of the paper on Irish Beehive querns, the writer suggested that even broader issues, such as the language problems raised by a Celtic La Tène Iron Age can be satisfactorily answered within the new interpretation (Caulfield, 1977, 129).

This present paper now looks at these broader issues and suggests that the model of a heterogeneous Iron Age best explains Celtic Ireland in early historic times. Five aspects of Early Historic Ireland will be dealt with: (1) archaeology, (2) proto-history and history, (3) sagas, (4) origin legends, (5) language.

ARCHAEOLOGY

The most common settlement type of the Early Christian Period is the ringfort of either earth or stone and the closely related crannógs. The writer has suggested that these structures go back into the Iron Age and constitute the southern non-La Tène Iron Age. There are two difficulties in attempting to prove this. Firstly, only a small number of habitations have been excavated in the southern half of Ireland and at only one published site are radiocarbon determinations available. Secondly if one insists on defining the Iron Age as equivalent to La Tène then the absence of La Tène from sites with iron objects will mean that these sites are usually dated post-Iron Age or into the Early Christian period. There are, however, a number of ringforts for which an earlier date than that assigned to them can be proposed.

RAHEENNAMADRA (Stenberger, 1966)

There are nine radiocarbon determinations from this site, six of which are publish-ed in the final report (Stenberger, 1966, 52f.). These six dates are:

Two post-ends in subterranean house (1)	1430 ± 130 a.d. 520
(2)	1260 ± 120 a.d. 690
Duplicate of No. 1	1280 ± 120 a.d. 670
Charcoal from hearth above hut trench	1300 ± 120 a.d. 650
Charcoal from same hearth fallen into souterrain	1360 ± 100 a.d. 590
Hearth 1, under-spread of boulder clay	1840 ± 110 a.d. 110

The dates as published in the final report suggest a consistency for the structures associated with the subterranean house in that all the dates fall within 170 years. If one accepts the post (1) duplicate then the span is just one century. The early date for the final sample is explained away as probably not being connected with the ringfort: 'There were no traces of any habitation layers on this lower level. The hearth probably belonged to a temporary dwelling before the site was constructed (for its age according to C14 analysis, see below)' (Stenberger, 1966, 41).

If however the group of eight determinations from four samples as published in *Radiocarbon* are examined it is clear that the consistency of the dates in the final publication is not wholly warranted.

Sample	A	B
1	1280 ± 120 670 a.d.	1430 ± 130 520 a.d.
2	1220 ± 110 730 a.d.	1260 ± 120 690 a.d.
3	1330 ± 110 620 a.d.	1300 ± 120 650 a.d.
4	1200 ± 110 750 a.d.	1360 ± 100 590 a.d.
5	1840 ± 110 110 a.d.	

Duplicate estimations vary in one case by more than a century and a half. Also, the standard error is comparatively large for all samples. There is also some confusion between the exact origin of the samples as given in the two publications. This is particularly relevant to the final sample (No. 5). In the primary publication the sample is given as 'charcoal from a dark layer assumed to be a hearth, in a trial trench within what was supposed to be a hut 114 cm below arbitrary datum'. It would seem as if the interpretation of hearth 1 in the final report is strongly influenced by the early radiocarbon determination and there seems to be a good chance that in fact this early 'date' represents the initial activity on the site.

KILTERA (Macalister, 1935)

Proudfoot (1970, 41) has pointed out that Kiltera had ceased to be a habitation site when it came to be used as a cemetery and that the ogam stones on the site were probably associated with this late burial phase. On the assumption that the ogam stones date to around the middle of the 1st millennium A.D. an Iron Age date can be suggested for the site.

FEERWORE (Raftery, J., 1944)

The main evidence used by the excavator to date this site to the Iron Age no longer holds the same significance following the recognition of the cultural dichotomy between the rath and the adjacent Turoe Stone. The fragment of iron fibula was found beneath the bank and therefore is likely to be associated with the La Tène presence in the vicinity. The transitional Bronze Iron Age technology argued for the socketed iron axe on which the excavator based an early Iron Age date is now recognised not to be as reliable an index of date as was originally thought because of the finding of such an axe in the apparently thirteenth-century A.D. context at Castell Degannwy in Wales (Alcock, 1972, 110n). However Raftery's case for the construction of the final phase of Feewore during the Iron Age still holds good. As he points out, the placing of a cremation burial in a cist dug into the bank of the ringfort indicates construction in pre-Christian times (Raftery, J., 1944, 41).

CARRAIG AILLE (Ó Ríordáin, 1949)

These two ringforts were dated to the eighth to tenth century on the basis of a number of late objects which came from them. But it is clear from the plans and sections that occupation at Carraig Aille 2 occurred when the site had virtually ceased to exist as a fort. A large stone house was built with one wall on the wall of the fort, the floor level at that stage being level with the wall-top due to the build-up of debris inside. There are however early items from these two forts and associated houses which should date their construction back into the Iron Age.

Pin no. 520 was identified as almost certainly an ibex headed pin, regarded as the prototype of the hand pin. 'Even if they continued to be manufactured to a

date contemporary with the earliest hand pins (in the first, second or third centuries A.D.) it leaves a strange chronological gap between this example and the
main bulk of the material from this site. If one remains cautious as to the object being a true ibex headed pin the form of the pinhead still points to a very early tradition' (Ó Ríordáin, 1949, 69). No. 254 is a Roman toilet implement for which an
excellent parallel can be found in the fourth-century A.D. occupation at Freestone
Hill (Raftery, B., 1969, fig 19, 63). Handpin no. 173 dated by Ó Ríordáin to the
seventh or early eighth century, is claimed by Duignan (1973, 222n) to be an adaptation of the form of a Romano-British pelta brooch. No. 30 is described as an
'imitation Roman coin' and Ó Ríordáin quotes Mattingly as saying that 'these coins
continued to be issued into the fifth century if not later'. Bateson (1973, 48)
described the coin as 'a Roman coin.. It is an extremely barbarous imitation of the
major issue of Constantius II (324-361) and is firmly associated with the 350s'.

Apart from one quernstone of Disc 3 type which is likely to be late and which
came from the area of the late house in Carraig Aille 2, all the other identifiable
querns are of the earlier Disc 1 type. Other material which is likely to be of early
date is the single-sided bone comb no. 13 from the house sites and the bone dice
from Carraig Aille I. Much of the material, e.g. the brooches, one of which was
found under the same stone as the Roman coin, could be earlier than the dates normally assigned to them. There is therefore at the Carraig Aille forts an amount of
material which points to an Iron Age date for their construction.

CUSH (Ó Ríordáin, 1940)

An exceptionally early date for these ringforts was suggested by the excavator on
the evidence of an urn burial thought to have been interred after Ringfort 5 was
abandoned as a habitation. When published in 1940 it was just credible that an
urn burial could postdate the souterrain and general occupation material from this
site. Since then urn burials tend to be dated to earlier in the Bronze Age while
rotary querns etc. cannot be pushed back to such an early date. It appears now that
Cush should be interpreted as analogous to Letterkeen (Ó Ríordáin and
McDermott, 1952) where an area previously used as a Bronze Age cemetery later
had a ringfort built on the site. The finds from Cush e.g. the Disc I type rotary
querns, the jet bracelets and the glass beads are not closely datable within the first
millennium A.D. but they are as likely to belong to the first as to the second half of
that millennium. However the likely Iron Age date does not depend on the finds as
much as on the general integration of forts with field systems and tumuli within
the Cush settlement. The excavated Tumuli 2 and 3 with cremated burials and the
bone plaque from Tumulus 2 represent a tradition distinct from the Bronze Age
Tumulus 1. The bone plaque is reminiscent of Iron Age dice and probably dates to
that period. A pre-Christian Iron Age date on these grounds can be suggested for
this ringfort complex.

AUGHINISH (Kelly, 1974)

A stone fort produced coarse bucket-shaped pottery, a tanged bronze chisel, two saddle querns and an iron horse-bit. In view of the horse-bit it is impossible to accept the excavator's view that the fort was built and occupied solely within the Late Bronze Age. The pottery, the tanged bronze chisel which is known to continue in use into the Iron Age on some British sites (Cunliffe and Phillipson, 1968, 223) and the saddle querns (see discussion on Cahercommaun below) all point to this site having been constructed early in the Iron Age. There was a second stone fort on Aughinish island which also produced pottery and is likely to be equally early.

CAHERCOMMAUN (Hencken, 1938)

This has been one of the most controversial sites of Iron Age/Early Christian date in Ireland. When published in 1938 it was dated to the ninth century on the basis of a silver brooch found in a souterrain and on the general similarity between the objects from Cahercommaun and from the then recently excavated Lagore Crannog in Co. Meath which, on historical evidence, was occupied from the latter half of the eighth until the tenth (Hencken, 1938, 3). By the time the Lagore report was published twelve years later (Hencken, 1950) an earlier 'historical' reference of 651 had been discovered for Lagore and Cahercommaun was (with Ballinderry 2) redated at least a century earlier. In 1972 B. Raftery dealt at some length with the sub-Roman origin of many of the Cahercommaun finds and suggested that 'this and a number of other Irish sites, hitherto dated to the second half of the first millennium A.D. may well have to be backdated by at least half a millennium' (Raftery, B., 1972, 53). Laing has taken issue with Raftery's redating and has suggested that the original dating was more valid (Laing, 1975, 147f). More recently (at the 6th International Celtic Congress in Galway in 1979) Raftery has himself rejected his own earlier dating for this site by holding that it cannot be dated before 500 A.D.

Yet it is difficult to see the case for placing the construction of this site in the Early Christian Period. One of the most telling artifacts must be the saddle querns, seven of which were found on the site. In the absence of any evidence to the contrary, it was reasonable in 1938 to suggest that the saddle querns continued in use in Ireland throughout the first millennium A.D. In fact, one found in a high level at Cahercommaun seemed to prove this. But subsequent excavations throughout Ireland have shown that the saddle quern in this country is very much a Bronze Age artifact and there is little evidence for its survival into Iron Age and certainly none for later times. The introduction of the rotary quern led in Ireland to the rapid abandonment of the saddle quern in exactly the same manner as in other Iron Age communities, as for example in the Atlantic province of Scotland (Caulfield, forthcoming). Cahercommaun, like Aughinish appears to have been constructed before the introduction of the rotary quern and thus could potentially have a B.C.

rather than A.D. date for its construction and initial occupation. While this is an exceptionally early redating of the site, it should be noted that many of the artifacts from the site including the lignite and glass bracelets and the iron penannular brooches and pins could well have such an early date. The small shears found on bedrock in structure 5 which shows considerable difference in size and form from the larger one found elsewhere on the site could also be of early date. The saddle-quern found at a high level on the site has no particular significance. Discarded saddle-querns became normal building stones and can be used and re-used as such indefinitely.

The early forts of Ireland can be paralleled in Atlantic Scotland where early sites in the west, for example, Duntroon (Christison, 1905, 274) and in the north at Clickhimin (Hamilton, 1968) show their general occurrence along the Atlantic seaboard. Their origin is exceptionally controversial, some seeing them as a purely indigenous development, others as due to external influences. That enclosed dwellings date back in Ireland to the Neolithic is not in question; the enclosure at Glenulra in Co. Mayo yielded a radiocarbon determination of 2510 ± 115 b.c. (Caulfield, 1978, 141). But the defensive element is not found in Neolithic times and it is only in the last millennium B.C. that strongly defended domestic and tribal forts appear. Elements found in the Irish forts of the south and west such as widely spaced multi-vallation and chevaux-de-frise are best paralleled further south along the Atlantic seaboard in Iberia. A merging of the central element of the defences of multivallate hillforts with the indigenous tradition of enclosed isolated farmsteads could account for the origin of the ringfort proper in Ireland. Any Iberian element introduced to Ireland in the latter part of the first millennium B.C. would not exhibit La Tène influence since the Iberian Iron Age did not come under the later Iron Age influence of the La Tène Celts. The Celtic element of northern and western Iberia is attributed to the pre-La Tène Iron Age expansion into the peninsula (Powell, 1958). It seems likely that any Iberian element in the Irish Iron Age would be exceptionally limited and the indigenous elements would always be numerically dominant. But one cannot rule out entirely the presence of Iberian influence among the artifacts as well as among the structural and defensive elements in the forts. Basic items such as the two-link iron horse-bit, the Disc quern, in particular that of Atlantic Scotland and the iron penannular brooch such as those found at Cahercommaun all occur in Iberia and are the counterpart of the fibula, the Beehive quern and the three-link bronze horse-bit found in La Tène contexts.

There is then in southern Ireland in the prehistoric Iron Age, an Iron Age which can be linked with the non-La Tène stone fort Iron Age of Atlantic Scotland and with its ultimate inspiration lying further to the south in Iberia. By early historic times this southern Iron Age of the forts has extended its influence to the entire country and the La Tène tradition has disappeared. An attempt will now be made to integrate this archaeological model with the history, sagas, origin legends and language of the Irish Celts.

HISTORY AND PROTO-HISTORY

One finds close agreement between the archaeological view of the immediately prehistoric period and the history and proto-history as seen by historians. At the dawn of history the Uí Néill are established at Tara, but have their roots at Cruachain from which they are thought to have expanded eastwards and northwards. 'Consistent tradition suggests that the ruling dynasty of northern and central Ireland obtained their power by military conquest, in the late fourth and early fifth century A.D. Meath with its rich soil and an ancient sanctuary would have been a tempting prize and it may be that the Connachta of Cruachain drove the Lagin from their stronghold and so established the lasting enmity between the Uí Néill and the Lagin' (Dillon and Chadwick 1972, 38). The Uí Néill also extended their power northwards to establish the Northern Uí Néill (Byrne, 1973). There is historical evidence for the contraction of the Ulaid to the east of the Bann and the spread of the Uí Néill influence northwards and eastwards. This spread from a Connaught base provides an historical context for the waning of the northern Iron Age and the universal distribution of the domestic forts. It is interesting to note that Cruachain is mainly a complex of ringforts and ritual sites in contrast to the northern and eastern royal sites with their hillforts at Clogher, Emain Macha, Tara and Dún Ailline. At Tara and at Clogher in Co. Tyrone one can see the late implantation of earthen ringforts on much earlier sites so that what exists today is a palimpsest of monuments which were clearly not in contemporaneous use. At Tara for instance the two ringforts, Tech Cormaic and the Forad, within the hillfort make little sense defensively and even less so does the Rath of the Synods which ignores completely the defences of Ráth na Ríg. Excavation has shown that the Ráthof the Synods was in fact built on a much earlier site of the Iron Age. At Clogher a similar situation obtains: here a ringfort was constructed in the sixth century A.D. within an earlier hillfort.

One is not necessarily here proposing the large scale migration of people from south to north but rather pointing to the major historical developments around the middle of the first millennium A.D. — the spread of the Uí Néill influence and power as the mechanism by which the La Tène tradition waned and the domestic forts gradually spread to all parts of the country.

ORIGIN LEGENDS

The political divisions apparent in the early historic period obviously do not come into existence overnight though in themselves they could have created barriers to a homogeneity of culture throughout the island. But in the corporate identity and origin legends of the different political powers one can recognise more than merely a difference of political affiliation. One version of the Milesian legend is of particular interest in that it agrees closely with the archaeological interpretation of the

Iron Age put forward above. It was suggested that there was a merging of the native with intrusive (military) elements from Iberia in the south with an expansion northwards at the expense of the northern Iron Age. In the Milesian legend two sons of Míl came to Ireland, one first into Munster who because of assistance in time of famine is chosen by the indigenous people as their king. The second son who comes later takes swordland in the north and the country is divided between the two brothers into Leth Chuinn and Leth Moga (Byrne, 1973, 199f). This division and legend would suggest that prior to the Uí Néill military expansion the limit of the southern group was in Leth Moga. The distribution of La Tène material, in particular the distribution of Beehive querns is so much confined to the Leth Chuinn limits that it would suggest that the late division of Leth Chuinn and Leth Moga between two dynasties acknowledging a common ancestry was along the line of a much more fundamental frontier of earlier times.

The basic agreement between the archaeological heterogeneous Iron Age model, proto-history and the origin legends may also find an echo in the Irish laws. 'The usual word for the free population in the laws is *Féni*, and the traditional law itself is called *fénechas* . . . Occasionally, in the law tracts we come across Ulaid — the men of Ulster — and the *Gáileóin* or *Laigin*, the men of Leinster, as distinct from the *Féni*' (Byrne, 1973, 8).

SAGAS

The distinction and animosity between the Connachta and Ulaid finds its greatest expression in the Táin saga. Over twenty years ago Professor Rynne (1961) suggested that the Irish La Tène material could be divided into early western and later northern groups which could represent distinct La Tène groups and be the basis of the Táin saga. Now the possibility of the more basic conflict between the La Tène and the non-La Tène groups could be the origin of the epic. At the same time it should be recognised that the world portrayed in the Táin is very much the world of the La Tène Celts and the chronological sub-division by Rynne was strengthened by the distribution of an earlier sub-type of Beehive quern in the west and of a later type in the northeast. In short, the new research on the Irish Iron Age agrees with Rynne that the Táin has an historical basis which is reflected in the archaeology and while it augments the evidence put forward by Rynne for an inter-La Tène conflict it also provides an alternative basis for conflict in the La Tène/non-La Tène division.

LANGUAGE

Finally the question raised in the opening quotation can be answered in the interpretation put forward above. The Goidelic language of Ireland with its archaic tradition could have had a late introduction into Ireland provided it originated in Iberia. Dillon, in discussing O'Rahilly's view of the Milesian legend, appears to accept on linguistic evidence, the authenticity of the Spanish origin. 'A more acceptable theory would be that the Milesian Goidels did come from Spain as the Book of Invasions says. The discovery of Q-Celtic inscriptions in Spain by Tovar shows that in that lateral area the older forms had survived' (Dillon and Chadwick, 1972, 37). The archaism of the Celtic language in Iberia would parallel the relative archaism of its Iron Age which was largely unaffected by the later La Tène developments. Archaic elements in a language such as one finds in Goidelic do not necessarily imply a remote ancestry within the country. In fact, it is acknowledged that the archaic Celtic language of Scotland dates to the late Dál Riada expansion. It should be noted however that the view of the integrated Atlantic fort culture put forward above would suggest that Celtic akin to Goidelic was introduced to Atlantic Scotland simultaneously with its introduction to Ireland.

With the view put forward above, the problem of the language of the ephemeral La Tène in the north is greatly diminished. There is no longer any need to expect a P-Celtic language to survive in Ireland given the major trends of southern expansion and northern contraction pointed out above. But it does raise the question as to whether any element of this branch of the Celtic languages can be recognised in Ireland. Celtic scholars seem to be divided on this issue. Ross (1970, 27) assumes its certain presence in Ulster. Byrne (1973, 8) mentions that Celtic dialects akin to Welsh have left their traces in Irish while Greene (1966, 7) thinks that it is very uncertain that Brittonic was ever spoken in this country. Greene's opinion as to the date of the introduction of Irish however is in close agreement with the views expressed in this paper. 'Neither archaeological nor traditional evidence is worth very much when we are dealing with language, but it seems to me that a date round about 300 B.C. is not likely to be more than two centuries out' (Greene, 1966, 7).

The Early Christian Period in Ireland, in particular in Munster, is one to which Professor O'Kelly by both excavation and artifact studies has applied his skills. It is a pleasure for me then to offer this paper on the background to that period to Professor O'Kelly on the occasion of his reaching his sixty-sixth birthday.

REFERENCES

Alcock, L., 1972. 'The Irish Sea zone in the Pre-Roman Iron Age'. In C. Thomas (ed), The Iron Age in the Irish Sea Province, 99-112.

Bateson, J.D., 1973. 'Roman material from Ireland: a reconsideration', Proc Roy Ir Acad C 73, 21-97.

Byrne, F., 1973. Irish Kings and High Kings. London.

Caulfield, S., 1977. 'The beehive quern in Ireland', J Roy Soc Antiq Ir 107, 104-38.

Caulfield, S., 1978. 'Neolithic fields: the Irish evidence'. In H.C. Bowen and P. Fowler (ed), Early Land Allotment, Brit Archaeol Rep 48, 137-43.

Caulfield, S. (forthcoming). 'Quern replacement and the origin of the brochs', *Proc Soc Antiq Scot* **109**.

Christison, D., 1905. 'Report on the society's excavations of forts on the Poltalloch estate, Argyll', *Proc Soc Antiq Scot* **39**, 259-322.

Cunliffe, B. and Phillipson, D.W., 1968. 'Excavations at Eldon's Seat, Dorset', *Proc Prehist Soc* **34**, 191-237.

Dillon, M. and Chadwick, N., 1972. *The Celtic Realms* (2nd ed). London.

Duignan, L., 1973. 'A hand-pin from Treanmurtagh Bog, Co. Sligo', *J Roy Soc Antiq Ir* **103**, 220-23.

Greene, D., 1966. *The Irish Language*. Dublin.

Hamilton, J.R.C., 1968. *Excavations at Clickhimin,Shetland*. Edinburgh.

Hencken, H. O'N., 1938. *Cahercommaun: A Stone Fort in Co. Clare*. Roy Soc Antiq Ir, Extra volume.

Hencken, H. O'N., 1950. 'Lagore Crannog: an Irish royal residence of the 7th to 10th centuries A.D.', *Proc Roy Ir Acad C* **53**, 1-247.

Herity, M. and Eogan, G., 1977. *Ireland in Prehistory*. London.

Kelly, E., 1974. 'Aughinish stone forts'. *In* T. Delaney (ed), *Excavations 1974*.

Laing, L., 1975. *Late Celtic Britain and Ireland*. London.

Macalister, R.A.S., 1935. 'The excavation of Kiltera, Dromore, Co. Waterford', *Proc Roy Ir Acad C* **43**, 1-16.

Olsson, J. and Kilicci, S., 1964. 'Uppsala natural radiocarbon Measurements IV', *Radiocarbon* **4**, 291-307.

Ó Ríordáin, S.P., 1940. 'Excavations at Cush, Co. Limerick', *Proc Roy Ir Acad C* **45**, 83-181.

Ó Ríordáin, S.P., 1949. 'Lough Gur excavations: Carraig Aille and "the Spectacles" ', *Proc Roy Ir Acad C* **52**, 39-111.

Ó Ríordáin, S.P. and McDermott, M., 1952. 'The excavation of a ringfort at Letterkeen, Co. Mayo', *Proc Roy Ir Acad C* **54**, 89-119.

Powell, T.G.E., 1958. *The Celts*. London.

Proudfoot, B., 1970. 'Irish raths and cashels: chronology, origins and survivals', *Ulster J Archaeol ser 3* **33**, 37-48.

Raftery, B., 1969. 'Freestone Hill, Co. Kilkenny: an Iron Age hillfort and Bronze Age cairn', *Proc Roy Ir Acad C* **68**, 1-108.

Raftery, B. 1972. 'Irish hill-forts'. *In* C. Thomas (ed), *Problems of the Iron Age in the Irish Sea Province,* 37-58.

Raftery, B., 1976. 'Dowris, Halstatt and La Tène in Ireland: problems of the transition from Bronze to Iron'. *In* S.J. De Laet (ed), *Acculturation and Continuity in Atlantic Europe mainly during the Neolithic period and the Bronze Age.* Dissertationes Archaeologicae Gandenses 16, 189-97.

Raftery, J., 1944. 'The Turoe stone and the rath of Feerwore', *J Roy Soc Antiq Ir* **74**, 23-52.

Raftery, J., 1972. 'Iron Age and Irish Sea: problems for research'. *In* C. Thomas (ed), *The Iron Age in the Irish Sea Province,* 1-10.

Ross, A., 1970. *Everyday Life of the Pagan Celts*. London.

Ross, A., 1974. *Pagan Celtic Britain*. London.

Rynne, E., 1961. 'The introduction of La Tène into Ireland'. *Bericht über den V. Internationalen Kongress für Vor- und Frühgeschichte, Hamburg 1958,* 705-9. Berlin.

Stenberger, M., 1966. 'A ringfort at Raheennamadra, Knocklong, Co. Limerick', *Proc Roy Ir Acad C* **65**, 37-54.

Waddell, J., 1978. 'The invasion hypothesis in Irish prehistory', *Antiquity* **52**, 121-28.

Post-Roman Drying Kilns and the Problem of Function: a preliminary statement

M.A. Monk

The three traits that have most impressed me about Professor O'Kelly as an archaeologist are his keen perception, his ability to integrate information and his appreciation of early technology. This latter understanding evolved during his early years in west Limerick where as a youth he witnessed many aspects of traditional farming and technology at first hand. I feel that it is therefore appropriate to present to Professor O'Kelly this paper on corn drying kilns, the study of which I am sure he will agree is integral to the better understanding of past agricultural societies.

Drying kilns have attracted considerable interest, not only amongst archaeologists but also agricultural historians and specialists in folk life, largely perhaps because such kilns were in use in many areas of northern Britain and Ireland until recently. In these areas drying kilns were of fundamental importance in cereal crop processing, especially to dry or ripen the crop after damp harvests and/or short growing seasons.

In the course of excavations in both Britain and Ireland archaeologists have recovered evidence of structures which, because of their similarity to the northern and western kilns and also because of the absence of artefacts relating them to metallurgy or ceramic manufacture, have been interpreted as corn drying kilns. There are numerous references in the archaeological literature to such structures but few general and interpretative statements have been published, apart from Goodchild's paper on the Roman kilns (Goodchild, 1943) and Scott's on later structures (Scott, 1951). In the near future it is hoped that more such publications will appear but until then perhaps this paper will serve as an interim statement on several little appreciated aspects of these structures.

The majority of drying kilns that have been investigated archaeologically in Britain are of Roman date and most of them form one type, the T-shaped kiln. In this case the stem of the T forms the flue and the cross forms the duct of the drying chamber, which would have been constructed above it (Goodchild, 1943, 151). Surprisingly enough, many of these structures have been found in southern Britain, an area not usually associated with regular damp harvests. On the present evidence most of these kilns are late Roman, third century and after. Although the second-century kiln at Park Street, Herts. may be an exception (Rivet, 1964, 107). Collingwood and Richmond (1969, 151) have argued that some early corn dryers may have been misinterpreted as hypocausts. The concentration of recognisable drying kilns at the later period in southern Britain has prompted some authors to suggest that their presence can be taken as an indicator of a deteriorating or damper climate towards the end of the Roman period (Scott, 1951, 205; Applebaum, 1958, 84; 1972, 5). Although the proponents of this argument did have some independent support from some early work on climate (Brookes, 1949, 299), more recent studies seem to indicate that the climate did not begin to deteriorate in Europe until about 450 A.D. (Lamb, 1977, 424-8). In any case the climatic argument does not take into account the other important functional aspects of corn drying kilns. The problem however remains that few corn dryers of an earlier or indeed later date have been identified. This under-representation may be more apparent than real; it may be that earlier kiln types were more flimsy above ground structures which have not left any recognisable traces or which have not been recognised for what they were during excavation.

It is the primary intention of this paper to stress a more functional approach to the question of corn dryers and in so doing present some preliminary results with which I am currently involved where an attempt has been made to understand more fully the question of function.

The drying of corn prior to threshing, following a damp harvest or a short grow-ing season, is just one of several functions that these kilns may have performed. In the northern Isles and some areas of the west it has always been necessary to dry the crop to harden the grain and therefore facilitate threshing. In southern Britain, in recent years at least, it has only been necessary to dry a crop artificially when the harvest has been too damp to allow it to dry stooked in the fields.

A little known and equally important function of a drying kiln which may have accounted for their wider distribution in former times was to harden the grain to allow effective milling (Scott, 1951, 196; Fenton, 1978, 375). The association of mill and corn drying kiln was common in many areas until recently (Wiliam, 1977, 15). In Scotland and Ireland, this association developed as part of an expanding and more centralised landlord system that destroyed the former smallholder com-munities in those areas (Gailey, 1970, 52; Fenton, 1978, 389). But regardless of the scale of the milling operation, parching the grain prior to grinding speeded up the process and saved labour, as experiments carried out using small rotary hand querns have demonstrated (Curwen, 1938, 151-2; Nielson, 1966, 19; Moritz and Jones, 1950, 2-4). These experiments have shown that the grain, without pre-roasting, would simply be rolled and clog the quern surface rather than be ground. In the case of the experiment described by Curwen undried grain took 3/4 hours to be ground into flour and had to be put through the mill 8 or 9 times. As Fenton suggests (1978, 375), it is quite likely that for small scale domestic flour production using a rotary quern the grain was simply dried in a round bottomed pot over a fire prior to grinding. According to Ó Danachair (1955, 7-8) it was the practice in Ireland until the nineteenth century to roll the grain in a wrapping of straw on heated stones. Similar small scale parching operations are even more likely to have taken place in the more distant past and this may in part account for the lower incidence of corn dryers in the early and pre-Roman periods. It could be argued therefore that drying kilns were most often associated with larger units of production, which may have developed in the later Roman period in Britain.

A most important feature of grain processing in the period prior to, during and after the Roman occupation was the removal of the tight fitting glumes of the hulled wheats, particularly emmer (*Triticum dicoccum*) and spelt (*Triticum spelta*). The primary spikelets of these wheats, once separated by threshing, had to be parched to make their robust glumes brittle enough to be removed by pounding and separated by secondary winnowing and cleaning (Hillman, 1980). In southern Europe this practice, according to Ovid (*Fasti* II 519, V1 313, after Curwen, 1933, 124-5), was carried out in small ovens. With the increased production of these hulled wheats and the larger scale of operations, kiln parching would have been an obvious development.

It is often argued that during the Iron Age the increased adoption of the reputed winter hardy spelt wheat allowed the development of autumn sowing. It is difficult to demonstrate that such a sowing regime was practised or whether it was more prevalent after the Iron Age than before, but in more recent times when autumn sowing was the norm an important function of the corn drier was to prepare the seed corn for sowing. The short time available between harvest and sowing in October necessitated the threshing of the crop before it had time to mature in the sheaf; normally the bulk of the harvest would be threshed in the winter after several months maturing in stooks and stacks (Wiliam, 1972, 103). It is tempting to speculate that the higher incidence of corn dryers in the later Roman period was related to an expansion in winter sowing practices.

A further important use of the corn kiln was in the production of malt; the roasting of the sprouted grain intended for the fermentation vats and ale production. The production of ale and hence malting is likely to date back to the pre-Roman period in Britain and Ireland (Strabo IV 5.5 and Dioscorides *De Mat. Med* I 88, after Applebaum, 1972, 206), but as yet little archaeological and archaeobotanical evidence has been recovered to substantiate this, although possible evidence now exists for the Roman period (Hillman, 1980 and Helbaek, 1964). Of the remaining functions of the corn drying kiln the most significant is the drying of grain to reduce the moisture content prior to storage, and to fumigate for insect pests like the grain weevil, *Sitophilus granarius*. It is argued by Buckland (1978, 45) that the ravages of this beast in Roman times may have necessitated increased grain production; and it might be added that this increased production could have led to the development of large scale kiln drying for fumigation purposes.

Cereals were not the only group of crops that were dried in a kiln. It is likely that pulse crops like beans and peas were similarly dried, if it was not possible to allow them to air dry in the open. In addition, other field crops like hemp and flax both have to be dried during processing. Nineteenth-century lime kilns are an example of a specialised kiln built for a specific purpose, although in Ireland it seems that former corn drying kilns were often used for other purposes including lime produc- tion and illicit poteen making (Gailey, 1970,53). Also in Ireland flax production was particularly prevalent until this century and one would perhaps have expected that specialised flax kilns would be constructed to dry the flax after retting. It is possible that this was the case in some areas although the only possible flax kiln described in the archaeological literature could on structural grounds equally suf- fice as a corn drying kiln (Davis, 1938, 79; Gailey, 1970, 57). The structural similarity between this Tyrone kiln and that recovered in Ó Ríordáin's excavations at the early christian site at Ballycateen, Co. Cork was commented on by the ex- cavators (Ó Ríordáin and Hartnett, 1944, 12). It is equally possible therefore that this structure and a similar though possibly later example identified and excavated by Ó Ríordáin at Emlagh townland near Leacanabuaile were corn dryers, but unfortunately no evidence relating to their function was recovered (Ó Ríordáin and Foy, 1941, 98-99).

The recent study by Ricketts (1975) examined in detail the structures of a number of post-Roman and medieval supposed corn drying kilns and he concludes that function cannot be ascertained on structural evidence alone and that the pro- blem is further compounded by the fact that many of them may have been multi- functional and/or changed functions during their period of use (Ricketts, 1975, 9-12).

The functional interpretation of suspected drying kilns identified during an ex- cavation cannot depend on one parameter alone. An important area of evidence which in the past was either totally ignored or not fully exploited is the analysis of charred plant remains associated with kiln-like structures. As has been noted above, most of the functions of a drying kiln involve the drying of plants. Because of the use of fire in the drying process the risks of accidental burning are relatively high (Fenton, 1978, 387; Evans, 1957, 123) and in consequence the chances of recovering charred remains of the crop or crops being dried in such a kiln are similarly high. However a distinction must be made between the charred remains of the plants being dried and the charred residue of the fuel.

In practice it may be difficult or impossible because of mixing to separate these two distinct charred residues (Hillman, 1980). If kiln cleaning was regularly practis- ed one might expect to find accumulations of mixed deposits in areas well away from the kiln itself, although perhaps in the general vicinity. This certainly seems to have been the case for normal domestic hearths in the Roman period and may well have been so for corn dryers (Monk, in progress). It is therefore important to take full account of all these possibilities when carrying out a systematic sampling programme of suspected corn dryers.

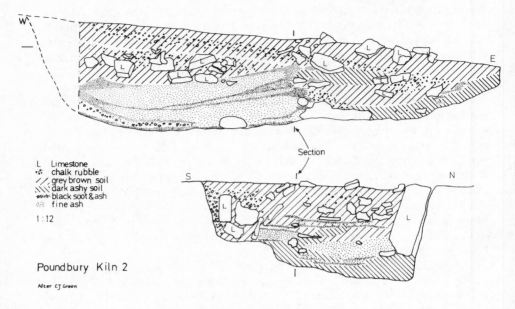

L   Limestone
·∴· chalk rubble
/// grey brown soil
\\\ dark ashy soil
～～ black soot & ash
∴∴ fine ash

1 : 12

Poundbury Kiln 2

After CJ Green

Fig 43: Poundbury, Kiln 2.

Over the past few years a few systematic archaeobotanical studies have been made of drying kilns in Britain and is is hoped that their publication will further our knowledge of these structures. One such study is being carried out by the author on several suspected corn dryers of post-Roman date at Poundbury near Dorchester, Dorset. To date, excavation has revealed five structures that on archaeological and archaeobotanical grounds have been identified as corn dryers. They form an important part of a whole complex of post-Roman settlement activity that superseded a late Roman christian cemetery (Green, 1974; and in progress). Apart from the fact that they all produced a large quantity of charred grain these structures had a number of other similarities in their layout, structural details and size.

GENERAL CHARACTERISTICS OF THE POUNDBURY KILNS

Only three of the five kilns have been fully investigated at present; this therefore can only be an interim statement. Each of the three kilns consisted of a sub-rectangular pit, the overall dimensions of which were 10-11 ft by 5-6 ft at their widest points and 2-2 ft 6 in at their deepest points, though in each case, particularly kiln 2, they were deeper at their wider end (fig. 43). It is possible that this

Poundbury Kiln 2

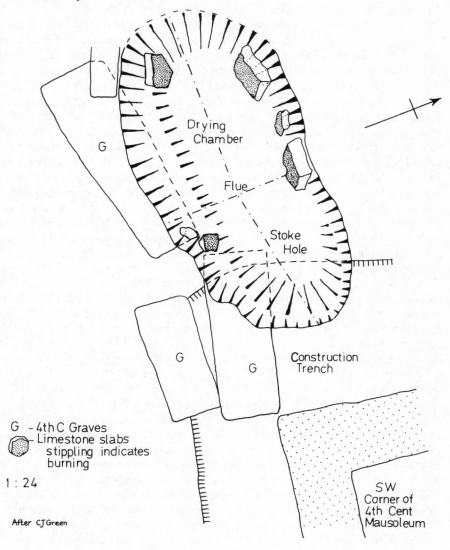

G – 4th C Graves
— Limestone slabs
  stippling indicates
  burning

1 : 24

After C J Green

Fig 44: Poundbury, Kiln 2.

overall shape could have resulted from the re-use of earlier graves but there is no clear evidence that this was the case. In two of the three structures, stone from the Roman cemetery and nearby buildings had been re-used in the construction. In all three instances the pits had battered sides and a narrow ledge (6-10 in wide) extending around the inside perimeter of their wider ends. The north side of the broad end of kiln 2 was lined with limestone blocks with some indication that this lining had formerly continued around the southern edge also. Unfortunately the other three pits did not produce similar evidence. In all three examples the charred plant remains came from the wider sections of the pits and in the fill of kiln 2 several lenses of charred remains were noted and sampled separately for identifiable material. In addition to these successive lenses of burnt material, the fill of kiln 2 showed in section a break in the stratigraphy at the point of juncture between the wider and narrower sections of the pit. In kiln 3 a large hamstone straddles the pit at this point although it was difficult to demonstrate archaeologically whether or not this stone was *in situ*. The suggestion is that the stone was either part of the flue wall or a baffle stone, and that the narrow end of this and the other pits was the stoking area that contained the fire while the broader compartments of the pits with their battered sides and ledges formed the sub-structure of the drying chamber, the drying floor having been supported on a stone lining that only partially survives in kiln 2. In addition to the structural aspects of these kilns, it is thought that their location could have an important bearing on their function. In the first place all three pits were situated in close proximity to three pre-existing mausolea and there are a number of indications, including a spread of charred grain inside one of these, that they may have functioned as granaries, although this spread of charred material could also have accumulated as dump material from kiln cleaning as there was no evidence that the mausolea had been burnt in any accidental granary fire. Another significant aspect of the location of these kilns is their orientation, as this and the local topography would have been important factors influencing the conduction of air and therefore the drying capability and efficiency of these kilns. It seems that kilns 1 and 3 at Poundbury were located to make the best use of a northerly air stream, being aligned north-south with their drying chambers at the southern end. Kiln 2 however is aligned east-west with its drying chamber in the west. Equally important is their location on the eastward slope of the site, affording shelter from the prevailing south-westerly winds while allowing sufficient air flow from the north and east, the winter winds, to cause the kiln fires to draw adequately. Recent ethnographic evidence from the north and west of Britain would further the suggestion that these kilns were more often in use in winter (Wiliam, 1977, 17; Fenton, 1978, 387). Control of the draught through the kiln was essential but despite constant vigilance accidents often occurred in recent times, and it is unlikely that such accidents were any less common in post-Roman times, as indeed the presence of charred grain would indicate.

THE CHARRED REMAINS

A broad based sampling programme was undertaken at Poundbury including the complete range of contexts revealed by excavation, the aim being to recover as much evidence as possible for localised crop processing and waste disposal.

Most of the charred material, including charcoal fragments, was however recovered from in and around the drying kilns. Of the samples from these contexts the most productive in terms of quantity of identifiable items was obtained from the basal fill at the 'drying chamber' ends of the pits. The samples from the narrower and shallower 'stoking areas' of the pits were relatively unproductive, suggesting that the fuel residue was cleaned out regularly, even in the last few firings of each kiln, the converse being the case for the sub-structures of the drying chambers. The accumulation of charred remains in kiln 2 was particularly marked, for in this instance several successive layers of charred grain and ash were found, suggesting a number of firings prior to abandonment. Although the evidence was not absolutely clear, it would seem that this kiln had been used to dry different crops before it went out of use. In the lowest lenses of charred material grains of barley, *Hordeum vulgare/hexastichum* (6-row hulled barley) and oats, *Avena sp.*, were dominant whereas in a stratigraphically later deposit only oats (including definite cultivated oats, *Avena sativa*) were dominant. A third cereal that was not well represented in these samples was the free threshing hexaploid wheat *Triticum aestivo-compactum* (a more compact form of bread wheat), an important addition to the plant economy at this time or slightly earlier (Monk, 1977, 338, 346). It is important to note, in connection with the increased production of this free threshing compact form of bread wheat, that drying is more essential prior to milling than it is for some of the harder wheats like spelt — perhaps a further cause of the higher incidence of drying kilns in the later Roman period.

Kiln 1 at Poundbury produced a similar range of cereal remains although material was only recovered from the lowest fill, and in this case there was more of an equal dominance of oats and barley. This may represent mixing of charred residue from two separate dryings although it is not impossible that a mixed crop was being dried, given that mixed crops of oats and barley called 'drage' are known to have been grown in medieval times on the Glastonbury estates in Dorset (Keil, 1965, 236). In contrast to the samples from the other two kilns those from kiln 3 produced a dominance of wheat, with oats being of secondary importance and barley being represented by only a few grains. The sample from this kiln, in common with most of those from the other kilns, had a high incidence of weed seeds, particularly *Galium* cf. *aparine* (goosegrass), *Vicias* (vetches) *Chenopodium album* (fat hen) and *Rumex sp* (the docks). The grain:weed seed ratio for kiln 3 was 1:0.3 and for kiln 1 the average was 1:0.4. This relatively high incidence of weed seeds is suggestive of an imperfectly cleaned crop, although mixing could have occurred if the 'chaff' waste (including weed seeds) was used for tinder in the initial firing of the kiln, a common practice in paperless societies (Hillman, 1980; Ricketts, 1975, 15-16). However, if one considers the grain:chaff ratio, the incidence of chaff and straw fragments is lower than would be expected if there had been much admixture with chaff used as tinder (the grain:chaff ratio in kiln 1 was 1:0.16 and in kiln 3 1:0.06). It is possible that a certain level of weed contamination was tolerated in a cleaned crop, especially if the grain was not intended for human consumption. However one or two seeds of poisonous plants do occur in the samples (in particular henbane, *Hyoscyamus niger* and fools parsley, *Aethusa cynapium*), and although there are only one or two seeds of these species in a few of the samples, they should normally be eradicated if the crop was intended for human or animal consumption (Field, 1967, 71, 87-8). Most of the other non-crop seeds present in these samples are from plants commonly found as weeds of cornfields, particularly those on calcareous soils.

At this stage in the analysis it is not clear what type of drying practice was being performed in the Poundbury kilns, though it is unlikely to have been malting; malting requires sprouted grain but in these samples such grain was only present in small quantities.

Given the low incidence of chaff elements (straw, rachis fragments, glume fragments etc) it is likely that the grain was either being roasted to facilitate glume removal, as might be the case for hulled barley, or the grain was being dried prior to storage. The high incidence of oats (many of which may well be the cultivated species *Avena sativa*, could be taken possibly to indicate that drying was taking place in preparation for groats production (Hillman, 1980).

STRUCTURAL PARALLELS TO THE POUNDBURY KILNS

To date very few post-Roman and Saxon corn dryers have been excavated and so parallels of the same date range are few. Most of those that have been identified and excavated are very different in structure and have not been adequately sampled for charred plant remains.

Of those post-Roman structures that have been excavated and interpreted as corn drying kilns, a number, particularly the six examples from Nottingham, are of the key hole type, consisting of a circular or oval drying chamber with battered sides, with a single rectangular combined flue and stokehole that may or may not have been enclosed (Ricketts, 1975, 39, 56-7; Cherry, 1972, 171-212). The Saxon example from Buckden, Hunts. was not as clearly defined and appeared to have an elliptical drying chamber with vertical sides and a curious curving flue. Burning was noted on one side of some broken limestone slabs that had fallen into the flue and may have formed part of the roof (Addyman, 1963, 12-14). The only other two groups of corn dryers of post-Roman/Saxon date, found at Hereford and Chalton Manor Farm, Hants., were very different in having an L-shaped plan. The examples from Hereford were found cut into the old ground surface beneath the medieval defences of the city, and pending C14 dating are thought to be Saxon on stratigraphic evidence (Rahtz, 1968, 242-6). According to the excavator, each kiln consisted of a firing chamber, a stoke pit and a single long lateral flue running off at right angles to the pit. These structures were partly built of stone and included fragments of two Roman altars and re-used Roman building stone coated with mortar. A large quantity of charred grain was recovered from these structures and analysed. The majority of the grain found was identified as *Triticum turgidum* (rivet wheat), but *Hordeum vulgare* (barley) and *Avena sp* (oats) were also present (Shoesmith, personal communication; Arthur, D.o.E. report no. 756422). Similar structures were found during excavations at Chalton Manor Farm, consisting of an oblong pit with a gully joining it at right angles, forming an L-shaped plan. The gully had the appearance of a flue, and like the Hereford examples was constructed of re-used Roman tile and mortar (Hughes, personal communication). Apart from this material, no other finds indicated a date for these structures, although in the upper fill of the flue a piece of possible tenth-century pottery was recovered. Apart from a mixed earthy fill, the pit also contained daub, ash and a very sooty primary fill. Both the sooty layer and the layer of ash and daub were sampled for plant remains and a range of cereal fragments was recovered, including mainly *Avena sp* (oat) but also probable grains of the free threshing wheat *Triticum aestivo-compactum* and *Hordeum vulgare* (six row barley). In addition a few charred weed seeds were recovered from the same samples including *Rumex sp* (the docks) and *Sinapis arvensis* (charlock), both weeds of cultivation (Monk, 1977, 321-5). As the samples were small and the amount of identifiable charred material limited, all that can be said is that this, like Hereford, probably was a corn drying kiln. During the course of the excavation at Chalton the excavator noted a similar structure on the edge of the trench which because of time was not excavated (Hughes, personal communication). Whatever their date, it will be noted that these structures are very different from the Poundbury examples. Although in general terms the Poundbury examples were similar to some early Roman examples of kilns from Atworth and Thundersbarrow Hill (Goodchild, 1943, 144-9; Curwen, 1933, 121), the nearest parallels to them so far excavated are in fact medieval.

The four examples from Stamford, described by Cherry (1973; Ricketts, 1975, 41-5) are classified by Ricketts as his type 1 kilns, being stone-built with a square or rectangular drying chamber with three or four sides battering outwards. The drying chamber in this type was connected to a walled or partly walled stokehole which could be of varying shape, rectangular or oval. These structures could have been free standing or contained within a building. The Stamford kilns had in addition short flues constricted by blocking stones along their sides. In the case of kiln 4 from Stamford and also possibly kiln 1 a baffle stone was found at right angles to the flue, the function of which was, judging by recent parallels from the northern Isles (Fenton, 1978, 377), to protect the drying chamber area from stray sparks from the fire in the flue/stokehole. The stone found in a similar position in kiln 3 at Poundbury represented either a displaced baffle stone or a fallen flue blocking stone. The Stamford kilns (two of which were found in the castle bailey and two on sites in the town) were thirteenth- or fourteenth-century in date but their apparent similarity to the Poundbury examples is significant in indicating an earlier tradition of kiln building of this type. The similarity lies not only in general shape and size but also in certain structural details, particularly the battered sides of the drying chamber and the short flue. However, as only one of the Stamford kilns produced charred grain from the area of the drying chamber and flue and the results of this analysis are not known, it is not yet possible to assess the functional similarity between the Poundbury kilns and their medieval counterparts.

THE SUPERSTRUCTURE OF THE POUNDBURY KILNS

Unfortunately there was very little indication from the surrounding archaeological evidence of the superstructure of the Poundbury kilns. Their proximity to the cemetery mausolea may suggest that they were roofed in some way, perhaps by a lean-to structure, but archaeologically this was impossible to ascertain.

The immediate superstructure of the kilns themselves was equally difficult to identify. Speculations on the basis of recent ethnographic evidence (Evans, 1957, 122-3; Fenton, 1978, 377; Knox, 1907, 270) could suggest that a grain drying floor was supported on the limestone slabs that were found lining the sub-structure of the drying chamber. In common with the Scottish and Irish examples, this floor may have consisted of a frame of wooden cross bars or hurdles on which threshed sheaves of drawn straw would have been spread. This drawn straw may in turn have carried a linen sheet or finely woven cloth of horsehair on which the grain would have been spread. Evans (1957, 122, citing Knox 1907, 270), estimated that the drying of grain in an Irish tobacco-pipe shaped kiln of the last century would take 24 hours to complete, but the drying time depended not only on the size of the kiln and the quantity of grain being dried at one time, but also on the species of grain, its condition and intended use. According to Eurwyn Wiliam in his description of the kiln attached to the Melin Bompren mill (reconstructed at the Welsh Folk Museum, St Fagan's, Cardiff), it would take three hours to dry oats which after twelve hours cooling would be ready for milling. This particular kiln was capable of drying four bushels of grain at a time. A Scottish kiln in recent use had a floor of 8 ft diameter and could hold four sacks of oats spread to a depth of 3 inches which, depending on the amount of heat generated and the amount of draught controlled by opening or closing a barn door, would take 6-8 hours to dry (Fenton, 1978, 387).

The fire risk in these kilns was considerable despite various structural precautions like the development of long flues and the use of baffle stones. The kiln would therefore have to be constantly attended by a member of the community who would also be responsible for turning the grain to allow even drying (Scott, 1951, 203; Fenton, 1978, 377; Gailey, 1970, 66-7). Because of the fire risk the early Irish laws stipulated that the kiln was not to be placed within so many paces of a dwelling house (Evans, 1957, 123).

The drying floor and chamber of these kilns would probably have been roofed over, even if the structures were temporary. The roof would have been of thatch and the walls of wattle and daub or stone as described by Scott (1951, 203) and also noted earlier by Knox when describing the recent Irish tobacco pipe kilns. These kilns were set into a bank and had a longish rectangular flue leading to a stone-lined circular drying chamber with a drying floor set within it, which was covered at ground level with a timber-framed thatched roof. In some cases these thatched roofs were detachable and were only placed over the drying chamber when it rained (Gailey, 1970, 62). Estyn Evans considers that these pipe shaped kilns were preceded by much smaller oven-like structures built entirely of wattle and daub. This may have been the case for the smaller scale operations but Gailey argues on the basis of the early Irish literary evidence that the forerunners of the tobacco pipe kilns were flueless kilns that were, like the recent examples from the northern Isles, attached to the barns where the rest of the crop processing took place (Gailey, 1970, 67; Fenton, 1978, 377-9; Scott, 1951, 197-200; Firth, 1974, 18-19). However, even in these areas small structures of wattle and clay were being used until relatively recently. Boswell in his travels of the northern Isles observed a barrel-like structure of wattle covered with clay close to a farmhouse at Rousay in the Orkneys which was used to dry corn prior to threshing — 'a little house kiln for drying corn . . . a little at a time . . . instead of having one (a kiln) to attend to in an outhouse. It was about the size of a hogshead; was made of wattles plastered with clay very firmly both on the outside and inside'. In the life of St Ciarán a similar structure of wattles set in sand over a fire is described in connection with corn drying (Scott, 1951, 204). The truth of the matter is probably that both small and large kilns were in use contemporaneously in the recent past, although in an evolutionary sense the smaller kilns were probably the earliest, perhaps originally developing in prehistory from multifunctional bread ovens. Although the Poundbury kilns were similar in size to the larger recent types, their superstructure probably consisted of materials like wattle, daub and thatch, materials more appropriate to the smaller kilns. Because of the perishable nature of these materials and the lack of supporting archaeological evidence it is not possible to progress further with their interpretation.

THE POSSIBLE SOCIAL AND ECONOMIC IMPORTANCE
OF THE POUNDBURY KILNS

As noted earlier, it is highly probable that the advent of recognisable corn dryers in the Roman period was part of a response to a need for larger scale production of cereal crops to meet a greater demand. Similarly perhaps the localisation of groups of medieval kilns around growing centres of population like Stamford and Lincoln was to meet local demand. Ricketts however would prefer to see the thirteenth-century concentration of kilns in this area of East Anglia as part of a wider trade network in malt or ale from the port of Kings Lynn (Ricketts, 1975, 35-6). Such demand and trade factors are important considerations and it is tempting to speculate that the presence of the five kilns at Poundbury may reflect a similar need; but this raises a number of very difficult though important questions about the post-Roman occupation of nearby Dorchester for which as yet there is very little archaeological evidence.

At the more specific level it is possible that the actual location of the drying kilns on the site may have some significance. From the earlier discussion it will be noted that all three kiln structures at Poundbury were located in close proximity to three pre-existing mausolea that formed the foci of the late Roman cemetery. From the evidence so far recovered it would seem that they continued to occupy an important position in the post-Roman settlement, but their function in respect to the corn drying kilns is not understood, though they may have been used as barns.

The association of the barn and the drying kiln is quite clear from recent evidence (Fenton, 1978, 77-9; Gailey, 1970, 67; Firth, 1974, 18) and was also close in the early historic period. The eleventh-century Anglo-Saxon estate document known as the *Gerefa* implies the close association of the kiln and the threshing floor, both of which would have been in the barn (Skeat, 1922, 573-6; Monk, 1977, 279). Gailey (1970, 67) also points out that the early Irish law tracts indicate this close connection between the threshing floor and the kiln, again suggesting that they were housed in the same building. The threshing barn and the corn kiln would of necessity be important centres of agricultural activity in a small farming community, particularly in the winter months, the main time of year when traditional agriculturalists would have had time to catch up on threshing, winnowing and kiln drying of crops. Crop processing and kiln drying required a cooperative effort on the part of a number of members of the community or workers on the estate. The communal effort was emphasised in the north and west by the common ownership of the corn drying kiln. Between November and March the people would gather in the barn to carry out the necessary crop cleaning tasks, but also in the evening to avail perhaps of the warmth given off by the drying kiln. In Wales the assembly at the kiln known as the 'Shimli' played an important part in the social life of the community and, we are told by Wiliam (1977, 17), was as popular a gathering place as the blacksmith's shop or the tavern. Similarly in the Orkneys John Firth in his reminiscences indicates that despite the discomforts connected with kiln drying he and others spent many an entertaining evening in the barn where the children played hide and seek while the older folks gathered round the fire and exchanged stories (Firth, 1972, 24). Although it is not possible for us to envisage the social importance of the Poundbury kilns in the same way, the centralised positioning of the mausolea and the associated kilns in regard to the layout of the post-Roman settlement at Poundbury is the only pointer we have to their significance in the community.

SUMMARY AND CONCLUSIONS

The main theme of this paper is the paucity of evidence for corn drying kilns in general and post-Roman types in particular, so that of necessity what has been said can be no more than an interim and somewhat speculative review of the evidence to date. Particular emphasis has however been laid on the functional aspects of these structures and it is now obvious that these kilns performed a number of functions, although most of these would have been connected in some way with the processing of field crops, particularly cereals. Preliminary archaeobotanical evidence from the Poundbury examples, obtained by careful sampling of discrete areas of the kiln fills, has in part been able to demonstrate this. Further evidence is however badly needed from a number of sites and it is suggested that excavation of potential corn dryers would be more fruitful if carried out in conjunction with an extensive sampling programme for charred plant remains.

The importance of the barn and the mill to traditional agricultural societies has survived in the folk memory, but the corn drying kiln, an important adjunct to these, has been nearly forgotten. If this paper does no more than point the way to a fuller understanding of the function of these structures through ethnological, archaeological and archaeobotanical evidence, then it has achieved what it set out to do.

ACKNOWLEDGEMENTS

It is appropriate to take this opportunity to acknowledge the immeasurable cooperation I have had throughout the course of this study from the excavator of Poundbury, Christopher Green, who has allowed me free access to his unpublished work on the site and has encouraged me with free discussion. I would also like to express my thanks to Mike Hughes, Ron Shoesmith, Bob Ricketts and Gordon Hillman who have also allowed me to refer to their unpublished work. Finally I would like to thank my wife Judith who drafted the drawings and helped with the final typescript.

REFERENCES

Addyman, P.V., 1963. 'Note on a kiln like structure at Buckden, Hunts.' *Medieval Archaeol* **6-7**, 12-14.
Applebaum, S., 1958. 'Agriculture in Roman Britain.' *Agr Hist Rev* **6**, 66 ff.
Applebaum, S., 1972. 'Roman Britain'. *In* H.P.R. Finberg (ed), *The Agrarian History of England and Wales*, Vol. I. pt i, A.D. 43-1042. Cambridge.
Brookes, C.E.P. 1949. *Climate through the Ages*. London.

Buckland, P.C. 1978. 'Cereal production storage and population: a caveat.' *In* S. Limbrey, J.G. Evans and H. Cleere (ed), *The Effect of Man on the Landscape: the lowland zone*, 21-27. CBA Res. Rep. **21**. London.

Cherry, J. 1972. 'Medieval Britain in 1971. Part II.' *Medieval Archaeol* **16**, 171-212.

Cherry, J., 1973. 'Medieval Britain in 1972' Part II. *Medieval Archaeol*, **17**, 153-88.

Collingwood, R.G. and Richmond, I., 1969. *The Archaeology of Roman Britain*. London.

Curwen, E.C. 1933. 'Excavations on Thundersbarrow Hill, Sussex'. *Antiq J* **13**, 109-33.

Curwen, E.C., 1938. 'Early agriculture in Denmark' *Antiquity*, **12**.

Davies, O., 1938. 'Kilns for flax drying and lime burning', *Ulster J Archaeol ser 3* **1**, 79-80.

Evans, E.E., 1957. *Irish Folkways*. London.

Fenton, A., 1978. *The Northern Isles: Orkney and Shetland*. Edinburgh.

Field, H.I., 1967. *British Poisonous Plants*. H.M.S.O. Bulletin 161, London.

Firth, J., 1974. *Reminiscences of an Orkney Parish*. Stromness.

Gailey, A., 1970. 'Irish corn drying kilns', *Ulster Folk Life* **15/16**, 52-71.

Goodchild, R.G., 1943. 'T-shaped corn drying ovens in Roman Britain', *Antiq J* **23**. 148-53.

Green, C.J.S., 1974. 'Interim report on the excavations at Poundbury, Dorchester 1973', *Proc Dorset Natural Hist Archaeol Soc* **95**, 97-100.

Helbaek, H., 1964. 'The Isca grain. A Roman plant introduction in Britain', *New Phytol* **63**, 158-64.

Hillman, G., 1980 forthcoming. 'Spelt kilning at Catsgore, Somerset' In R. Leech (ed), *Excavations at Catsgore, Somerset*. H.M.S.O. Monograph.

Keil, I., 1965., 'Farming on the Dorset estates of Glastonbury Abbey in the early fourteenth century', *Proc Dorset Natural Hist Archaeol Soc* 87, 234-49.

Knox, H.T., 1907. 'Notes on gig-mills and drying kilns near Ballyhaunis Co. Mayo', *Proc Roy Ir Acad C* **26**, 265-74.

Lamb, H.H., 1977. *Climate Present, Past, and Future*, Vol. 2. *Climatic History and Future*. London.

Monk, M.A., 1977. The Plant Economy and Agriculture of the Anglo-Saxons in Britain: with particular reference to the 'Mart' settlements at Southampton and Winchester. Unpublished M Phil thesis. Southampton University.

Moritz, L.A. and Jones, C.R., 1950. 'Experiments in grinding wheat in a Romano-British quern', *Milling* June 1950, 2-4.

Moritz, L.A., 1958. *Grain Mills and Flour in Classical Antiquity*. Oxford.

Nielson, S., 1966. 'Eksperiment', *Skalk* **3**, 13-23.

Ō Danachair, C., 1955. 'The flail and other threshing methods.' *J Cork Hist Archaeol Soc* **60**, 6-14.

Ō Ríordáin, S.P. and Foy, J.B., 1941. 'Structure in Emlagh townland', *J Cork Hist Archaeol Soc* **66**, 98-9.

Ō Ríordáin, S.P., and Hartnett, P.S., 1944. 'The excavation of Ballycatteen fort, Co. Cork', *Proc Roy Ir Acad C* **49**, 1-44.

Rahtz, P., 1968. 'Hereford.', *Curr Archaeol* **1**, 242-6.

Ricketts, R.J., 1975. Post Roman and Medieval Drying Kilns. Unpublished BA dissertation. University College, Cardiff.

Rivet, A.L.F., 1964. *Town and Country in Roman Britain*. London.

Scott, Sir Lindsay, 1951. 'Corn drying kilns', *Antiquity* **25**, 196-208.

Skeat W.W., 1922. 'The Gerefa'. *In* W. Cunningham, *The Growth of English Industry and Commerce during the Middle Ages*. Cambridge.

Wiliam E., 1977. *Melin Bompren Corn Mill*. National Museum of Wales, Cardiff.

The Date of the
Moylough Belt Shrine

Peter Harbison

In the concluding section of his exemplary technical examination of the Moylough Belt Shrine, Professor O'Kelly (1965) summarised the dates which had previously been suggested for this important example of early Irish metalwork, without countenancing any one of them in particular. With the great majority of earlier commentators (O'Kelly, 1965, 187n) agreeing on an eighth-century date, most recent opinions hover close to 700 (Lucas, 1973, fig 67; Laing, 1975, 359; L. de Paor, 1977, fig 21; M. de Paor, 1979, 30; Haseloff, 1979, 238). Yet the possibility of a later date was left open by Professor O'Kelly when he compared certain features of the Shrine with those on High Crosses, which are scarcely much earlier than 800. As a contribution to this congratulatory volume in honour of Professor O'Kelly, I should like to offer some thoughts which could strengthen the possibility of a date later than the one currently favoured, and explore briefly some consequences which the acceptance of such a later dating might have in our understanding of some other pieces of Early Christian metalwork in Ireland.

One of the arguments put forward for an early date for the Belt Shrine is the similarity of some of its spiral ornament to that in the Book of Durrow (O'Kelly, 1965, 187), which is normally dated to the second half of the seventh century. It ought not to be forgotten, however, that variations of the same type of spiral ornament continued in use into the ninth century. The 'fleshiness' of the lobes of the spiral terminations of some of the Shrine's silver plaques (e.g. Pl XII) is encountered, for instance, on the famous Chi-Rho page, f. 34ʳ of the Book of Kells or on the south side of the Bealin cross — a monument which may be ascribed roughly to the first half of the ninth century (Henry, 1965, 143-4). Furthermore, the pelta ornament on one of the triangular silver panels (Pl XII) may be compared to that on the underside of the ring of the Termonfechin cross (Stokes, 1901, Pl XLIII and XLV),which is scarcely earlier than the first half of the ninth century. The loose interlacing on two of the other silver plaques (e.g. Pl XIII) would equally not be out of place in the same period.

In a recent publication (Harbison, 1978, 46 and 57), I followed current dating and suggested that the Shrine's cross-shaped medallions (e.g. Pl XIV) showed an experimental stage in the development of the 'Celtic' ringed cross around 700. If the Shrine really is as early as 700, it could be described as perhaps the earliest surviving experiment in integrating the cross form with a ring which has a smaller diameter than the width of the cross-arms (compare also the Whitby mount — Wilson, 1964, No. 107 with Pl XXXIX). But, leaving aside the Shrine's cross-medallions for a moment, we must come to the conclusion that there is no reliably dated example of a ringed cross in Ireland before the ninth century, with the possible exception of the Ailill aue Dunchatho graveslab from Athlone (Fanning and Ó hÉailidhe 1980, 7-9). Certainly, there is no *proof* that any of the great stone High Crosses, such as those at Ahenny or Moone (to the latter of which Professor O'Kelly compared the Shrine's medallions), are much or any earlier than 800 (*pace* Henry, 1965, 138-42 and Roe, 1969, 9). Perhaps the earliest reliably dateable expression of a cross-shape fused with the narrower ring is found on some initials of the Dagulf Psalter in the Austrian National Library in Vienna, a manuscript painted for Charlemagne sometime between 783 and 795. One of these initials, the Q of f. 67ᵛ (Pl XIV), shows three circled crosses one above the other, and the little dot at the top and bottom respectively could imitate nail-heads, suggesting that the design may have been modelled on metal appliqué crosses. What may well be a copy of this ornament is found in another letter Q on f. 1ᵛ of a late eighth century Freising manuscript (Clm 6237) in the State Library in Munich, which Katharina Bierbrauer (1979, 10, 13 and 110 with Taf. 41) considered to be the only ornament in the whole manuscript to be of purely continental origin. But in view of the fact that its author, Peregrinus, was an Anglo-Saxon monk, and because of its similarity to 'insular' crosses, the possibility of ascribing this motif along with the rest of the manuscript's ornament to an 'insular' origin ought to be left open for consideration. Another manuscript bearing ornament in the shape of a ringed cross is the Codex O. IV. 20, f. 2a in the National Library in Turin (Alexander, 1978, Pl 280), which may belong to the first half of the ninth century, while a more complicated version may be found on f. 4a of the Gospel of Arnaldus in the Cathedral at Nancy (Köhler, 1930, Taf. 38a), which was written between 834 and 843. As it seems to me to be comparatively unlikely that the ringed crosses of the Belt Shrine's medallions would pre-date the earliest reliably dateable example by as much as three-quarters of a century — which is what an early eighth-century dating for the Shrine would imply — a date for the Shrine rather later in the century must be considered as a serious possibility.

This notion finds further support in the beast heads of the Belt Shrine (Pl XII and XIII). One of their characteristic features is that the upper jaw curls up into a spiral at the end. Perhaps the earliest surviving manuscript occurrence of a curling upper jaw of this kind is found on page 5 of the Codex numbered 60 in the Stiftsbibliothek in St Gall (Alexander, 1978, 80, no. 60 with Pl 283), which may be as late as the first half of the ninth century. It is, however, much more common on metalwork, where it is encountered on the Tara and Killamery brooches, the Emly Shrine and the D-shaped panels in the National Museum of Antiquities at St Germain, while its presence on stonework may be noted on the south cross at Ahenny and on the Killamery cross (for drawings, see Harbison, 1981). Although none of these works can be dated precisely, the D-shaped panels in St Germain are decorated in the 'boss style' which many would place no earlier than towards the end of the eighth century (Bakka, 1965, 39-40; compare Small, Thomas and Wilson, 1973, 142-3 and M. and L. de Paor, 1978, 119). The beak-shaped projection pointing backwards behind the eye of the animal-head on the Shrine's buckle (Pl XII and XIII) is found also in the St Gall Codex 60 and on the D-shaped plaques in St Germain (Pl XV). Thus, the combination of the upper jaw curling into a spiral and the beak-shaped extension of the eye could be seen to argue in favour of a date scarcely earlier than the later eighth century for the Shrine.

The L- and T-shaped fields of enamel on the Belt Shrine are of a kind which is notoriously difficult to date precisely. However, one rare feature of the enamel decoration which may be of value for dating purposes is the presence on the buckle of two fields in the shape of an angular S (Pl XII). Perhaps the best comparison for this is offered by the Ekerö crozier in the National Museum in Stockholm. On the facetted shaft, between the knop and the volute head of the crozier, we find two examples of a very similar S (Pl XV; Holmqvist, 1955; Lundström, 1978, 26; Werner, 1978; Graham-Campbell and Kidd, 1980, 178), which however lacks the final turn on each end of the S of the Belt Shrine. As Holmqvist (1955) was the first to point out, the Ekerö crozier shares certain ornamental features with the D-shaped plaques from St Germain (Pl XV), so that if a late eighth-century date is acceptable for the St Germain plaques, it could also be acceptable for the Ekerö crozier (*pace* Werner, 1978) and, *mutatis mutandis*, for the Moylough Belt Shrine as well.

The millefiori design on the bottom left-hand corner of the rectangular frame of that part of the buckle seen on Pl XII, whereby a square is sub-divided into nine roughly equal squares of which the central and corner ones are decorated (O'Kelly, 1965, Pl 27), is reflected on top of the central boss of the Antrim cross in the Craggaunowen Museum in Plassey near Limerick, for which I have elsewhere (Harbison, 1981) suggested a date in the late eighth century or close to 800 on the basis of the animal ornament among other things.

The glass studs of the Shrine's buckle (Pl XII and XIII) (O'Kelly, 1965, Pl 24-25) obviously belong to the same general family as those on the Ardagh Chalice and the Tara Brooch, as well as the individual fragment found at Ekerö (references in O'Kelly, 1965, 185n). One of these (O'Kelly 1965, Pl 25) bears a very striking resemblance to those on the ring of the west face of the Tall Cross at Monasterboice, which dates from the second quarter of the ninth century. Of considerable interest, too, are the glass studs with three C-shaped wires, touching each other back to back so as to leave a spherical triangle between them (Pl XIII, centre top and bottom) (O'Kelly, 1965, Pl 26). To the close parallel forming the eye of the open-mouthed beast on the Ekerö crozier (Pl XIV) and that using beaded gold wire on the Ardagh Chalice (Organ, 1973, 263, fig 59) already adduced by

Fig 45: Processional cross in Santa
Maria in Valle in Cividale, northern
Italy (after Cecchelli).

Professor O'Kelly (1965, 118), we may add the Derrynaflan paten (Ó Ríordáin
1980, Pl XXIII, b), a cloisonné example forming part of a ring found in Ireland in
the 19th century (Ross 1933), a lost disc from the Trewhiddle hoard deposited *c.*
875 (Wilson 1961, Pl XXII and XXVII, b), a hanging bowl escutcheon from
Anskvoll in Norway (Henry, 1936, Pl XXXVI, 4), and the filigree example used on
the Tara Brooch (Henry, 1965, Pl 41, lower left). Filigree is also used for the
C-shaped wires, placed in a roughly similar fashion, though four in number, on
the 'Cavan' brooch (Cone, 1977, Pl 41), for which a date late in the eighth century
has been proposed (Lucas, 1973, 98, caption to Pl 28). A variant of the type with
four C-shapes occurs in the Book of Lindisfarne (Alexander, 1978, Pl 38), and Ross
(1933) and Elbern (1954, 9) have pointed to a number of instances where these
C-shapes are found on Langobardic and Coptic metalwork probably of the
seventh and eighth centuries. A most interesting metalwork example,
geographically closer to Ireland, is found on the portable altar from the former
Adelhausen monastery in Freiburg i. Br. in Germany, and now in the Augustiner
Museum in the same city. Here we find both three and four C-shaped wires in the
medallions of the crosses at each end of the altar (one of the ends being illustrated
here on Pl XV). They are executed in cloisonné enamel — a technique different

Fig 46: Unprovenanced fibula in the
British Museum (after Haseloff).

Fig 47: Enamelled brooch from York
(after Addyman).

from that used in the glass studs of the Belt Shrine but, as closely comparable pieces of the metalworker's art, rather than a manuscript pattern, they are nevertheless sufficiently close in design to be relevant in assessing the date of the Belt Shrine.

In 1954, Elbern (1954, 18) suggested for the Adelhausen portable altar a date in the first half of the ninth century, but subsequently (Elbern, 1962, 83, no. 284) he preferred a date in the second half of the eighth century, or towards 800, which coincides with the late eighth-century dating proposed by Lasko (1972, 9). Recently, Haseloff (1978, 33-34) has rightly compared the cross-in-circle ornament on the borders of the long side of the altar to the so-called cross-enamel (*Kreuzemail*) fibulae, some of the examples of which may be dated to the second half of the eighth century through the horizontal stratigraphy worked out by Wegewitz (1968) in the cemetery at Maschen, Kr. Harburg.

However, a date closer to the middle of the eighth century could be suggested by the shapes of the ends of the cross-arms on the portable altar, which resemble two D-shapes placed back to back. The shape is perhaps best understood (Elbern, 1954, 6) as a stylised version of the 'half-palmettes' found in the same position on crosses from Stabio in the southern Swiss canton of Ticino (Elbern, 1954, Abb. 4) and that (fig 45) in the church of Santa Maria in Valle in the north Italian town of Cividale (Cecchelli, 1943, Tav. LXXXI), with which one may also compare the silver cross from S Agnello in the Archiepiscopal Museum in Ravenna (Ricci, 1905, Tav. 154-55). The stylised form as found on the cross of the portable altar is also encountered on an undateable fibula (fig 46) in the British Museum (Haseloff, 1978, 29, Abb. 8,7), and in an even more stylised form on the older Lindau book-cover now in the Pierpoint Morgan Library in New York (Lasko, 1972, Pl 2). But, more importantly, a shape similar to that on the portable altar occurs on a fibula found recently on the site of a new swimming-pool at York (Addyman, 1977, 55), where it was accompanied by coins of Eadbert (737-758). This significant coin-dated example (fig 47) could be seen to favour a date of around the middle third of the eighth century for the Adelhausen portable altar.

It may be noted here that the shape of the ends of the arms of the portable altar, the unprovenanced fibula in the British Museum and also of the fibula recently discovered at York, resemble closely that of the two D-shaped plaques from St Germain when placed together, but with the difference that the outer sides of the St Germain plaques are straight, whereas those of the other examples are slightly concave. These St Germain plaques were imaginatively reconstructed by the late John Hunt (1956) as being the finials for a sarcophagus. But the constant recurrence of similar D-shaped forms on the crosses of the portable altar and the two fibulae make a strong case for seeing in the St Germain plaques, and their virtual twins found at Gausel in Norway (Bakka, 1965, 39 with Pl 4b), the ends of the arms of a bronze altar or processional cross somewhat smaller in size than that from Cividale mentioned above which measures 94 × 86 cms and for which Cecchelli (1943, 241) suggested a date in the early ninth century. The only difficulty in such a reconstruction for the St Germain plaques is the angle at which the animal heads project at the bottom end, which could be difficult to fit into the adjoining round form as found on the Adelhausen altar. The dating provided by the York fibula need not, incidentally, be applied to the St Germain plaques, as the latter's straight outer sides could be seen as a half-way stage between the concave form found on the portable altar and the York fibula on the one hand, and the straight sides found in more stylised ends of the Ardennes cross (Elbern, 1962, Taf. 288-89), on the other, for which Lasko (1972, 39-40) has proposed a date of c. 830.

If, with the aid of the York fibula, we date the Adelhausen portable altar to around the middle third of the eighth century, we must then pose the question as to whether the C-shaped ornament of the Belt Shrine's studs is to be derived from those on pieces like the Ardagh Chalice or the Tara Brooch, or whether they may be derived from continental examples such as the Adelhausen altar? The answer, of course, depends upon how we date the Ardagh Chalice and the Tara Brooch, both of which are often dated to the earlier eighth century or even as early as 700. If these two great metalwork masterpieces date from closer to the beginning than to the end of the eighth century, as current opinion would appear to believe, then they would obviously be the most likely source for the C-shaped studs on the Belt Shrine. However, it ought to be mentioned that the animals projecting outwards from the rim of the Tara Brooch have the same curling upper jaw as found on the Belt Shrine animal heads. Other animals on the Brooch bear a remarkable similarity to those on the Steeple Bumpstead boss (Henry, 1965, Pl 43) which also features an animal in relief which finds its closest parallel in the St Ninian's Isle hoard (Small, Thomas and Wilson, 1973, II, Fig 23 with Pl 24-25) dateable to the 'latish eighth century' according to Wilson (1978, 8). One of the earliest appearances of such an animal is in the letter V of the word AVTEM on fol. 11 of the

Codex Aureus in Stockholm (Alexander, 1978, Pl 152), a Canterbury manuscript dating possibly from around the middle of the eighth century (Nordenfalk, 1977, 29), but in Ireland variant members of the same animal family occur on a number of High Crosses (Harbison, 1977, 293-94) dating probably from the first half of the ninth century. In addition, the toothful yet tongueless animal-head with jaws opening to an angle of about 130° incised below the handle escutcheons of the Ardagh Chalice (Lucas, 1973, 104, Fig 64, bottom left and right) is closer to those of the St Germain plaques and the Ekerö crozier than to the examples in manuscripts of the late seventh or the first half of the eighth century, e.g. f. 12ᶜ of the Book of Lindisfarne (Kendrick, 1960, 204, Fig 42, h) or page 5 of the Book of Lichfield (Alexander, 1978, Pl 76). As the enamel studs of both the Tara Brooch and the Ardagh Chalice seem to be close in style to those of the Moylough Belt Shrine, a case could thus be made for envisaging the Brooch and the Chalice as being works which could conceivably be ascribed to the middle or second half of the eighth century.

If, then, the Tara Brooch and the Ardagh Chalice, as well as the Moylough Belt Shrine, are seen as being all roughly contemporary, and dating from the middle or second half of the eighth century, then it is quite conceivable that the C-shaped decoration on the Belt Shrine may owe its immediate origin to pieces like the Brooch and the Chalice, but its ultimate origin to continental Europe, where it is found on objects like the Adelhausen portable altar. It is interesting to note that the cloisonné technique used on the cross of the Adelhausen altar, and on the ring from Ireland referred to above, is one practised in the Byzantine world in the eighth century, and that the Byzantine Silver Chalice in the Museum of Fine Arts in Boston (Dodd, 1973, 15, Fig 7) suggests that the ultimate origin for the shape of the Ardagh Chalice is probably Byzantine also.

In conclusion, it may be said that comparisons with the Adelhausen Altar on the one hand, and with the Tall Cross at Monasterboice on the other, suggest that the Moylough Belt Shrine was made between 750 and 850, rather than around 700 as current opinion would hold. Other considerations favouring a date in the late 8th or early 9th century also rest within these parameters. However, such a dating must still be regarded as tentative, based as it is on examination of only a few individual traits of the Belt Shrine, whereas a complete analysis of all the traits might lead to rather different conclusions. But, hopefully, the foregoing remarks will have shown how weak are the foundations on which the chronology of Early Christian Irish metalwork is based, and how necessary it is to review them afresh. Perhaps the recent discovery of the hoard of ecclesiastical metalwork at Derrynaflan in Co Tipperary will give the necessary impetus to review the whole subject anew.

ACKNOWLEDGEMENTS

I would like to express my thanks to my wife, Edelgard, for the drawings accompanying this paper. For photographic illustrations, I am grateful to Bord Fáilte, the National Museum of

Ireland, the Austrian National Library, the National Museum of Antiquities in Stockholm (through Hilary Richardson), and the Augustiner Museum, Freiburg i. Br.

REFERENCES

Addyman, P., 1977. 'Urban excavations in York. 2: Anglian and Viking York' *Illustrated London News*, April 1977. 55-57.

Alexander, J.J.G., 1978. *Insular Manuscripts, 6th to the 9th century*. Harvey Miller, London.

Bakka, E., 1965. 'Some decorated Anglo-Saxon and Irish metalwork found in Norwegian Viking graves'. *In* A. Small (ed), *The Fourth Viking Congress, York, August 1961*, 32-40. University Press, Aberdeen/Edinburgh/London.

Bierbrauer, K., 1979. *Die Ornamentik frühkarolingischer Handschriften aus Bayern*, Bayerische Akademie der Wissenschaften, Philosophisch-Historische Klasse, Abhandlungen, Neue Folge, Heft **84**.

Cecchelli, C., 1943. *I Monumenti del Friuli dal secolo IV all XI*. Rizzoli, Milan/Rome.

Cone, P., 1977. *Treasures of Irish Art, 1500 B.C. - 1500 A.D.* Metropolitan Museum of Art, New York.

De Paor, L., 1977. 'The Christian triumph: the Golden Age'. *In* P. Cone (ed), *Treasures of Irish Art 1500 B.C. - 1500 A.D.*, 93-104. Metropolitan Museum of Art, New York.

De Paor, M., 1979. *Early Irish Art*. Department of Foreign Affairs, Dublin.

De Paor, M. and L., 1978. *Early Christian Ireland*, 2nd ed. Thames and Hudson, London.

Dodd, E.C., 1973. *Byzantine Silver Treasures*. Berne.

Elbern, V.H., 1954. *Der Adelhausener Tragaltar — Formenschatz und Ikonographie*. Nachrichten des Deutschen Instituts fur merowingisch-karolingische Kunstforschung 6/8. Erlangen.

Elbern, V.H., 1962. *Das Erste Jahrtausend. Kultur und Kunst im werdenden Abendland an Rhein und Ruhr. Tafelband*. Schwann, Düsseldorf.

Fanning, T. and Ó hÉailidhe, P., 1980. 'Some cross-inscribed slabs from the Irish midlands'. *In* H. Murtagh (ed), *Irish Midland Studies, Essays in commemoration of N.W. English*, 5-23. The Old Athlone Society, Athlone.

Graham-Campbell, J. and Kidd, D., 1980. *The Vikings*. British Museum Publications, London.

Harbison, P., 1977. 'On some possible sources of Irish High Cross decoration'. *In* O.-H. Frey and H. Roth (ed), *Festschrift zum 50-jährigen Bestehen des Vorgeschichtlichen Seminars Marburg*, Marburger Studien zur Vor- und Frühgeschichte **1**, 283-297. Verlag Kempkes, Gladenbach.

Harbison, P., Potterton, H. and Sheehy, J., 1978. *Irish Art and Architecture from Prehistory to the Present*. Thames and Hudson, London.

Harbison, P., 1981. 'The Antrim Cross in the Hunt Museum', *N Munster Antiq J.* **21**,17-40.

Haseloff, G., 1978. 'Der Einband des Ragyndrudis-Codex in Fulda, Codex Bonifatianus 2'. *In* A. Brall (ed), *Von der Klosterbibliothek zur Landesbibliothek. Beiträge zum zweihundertjährigen Bestehen der Hessischen Landesbibliothek Fulda*, 1-46. Hiersemann, Stuttgart.

Haseloff, G., 1979. 'Irland'. *In* H. Roth (ed), *Kunst der Völkerwanderungszeit*. Propyläen Kunstgeschichte, Supplement IV, 223-43. Propyläen Verlag, Berlin.

Henry, F., 1936. 'Hanging Bowls'. *J Roy Soc Antiq Ir* 66, 211-46.

Henry, F., 1965. *Irish Art in the Early Christian Period (to 800 A.D.)*. Methuen, London.

Holmqvist, W., 1955. 'An Irish crozier-head found near Stockholm', *Antiq J* 35, 46-51.

Hunt, J., 1956. 'On two "D"-shaped bronze objects in the St Germain Museum', *Proc Roy Ir Acad C* 57, 153-57.

Kendrick, T.D. *et al.*, 1960. *Evangeliorum Quattuor Codex Lindisfarnensis* II. Urs Graf Verlag, Olten and Lausanne.

Köhler, W., 1930. *Die Karolingische Miniaturen — I. Die Schule von Tours*, Teil I. Deutscher Verein für Kunstwissenschaft, Berlin.

Laing, L., 1975. *The Archaeology of Late Celtic Britain and Ireland c. 400 - 1200 A.D.* Methuen, London.

Lasko, P., 1972. *Ars Sacra 800-1200*. Pelican, Harmondsworth.

Lucas, A.T., 1973. *Treasures of Ireland. Irish Pagan and Early Christian Art*. Gill and Macmillan, Dublin/Unesco.

Lundström, A., 1978. 'Helgö, a pre-Viking trading center', *Archaeology* 31, 4, 24-31.

Nordenfalk, C., 1977. *Celtic and Anglo-Saxon Painting. Book Illumination in the British Isles 600-800*. Chatto and Windus, London.

O'Kelly, M.J., 1965. 'The Belt-Shrine from Moylough, Sligo', *J Roy Soc Antiq Ir* 95, 149-88.

Organ, R.M., 1973. 'Examination of the Ardagh Chalice - a case history'. *In Application of Science in Examination of Works of Art, Proceedings of the Seminar, 1970*, 238-71. Museum of Fine Arts, Boston.

Ó Ríordáin, B., 1980. 'The Derrynaflan hoard', *Antiquity* 54, 216-7.

Ricci, C., 1905. *Raccolte Artistiche di Ravenna*. Instituto Italiano d'Arte Grafiche, Bergamo.

Roe, H.M., 1969. *The High Crosses of Western Ossory*. Kilkenny Archaeological Society.

Ross, M.C., 1933. 'An Irish cloisonné enamel', *Down Connor Hist Soc J* 5, 43-6.

Small, A., Thomas, C. and Wilson, D.M., 1973. *St. Ninian's Isle and its Treasure*. Vol. I. University Press, Aberdeen/London.

Stokes, M., 1901. 'Notes on the High Crosses of Moone, Drumcliff, Termonfechin, and Killamery', *Trans Roy Ir Acad* 31, 541-78.

Wegewitz, W., 1968. *Reihengräberfriedhöfe und Funde aus spätsächsischer Zeit im Kreis Harburg*. Göttinger Schriften zur Vor- und Frühgeschichte, 10.

Werner, J., 1978. 'Jonas in Helgö', *Bonner Jahrbücher* 178, 16-42.

Wilson, D.M., 1961. 'The Trewhiddle hoard', *Archaeologia* 98, 75-122.

Wilson, D.M., 1964. *Catalogue of Antiquities of the Later Saxon Period. I, Ornamental Metalwork A.D. 700-1100*. British Museum, London.

Wilson, D.M., 1978. 'The Art and Archaeology of Bedan Northumbria'. *In* R.T. Farrell (ed), *Bede and Anglo-Saxon England* (Brit Archaeol Rep 46), 1-22.

KEVIN A O'BRIEN

Fig 48: Conjectural reconstruction of an Early Christian cemetery and settlement based on the excavations at Reask, Co. Kerry.

Early Christian Sites in the Barony of Corkaguiney

Thomas Fanning

Co. Kerry has a rich heritage of archaeological sites particularly sites belonging to the Early Christian Period. Almost certainly the best known and probably the most important of the early monastic sites is Skellig Michael lying about eight miles off the coast of the Iveragh peninsula. This famous site has not been excavated but a survey has been published (de Paor, 1955) and an account of the monastery is also included in the survey of early monasteries around Cahirciveen and Waterville (Henry, 1957). Church Island, near Valencia, stands alone amongst these sites as the only excavated example and the excavations conducted there in 1955-6 by Professor M.J. O'Kelly have provided us with a very complete picture of the nature and sequence of both the ecclesiastical and domestic features to be found on such sites (O'Kelly, 1958). His more recent comments on the nature of monastic sites in the west of Ireland have given scholars in this field much room for thought and highlighted some of the major problems attached to the study of such sites for which little or no historical records have survived (O'Kelly, 1974).

From 1972 to 1975 the present writer was engaged in the excavation of such a site at Reask on the western tip of the Dingle peninsula across the bay from Valencia. These excavations, recently published (Fanning, 1981)[1], owed much to the earlier research of Professor O'Kelly and it is with a deep sense of gratitude that the writer offers the following paper as a contribution to this *Festschrift* in his honour. Whilst working at Reask most of the Early Christian sites in the Barony of Corkaguiney (roughly coterminous with the Dingle peninsula) were visited for comparative material. Notes were taken and a descriptive survey compiled[2]. What follows below is a summary account of the results of these visits in the hope that it may stimulate more detailed study of these important Early Christian monuments.

The majority of the Early Christian enclosures or cemeteries in the Dingle peninsula are marked on the O.S. six inch maps as 'Calluragh burial ground (disused)'. The word calluragh, or *ceallúnach* as it is called locally, is used to denote these sites as places of interment for unconsecrated burial especially of unbaptized children. Although a few sites so marked were chosen for this type of burial simply on account of their antiquity, e.g. ringforts or clochauns, in most instances an early ecclesiastical association had survived either in their obvious remains or in folk memory or both and was the primary factor in their re-use as *ceallúnachs*. It would appear that most of these sites had been abandoned as cemeteries and settlements by medieval times and the only continuity, or more properly, re-utilization after that period is for clandestine burial which is known to have continued even into modern times.

Every site so designated as a calluragh was visited even though the surface indications, in some cases, were slight and unpromising and, in a few instances, contained no obvious ecclesiastical features. Graveyards containing the ruins of medieval churches and still in use as consecrated burial grounds were also visited as it was felt that some might contain features belonging to the Early Christian period. This search proved to be largely negative.

Of the fifty-six sites in the Dingle peninsula which could be thought of as Early Christian cemeteries at least seventeen can be regarded as major sites or developed cemeteries as defined by Thomas (1971, 51). These include sites like Inishtooskert and Inishvicillane on the Blasket Islands; Maumanorig and Kilvickadownig near Ventry harbour; Reask, Ballywiheen, Gallarus, Kilmalkedar and Currauly around Smerwick harbour; Kilfountain and Ballymoreeagh near Dingle; and Illauntanig on the Maharee Islands. These sites compare very favourably in their surviving features and remains with the major sites in Iveragh such as Skellig Michael, Church Island, Killabuonia, Illaunloughan and Kildreelig (Henry, 1957).

The seventeen Corkaguiney sites contain most of the following diagnostic features: a sub-circular, dry-built enclosing wall; a small drystone oratory; a small rectilinear grave enclosure or *leacht*; a cross-inscribed pillar or slab or a plain cross; an internal dividing wall and the remains of beehive or clochaun structures. Other features such as souterrains and ogham stones although their occurrence is not so widespread could also be regarded as diagnostic. Holy wells are associated with many of the sites but in most instances are located outside the enclosure. With the notable exception of Kilmalkedar few sites contain any definite medieval remains.

Although only a relatively small number of sites contain all these features as visible antiquities, excavation as at Reask would undoubtedly reveal additional structures. The conjectural reconstruction of the structures and features of such a site as shown in fig 1 is largely based on the evidence from the excavations at Reask.

An important antiquity which is not found in the Dingle peninsula is the gabled shrine or special tomb as known from Iveragh e.g. at Killabuonia (Henry, 1957, Pl XXXIXb; Hughes and Hamlin, 1977, fig 3). However, the excavations at Reask did reveal a very early form of shrine known as the slab-shrine (Fanning, 1981, 85) and perhaps more await discovery. On the other hand the small rectilinear grave enclosure or *leacht* often covered with quartz pebbles is a feature of many of the sites visited e.g. Inishvickillane (Pochin Mould, 1972, fig 104) and it may be linked with the location of early burials or a shrine (Thomas, 1971, 143). It should be stressed, however, that the evidence from the excavations at Reask indicates that the form of rectilinear grave enclosure as found in the Dingle peninsula is more likely to be a late feature associated with the calluragh phase.

The majority of the cross-inscribed pillars and slabs can be regarded as pre-tenth century in date though it would be unwise to offer a firm date for most of them.

However, the cross forms at Arraglen and Coumduff or Knockane (Henry, 1937, pls XXV, XXVII) which have the Chi-rho motif and the Greek crosses with widely expanded terminals and curvilinear ornament as at Reask and Kilvickadownig (Macalister, 1899, 214) exhibit significant parallels with the decorative motifs displayed in the early insular manuscripts of the seventh century A.D. The curvilinear designs, also found on the alphabet stone at Kilmalkedar (Romilly-Allen, 1892, 268), Currauly (Crawford, 1912, 231) and the recent find at Ardamore[3] may well be derived from or inspired by an ultimate La Tène tradition. Inscriptions where they occur are in an early form of Irish script like the contraction DNE at Reask and offer another link with the manuscripts. The finding of the peacock design at Reask (Fanning, 1981, fig 31) coupled with the evidence of slabs such as Loher in Iveragh (Henry, 1957, Pl XXIXa) are indicative not only of an early date but perhaps too of a direct continental and east Mediterranean influence in this coastal region.

Pillar stones like the well-known example at Reask could have demarcated the boundary of the primary cemetery or could have been set up over an early grave, perhaps the founder's grave, as at Church Island (O'Kelly, 1958, 131). Some of the slabs appear now to be in a secondary position as part of the rectilinear grave enclosure as at Ballywiheen (Henry, 1937, Pl XXXV). The cross-slab at Gallarus may also be re-used in a similar fashion as there are clear traces of a small rectilinear enclosure on the northern side of the famous oratory.

Ogham stones with inscribed crosses occur on a number of sites e.g. Maumanorig (Henry, 1937, Pl XXVI, 2, and Ballymorereagh (Romilly-Allen, 1892, 276) but are more numerous as isolated antiquities. Some of the latter as at Trabeg (Crawford, 1912, 236) are also inscribed with crosses. The presence of so many ogham stones (nine in all) at Ballintaggart (Romilly-Allen, 1892, 256-61) raises the question that some of these sites could have been pagan pre-Christian burial places. This is a plausible theory but is not borne out by the evidence from the excavations at Reask. At Maumnahaltora (Ó Conchúir, 1974, 13) the Bronze Age wedge tombs were re-used as places of Christian devotion but the site was not adapted as a Christian cemetery. At Coumduff (Knockane) only excavation could tell us to what period the cist-like structures belong though the surface traces would appear to link the features with the *ceallúnach* graves at Reask and not with any tumulus or megalith as suggested by Henry (1937, 276).

Most of the developed cemeteries contain the remains of an early drystone oratory — Illauntanig has two examples (Dunraven, 1875, facing p. 128). That at Gallarus is unique in its state of preservation and its dating has been the subject of some debate — the most recent assessment (Harbison, 1970) favouring a late, possibly even a twelfth-century date, for its construction. In this regard it should be pointed out, however, that the O.S. six inch maps show the existence of three oratories at nearby Kilmalkedar. Two of these survive — one a few fields to the N.W. of the site and the second almost directly outside the graveyard wall on the

N.E. In all probability these oratories should antedate the building of the Romanesque church. The evidence from the excavations at Church Island and Reask has shown that whilst the stone oratories at both sites were not contemporary with the primary burial phases they were, apparently, constructed sometime between the eighth and tenth centuries.

It seems reasonable to suggest that the stone oratories belong to a phase of development which also included some form of eremitic monastic settlement as evidenced by the beehive or clochaun structures. The internal dividing wall may well be a contemporary feature dividing the sacred and domestic areas with the former containing the oratory, cross-slabs and cemetery in the eastern and upper segment of the site as at Reask and Gallarus. No visible traces of a primary cemetery composed of lintel or simply dug graves (Thomas, 1971, 49) will be evident without excavation though its position may be indicated by a cross-slab or pillar. The simple stonemarkers to be seen at some sites e.g. at Reenconnell are part of the later *ceallúnach* phase. At Reask the primary lintel graves lay well below the level of the *ceallúnach* burials extending in a long crescent in the eastern sector with the cross-inscribed pillar providing the only visible indicator. As the investigations at Church Island revealed — and to a lesser extent at Reask — most of the primary domestic and religious structures were probably built of wood.

The enclosure wall where it has not been interfered with by later field fences is usually, but not exclusively, sub-circular in form and is probably an early feature related to the primary cemetery. Due to the later interference it is often difficult to determine the original plan but from an examination of the O.S. maps and aerial photographs it is clear that some of the enclosures were quite large. At Ballymorereagh the line of the almost circular enclosure can be followed across two fields and at Reask the area enclosed measures approximately forty-five metres in diameter. Well-built, cashel-type walls are in evidence at both the above sites and at Ballywiheen whilst the cashel wall on Illauntanig can be compared to the walls at stone forts such as Leacanabuaile.

Few of the beehive structures survive to any great height and only the single example on Inishtooskert and the three examples on Illauntanig (Pochin Mould, 1972, fig 14) can be compared to the well-preserved cells on Skellig Michael. At Kilfountain and Currauly excavation could reveal substantial foundations similar to Reask (Fanning, 1981, fig 2) where the remains of seven clochauns or beehives were exposed and conserved though traces of only two such structures were visible prior to the excavations.

On the enclosures which could be regarded as undeveloped cemeteries (Thomas, 1971, 51) a number of comments can be made. Some, like Lateevemanagh, consist of little more than a small, enclosed stony area with a low mound of stones containing a cross-slab. This type of site could, conceivably, be the remains of a larger enclosure of which all other visible traces had disappeared. On the other hand, in quite a few instances the calluragh when visited proved to be nothing more than a stony area in the corner of a field e.g. at Ballynabuck. Such a site might well be of fairly recent origin of little or no antiquity and with no Early Christian associations. It is known that unbaptized infants were sometimes buried simply in a plot near the house or beside townland boundaries (Ó Súilleabháin, 1939, 148). Some of the sites turned out to be the remains of ringforts or clochauns with no ecclesiastical features or associations but which were re-used as calluraghs and marked as such on the maps e.g. at Ballybowler South and Puckisland.

One must also consider the locations of some important cross-slabs such as the cross-inscribed ogham stone at Arraglen and the recent find at Ardamore. These stones are certainly indicative of Early Christian activity but the latter, at least, may have been moved some distance from its original location. The site at Fohernamanagh on the southern slopes of Masatiompan should also be mentioned. The structural remains here are very interesting as is the eremitic location though there are no visible traces of a grave or cemetery.

Almost all the major sites i.e. developed cemeteries lie to the west of the town of Dingle with particular concentrations in the townlands around Smerwick and Ventry harbours and two major sites on the Blasket islands of Inishtooskert and Inishvickillane. The one outstanding major site to the east of Dingle is located on Illauntanig on the Maharee Islands. This coastal distribution agrees with the pattern in the Iveragh peninsula and may very well indicate a seaborne introduction of Christianity direct from Gaul and Spain or even from the eastern Mediterranean. Such connections could account for the emphasis on the eremitic tradition and explain the other associations such as the B-ware and the peacock motif at Reask (Fanning, 1981, 159). The spread of this Early Christian monastic movement along the western Atlantic seaboard is also demonstrated by the distribution of similar sites and comparable cross-inscribed stones in counties Galway, Mayo, Sligo and Donegal (Henry, 1937).

We do not know how long these enclosures remained in use as the foci of the Early Christian communities of the west. Apart from Kilmalkedar none of the Corkaguiney sites appears to have achieved any prominence in medieval times and only the latter site received any attention in the scanty, historical documentation now available to us. From the very fact, however, that these Early Christian cemeteries are set apart from the medieval church sites and graveyards it would appear that they were abandoned probably by the time of the Norman invasion except for their more or less clandestine use as calluraghs by which designation they can still be located to-day.

NOTES

1 The excavation at Reask was undertaken on behalf of the National Parks and Monuments Branch of the Office of Public Works.

2 This survey will be published shortly in a forthcoming number of *J Kerry Archaeol Hist Soc*. An appendix to the Reask report contains a list of Early Christian sites in the Barony of Corkaguiney.
3 Information received from the excavator, Mr Conleth Manning of the Office of Public Works.

REFERENCES

Crawford, H.S., 1912. 'A descriptive list of early cross-slabs and pillars', *J Roy Soc Antiq Ir* **42**, 217-44.
De Paor, L., 1955. 'A survey of Sceilg Mhichil', *J Roy Soc Antiq Ir* **85**, 174-187.
Dunraven, E. (ed. Stokes, M.), 1875. *Notes on Irish Architecture*, 2 vols. London.
Fanning, T., 1981. 'Excavation of an early Christian cemetery and settlement at Reask, Co. Kerry', *Proc Roy Ir Acad C* **81**, 67-172.
Harbison, P., 1970. 'How old is Gallarus Oratory? A reappraisal of the role of Gallarus Oratory in early Irish architecture', *Med Archaeol* **14**, 34-59.
Henry, F., 1937. 'Early Christian slabs and pillar stones in the West of Ireland', *J Roy Soc Antiq Ir* **67**, 265-79.
Henry, F., 1957. 'Early monasteries, beehive huts and drystone houses in the neighbourhood of Cahirciveen and Waterville (Co. Kerry')', *Proc Roy Ir Acad C* **58**, 45-166.
Hughes, K. and Hamlin, A., 1977. *The Modern Traveller to the Early Irish Church*. London.
Macalister, R.A.S., 1899. 'On an ancient settlement in the south-west of the barony of Corkaguiney, County of Kerry', *Trans Roy Ir Acad* **31**, part y, 209-344.
Ó Conchúir, D., 1973. *Corca Dhuibhne*. Dublin.
O'Kelly, M.J., 1958. 'Church Island near Valencia, County Kerry', *Proc Roy Ir Acad C* **59**, 57-136.
O'Kelly, M.J., 1974. 'Monastic Sites in the West of Ireland', *Scot Archaeol Forum* **5**, 1-16.
Ó Súilleabháin, S., 1939. 'Adhlacadh leanbhaí', *J Roy Soc Antiq Ir* **69**, 143-151.
Pochin Mould, D., 1972. *Ireland from the Air*. Newton Abbot.
Romilly Allen, J., 1892. 'Notes on the antiquities in Co. Kerry visited by the Royal Society of Antiquaries of Ireland and the Cambrian Archaeological Association, August, 1891', *J Roy Soc Antiq Ir* **22**, 255-84.
Thomas, A.C., 1971. *The Early Christian Archaeology of North Britain*. Oxford.

Anglo-Norman Dublin:
Continuity and Change

Patrick F. Wallace

While it might have been simpler to entitle this essay 'the archaeology of thirteenth-century Dublin' which is its real concern, the present title has been adopted because it makes it less easy to ignore the apparent gap in our archaeological data for the generation or so after the siege of Dublin in 1171. The general labelling in this way of the physical culture of this period, though arguably provocative, is also useful for it seeks to compare and contrast the material remains of the Hiberno-Vikings of the pre-Norman period with that of the Anglo-Normans and invites an assessment of the elements which continued unchanged from one period to the next. The comparison of the two periods will be preceded by a description of the material remains of the Anglo-Normans. It is also felt that a general survey of the urban archaeology of this period is overdue, for, not only is it only now gaining general acceptance in our university courses, but also because in the popular mind our medieval urban archaeological remains have been dominated by the Vikings. People rarely talk about preserving their Anglo-Norman medieval remains and will persevere in thinking of the National Museum's archaeological excavations in Dublin as being concerned with the Vikings only when, in fact, on present experience, our levels go on to about the middle of the fourteenth century. By drawing attention to the archaeological remains of this relatively neglected period and to some of its problems, it is hoped that this essay will go some little way towards redressing this imbalance. An attempt is also made to place the archaeological evidence into a general historical framework, though the danger of 'fitting' archaeological evidence to historical fact must be avoided.

Two notes of caution are necessary. Firstly, the archaeological discussion presented here is based purely on the results of the Dublin excavations and does not treat of architectural evidence, either surviving or documentary. Secondly, as the type of site I have excavated is different for the period after the Norman invasion from what it is before, this may have an effect on a comparison of the material culture of the two periods. For, while our evidence for the tenth, eleventh and early twelfth centuries is derived from waterfront and urban habitation sites, that for the thirteenth and early fourteenth centuries, comes largely from the reclamation infill dumped behind the waterfront. Given that the dumped infill consists in part of urban refuse, which contains artifacts which must be generally representative of the contemporary urban scene, and that both site types are blessed with similar anaerobic qualities, it would seem that a comparison between aspects of the material culture of the two periods is not only possible but desirable, although the different sources of evidence militate against statistical comparisons and a comparison of the environmental remains.

The archaeology of Anglo-Norman Dublin can conventionally be dated to after the 1169 invasion or, more properly, to after the surprise capture of Dublin by the Normans under de Cogan and le Gros in September 1170 or, to the raising of O'Connor's futile siege a year later (Orpen 1911, i 210-11, 225-30). However, this approach conflicts with the political (Warren, 1969, 9), mercantile (Westropp, 1912-13, 375-6; Wood, 1915, 258) and ecclesiastical history of the late eleventh and early twelfth centuries (Warren, 1969, 8) when the church in Dublin was organised, not under Armagh, but until 1140 under Canterbury (Watt, 1972, 1-7) and Irish kings took an interest in the political affairs of the Norman world (Ryan, 1942-3, 20, 38) and when at least one Norman king appears to have contemplated an invasion of Ireland (Orpen, 1911, i 82). It would also appear that by the beginning of the twelfth century, the direction of Ireland's foreign trade had shifted away from the old northern trade routes frequented by the Vikings in the tenth and eleventh centuries and was increasingly concentrated on the seas between south-west England and northern and western France (Haskins, 1918, 144; Slover, 1926, 42-8; Ryan, 1942-3, 20). The evidence from the archaeological excavations conducted in Dublin by the National Museum, especially the Fishamble Street and Wood Quay sites which I have directed since 1974, tends to confirm an early involvement of the Anglo-Normans in Dublin's affairs well before 1170 and to support the view of the Norman invasion as the inevitable development rather than the beginning of a series of historical events. The nature of the pottery imports, the standardisation of smaller metal ornaments like bronze stick- or cloak-pins as well as the growing use of heavier timbers such as ground sills in houses, all argue for an early twelfth-century watershed in the material culture of Dublin rather than for major changes after the invasion. It seems that it was not until the first couple of decades of the following century that we can see the real effects of the invasion, when King John's interest in Ireland, coupled with Dublin's growing trade prosperity, led to another great watershed.

The take over of Dublin by the Normans from the Hiberno-Vikings or Ostmen who migrated (Curtis, 1938, 403), were compelled to migrate (Curtis, 1908, 210) or were banished (Clarke, 1979, 37) to Oxmanstown north of the Liffey, where they may already have had a settlement, led to a growth in civic (Edwards, 1938, 2-10) and ecclesiastical institutions like the setting up of a merchant's guild which was first legally recognised in John's 1192 charter (Webb, 1929, 44-8) and in the early thirteenth century to the purchase of the fee farm from the King in 1215 (Gwynn, 1947, 281) and to the establishment of the office of mayor in 1229. These administrative changes followed Henry II's grant of Dublin to the men of Bristol and were formalised in the charters of John (Curtis and McDowell, 1943, 24-27).

The growth of civic institutions and the fortification of the castle in the early thirteenth century (*c.* 1220) occur at a time when major engineering feats, such as the 1215 building of a bridge over the Liffey, the provision of an embanked freshwater supply from outside the town (Berry, 1891, 557-8) and, as recent excavations have shown, a major redevelopment of the port were undertaken. The commencement of the nave of Christchurch about 1212 (Waterman, 1970, 71) is also indicative of this early thirteenth-century rise of Dublin as is the expansion of the city beyond the west walls (Sweetman, 1886, 48). This apparent bustle of urban activity, which is discernible at the beginning of the thirteenth century, is possibly not unconnected with the loss of Normandy (Warren, 1969, 17) which forced the Norman barons to concentrate on their Irish interests and to develop Irish trade. It is not surprising, therefore, to find such large quantities of imported pottery in Dublin from precisely this period.

It would seem that for about thirty years or so after the initial invasion, no major concerted effort was made to develop, improve and enlarge the city, though this impression could be due to the absence of historical data and it must be admitted that Dublin's municipal status, if nothing else, was in the ascent, if Henry II's 1171-72 and 1174 and John's 1192 charters are anything to go by. A possible clue to a twenty-year delay in Dublin's development may be afforded by the evidence of the charters for it is the second and not the original which gives the go-ahead for laying out the town in messuages, some of which were to be extended into the river. Elsewhere, there is also a suggestion of growth outside the western boundary of the town from 1200 (St J Brooks, 1936, 47, 56) and for the reclamation of the Liffey in 1202 (McNeill, 1950, 29). However, as it seems that the archaeological record is relatively poor for this period and as we appear to have few remains (especially pottery) which can be conclusively ascribed to it, it seems that there was relatively little urban development or activity until after the initial conquests, possibly due to the threat posed by native resistance. However, we must be warned against sweeping conclusions at this early stage in the study of the material culture of the period, especially as it must be remembered that there is a written reference to the presence of a 'crocker's (i.e. potter's) lane' as early as 1190 (St J Brooks, 1936, 22) which implies that local kilns possibly stimulated by imported wares (from south-west England?) were established by this time and that archaeologists may yet find compelling reasons to bring forward some of the dates for the earlier pot types, conventionally dated to the thirteenth century (Barton, 1974).

The expansion of the port, just mentioned, was achieved by constructing a series of waterfronts (one succeeding the other) at the riverward side of the city wall in pursuance of a number of advances into the river which had their origins in the early tenth century (Wallace, 1981a). The first of these was built about, or slightly before, 1200 and consisted of a post and wattle reinforced embankment which ran for at least 35m from east to west about 20m north of the stone wall. The embankment was comprised of available gravel, estuarine mud and organic debris dumped on the waterfront. This may have been intended as a temporary measure and was shortlived as the west part collapsed shortly after it was erected. There was already a series of parallel post and wattle fences issuing from the wall into the water before the building of this bank which may have been 'messuages' and possibly those referred to in John's 1192 charter. They now assisted the reclamation infill between the embankment and the stone wall.

The next major advance into the bed of the Liffey was made about 1210 when a stout wooden quay-wall or oak revetment was constructed roughly parallel to the embankment which it replaced. This was built in a straight line in at least six 12m wide sections, each probably reflecting the response of the burgess who was responsible for the relevant section of the waterfront. This front braced revetment belongs to the vertical type of the contemporary north European harbour wall building tradition (Milne, 1979, 145-53) and is comprised of horizontally laid lapped boards placed on edge behind squared oak posts which are morticed into horizontal baseplates which are braced on the front, at the riverward side. The heels of the braces are sometimes bedded in the gravelly foreshore but are also morticed into subsidiary baseplates at right angles to the main series to which they are often morticed. The revetment was completed by infilling the area behind with estuarine mud, gravel and dumped organic refuse from the town. Thereby, the accommodation at the port was increased and improved especially when pathways, streets and warehouses were laid on top of the newly reclaimed ground and the docking facilities were ameliorated by the provision of these vertical wooden quay walls which could be approached by ships. Indeed, apart from the general desire to improve the port which is implicit in the wooden quay fronts, there was also a desire to increase the draught of available water to float the larger ships which had been introduced into Ireland by the Anglo-Normans (Wallace, 1976, 22-4). In the absence of dredging, it was probably felt that the depth of water would be increased by encroaching on the river. While there is also literary evidence that the river was reclaimed from the other side in the thirteenth century by the monks of St Mary's Abbey (Carville, 1972, 41) the upstream position of their harbour or 'pill' cannot be seen as evidence of a concerted attempt to contain both banks of the Liffey. The shallowness of the river persisted into the fourteenth century (Sweetman, 1886, 135) and as late as 1358, long after the erection of the wooden waterfronts and the later stone wall which replaced them, the merchants of Dublin still complained of the want of water and of how Dalkey had become the deep-sea anchorage for the city to which goods had to be transshipped in lighter vessels (Gilbert, 1895, 19-20).

The early thirteenth-century wooden revetment or quay wall was provided with a 'buffer' device, probably to absorb the pressure of docking ships. One of the six known sections was extended farther out in the bed of the river shortly after the erection of the revetment. Here, a series of nailed ships' planks was stood vertically on a baseplate and front braced, but collapsed soon after construction. The extension was linked to the main revetment by a post and wattle breakwater.

Two further wooden revetments were built farther out in the river bed later in the thirteenth century — each crossing the site from east to west and each parallel to one another as well as to the original revetment and to the river. The first of these was back braced and had a right angled turn at its east end — the present Fishamble Street where we know from later documents was a 'Fish Slyppe' (Gilbert, 1889, 223, 290, 469; Clarke, 1979, 37). An elaborate brace to protect the vulnerable scarf-joint of the baseplates of this revetment was featured near its west end. The final wooden revetment was built even farther out in the bed of the river and was provided with a series of pegged tie-backs which projected through the planking. This was replaced by a stone quay wall about 1300, the latter being about the ninth in a series of waterfronts unearthed in the present excavations at Wood Quay. Of these waterfronts, four are pre-Norman while the others are post-Norman and are almost entirely of thirteenth-century date.

A general switch over to heavier timber framed building and an increased use of stone as a building medium seem to be the two main influences of the Normans on Dublin's houses. Heavy squared ground sills with morticed vertical posts, as used in the waterfront revetments or as a framework for grain and wine cellars and rubbish pits and drains which were lined with vertical or horizontal weather-boarded planks, are common in the thirteenth and early fourteenth centuries (Ó Ríordáin, 1971, 76). The same kind of building was evident in the heavy thirteenth-century cagework warehouses along Wood Quay. The large squared timbers of the warehouses (?) have mortices in their upper surfaces, presumably to hold upright posts, the intervals between possibly having been filled with wattle screens. Although it is tempting to attribute this form of construction to Norman influence and while there is little doubt that it was popularised after the arrival of the Normans, it should be remembered that there is limited evidence for the use of ground sills and squared vertical posts in the early twelfth-century houses at present (July 1980) being excavated on the Fishamble Street 111 site.

An increasing number of stone buildings is evident from the numbers of floor and roof tiles as well as roof ridge tiles and chimney pots which are almost certainly derived from the stone supported roofs of either secular or ecclesiastical buildings, or both. The Christchurch Place site contained the remains of a mortared stone building of the late thirteenth/early fourteenth century (Ó Ríordáin, 1974, 206; 1973, 152). The gradual substitution of stone for wood in the castles of the countryside from about the turn of the century (Martin, 1967, 138), may have been accompanied by a concomitant change from post-and-wattle to stone for the more substantial town houses or a least by a shift from post-and-wattle to timber framing, though most houses probably continued to be built in post-and-wattle in the post-invasion period (Ó Ríordáin, 1971, 76).

Stone was also used in thirteenth-century drains of which there are examples in excess of 30m from Christchurch Place (Ó Ríordáin, 1973, 151-2; 1974, 206) and

Wood Quay (Wallace, 1975-76, 31-32). Drains were a major feature of the site at Wood Quay where they were first built of wood and later of stone. Some were built of re-used ships' timbers and all ran roughly north-south at right angles to the city wall and the revetments. They appeared to issue from cesspools outside the wall. The longest was over 40m in length, averaged 1.50m wide by 1.75m high and was built in six stages having uprights, soleplates and headplates as well as sheeting along the sides, which was held in place by the pressure of dumped infill. The top decking was used for a time as a footpath.

As will be apparent from the size and length of the wooden revetments just described, it is not surprising that thanks to our excavations, we are now in possession of a dictionary of thirteenth-century carpentry joints and techniques which can be usefully compared with those of the horizontal mills of early historic Ireland (Lucas, 1953, 1-36) and more pertinently with those of the pre-Norman period from the Fishamble Street and other Viking period excavations on the one hand, and with the few surviving late medieval details of carpentry as at Dunsoghley Castle, Co. Dublin (Leask, 1941, 118-121) and the Cashen Bridge, Co. Kerry (O'Kelly, 1961, 135-52) on the other. Recent examination (Wallace, 1981b) of these joints shows that the basic techniques employed in the main (1210) revetment, such as simple pegged scarf jointing, the axing of baseplates and the general use of the axe in dressing heavy beams and planks, the apparent lack of understanding about the increased stress bearing qualities of timbers laid on edge rather than on the flat, all make it possible for this carpentry to have been the product of locally based craftsmen to whose ancestors this repertoire of techniques and joints was known in Viking and — as the evidence of the horizontal mills seems to indicate — since early historic times where their introduction into Ireland may have been from the Roman world. While the mortice and tenon joint is well attested in early historic mills, only the more basic notch and tenon version was known to the tenth- and eleventh-century Dublin house builders. Generally, it seems, in spite of the recurrence of the proper mortice and tenon and the preference of the thirteenth-century carpenter for oak, which was not generally used in the pre-invasion period, any new techniques which were introduced by Henry II's prefabricated wooden castles (Lydon, 1972, 41) or by the carpenters known to have come to Dublin with John to perform the 'King's works', (Browne et al., 1963) were not subsumed within the local repertoire; the early Norman carpentry of the Dublin waterfront drew on native skills and craftsmen. The second revetment may have been an exception, as here we see the use of notch-joints which appear to be innovative, possibly the work of sappers, and rather short-lived as the surviving evidence from the third revetment suggests, as the latter seems to be comprised of the joints known in Ireland at the time of the first wooden revetment, if not earlier.

The craft of shipbuilding was close to that of carpentry in medieval times. Fortunately, the excavations have revealed considerable evidence of thirteenth-century shipbuilding, especially at Wood Quay where considerable quantities of nailed ships' planks have been unearthed. These were particularly conspicuous in the extension to the first revetment where part of the dismembered side of a ship was stood on its side to form a waterfront revetment. The use of ships' timbers in this way is paralleled in a similar situation at the Seal House site, London (Schofield, 1975, 56). Caulking and evidence for the use of Stockholm tar are also found, as are different widths and lengths of ships' planks, suggestive of different ship sizes and functions. Other, and to the ship archaeologist, more diagnostic parts of Norman-period ships have also come to light from the excavations. These include bulkheads, a mast step, a keel, beam-knees, a stealer, numerous ribs (generally reused as uprights for drains), oar port, paddles, oars, possible decking, a possible thwart and two 'Y' shaped mast crutches or *mykes*. Dendrochronological analysis (Baillie, 1977, 260) of the Wood Quay ships' timbers suggests that the ships were locally made and of local oak and that they had a useful life of about thirty years (i.e. by subtracting their dendro-dates from those of the revetment in which they were incorporated) after which they were either dumped as part of the reclamation in the expanding harbour outside the city wall or reused and incorporated in drains or revetments. It appears that the timbers of some of the ships found in early thirteenth-century contexts at Wood Quay were felled about 1180. Preliminary results of the examination of the ships' timbers suggest that the ships were enlarged versions of their precursors in the Viking period, not unlike those depicted on the Bayeux Tapestry or that on the roughly contemporary early thirteenth-century pewter ampulla (see below) from Canterbury which was found at Wood Quay. Even more so than carpentry, shipbuilding techniques do not appear to have been subjected to change with the coming of the Normans as the more recently found ships' timbers of the Viking period tend to show.

Turning our attention from structures to artifacts, we find that pottery is the most abundant artifact recovered in the excavations of medieval Dublin where it was commonly employed for a variety of domestic and architectural purposes, especially in the thirteenth century, as kilns were established locally and a plentiful supply of English, French and other continental types was imported. Whereas pottery is rare in the early tenth century, it becomes increasingly common in the later eleventh and early twelfth centuries with the apparently increased importation of unglazed and French gray-wares, red-painted and Normandy gritted wares and glazed Ardennes wares (Hurst, 1976, passim; Hodges, 1977, 239-255) which turn up from the later eleventh-century levels. Examples of these wares argue for active trade links with the Norman world and Norman England long before the 1169 invasion and were recovered from the layers behind the old city wall which is also of pre-invasion date and is itself reflective of Dublin's wealth about 1100.

The production of pottery presents one of the greatest differences between the Vikings and the Normans for, whereas the former imported pottery in relatively small amounts, the latter not only imported it in huge amounts but set up local kilns, the output of which made them the closest thing to factories before the Industrial Revolution.

It comes as no surprise that the most commonly imported wares of the post-invasion period came from the Bristol Channel-Severn Valley area of south-west England, especially from Bristol itself. This was an area of England closely associated with pre-Norman Dublin with which trade links had long been forged and which was even more strongly linked with Dublin after Henry II granted Dublin to his men of Bristol 'for them to inhabit' (Gwynn, 1947, 275-86), an opportunity which they seized, as is evident from the proportion of people from that area (Otway-Ruthven, 1965, 75-84) who feature in a 1226 list of citizens (Webb, 1929, 4-11). The well known Bristol wares especially from the Ham Green kilns are the most conspicuous (Barton, 1964, 95-126). Of these, the lead-glazed thirteenth-century 'B' wares with their characteristic bridge spouts, slash decoration, internal buff slip and applied strip decoration as well as the unglazed comb-decorated cooking wares are more common than the often roulette decorated 'A' wares with the better made fourteenth-century Bristol wares less in evidence due, perhaps, to the by then flourishing state of local potteries. From the Bristol area also came a number of three-spouted puzzle-jugs, including the knight-jug variety, because of the applied knights-in-armour which adorn their necks. Gloucestershire's large tripod pitchers, with their characteristic pocked internal surface, applied tubular spout and sparing use of lead glaze were also commonly imported. The Gloucester pitchers are often regarded as earlier than the late twelfth century and it may be that they were the earliest English imports shipped to Dublin from Bristol after Henry II's grant. Gloucester's historical links with Dublin are also well known (Lydon, 1972, 41). A series of squat jugs with thumb-frilled spouts and applied rouletted strips of body decoration which were often generously lead-glazed and had a characteristic lozenge sectioned rim is usually ascribed to the Cheshire region and may have been shipped through Chester. The south-western area of England may also have produced the unglazed bee-skips, fire covers or curfews and grain measures which also turn up in Dublin while many others of our, as yet unidentified, potsherds probably also came from thirteenth-century England. These may include specimens from Scarborough and also fairly fine wares with complex rouletting.

The impact of these imports, especially those from Bristol, on Dublin and on other Irish towns, must have been enormous and must have given rise to the establishment in them of pottery kilns as is evident from the shape, appearance and abundance of thirteenth- and early fourteenth-century locally produced wares, the most usual vessels of which were jugs, storage jars and cooking pots.

Barton (1974) has distinguished three basic Dublin wares. The 'A' group (especially jugs) is strongly influenced by Ham Green 'B' products especially in respect of rim type, the characteristic bridge spout, the slashing of the strap handles and the occasional application of body strips to a more generally preferred plain body. These wares were made in a micaceous clay, the fabric being tempered with mica and fired in a kiln designed to produce an oxidising atmosphere. They have a brick-red finish with a slate-grey reduced internal sandwich colour. The 'B' wares were contemporary with the 'A' group, had a dull grey fabric, often with a muddy finish, were infrequently glazed and were fired in a reducing atmosphere. Large cooking vessels appear to have been more common than jugs in the 'B' group, which includes a distinctive series of pipkins with trumpet-shaped handles, a number of decorated cooking wares with thickened flat rims and large-handled pottery tubs. The Dublin 'C' cooking wares were fired in a reducing atmosphere and are very coarse, hard finished vessels of simple crude appearance with large quartz grits in the fabric. Despite variations in firing, glazing and in the quality of the wares, Barton maintains that Ham Green 'B', Dublin 'A' and to a lesser extent, Dublin 'B' are contemporary and together with the bulk of the south-west French material are probably ascribable to the late thirteenth and early fourteenth centuries when the Dublin potters could have been copying a late and undecorated variety of Ham Green 'B'.

Thanks partly to the stimulus of the late thirteenth-century fine wares from France, the early fourteenth century saw the appearance, among the Dublin 'A' wares of plain and twisted rod handles, tubular spouts and wider slashed strap handles as well as apparently new vessel forms like shallow rectangular meat dishes with internal glazes, dripping trays, handled baking vessels and internally glazed skillets as well as a double shell lamp. The Dublin puzzle-jugs with their fish mouth pouring spouts, which may have been an imitation of the Bristol type, were also produced about this time. The apparent use of a white slip under the characteristic green lead glaze may have been an attempt by local potters to recreate the effect of the probably more expensive French polychromes. The rod handles of Rouen and the occasional projecting base may have been in response to the French Saintonge series just as the rare applied bird motifs may literally have been a plastic imitation of the ravens which feature on the Saintonge polychrome jugs. The applied 'ram's-horns' which sometimes feature around the spouts may have been derived from Ham Green and Chester-area prototypes. While it is not usual for vessels in one medium to copy, or be influenced by, the shapes of those produced in another, the angular lug handles which occur on the fourteenth-century Dublin pots were probably styled on the more highly prized contemporary bronze cooking vessels and skillets. In their turn, the ceramic forms influenced at least one wooden jug- or treen-maker who carved a vessel out of a simple piece of wood with a basal foot and profile reminiscent of a contemporary ceramic jug.

The development of the local pottery industry also witnessed the production of products for functions other than domestic cooking especially the manufacture of roof and floor tiles and their allied products (like chimney finials). Heavy roof ridge tiles with characteristic slashed cockscomb lugs and the more rare variety with hooks on the crest were produced in local fabrics, as were shingles, although ridge tiles could have as easily capped slates as tiles. The thirteenth-century inlaid floor tile is only rarely found in the excavations and the typical line-impressed tiles of the four-teenth and fifteenth centuries are slightly more numerous. Future excavations may show that both roof and floor tiles were used in town houses as well as on ec-clesiastical buildings. For all our information on medieval Dublin pottery types, we have not as yet any trace of an actual kiln despite the occasional discovery of wasters or stackers. From the written reference to 'crocker's lane', it appears that the kilns were situated to the west of the city, outside the walls where they posed less threat of fire.

The grey unglazed wares from northern France with their typical applied flatten-ed strip and roulette decoration and their characteristic rim form came to Dublin from the late eleventh to the thirteenth centuries. However, in the thirteenth cen-tury, the most commonly imported French pottery type was the lead glazed parrot-beak spouted jug with the projecting basal edge and characteristic mottled green appearance which resulted from the inclusion of copper filings in the glaze. These were produced in the region of La Chapelle de Pots in the Saintonge region (north-east of Bordeaux) of south-western France (Barton, 1963, 201-214). Many of the bases of these jugs have a carved geometric symbol, possibly a merchant's mark, to indicate a particular consignment or batch. These can vary from stars-of-David to crosses and triangles and more obscure marks.

It is possible that the influx of Saintonge pottery into thirteenth-century Dublin (and other Irish towns) (Dunning, 1974, 110) is related to the acquisition of Aquitaine as part of the dowry of Eleanor, wife of Henry II and to the loss of Normandy earlier in the thirteenth century, during the reign of John. Both events must have contributed to a shift southwards in France by Anglo-Norman traders, shippers and wine merchants. This shift appears to be reflected in the relative quantities of French pottery from thirteenth-century Dublin. It is possible also that the bulk of Dublin's imports from south-west France came from a small area of the Saintonge which may have specialised in the production of pots (and wines?) for export to Dublin (Bob Thompson, personal communication). This possibility emerged recently at the Hull pottery conference (Davey and Hodges, 1981) where, despite their overall similarity to the south-western French jugs and pots imported through Southampton, the Dublin series is still rather distinctive and includes many specimens not found at southern English ports. These include jugs which sometimes have a wide lid-seating, specimens with dummy spouts and, especially, examples with applied thin wavy strips of brown slip. Dublin has also produced cruets and trumpets of Saintonge origin as well as specimens of both glazed and unglazed squat Pégau jugs with their characteristic wide strap handles and large spouts in which the body of the pot was cut back to facilitate pouring.

Saintonge polychrome jugs with their characteristic greens, yellows and blacks on their clear-glazed white body surfaces are also in evidence among the Dublin im-ports but are not as common as might appear. Saintonge sgraffito jugs are even more rare while there are also other rare types from south-western France, including an intact specimen with an overall chequer board design (N[ational] M[useum of] I[reland], 1973, Cat. 104, 35) and a brown and cream jug of which the fabric, if not the decoration, appears to be from the Bordeaux region (N.M.I., 1973, Cat. 101, 35). This decoration resembles that of the patterns in brown slip under a clear cream glaze found on the rather coarser, thicker and whiter fabrics, which probably came from western France.

The distinctive Rouen type (Barton, 1965, 73-85) jugs with their clear glaze over a red haematite slip, their characteristic rouletted thin applied strips and pellets and their very distinctive rod handles topped with pairs of pinched lugs form a considerable proportion of the thirteenth-century quality imports. A rather similar series with long necks and hollow rod handles and differing in that their glaze includes copper filings which gives them a greenish rather than a creamy 'Rouen' appearance is much less in evidence. These may have originated from the Paris region (Barton, 1966, 59-73) while other green-glazed French jug varieties including specimens with deeply scored lines and applied scales may have been brought to Dublin from places like Orleans and Caen. There are examples of other fine wares of probable French origin to which an actual region of origin cannot at present be ascribed. These include at least two varieties in which a brown slip has been painted on applied strips (vertically placed in one, and in bands of curves in the other) under a fairly clear glaze with few copper filings. There are also green-glazed jugs with distinctive incised cable decoration along rim and spout edges and these may have come from western France.

A variety of French ceramic mortars appears in Dublin. These range from flint-gritted types with brown slips under lead glaze to more finely finished green glazed types with heavy ledge rims to specimens with moulded human face masks to others in which human face masks are incised into a wide flattened rim which often bears stamped decoration. Other ceramic products of thirteenth- and fourteenth-century France which have been unearthed in Dublin include aquamaniles, roof finials (including an elaborate louvre finial fragment with smoke openings at the side), money-boxes, oil lamps and candlesticks.

Other pottery imports include exotic painted wares and blue-grey skillets. The painted ware sherds are representative of jugs painted in yellow with brown tendril patterns, others in red with encircling yellow bands and blue panels, a handle with brown 'C' curves, a bodysherd with multicoloured horizontal daub marks and another with a painted human face mask. These probably late thirteenth-century exotic painted wares appear to have been brought from southern France and Italy. If they are Italian, they can be regarded with the bulla of Pope Innocent III (N.M.I., Cat. 180, 42) and a pilgrim's badge from Rome (N.M.I., Cat. 178, 42) as among the few surviving artifacts of such an origin to have been found on the Dublin excavation. In the absence of written sources it would be concluded from the archaeological evidence that Italy's trade links with thirteenth-century Dublin were fairly inconsequential when compared with those of France. We know however that Italian merchant bankers and traders played a huge part in the mercantile and fiscal affairs of thirteenth-century Ireland (Westropp, 1912-3, passim; O'Sullivan, 1962, passim), so much so that they may even have been in charge of the French pottery trade.

Spanish amphorae are very scarce and there is also a handful of sherds of archaic majollica from about 1300. The Dublin excavations have also revealed late Saintonge sgraffito and polychrome chafing dishes as well as later majollica wares from the fifteenth and sixteenth centuries. There is also evidence for the importation of German blue-grey wares in the form of the characteristic handled cup or 'Paffrath' skillet although, on pottery evidence at least, Dublin's thirteenth-century trade with Germany and the Low Countries cannot have been very great, the axis being very much tilted in the direction of south-western France.

Apart from objects made in pottery, artifacts made of metals like iron, bronze, lead and pewter, with very little silver and gold, organic materials like wood and leather, as well as stone, glass and amber have all been found in thirteenth-century Dublin levels. Such an array of objects considerably helps with a reconstruction of life in medieval Dublin. Apart from information on the nature of the contemporary household and related chores furnished by wooden objects like bowls, plates, platters etc. carved out of single pieces of timber, stave-built buckets, tubs and barrels, spoons and beatles, wooden shovel blades, bronze items like keys, skillets and spoons, stone mortars, bone needles, pins, plain-headed and simply ornamented bronze needles and bodkin-needles as well as stone, pottery and pewter candlesticks and lamps, these objects tell us of the variety and skills of the craftsmen necessary to supply the requirements of the medieval townsman. The crafts of the cooper, blacksmith, bronzesmith, leather-worker, harness-maker, locksmith, bone and antler worker, carpenter, builder, shipwright, fisherman, weaver, spinner, basketmaker are all in evidence as are the goods bought and sold by a variety of merchants and shopkeepers. The proximity to the city of the land and evidence of animals is clear not only from the surviving bones of the various animals butchered in Anglo-Norman Dublin, but from the objects like combs, gaming pieces, dice, harp pegs, pins and needles which were carved from the discarded bones of these animals and the collected antlers of the red deer. The discovery of items such as iron sickle blades probably shows that farmers were kitted out by the urban craftsmen with whom they must have traded extensively, given the nature of the toll items listed in contemporary murage grants (O'Sullivan, 1962, 106) and of the main items of export through the port of Dublin (Russell, 1972, 130-7; MacNiocaill, 1964, 505-38).

The cloth industries of spinning and weaving are represented not only by surviving textile fragments but also by stone and lead spindle whorls, iron shears and a variety of needles in bone and bronze. Stone moulds and crucibles, as well as iron slag, are other evidence of craft industries. Other stone products like large lugged mortars, quernstones, moulds, astragals and other building stones need not all have been produced locally. Some oolitic limestones, especially from Dundry Hill, were imported from Somersetshire (Waterman, 1970, 63-75) and were used locally. Though usually corroded in the thirteenth- and fourteenth-century levels, the iron products, especially those connected with horses, are significant. These include, horsebits, horseshoes, prick-spurs, nails(?) and, possibly from a later period, rowel spurs. An iron claw-hammer may more easily be attributed to the blacksmith than to the carpenter who appears to have used nails more sparingly, though it is difficult to be certain. Another heavier iron hammer head and a couple of iron chisels could have belonged to a stone mason. The ironworker's craft is also represented in the numerous ships' nails and roves or washers, iron keys, barrel padlocks and their keys, fishhooks, as well as rings and chains of unknown purposes, which are found in the course of the excavation.

Leather working is attested not only by ornamented knife sheaths and other pieces but by boots and shoes and their repair scraps as well as by cobbler's tools including awls with lathe-turned wooden handles. Similarly, bone and antler working is borne out by finished articles as well as by unused off-cuts. As we have seen, there is now little doubt that both the carpenter and the shipwright were very important in Anglo-Norman Dublin and while they, like the other crafts, have left considerable evidence of their work, there are other crafts (Webb, 1929, 9) such as that of fishermen for which we only have lead sinkers and iron fishhooks, and even others like rope makers and basket makers for which we have even scantier surviving evidence. This serves to underline the limitations of archaeological evidence which, for all its value for the materials which survive, still supplies only part of a picture which has to be supplemented by literary references and illustrations (where they survive) for areas of social life for which material artifacts no longer exist.

Personal ornaments are represented by bronze buckles, bronze and silver annular brooches, worn at the throat to fasten the slits of neck garments, bronze stick or cloak pins, most of which are plain headed but some of which have more elaborately cast heads often crooked and chiselled or in the shape of a horse's head. Personal ornaments also occur in wood in which were carved buckles and strap tags, as well as in amber (beads), iron (knives), lead (pendants) and leather (knife-sheaths). It would appear that the iron knife was the most common contemporary item of personal ornament. The iron knife was tanged and fitted with a wooden, antler or bone handle (the small grinding stones from the excavations were probably for sharpening these knives). The handle was often of polished bone and sometimes decorated with dot and circle designs. One thirteenth-century knife handle from Wood Quay is carved in the shape of a crowned(?) human figure which clasps a chain or cloak string with its right hand. The knife was usually carried in a decorated leather sheath which was fastened to the belt of the wearer by leather thongs. In excess of forty examples of these sheaths have come from the

Wood Quay site alone. The designs tend to be simple, geometric and repetitious, almost as if they were mass produced. The designs were sometimes stamped or bluntly incised. One of the most unusual thirteenth-century personal ornaments was a child's bracelet in which the links were all carved out of a single piece of wood. Closely related to personal ornaments are toilet implements. Of these, the most obvious examples are combs single or double sided, usually of bone and antler, rarely of wood and bronze, tweezers including some with finely chiselled rectilinear designs.

Apart from coins which are scarce in the twelfth and thirteenth centuries, save for a few of Henry II, John, and Henry III, as well as French *deniers tournois*, Bordeaux oboles (Ō Ríordáin, 1972, 168), Westphalian(?) coins and the spectacular hoard of over two thousand thirteenth-century tavern tokens (of eighteen varieties) (Dolley and Seaby, 1971), found in a Winetavern Street pit with southwestern French pottery, other objects connected with trade include bracteates, pottery money boxes, pans, beams and suspension holders for weighing scales. There is also a lead weighted bronze jetton or reckoning counter, a notched wooden tally stick possibly used by shopkeepers and a pewter lid which probably came from the lid of a box which contained a set of nested weights. The Wood Quay site has also produced a fifteenth-century wool-merchant's lead seal with the arms of the city of Rouen (Platt and Coleman Smith, 1975, ii, 270) which had a long trading history with Dublin.

Evidence for Norman games and pastimes comes from bone dice, discoidal bone and wooden counters, sometimes incised with dot and circle patterns, stone and slate gaming boards, usually incised with three rectangles (one inside the other), and said to be for playing Nine-Mens-Morris of which there is a late medieval French tapestry illustration (Evans, 1969, pl. 62 and p. 236). Two chessmen deserve special mention. One is a carved king or vizier/queen of possible arabic derivation and the other is a bishop(?) carved in antler (N.M.I., Cat. 90, 33). Bone harp pegs and bone whistles also turn up in the thirteenth century while there is also a variety of spinning tops and possible horn and wood diabolos(?).

A number of objects from the Anglo-Norman levels of the Dublin excavations may be said to have historical associations. These include pilgrims' souvenirs in the form of ampullae or miniature flasks and badges. Four thirteenth-century flasks are now known, each made of pewter, three being from Canterbury and the other from St Wulfstan's Shrine at Worcester. These flasks were intended to contain healing or holy water and were worn around the neck. The three which commemorate St Thomas à Beckett of Canterbury include one in the shape of a ship which depicts the scene of St Thomas's martyrdom on one side and the saint's head on the other. It exhibits some interesting ship details including pronounced external keel, side oar-ports and a double-ended appearance reminiscent of the ships in the Bayeaux tapestry. More recently, a pit at the John's Lane end of Wood Quay contained another ampulla which also depicts the scene of St Thomas's martyrdom on one side and his head on the other. Both are made to look more expensive by being given a tin flashing. The third Canterbury ampulla which, like the others from the same shrine, was also found at Wood Quay, is in the form of a sword scabbard, the sword being the instrument of St Thomas's martyrdom. Wulfstan is featured on one side of the ampulla from his shrine, with the Virgin Mary on the other. The latter was found at High Street (N.M.I. Cat. 179, 42). Pilgrims' badges were sewn on to pilgrims' hats to prove they had visited the shrine. One of the badges bears the figures of SS Peter and Paul and was undoubtedly brought to Dublin in the early thirteenth century by a pilgrim from Rome (N.M.I. Cat. 178, 42). The other, from Wood Quay, is in the form of a lion within a circular band. It cannot now be identified with a particular place of pilgrimge. An item with a definite historical association which can be connected with a person is the lead seal or bulla of Pope Innocent III (N.M.I., Cat. 180, 42) which probably came to Dublin attached to an important document relating to the archbishopric. A much lesser known, but no less real, historical person was Adam Burestone whose name is inscribed on a lead seal matrix which like the bulla was also found at High Street (N.M.I., Cat. 181, 42).

Apart from the objects with religious connections which have just been mentioned in the context of finds with historical associations, the excavations have also yielded a cabochon mount which could have come from a medieval Irish shrine. It consists of an oval unfaceted rock crystal set in a bronze mount. A sheet gold mount in the shape of a sheep's head may also have come from a reliquary.

This survey of the material remains of the Anglo-Norman Dubliners shows both continuity and contrast with the archaeology of the preceding Viking and Hiberno-Viking periods. Such an impression is based on a general reflection on all the excavations carried out to date. As has been said, there appears to be no one date which can be regarded as a watershed, but it is now possible to speak in general of the material culture of the earlier half of the tenth century, while the material from the earlier eleventh century, the late eleventh, early twelfth century and the thirteenth century each contains a broadly defined but distinguishable assortment of structures and artifacts.

In general it appears that the Anglo-Normans used less amber, less gold and silver, fewer glass beads and less lignite than did the Vikings. They seem to have had little use for or need of the motif or trial-pieces which are so characteristic of the preceding age but used pottery for all kinds of things, unlike their predecessors who only used it sparingly. Both cultures seem to have used amounts of stone — the earlier for querns, moulds and bowls and the later for querns, moulds, mortars and building. The Norman period ushered in a much greater use of pewter and heavier bronze utensils like cooking vessels and skillets. The abundance of artifacts concerned with the fireplace and cooking as well as with horses from the Norman period contrasts with the preceding period which has yielded more personal ornaments and *objets d'art*. For example, plainer metal finger-rings sometimes with stone settings became common in the thirteenth century while bronze cloak or stick pins appear to have become less ornate and smaller. The number of buckles increased in the Norman period as did stone spindle whorls, iron spurs and horseshoes. Both periods have produced considerable evidence of crafts and trades especially those based on wood and leather and the importance of ships and ship-building is also commonly shared.

There appears to have been a continuity of tradition in craftsmanship, especially in the production of domestic utensils, which persisted after the Norman invasion. The stave-built wooden buckets, lathe-turned wooden bowls and other vessels hollowed out of single pieces of wood of the thirteenth century resemble those of the preceding period. It is likewise with other domestic crafts, such as the spinning and weaving of textiles, the production of bone and antler combs, pins and needles and probably the same with ironworking. Bronze stick pins remained in use as did fasteners and only differed in that they appear to be more standardised and repetitious in the choice of terminal shapes and designs. Shoemaking and leather-working seems to have changed little, except for the absence of originality in the choice of decorative patterns evident in the thirteenth-century examples. Most if not all the carpentry techniques found in the thirteenth-century revetments already existed in the Viking period. Reliance on the axe and adze, the comparative rarity of the saw, and the use of radially cut boards and the use of pegs rather than nails (except in ships) persist throughout. However, a greater reliance by the Normans on oak, in contrast to the former widespread use of ash for heavier buildings appears to represent change. There appears to have been a greater tendency to employ squared larger building beams in the Norman period when there was also a much greater use of mortice and tenon joints. A complex stop-splay joint which appears in a tenth-century ship's keel from Fishamble Street was not used in the revetments of the later period when the simpler scarf joint was almost invariably preferred. It should be borne in mind that this suggested continuity of carpentry tradition from the Viking to the Norman period was probably much more deeply rooted and closely related to the native tradition. This continuity of carpentry, evident from the Dublin excavations and the apparently similar conservatism in the other domestic crafts and trades suggests that either the newcomers (whether they were Vikings or Normans) brought few new techniques with them or, more likely, if they did they had little impact on the technical repertoire of the native craftsmen who had mastered locally available raw materials as well as the limitations of tools and the requirements of the environment and who were probably retained and patronised by each successive wave of newcomers. Curtis's view that the old Scandinavian element was the basis of the later population of Dublin and the other Norman towns would seem to be correct, at least as far as the crafts are concerned (Curtis, 1938, 409).

Aside from this obvious continuity of tradition in domestic crafts from the Viking to the Norman periods, there are many more changes than parallels in the material culture of the two periods. Apart from the well documented historical Norman introductions like the appointing of urban officers such as that of mayor and the establishment of a bureaucracy which tied Dublin to the English king's interests, the principal physical difference seems to have been in the scale of engineering. The Normans built bigger structures and used more stone than did their predecessors. Dwelling-houses are more commonly built of stone than before and stone buildings, especially castles and abbeys, make their appearance in contrast to the infrequent use of stone in the preceding period when only the rather insubstantial city wall was built in that medium. Not only are houses bigger, docks and ships are larger. The latter, because of their increased size, derived from ships of the preceding period probably led to the creation of larger and more commodious docks.

The undertaking of a large-scale civic development, urban expansion, dock building and reclamation in the thirteenth century contrasts with the Viking phase when only earthen embankments and a narrow stone wall probably backed in part by an earthen embankment were attempted. The impact of individual burgesses or town property owners, which appears evident in the structural sections of the waterfront, has no comparable echo in the tenth and eleventh centuries when a royal command was probably responsible for any military response or civic improvement like the building of a bank around the town.

The Norman approach to town layout may also have differed from that of the foregoing period, for while the newcomers may have accepted the plots or garths of their predecessors, they appear to have preferred a more rectilinear approach, at least in the waterfront at Wood Quay, where their grander scale of building along relatively straight lines would have allowed straighter streets and lanes. Modern-day Fishamble Street is a case in point. For, while the curved nature of its high southern part may have derived from an underlying tenth-century predecessor on which the trapezoidal house plots recently excavated appear to have converged, its comparatively straight northern line seems due to its being on the site of a fifteenth-century 'Fish-Slyppe', which was probably built on the line of the thirteenth-century revetment corners which made right-angled turns in that direction. The straight line of the east-west waterfronts and the later quay wall and the straight north-south line of the east corner at Fishamble Street probably prompted the layout of a rectilinear medieval street/lane plan in this reclaimed area — a pattern which is reflected in the eighteenth- and nineteenth-century topography, much as the radial lines of the earlier Viking period properties seem to have determined a differently aligned layout at the south-east corner of the Wood Quay site.

Insofar as they are reflected by surviving archaeological artifacts, the trade patterns of the two periods also seem to differ. For, while the north-west seaways route, along which was probably traded the amber, lignite, steatite and walrus ivory, and the Irish Sea routes to England, along which probably came the late Saxon pottery, Anglo-Saxon coins and possible Saxon ironwork, continental fine fabrics and glasswork which survive from the tenth- and early eleventh-century levels appear to have had a northern, as well as a north-west, European import bias, the growing amount of north French wares from the late eleventh and twelfth centuries, shows a shift southwards of the trade axis probably increasing after the Norman conquest of England in 1066. This is not unconnected with the rise of Bristol. This trade bias was maintained after the Norman invasion when Bristol and the ports of south-west Britain traded extensively with Dublin as is evident from the abundance of potsherds from this area, which have been found in the urban excavations of Dublin and Wexford. Chester and its region, which was an important trading contact of Dublin in the tenth century, is of much lesser importance to judge from the relative amount of imported pottery attributed to that region found in Dublin. France and especially the port of Bordeaux, through which wine and Saintonge pottery were exported to Ireland continued to be very important. The Mediterranean area also traded with Dublin (O'Sullivan, 1962, passim; Westropp, 1912-13, passim), though except for a few painted potsherds and part of a thirteenth-century Syro-Frankish enamelled glass beaker (Ó Ríordáin, 1971, 76), there is little archaeological support to substantiate the overwhelming historical evidence.

It is not surprising that, because of their cultural and religious background, their piety and interest in pilgrimages and crusades, the Normans have left items connected with places of pilgrimage, popes, saints and religious objects which have no parallels in the Viking period. It is probably the attitude to art and ornament implicit in their material remains which best illustrates the cultural difference between the Vikings and the Normans. For, whereas the former by lavishing individual artistic attention on simple objects like brooches and pins, swords, buckets, walking-sticks, gaming-pieces, jewel boxes, ships' timbers, scabbards and sheaths which they cast, engraved, incised, scored, carved and embossed in their rich abstract animal interlacements, the latter seem more concerned with the quantity rather than the quality of their products and tended to mass produce articles like leather sheaths, pottery vessels and gaming-pieces which they simply decorated with repetitious stamped patterns and simple dot-and-circle designs. A more modern mercantile era of mass production was introduced by the Normans who consigned art to the sculpture and architecture of their churches and monasteries and the vessels they used in them, and introduced simple designs and ornament on articles in everyday use which the comparatively more leisurely pace of the Viking Age had time to beautify and give full expression to contemporary art.

It is unfortunate that there is as yet in Dublin no good evidence for continuous and undisturbed stratigraphy from the early tenth to the mid-fourteenth centuries. The Cork city excavations, which were directed by Dermot C. Twohig, and in which Professor O'Kelly has for so long had an active interest, have not as yet unearthed pre-Norman layers, but have provided an apparently unbroken stratigraphy from early medieval through to post-medieval times. The absence of similar higher and later archaeological levels from Dublin has been seen as due to the intrusion into them of Georgian and Victorian cellars and perhaps the growing tendency to dump rubbish properly in later medieval centuries also played a part. It is vital that future urban excavations should be undertaken with an awareness of this gap in our knowledge and where possible they should be concentrated where the maximum sequence of layers is known to exist so that a full succession of townscapes, their impact on one another as well as the continuity or otherwise of street positions, house dimensions and property boundaries may be unearthed.

It is especially important that there should be thorough examination of all available topographical evidence from the half century on either side of the Norman invasion. For, while our recent work at Fishamble Street has expanded our data on town layout, property size and housing from the early tenth up to the early twelfth centuries, we are not as yet able to demonstrate whether the property boundaries which had such long continuity in unchanged positions before the coming of the Normans actually survived into the late twelfth century and afterwards. Did the Normans change the layout of the streets and of the related properties and their sizes when the Hiberno-Vikings were expelled or went to Ostmanstown or, more likely, did they take over the already existing properties with the minimum modification except where the town was expanded? That they probably accepted the earlier property lines seems likely from the later topographical layout along the west side of Fishamble Street as has been seen. However, only future excavation in the right place will really tell whether Anglo-Norman Dublin was laid out on the lines of the Viking town or whether the layout was altered by the late twelfth-century planners.

ACKNOWLEDGEMENTS

I wish to acknowledge the expert advice and assistance I have had over the years from A.B. Ó Ríordáin, Kenneth J. Barton, John G. Hurst, Sean McGrail, Michael Baillie, Brian Spencer, Raghnall Ó Floinn, Tommy Healy and Michael Dolley, as well as the numerous site assistants at Wood Quay, with whom I have had many fruitful discussions, and Siobhán Denner for her typing.

REFERENCES

Baillie, M.G.L., 1977. 'Dating of ships' timbers from Wood Quay, Dublin'. *In* J. Fletcher (ed), *Dendrochronology in Europe*, B.A.R. Int Series **51**, 259-62.
Barton, K.J., 1963. 'The medieval pottery of the Saintonge', *Archaeol J* **120**, 201-14.
Barton, K.J., 1964. 'A medieval pottery kiln at Ham Green, Bristol', *Trans Bristol Gloucester Archaeol Soc* **82**, 95-126, 201.
Barton, K.J., 1965. 'Medieval Pottery at Rouen', *Archaeol J* **122**, 73-85.
Barton, K.J., 1966. 'The medieval potter of Paris', *Medieval Archaeol* **10**, 59-73.
Barton, K.J., 1974. 'Dublin's medieval pottery' (unpublished).
Berry, H.F., 1891. 'The water supply of ancient Dublin', *J Roy Soc Antiq Ir* **21**, 557-73.

Browne, R.A., Colving, H.M., and Taylor, A.J., 1963. *The History of the King's Works*, I-II. London.

Carville, G., 1972. 'The urban property of the Cistercians in medieval Ireland', *Studia Monastica* (Barcelona) **14**, 35-47.

Clarke, H.B., 1979. 'The medieval Liffey', *Dublin Arts Festival*, 32-8.

Curtis, E., 1908. 'English and Ostmen in medieval Ireland', *Engl Hist Rev* **23**, 209-19.

Curtis, E., 1938. *A History of Medieval Ireland*. London.

Curtis, E., 1942. 'Norse Dublin', *Dublin Hist Rec* **4**, 96-108.

Curtis, E., and McDowell, R.B., 1943. *Irish Historical Documents, 1172-1922*. London.

Davey, P.J., and Hodges, R.A., 1982. *Ceramic and trade: the production and distribution of late medieval pottery in north-west Europe* (forthcoming).

Dolley, R.H.M., and Seaby, W.A., 1971. *Spink's Numismatic Circular*, Dec. 1971.

Dunning, G.C., 1974. 'Pottery mortars in North West France' (with map and distribution list) *In* L.A.S. Butler, 'Medieval finds from Castell-y-Bere, Merioneth', *Archaeol Cambrensis* 78-112 esp. p. 110.

Edwards, R.D., 1938. 'The beginnings of municipal government in Dublin', *Dublin Hist Rec* **1**, 2-10.

Evans, J., 1969. *Life in Medieval France*. London.

Gilbert, J.T., 1889. *Calender of the Ancient Records of Dublin*, I. Dublin.

Gwynn, A., 1947. 'Medieval Bristol and Dublin', *Ir Hist Stud* **5**, 275-86.

Haskins, C.H., 1918. *Norman Institutions*. Cambridge, Mass.

Hodges, R.A., 1977. 'Some early medieval imported wares in the British Isles; an archaeological assessment of the French wine trade'. *In* D.P.S. Peacock (ed), *Pottery and Early Commerce*, 239-55. London.

Hurst, J.G., 1976. 'The pottery'. *In* D.M. Wilson (ed), *The Archaeology of Anglo-Saxon England*. London.

Leask, H.G., 1941. *Irish Castles*. Dundalk.

Lucas, A.T., 1953. 'The horizontal mill in Ireland', *J Roy Soc Antiq Ir* **83**, 1-36.

Lydon, J.F., 1972. *The Lordship of Ireland in the Middle Ages*. Dublin.

Martin, F.X., 1967. 'The Anglo-Norman invasion'. *In* T.W. Moody and F.X. Martin (ed), *The Course of Irish History*. Cork.

Milne, G., 1979. 'Medieval riverfront revetment construction in London'. *In* S. McGrail (ed), *Medieval Ships and Harbours*, B.A.R. Int Series **66**, 145-53.

McNeill, C. (ed), 1950. *Calender of Archbishop Allen's Register, c 1172-1534*. Dublin.

MacNiocaill, G., 1964. *Na Buirgéisí*, II. Dublin.

National Museum of Ireland, 1973. *Viking and Medieval Dublin, National Museum Excavations 1962-73*. Catalogue of Exhibition. Dublin (reprinted 1976).

O'Kelly, M.J., 1961. 'A wooden bridge on the Cashen River, Co. Kerry', *J Roy Soc Antiq Ir* **91**, 135-52.

Ó Ríordáin, A.B., 1971. 'Excavations at High Street and Winetavern Street, Dublin', *Medieval Archaeol* **15**, 73-85.

Ó Ríordáin, A.B., 1972. 'Dublin'. *In* L.E. Webster and J. Cherry (ed), 'Medieval Britain in 1971', *Medieval Archaeol* **16**, 168.

Ó Ríordáin, A.B., 1973. 'Dublin'. *In* L.E. Webster and J. Cherry (ed), 'Medieval Britain in 1972', *Medieval Archaeol* **17**, 151-2.

Ó Ríordáin, A.B., 1974. 'Dublin'. *In* L.E. Webster, and J. Cherry(ed), 'Medieval Britain in 1973, *Medieval Archaeol* **18**, 206.

O'Sullivan, M.D., 1962. *Italian Mechant Bankers in Ireland in the 13th Century*. Dublin.

Orpen, G.H., 1911. *Ireland Under the Normans*. Oxford.

Otway-Ruthven, A.J., 1965. 'The character of Norman settlement in Ireland'. *In* J.L. McCracken (ed) *Hist Stud* **5**, 75-84. London.

Ponsford, M., Dawson and Jackson, 1972. 'Medieval Wasters from St Peter's Church, Bristol', *Trans Bristol Gloucestershire Archaeol Soc* **121**.

Platt, C., and Coleman Smith, R., (ed), 1975. *Excavations in Medieval Southampton 1953-69*. Leicester.

Russell, J.C., 1972. *Medieval Regions and their Cities* .

Ryan, J., 1942-3. 'The O'Briens in Munster after Clontarf', *N Munster Antiq J* **3**, 1-53.

Ryan, J., 1949. 'Pre-Norman Dublin', *J Roy Soc Antiq Ir* **79**, 64-83.

Scholfield, J., 1975. 'Seal House', *Curr Archaeol* **49**, 54-7.

Slover, C.H., 1926. 'Early literary channels between Britain and Ireland', *Studies in English* (University of Texas) **6**, 5-52.

St John Brooks, E. (ed), 1936. *Register of the Hospital of St John the Baptist within the New Gate, Dublin*. Dublin.

Sweetman, H.S. (ed), 1886. *Calender of Documents relating to Ireland 1302-1307*. London.

Wallace, P.F., 1975. 'Wood Quay'. *In* T.G. Delaney (ed), *Excavations 1975-76*, 31-2.

Wallace, P.F., 1976. 'The Growth of 13th century Dublin', *Dublin Arts Festival*, 22-4.

Wallace, P.F., 1981a. 'Dublin's medieval waterfront at Wood Quay'. *In* G. Milne and B. Hobley (ed), *C.B.A. Research Report on Medieval Waterfronts*.

Wallace, P.F., 1981b. 'Carpentry in Ireland 900-1300'. *In* S. McGrail (ed), *Greenwich Conference on Woodworking Techniques*, B.A.R. (forthcoming).

Warren, W.L., 1969. 'The interpretation of twelfth-century Irish history', *Hist Stud* **7**, 1-19.

Waterman, D.M., 1970. 'Somersetshire and other foreign building stone in medieval Ireland, c. 1175-1400', *Ulster J Archaeol ser 3* **33**, 63-76.

Watt, J., 1972. *The Church in Medieval Ireland*. Dublin and London.

Webb, J.J., 1929. *The Guilds of Dublin*. Dublin.

Westropp, T.J., 1912-13. 'Early Italian maps of Ireland from 1300-1600 with notes on foreign settlers and trade', *Proc Roy Ir Acad C* **30**, 361-428.

Wood, H., 1915. 'Commercial intercourse with Ireland in the middle ages', *Studies* **4**, 250-66.

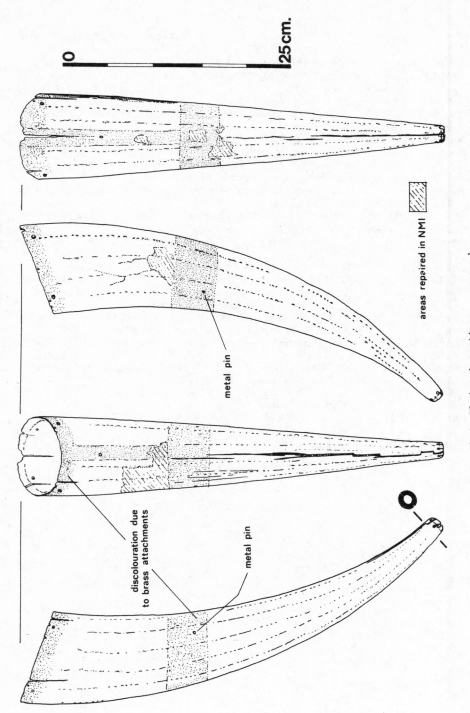

25 cm.

metal pin

areas repaired in NMI

discolouration due
to brass attachments

metal pin

metal pin

Fig 49: The ivory horn with mounts removed.

The Kavanagh 'Charter' Horn

Raghnall Ó Floinn

In 1976 an ivory horn with brass mounts, hitherto in the possession of the Kavanagh family of Borris House, Co. Carlow, was acquired by the National Museum (Reg. no. 1976:2). The object is composed of a curved elephant tusk, oval in cross-section and faceted with sixteen sides (fig 49). The lip is bevelled internally and below this are four perforations through which the rivets of the present mount pass (fig 50). Set closer to the rim are the remains of eight smaller perforations, probably belonging to an earlier mount. The narrow end of the horn is chamfered and has two perforations for the attachment of the present brass ferrule. It also contains five other rivet holes belonging to an earlier mount. Two metal pins set in the body of the horn opposite one another under the central mount indicate that here, also, the present mount is not the original.

Three mounts encircle the horn (Pl XVI). The rim mount, 6.5 cm wide, is flanged and has two components: an inscribed band, the lower end of which fits inside the lip of the horn and a scalloped decorative band with a debased egg-and-dart motif (Pl XVII). The latter is soldered to the lower edge of the inscribed band, covering the outer lip. The whole is secured by four tubular rivets. The inscription (set upside down and legible only when the horn is inverted) is in black letter characters against a hatched ground. It reads:

TIGERNANUS . O . LAUAN . ME . FECIT . DEO . GRACIAS . IHC.

The central mount is faceted and bordered by bands imitating twisted wire and has lobed edges. It is made from a brass sheet, 7.5 cm wide, bent into a tube. The ends are keyed and held in position by a plain metal plate, soldered to the outside. The rim and central mounts are linked by two plain straps secured by hinges at each end. Each strap is further secured to the horn by a modern screw set mid-way along its length.

The legs consist of curved bars, octagonal in section, ending in plates cast in the form of webbed birds' feet. The upper ends are T-shaped with three circular pins which fit into tubular sockets attached to the central mount. On one side, a rectangular repair strip has been inserted between mount and sockets. The legs are also secured by a pair of diagonally set struts, octagonal in cross-section, rebated at either end to fit into tubular sockets. Each foot bears a pair of punched holes, presumably for attachment to a flat surface (these may be modern additions). An interesting feature is that when the horn is removed, the supporting mount is freestanding. The ferrule is funnel-shaped, attached to the horn by a pair of rivets (fig

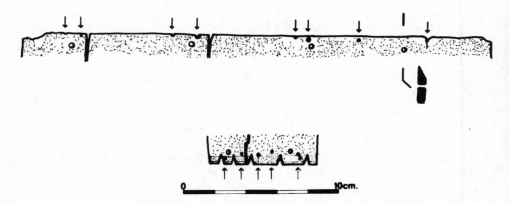

Fig 50: Rim and terminal of the ivory horn showing rivet holes for earlier mounts (indicated by arrows).

51). It is decorated with bands of incised lines and is scalloped at its wider end. The narrower end is closed and bears a series of incised concentric circles. The horn stands to a height of 42 cm and is 52.5 cm in overall length.

The earliest reference to the horn is contained in the Civil Survey of Co. Carlow, 1654-56. In discussing the lands of the Kavanagh family in the barony of Idrone it is stated: 'This house of Garrchoyle, for a testimony that they were the eldest of the Kavanaghs and, descended from the stock of the kings of Leinster, had a great seate and a vessell or cup to drink out of called Corne-cam-more . . . .' (Simington, 1961, 9). Given the coincidence of location and the undoubted antiquity of the piece under discussion, there is little doubt that our horn and that mentioned in the Civil Survey are one and the same. The 'house of Garrchoyle' referred to was the Garryhill branch of the Kavanagh family whose seat was at Rathnageeragh Castle, 6 miles north-east of Borris (Hughes, 1873, 297). By the eighteenth century, the horn was in the possession of the Kavanaghs of Borris House, Co. Carlow. Vallancey described and illustrated it in his *Collectanea* and when he wrote it had been transferred by Thomas Kavanagh to the Trinity College Museum (Vallancey, 1786, 25), where it remained for almost a century. According to another source the horn, and the other Kavanagh heirlooms were removed to Dublin for safe keeping at the outbreak of the 1798 rebellion (MacCormick, 1963, 28).

While it was displayed in the Trinity College Museum it passed largely unnoticed by nineteenth-century antiquarians. A short description and illustration was published in the *Dublin Penny Journal* (1832, 76-77) and a facsimile of the horn was illustrated by Wilde (1861, 266). The shrine of the Book of Mulling was returned to Borris House in 1895 but it seems that the Charter Horn may have been returned at an earlier date, sometime before 1887. A short note on the horn by Walter Kavanagh was later published in an article on horns (Bridge, 1905, 135-6).

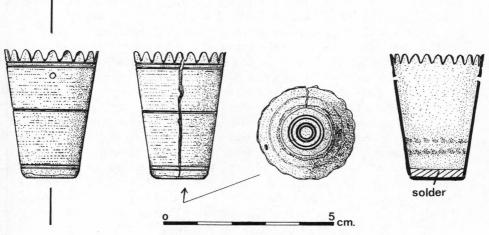

Fig 51: The brass ferrule at the narrow end of the horn.

The occurrence of horns and trumpets for military or ceremonial use is well attested for the prehistoric period in Ireland during the Later Bronze and Early Iron Ages. Decorated drinking horns (Henry, 1965, 59) are known from Early Christian Ireland mostly in the form of bronze terminals ending in bird or animal heads, dating from the eighth century and later. A complete example found in Norway is of aurochs horn (Petersen, 1940, 71). An early twelfth-century example, possibly made in the same workshop as the Shrine of St Lachtin's Arm, is preserved in Brussels (Henry, 1970, 106 and Pl 1). A decorated wooden hunting horn or trumpet, of eighth-to-ninth-century date, was dredged from Lough Erne in 1956 (Waterman, 1969). The Annals also mention war trumpets in use in the ninth and tenth centuries in Ireland (Radner, 1978, 123, 127, 141, 155). None of these horns is made of ivory but they point to the existence in Ireland of a long tradition for the use and manufacture of drinking horns and war trumpets.

There are many references to decorated horns or chalices in church treasuries in twelfth-century Ireland donated by wealthy patrons. In 1115 Turlough O'Connor, king of Connaught, presented a horn ornamented with gold (*corn go nór*) along with a gold cup and a gilt copper paten to the abbot of Clonmacnoise (O'Donovan, 1854, II, 1001). When the altar of the great church at Clonmacnoise was robbed in 1129 a similar horn (possibly even the same one) and the horn of Ua Riada, king of Araid, were taken (O'Donovan, 1854, II, 1033). The church of Doire Choluim Cille suffered a similar fate in 1197 when the four best horns in Ireland (*ceithre corn is ferr*) were stolen and their jewelled mounts were torn off (O'Donovan, 1854, III, 111; also recorded in the Annals of Ulster and the Annals of Loch Cé *sub anno* 1196). These latter bore individual names and included the horn of O'Doherty (*Cammcoraind Uí Dhochartaigh*). The word *corn* in many cases must refer to a horn as these annalistic references distinguish between various types of vessel, including *cailech* (chalice), *bleide* (drinking cup, goblet) and *copán* (cup, goblet). The use of the adjective *cam* clearly refers to a bent horn, such as that of an ox. That some of these horns were used as reliquaries is suggested by Giraldus Cambrensis, who in his *Topography of Ireland*, records a story about a Welsh monk who wore around his neck a relic of St Patrick in the form of a brass horn (Wright, 1887, 146-7). A reference to a horn in a secular context occurs in the Annals of the Four Masters for the year 1189 when, as part of a settlement, Donnell O'Brien was given a horn ornamented with gold (O'Donovan, 1854, III, 87).

In the later Middle Ages there are a few references to horns in wills and inventories. An inventory of the goods of Geoffrey Fox and Agnes Laweless in 1476 refers to a mazer and a horn worth 6s 8d (Berry, 1898, 134) and another of Thomas Hygdon and Agnes Duff dated 1468 refers to horns worth 3s (ibid, 6). A list of the plate belonging to the Earls of Kildare, dated 1518 included 'a great horne, bownd with silver and gylt' (Bryan, 1933, 272). The will of Thomas, 7th Earl of Ormond, who died in 1515, mentions 'a lytle white horne of ivory, garnished at both thends with gold, and corse thereunto of white sylke, barred with barres of gold and a tyret of gold thereupon, which was mine ancestors at fyrst time they were called to honour' (Astle, 1775, 20). The description clearly refers to a ribbon ('corse'), indicating that the horn was carried over the shoulder and may have been used in hunting rather than as a drinking horn. Another horn associated with an Irish family was kept at Garvagh, Co Derry. This consisted of a plain ox horn, carved with the initials I O'K and reputedly in the hereditary possession of the O'Kanes (information from National Museum files).

Finally, one must include in this survey of Late Medieval decorated vessels the remarkable Dunvegan Cup. This is essentially a wooden mether-like vessel encased in decorated silver gilt mounts standing on four feet. Its inscription contains the opening words of the 144th Psalm and suggests that the object was used as a chalice. It is at present preserved at Dunvegan Castle on the Isle of Skye, where it has been since the sixteenth century but its inscription states that it was commissioned by Katherine O'Neill, wife of Niall Maguire, Lord of Fermanagh, in 1493 (MacLeod, 1912-13).

Two main classes of decorated horns are found on the Continent during the Middle Ages. The majority of ivory horns in church treasuries throughout Europe were made by Muslim craftsmen working in Southern Italy in the tenth and eleventh centuries and were used to contain the relics of saints (Koechlin, 1924, 458-9; Kühnel, 1971, 6-19). They are rarely plain and are often richly carved with circus and hunting scenes, grotesques and interlaced animals.

Drinking vessels made of ox or ivory horn with brass, copper or silver mounts are most common in Northern Europe, especially in Scandinavia. Olrik (1909) lists some forty examples dating from the fourteenth to the seventeenth centuries in the National Museum at Copenhagen. There are a number recorded from Britain also

(Pegge, 1775; Jackson, 1911, 589-95). Most of the fifteenth-century examples are provided with a pair of legs in the form of claws and in their general construction they resemble the Kavanagh horn. Some of these are inscribed with the names of the three Magi or invoke the intercession of the Blessed Virgin (Olrik, 1909, nos. 11-23). Most, however, are made from the horns of wild oxen or bison.

The closest parallel for the plain faceted ivory horn such as the Kavanagh example is the Savernake horn (reputed to be the tenure horn of the forest of Savernake), now in the British Museum (Camber and Cherry, 1977). The horn itself is considered to be twelfth or thirteenth century in date while the enamelled mounts are of early fourteenth-century English workmanship. Another plain faceted ivory horn with fifteenth-century French silver gilt mounts is in the Treasury of St Servais, Maastricht (Koechlin, 1924, Pl CCVI). A faceted ivory horn carved with scenes from the life of St Hubert or St Eustace dating to the early fourteenth century is also similar although there are some doubts as to the authenticity of this piece (Longhurst, 1929, 51). Finally, the ivory Leys Tenure Horn, the hereditary symbol of the Burnett family of Leys, Kincardineshire, is multifaceted but is of uncertain date (Wilson, 1863, 501). None of the above examples were used as drinking horns. Similar faceted hunting horns, most probably of ivory, are depicted on the so-called Unicorn Tapestries, probably woven in Flanders around 1500 (Freeman, 1974). These were copied by potters in Germany and France throughout the Middle Ages and fragments of one of these ceramic horns, made in the Saintonge area of south-western France, have been found in late thirteenth-century levels at Wood Quay, Dublin.

The rim mount on the Kavanagh horn can be dated to the fifteenth century. The scalloped lower edge with its debased egg-and-dart motif can be readily paralleled on a horn of similar date in Copenhagen (Olrik, 1909, fig 12) and similar borders appear on many English mazer mounts of the period (Jackson, 1911, figs 830, 835). The motif is also found on the gilt silver casing of the Shrine of St Senan's Bell (Raftery, 1941, Pl 82) and St Mura's Bell Shrine (ibid, Pl 81) and, in an altered form, on the rim of the Dunvegan Cup (MacLeod, 1912-13, figs 3-6).

The epigraphy of black letter inscriptions in Ireland has not yet been sufficiently studied and cannot help in suggesting a close date for the rim mount. The earliest dated occurrence of black letter in metalwork is on the Shrine of the Book of Mulling, made in 1402 and it continues in use on church plate into the first quarter of the sixteenth century (Buckley, 1943, fig 3). It is found on stone sculpture in Ireland between *c* 1400 and 1550, the earliest occurrence being on the O'Kelly tomb at Knockmoy, Co Galway, which dates to shortly after 1403. Comparisons with the inscription on the Dunvegan Cup and with English metalwork, however, would suggest that the inscription on the Kavanagh horn should be dated to the late fifteenth century. It is almost certain that the central and terminal mounts were added at the same time. The style of the clawed feet suggests that they were added later, possibly in the sixteenth century. Comparable clawed feet occur on a horn in Copenhagen, dated c 1600 (Olrik, 1909, fig 31). The socket attachment of the feet cannot be paralleled in Irish or Continental metalwork of the period.

The Kavanagh 'Charter' Horn in its present form is therefore of a type current in Northern Europe in the later Middle Ages. The inscription indicates that the mounts were made in Ireland by an Irish craftsman but what of its provenance? The name O'Lavan (Ó Láimhín, probably a corruption of Ó Flaithimhín) is a Roscommon name, associated with the MacDermotts and the name Tighearnán as a Christian name is more common in the northern half of the country. The MacDermotts were lords of Moylurg but there is no documentary evidence to connect them or the O'Lavans with the Kavanaghs. There is a tantalising entry in the Annals of the Four Masters sub anno 1375 which records the death of Donough MacDermott of Moylurg, son of Conor of the Cup (Donnchadh mac Conchubhair an Chopáin) (O'Donovan, 1854, IV, 663; also recorded in the Annals of Ulster and the Annals of Connacht) but it would be rash to suggest any significance in this although the coincidence is interesting. The inscriptions on other pieces of Irish late medieval decorative metalwork also indicate that they were made by native Irish craftsmen. There is nothing particularly Irish in the style of the Kavanagh horn mounts although the scalloped central mount bears a superficial resemblance to the narrow diagonal strips separating the inscribed plates on the front of the Bearnán Conaill bell shrine kept until the nineteenth century by its hereditary keepers at Inishkeel, Co Donegal (Crawford, 1922, Plate III). In its general construction, the rim mount on the Kavanagh horn is similar to that on the Dunvegan Cup, dated 1493. Many of the surviving late medieval Irish shrines are provenanced to the north-west of the country and indicate the presence of several skilled metalworkers in this area. In view of the restricted occurrence of the surname O'Lavan in North Roscommon and the similarities to the Dunvegan Cup (commissioned by a Co. Fermanagh family) it is possible that the mounts on the Kavanagh horn (with the possible exception of the feet) were made by a craftsman working or trained in the west Ulster/north Connaught area around 1500. It is even conceivable that the horn and the Dunvegan Cup were products of the same workshop. The uncertainty underlines how few pieces of decorative metalwork survived the Reformation in Ireland.

By tradition, the horn is associated with the kingship of Leinster. In this connection Professor F.J. Byrne remarks on the frequent references to drinking horns as tuarastal distributed by Leinster kings and also states that drinking horns of wild ox — coirn buaball — were symbols of royal power among the Laigin (Byrne, 1973, 153). According to one writer, the horn was given to Donal Kavanagh, the son of Dermot Mac Murrough, in 1175 by Henry II to hold his lands in fief from the Crown (MacLeod, 1959, 16), but there is no historical justification for such an assertion. The Kavanaghs trace their claim to the kingship of Leinster directly back to Diarmait mac Maíl na mBó who assumed the kingship in the mid-eleventh century and continued to style themselves as such until the time of the Anglo-Norman invasion. The title was revived in the fourteenth century when Donnell Mac Art, a direct descendant of Dermot Mac Murrough was chosen king *c* 1327. In the late fifteenth and sixteenth centuries the kingship was largely in the hands of the Wexford septs, Cathaoir *mac na h-inghine crosda* (a descendant of Gerald, Lord of Ferns) who died in 1531, being the last person to accept the title.

The Kavanagh horn is also regarded as the symbol of tenure by which the Kavanagh family of Borris held their lands and it is stated that it had been at Borris 'from a very early period'. The source for this appears to be a note appended to the pedigree of the Kavanagh family drawn up by the Ulster King of Arms in 1817 (Ryan, 1833, 382). The term 'Charter Horn' was first used by Vallancey in 1786 but he does not explain why and it may be purely fanciful. He may have taken the term from a paper on Charter Horns in Britain published ten years earlier in the journal *Archaeologia* (Pegge, 1775), where their use as symbols of the conveyance and tenure of land is well attested (Trowsdale, 1879-80; Bridge, 1905).

The *Civil Survey*, however, clearly states that the horn was in the possession of the Garryhill sept in the mid-seventeenth century. If the horn had belonged to the late medieval kings of Leinster as an item of regalia, the Garryhill sept, which descended from Muircheartach Óg, a son of Murchadh Ballach, king of Leinster from 1476 to his death in 1511, may have inherited it as nearest of kin to Muircheartach Óg's brother Cathaoir *mac na h-inghine crosda*, the last to enjoy general recognition as king of Leinster. In the rising of 1641 a rumour ran among the English settlers in Co Carlow that the then head of the sept, Murtagh Oge, was to be made king of Leinster (Trinity College, Dublin, MS F.2.5). The last known representative of the Garryhill family was this Murtagh Oge's son, Captain Maurice Kavanagh of Ballinrush, who was outlawed as a Jacobite in 1689 (Simms, 1960, 41). It was perhaps after his death or departure from Ireland that the horn was transferred to the Borris family, the only important branch of the Kavanaghs to retain their lands and position in the eighteenth century.

The Kavanagh horn was used as a ceremonial drinking cup at least as early as the end of the fifteenth century. The evidence of earlier mountings suggests that it may originally have had a quite different appearance and, as the narrow end of the horn was originally hollow, it could equally have been used as a hunting horn or trumpet.

In the tract known as the *Bórama Lagen* in the Book of Leinster, it is recorded that a horn was given by the high-king, Áed mac Ainmerech, to the messengers of Brandub, king of Leinster, which is referred to as *Corn Lagen*, 'the horn of Leinster' (Best and O'Brien, 1967, V, 1292-3). This text was written probably in the mid-twelfth century and suggests that a horn with that title was in existence at that time. Brandub, significantly, was one of the few Uí Chennselaig kings of Leinster before Diarmait mac Maíl na mBó assumed the title in the later eleventh century. Can we see in this story a bolstering of the Uí Chennselaig claim in which a drinking horn plays a symbolic part? It is unlikely, though not impossible, that the ivory horn is as old as the time of the first Mac Murrough kings of Leinster in the mid-eleventh century. Ivory was seldom used as a raw material in early medieval Ireland or indeed throughout the middle ages. The most notable example of its use is the crozier crook from Aghadoe, Co Kerry, which is of early twelfth-century date (Henry, 1970, 114-5 and Pl 85). It was not until the twelfth century, with the Norman conquest of Sicily and the Crusades, that elephant ivory became widely available in Europe. In addition, even if the horn dates from the twelfth century, it does not necessarily follow that it was in Ireland at that time.

If the horn did symbolise the Kavanaghs' claim to the kingship of Leinster it is surprising that there is no reference to it in the literature and that it is not more elaborately decorated. It is strange that the mounts are all in a base metal whereas the Butler and Fitzgerald horns referred to earlier bore gold and gilt silver mounts respectively and all the major shrines of this period either contain panels of silver or are partly gilt. Even more surprising is the fact that the inscription refers only to the maker. Every other piece of inscribed metalwork of fourteenth- or fifteenth-century date bears the name of its owner or the person who commissioned it, in addition to the name of the craftsman. It seems highly unlikely that the significance (if such existed) of the horn was forgotten at the time when the present mounts were added. By contrast, we are left in no doubt as to the person who caused the Shrine of the Book of Mulling — another Kavanagh heirloom — to be repaired. Underneath the central crystal on the lid of this much denuded shrine is a black letter inscription which refers to 'Arthurus Rex Dominus Lagenie' and the date 1402 (Macalister, 1949, 23 and Pl V). The shrine was thus refurbished when Art Oge MacMurrough, king of Leinster, was at the peak of his military career and only three years after he successfully thwarted Richard II's second attempt to recover Leinster. The Kavanagh family in Borris were also in possession of what is referred to as the crown of the kings of Leinster. This was reputedly removed to the Museum of Trinity College along with the Charter Horn at the end of the eighteenth century and appears to have subsequently vanished (MacCormick, 1963, 28-9). Walter Kavanagh stated that a facsimile of the crown was fitted as a cap to a copy of the Horn given to his great-grandfather, Arthur, who died in 1789 (Bridge, 1905, 136) but neither crown nor facsimile survive and there is no description of the crown. Nevertheless, the tradition associating the horn with the kingship of Leinster was well established in the literature a century and a half after the present mounts were added at the end of the fifteenth century. At that time, the kingship passed in rapid succession to a number of members of the family and it is not possible to suggest which was responsible for the refurbishing of the horn.

Whether the Kavanagh Charter Horn was associated with the kingship of Leinster centuries before it is first mentioned in the mid-seventeenth century is impossible to say given the lack of documentary evidence. Its refurbishing in the later fifteenth century, however, fits in well with the renewal of the MacMurrough Kavanagh claims to the kingship and with the Gaelic revival of fourteenth- and fifteenth-century Ireland in general so well attested in the redecoration and commissioning of many of our most important shrines. Whatever the historical paradoxes which remain to be resolved about this enigmatic object, its historical attributions are unique and it remains the most important extant piece of secular metalwork of medieval date.

Finally, the Kavanagh Horn may well have served as a model for possibly the last example of a ceremonial drinking horn, made in London in 1813 probably for an Irish client (Los Angeles, 1962, 35 and cover). The horn is of ivory, faceted and bearing silver gilt mounts with an inscription in Irish translated as 'Peace and Plenty'.

ACKNOWLEDGEMENTS

I am grateful to Mr William O'Sullivan, Keeper of Manuscripts, Trinity College, Dublin for information on the date of the return of the horn to Borris House and to Mr G. Slevin, Chief Herald, Genealogical Office, Dublin, for information on the surname O'Lavan. In addition, my thanks are due to the following for their assistance and helpful comments: Professor F.J. Byrne, Department of Early and Medieval Irish History, University College Dublin; Mr David H. Caldwell, National Museum of Antiquities of Scotland; Mr John Cherry, Department of Medieval and Later Antiquities, British Museum; Mr John Lewis, Department of Archaeology, National Museum of Wales; Mr Fritze Lindahl, National Museum, Copenhagen and Mr A.R.E. North, Department of Metalwork, Victoria and Albert Museum. I also extend my thanks to Dr Joseph Raftery, former Director of the National Museum of Ireland, who initially suggested I undertake this work. To Messrs A. Siggins and B. Byrne of the National Museum of Ireland on whose work on the horn during conservation I have freely drawn and to Mr B. Doyle, also of the National Museum who did the photography, I must also express my indebtedness. Further, I am grateful to Edel Bhreathnach, U.C.D., for the reference to *Bórama Laigen*.

REFERENCES

Astle, T., 1775. 'Extract from the will of Thomas Earl of Ormond, dated July 31, 1515', *Archaeologia* **3**, 20-1.

Berry, H.F., 1898. *Register of Wills and Inventories of the Diocese of Dublin in the time of Archbishops Tregury and Walton, 1457-1483*. Roy Soc Antiq Ir, Dublin.

Best, R.I. and O'Brien, M.A., 1967. *The Book of Leinster*, Vol. V. Institute for Advanced Studies, Dublin.

Bridge, J.C., 1905. 'Horns', *J Chester Archaeol Soc* **2**, 85-116.

Buckley, J.J., 1943. *Irish Altar Plate*. Dublin.

Bryan, D., 1933. *The Great Earl of Kildare*. Dublin.

Byrne, F.J., 1973. *Irish Kings and High Kings*. London.

Camber, R. and Cherry, J., 1977. 'The Savernake horn' in *Brit Mus Yearbook*, **2**. *Collectors and Collections*, 201-211, London.

Crawford, H., 1922. 'Notes on the Irish bell-shrines in the British Museum and the Wallace Collection', *J Roy Soc Antiq Ir* **52**, 1-10.

Freeman, M., 1974. 'The unicorn tapestries', *Bull Metropol Mus Art* **32**, 177-224.

Henry, F., 1965. *Irish Art in the Early Christian Period*, London.
Henry, F., 1970. *Irish Art in the Romanesque Period*, London.
Hughes, J., 1873. 'The fall of the Clan Kavanagh', *J Roy Soc Antiq Ir* 12, 282-305.
Jackson, 1911. *An Illustrated History of English Plate* II. London.
Koechlin, R., 1924. *Les Ivoires Gothiques Français*. Paris.
Kühnel, E., 1971. *Die islamische Elfenbeinskulpturen VIII-XII Jahrhundert*. Berlin.
Longhurst, M.H., 1929. *Catalogue of Carvings in Ivory. Victoria and Albert Museum*. Part II, London.
Los Angeles, 1962. *Catalogue of Old English and Early American Silver Work*. Los Angeles County Museum of Art, Los Angeles.
Macalister, R.A.S., 1949. *Corpus Inscriptionum Insularum Celticarum* II, Dublin.
MacCormick, D., 1963. *The Incredible Mr Kavanagh*. Dublin.
MacLeod, I., 1959. 'The family of the Mac Murrough Kavanaghs', *Carloviana* 1, 3, 13-17.
MacLeod, F.T., 1912-13. 'Notes on the relics preserved in Dunvegan Castle, Skye', *Proc Soc Antiq Scot* 47, 99-129.
O'Donovan, J., 1854. *Annals of The Kingdom of Ireland, by the Four Masters from the earliest period to the year 1616*, 7 vols. Dublin.
Olrik, J., 1909. *Drikkehorn og Sølvtøj fra Middelalder og Renaissance*. Copenhagen.
Pegge, 1775. 'Of the horn, as a charter or instrument of conveyance', *Archaeologia* 3, 1-12.
Petersen, J., 1940. *Viking Antiquities in Great Britain and Ireland: Part V. British Antiquities of the Viking Period in Norway*. Oslo.
Radner, J.N., 1978. *Fragmentary Annals of Ireland*. Dublin.
Raftery, J., 1941. *Christian Art in Ancient Ireland*, II. Dublin.
Ryan, J., 1833. *History and Antiquities of Carlow*. Dublin.
Simington, R.C., 1961. *The Civil Survey 1654-6*, X *Miscellanea*. Dublin.
Simms, J.G., 1960. 'Irish Jacobites' *Analecta Hibernica* 22.
Trowsdale, B., 1874-80. 'On horn tenures', *The Reliquary* 20, 157.
Vallancey, C., 1786. *Collectanea de Rebus Hibernicis*, IV. Dublin.
Waterman, D., 1969. 'An Early Medieval horn from the River Erne', *Ulster J Archaeol ser* 3 32, 101-4.
Wilde, W., 1861. *A Descriptive Catalogue of the Antiquities of Animal Materials and Bronze in the Museum of the Royal Irish Academy*. Dublin.
Wilson, D., 1863. *Prehistoric Annals of Scotland*, II. London.
Wright, T., 1887. *The Historical Works of Giraldus Cambrensis*. London.

A Pietà from Cloran Old Near Fethard, Co. Tipperary

Mary Cahill

INTRODUCTION

A few years ago while engaged in fieldwork in the Fethard area the writer came across a carved representation of a pietà (exact location: O.S. 71, Td. Cloran Old, Par. Cloneen, Bar. Middlethird, Co Tipperary. 2.9 cm from W; 35.7 cm from S) which so far has gone unrecorded in the literature. Its discovery increases to seven the known representations in stone of the type — three of which, although varying in date and detail are in the south Tipperary area (Clonmel, Cloran Old and Kilboy, near Killenaule; see Hunt, 1974). The Ordnance Survey sheet (1904 revised edition, 1928 reprint) for the area indicated that in the townland of Cloran Old a 'Grave Yard, Disused' within the boundaries of which, another monument noted as 'Laghtnavar', would be found. The 1840 edition does not record the existence of any monuments in this field. A visit to the site disclosed that the 'graveyard' is barely perceptible from the surrounding field and that 'Laghtnavar' is a long, narrow stone now lying prone. No tradition of burial in this field exists in the neighbourhood nor is there any reference to it in the Ordnance Survey Letters or Field-Name Books for the parish. Thus it was all the more surprising to find a pietà depicted on a limestone slab lying against the field-fence. However, further discussions with the owner disclosed that a number of other stones, which from the description appear to have been bullaun stones, were removed from the site some years ago.

DESCRIPTION

The pietà (see Plate XVIII) is carved on a limestone slab measuring 64 cm by 58 cm by 15 cm approx. The words IHS and MARIA appear at the top of the slab on either side of the Virgin's head. The figure of the Virgin is depicted seated on a throne. She is clothed in a full-length, round-necked robe with a belt or girdle at the waist. The robe falls to the 'ground' from the waist in heavy folds or pleats of which there are eight — four on either side of a central panel of drapery. This central panel consists of four V-shaped folds executed in high relief giving a good impression of depth and texture. The gathering or pleating of the bodice from the neck band into the girdle is also indicated in a manner similar to that on some of the fifteenth and sixteenth century effigies of civilian women and female saints. The head is covered with a very large voluminous veil which is arranged to reach shoulder level at the front and falls from the back of the head on the left hand side to a point somewhat below the seat of the throne. The veil is not as long on the right and reaches only to waist level. The left arm is raised and the hand touches the veil in a gesture common amongst English examples. The fingers are only slightly in-dicated. The right hand, emerging from the veil, supports the head of Christ. The Virgin's face is long and rectangular in shape and almost expressionless with only slight indications of forehead, eyebrows and nose. Christ's face is carved in a similar way although this lack of detail and expression may be due, partly, to weathering.

The body of Christ rests upon the knees of the Virgin and in comparison to the proportions of her figure seems very slight — the ratio being approximately 1.5:1 — this also being a common attribute of pietà groups in all mediums. The head is tilting downwards slightly leaning on the right shoulder and further supported by the Virgin's hand. The right arm hangs loosely from the shoulder, the outer surface facing the viewer. The left arm, slightly crooked at the elbow, rests on the left hip. The torso, for the most part, is treated simply and naturally, the chest, waist and hips being clearly indicated although it might be said that the waist is a little over-accentuated. The figure is clad in a simple loincloth with a suggestion of loose pleating on the left hand side. The legs, which are very thin, fall almost vertically from the knees. The feet, which like the hands, are lacking in detail, appear somewhat awkwardly placed.

DISCUSSION

Although the concept of Mary contemplating the death of her Son while holding him on her lap developed in Germany around 1300 (Schiller, 1972), the first Irish representations do not occur until the middle of the fifteenth century. The theme had made its appearance in England somewhat earlier. Two variations in the at-titude of the Virgin are distinguishable; firstly, the gesture of touching the veil with the left hand which indicates sorrow or secondly, the Virgin supporting Christ's body with her left hand. Of the Irish examples only two show the Virgin touching the veil — the slab at Cloran Old and the cross at Balrath, Co. Meath — whereas this is the preferred attitude of the surviving English examples. Peter Harbison has suggested a Rhenish model for the two freestanding examples from Ennis and Kilmurry, Co. Clare, in which the Virgin supports Christ with her hand (1975, 41) and, by implication suggests that those which prefer the first attitude must be based on an English original. However, it is possible that both models are of German origin as pietà groups of the first variation are known from Bohemia and the Rhineland at the beginning of the fifteenth century (Schiller, 1972, Pls 629 and 638). The choice of one gesture rather than the other may be simply a reflection of a regional preference.

The purpose of this particular iconographic grouping of the Virgin and Christ was to imbue a sense of pious contemplation in the viewer and to reiterate the redemption of mankind by the supreme sacrifice of Christ. For this reason the pietà was usually placed at a secondary altar where presumably this response might be more readily evoked in the individual penitent. It seems likely that, as freestanding sculptures, the Ennis and Kilmurry pietàs would have served this purpose also. The pietà at Balrath would also have emphasised this ideal having been united with the cross itself. The remaining examples at Clonmel, Cloran Old, Kilboy and Srade (Co. Mayo) form or would have formed parts of tomb-chests or altar reredos and as such their purpose may have been slightly different in that the image in such a position becomes more public and in the case of tomb components may have functioned as an aid to mourning.

The Cloran Old pietà is also unusual in the group because it is the only one with an inscription (noted above). The form of the letters suggests a mid-sixteenth century date for the slab corroborating the evidence of the group itself. How and when it came to its present isolated position remains to be answered.

ACKNOWLEDGEMENTS

My thanks to Dr Peter Harbison for drawing my attention to the Balrath pietà and for useful discussion, to Michael Ryan for providing the photograph and to Victor Shea and Mrs Shea of Cloran House for allowing me access to the site.

REFERENCES

Harbison, Peter, 1975. 'The pietà from Kilmurry Ibrickane, Co. Clare' *N Munster Antiq J* **17**, 39-41.

Hunt, John, 1974. *Irish Medieval Figure Sculpture, 1200-1600*.

Hunt, John, 1975. 'The influence of alabaster carvings on medieval sculptures in Ennis Friary', *N Munster Antiq J* **17**, 35-39.

Schiller, Gertrude, 1972. *Iconography of Christian Art*.

ANCILLARY
DISCIPLINES

Field Boundaries in Ireland[1]

W. Groenman-van Waateringe

To Brian O'Kelly, in remembrance of a marvellous day while looking for stone walls, 6 April 1978

While reading *Compert Con Culainn* in a Dutch translation by Draak & de Jong (1979, 34), I was struck by the sentence: *Ní-bíth clad na airbe na caisel im thír i n-Ére ind aimsir sin acht magi rédi*[2] ('there were no dikes or fences or stone walls |around the land (field)| in Ireland at that time, only the open plain').[3] Any archaeologist with some knowledge of the prehistoric field walls, which have been discovered in Ireland in the past few years (Herity, 1971; Herity and Eogan, 1977, 50; Caulfield, 1978) will wonder what this phrase means. Was there at any time a situation that could be described by the above sentence?

To answer this question let us first look at the meaning of field fences, their structure and their dating in a wider European context. Field fences are multi-purpose, but amongst their main functions may be mentioned

1. marking boundaries between separate territorial units, personal or communal property (cf. Ó Riain, 1972);
2. protecting arable fields against wild and domestic animals;
3. enclosing domestic animals and protecting them from predators;
4. preventing soil erosion by down wash;
5. lessening the wind velocity, thus preventing erosion by wind and giving shelter to cattle and crop.

It depends on one's viewpoint which of these functions is considered to be the most important.

The structure of field fences is also highly variable and can range from hedges, twigs woven between trunks, dead wood, stone and earth walls (overgrown or not), and ditches to barbed or electric wire (cf. Jessen, 1937; Evans, 1967a, 40-43; Evans, 1967b, 100-113). The kind of fence used, save for the modern ones of barbed or electric wire, is highly dependent on the nature of the surroundings (cf. Jessen, 1935; Evans, 1967a, 42; Mead, 1966): stone walls in barren land as in the West of Ireland, hedges in more sheltered areas and ditches in the coastal marshlands (cf. Bakker *et al.*, 1977). In its most complete form a field boundary consists of a ditch (the primary feature) and bank (of earth or stone) and on top of this or on its flanks, a vegetation cover, mostly of prickly bushes such as hawthorn, wild rose, sloe, blackberries, furze, but also oak, willow, hazel and beech. The vegetation provided people with useful wood, wild fruits and nuts. Of the furze it is known both from Brittany (Hartke, 1951, 146) and Ireland (Lucas, 1960) that it is highly favoured for horse and cattle fodder, as bedding material for animals etc. The vegetation cover can develop naturally, but is mostly planted intentionally (cf. Lucas, 1960, 33-34).

A growing interest on the part of nature conservancy and ecological authorities as well as those concerned with agricultural and especially economic considerations, has provided us with numerous studies dealing with field fences in general and with hedges in particular. More recently, the history of hedges has attracted attention (Moore, Hooper and Davis, 1967; Hooper, 1971), but these studies only rarely touch on their presence in prehistoric times. Direct evidence therefore has to come from archaeological surveys and excavations (cf. Bowen and Fowler, 1978; Müller-Wille, 1979) or aerial photography (Norman and St Joseph, 1969). Indirect evidence can be obtained from palaeobotany (cf. Groenman-van Waateringe, 1971, 1978; Schweingruber, 1973), or from analysis of molluscs (cf. Bowen, Evans and Race, 1978).

A landscape partitioned by field boundaries into small units is called an enclosed landscape as opposed to an open landscape. The correlation between the kind of settlement, its agricultural practice and the social and economic pattern (nucleated vs. dispersed settlement, stock-breeding vs. arable farming, enclosed vs. open landscape, private vs. shared ownership of the land) is highly complicated and has not always been handled in publications with enough care. There is a tendency to see a direct correlation between an enclosed landscape, private ownership and dispersed settlement, but the landscape being enclosed or not is in the first place dependent on the motives for fencing. And these can be of many kinds, of which private ownership is only one. For example, when one has to prevent soil erosion, either because of downwash of soil on a hill flank (cf. Troll, 1951) or because of wind erosion of the ploughed top soil (Groenman-van Waateringe, 1979), fencing can be a common undertaking. The same holds true if the fence is intended to serve as a demarcation between cleared and unreclaimed land. The kind of agricultural practice, e.g. infield-outfield system or a regular alternation between arable farming for about two years and grazing for five to eight years (cf. Jessen, 1937, 15) or the need to provide enough shelter in bad weather conditions for cattle and/or crops, will also have encouraged the development of an enclosed landscape. Rough grazing will perhaps not have taken place very much in prehistory because one needed the manure badly for the arable fields. The domesticated animals had to be protected from predators such as wolves, or one had to prevent sexual interference by wild bulls or boars.

The history of the enclosed areas of today is not very old. For the most part their origin can be traced back to the seventeenth or eighteenth centuries, but recent research into the botanical composition of hedges gave evidence for a considerably greater age in the case of some, i.e. pre-enclosure hedges going back to medieval times. Organised planting and walling can for example be traced back to the seventeenth century in England (Mead, 1966, 103), and in Ireland mainly to the nineteenth century, when the rundale village system was broken up and the land redistributed. Nowadays many of the field boundaries are demolished by re-allotment for practical and economical reasons. Thus we see an alternation, even in historic times, of open and enclosed landscapes. Hartke (1951, 147, Abb. 8a) gives an example in which a strip of land bordering on unreclaimed woodland is fenced, whereas the fences in the centre of the area in which the clearing started, save for the immediate surroundings of the farm/hamlet/village, had already been removed.

How far back can we trace the existence of field boundaries in northwestern Europe using direct or indirect evidence? Through indirect evidence, i.e. botanical data, this is possible for the earliest Neolithic settlement in Western Europe, i.e. the Bandkeramik period (Groenman-van Waateringe, 1971, 1978; Schweingruber, 1973) and later (cf. van Zeist and Casparie, 1974, 425). Dated evidence, either find circumstances or C14 dating, is only known from Ireland (cf. Collins and Waterman, 1955, 8; Caulfield, 1978; probably also Pilcher, 1969). Although there is no C14 dated evidence for field walls in Ireland of the later periods, find cir-cumstances point to both Bronze Age (Lynch, 1981) and Iron Age datings (Norman and St Joseph, 1969, 38-72). Field systems dated to the Middle Bronze Age, Iron Age and later are well known by now from several sites in England (Bradley, 1978; Müller-Wille, 1979). From the marshy western parts of Holland field systems surrounded by ditches (Bakker *et al.*, 1977) are known from the Middle Bronze Age; so-called Celtic fields are dated in the Netherlands from the middle of the first millennium B.C. The same holds good for Celtic fields in NW Germany, Denmark and Sweden (Gotland) (cf. Müller-Wille, 1979).

Several of the above-mentioned motives for fencing can be applied to these early boundaries:

1. marking off the cleared area from the uncleared forest;
2. protecting the domesticated animals against predators and/or wild male animals;
3. protecting the crops against browsing animals, wild or domesticated;
4. protecting against downwash (when situated on slopes) or wind erosion (in exposed areas like the West of Ireland);
5. giving shelter to cattle and crops, although in a humid climate there are disadvantages too. In the West of Ireland with high rainfall and strong winds one has to consider the advantage of wind protection but also the disadvantage of higher humidity.

Under the oceanic climatic conditions in the West of Ireland the Neolithic farmers must have quickly learned that downwash of the soil and wind erosion were the results of removing the woodland cover, even only on a small scale. The only thing they could do against this was to build protecting walls around their fields. Thus the need for solid field boundaries was perhaps more strongly felt here than anywhere else, although one must be well aware that only in areas with a present-day blanket bog cover will the prehistoric palimpsest be better preserved than anywhere else.

The field walls excavated by Caulfield seem unequal to any of the above mentioned tasks, being low and with their stones rather widely spaced. But how representative of their original form is their present appearance? Was there possibly a vegetation cover that was more effective, consisting of prickly bushes such as hawthorn, sloe, wild rose, blackberry or furze? There is evidence for the occurrence of *Crataegus* (hawthorn) for the Boreal period in Ireland. *Prunus spinosa* (sloe) is recorded from Ireland in the Sub-Boreal, as is *Rubus fruticosus* (blackberry) from the Atlantic period onwards. *Rosa sp.* is known from a Sub-Atlantic findspot in Ireland, but is known from a much earlier date in England. Though *Ulex* (furze) is unknown in any prehistoric context in Ireland, there is according to Godwin (1975, 177) no reason to think of any climatic control that could have prevented its occurrence. The distribution of the *Ulex* species is 'all very typically western European'.

As has been established through experiments (cf. Groenman-van Waateringe, 1979) an open hedge is more effective as a wind barrier than a solid screen, and has the additional advantage of preventing too high a degree of humidity developing in the enclosed space; cf. the 'flimsy lace-like appearance when seen against the sky' of boulder walls in the West of Ireland (Evans, 1967b, 105).

To return to the phrase in the story of *Compert Con Culainn*, it is highly improbable that there ever was a period in Ireland since Neolithic times which was entirely without dikes, fences or stone walls around the fields. And as we now know Ireland had, before the Neolithic occupation, a thick woodland cover (Mitchell, 1976), at least from the Boreal period onwards. How then can the sentence be explained? Does it only mean 'very long ago', thus referring to a situation, unknown to the narrator, but supposed by him to have existed or does he refer to a situation which through oral tradition he knows to have existed or is still existing, but only in certain parts of Ireland? Another explanation, and to me the most probable and elegant one, is that of Professor A. Maartje E. Draak, Emeritus Professor in Celtic Languages and Literature at the University of Amsterdam (personal communication). She said, 'well, it is simply this: when the narrator tells the audience that Conchobor and the nobles of Ulster became so angry seeing their land ruined by a flock of birds that they got their chariots ready and chased the birds, which flew at will before them, someone in the audience must have made a remark about how could such a thing be possible with all the fences in the land. So the narrator invents, on the spur of the moment, the explanation, that there were no dikes or fences or stone walls around the land in Ireland at that time, only the open plain'.

NOTES

1 Thanks are due to Dr Ann Lynch and Drs Carol van Driel-Murray for correcting the English.

2 Translation, Kinsella, 1970, 21-22; material in square brackets is omitted by Kinsella. For an edition see Thurneysen, 1912, 35.

REFERENCES

Bakker, J.A. *et al.*, 1977. 'Hoogkarspel-Watertoren: towards a reconstruction of ecology and archaeology of an agrarian settlement of 1000 BC'. *In* B.L. van Beek, R.W. Brandt, & W. Groenman-van Waateringe (ed), *Ex Horreo* (Cingula 4.), 187-225. Amsterdam.

Bowen, H.C., Evans, J.G. & Race, E., 1978. 'An investigation of the Wessex linear ditch system'. *In* Bowen & Fowler, 149-53.

Bowen, H.C. & Fowler, P.J., 1978. *Early land allotment. A survey of recent work* (Brit Archaeol Rep **48**).

Bradley, R., 1978. *The prehistoric settlement of Britain*. London.

Caulfield, S., 1978. 'Neolithic fields: the Irish evidence'. *In* Bowen & Fowler, 137-43.

Collins, A.E.P. & Waterman, D.M., 1955. *Millin Bay, a Neolithic cairn in Co. Down. (Archaeological research publications (Northern Ireland)* 4.) Belfast.

Draak, M. & de Jong, F., 1979. *Van helden, elfen en dichters. De oudste verhalen uit Ierland.* Amsterdam.

Evans, E.E., 1967a. *Irish heritage, the landscape, the people and their work.* 9th ed. Dundalk.

Evans, E.E., 1967b. *Irish folk ways.* 4th ed. London.

Godwin, H., 1975. *The history of the British flora. A factual basis for phytogeography.* 2nd ed. Cambridge.

Groenman-van Waateringe, W., 1970-71. 'Hecken im westeuropäischen Früh-Neolithikum', *Berichten van de Rijksdienst voor het Oudheidkundig Bodemonderzoek* **20-1**, 295-99.

Groenman-van Waateringe, W., 1978. 'The impact of Neolithic man on the landscape in the Netherlands' *In* S. Limbrey & J.G. Evans (ed), *The effect of man on the landscape: the Lowland Zone* (Counc Brit Archaeol Res Rep **21**), 135-46. London.

Groenman-van Waateringe, W., 1979. 'Nogle aspekter af jernalderens agerbrug i Holland og NV Tyskland'. *In* H. Thrane (ed), *Fra Jernalder til Middelalder. (Skrifter fra Historisk Institut, Odense Universitet,* **27**) 75-86, Odense.

Hartke, W., 1951. 'Die Heckenlandschaft: der geographische Charakter eines Landeskulturproblems'. *Erdkunde* **5**, 132-52.

Herity, M., 1971. 'Prehistoric fields in Ireland', *Ir University Rev* **1**, 258-65.

Herity, M. & Eogan, G., 1977. *Ireland in prehistory*. London.

Hooper, M.D., 1971. 'Hedges and local history', *In Hedges and local history,* 5-13. London.

Jessen, O., 1937. 'Heckenlandschaften im nordwestlichen Europa', *Mitteilungen der geographischen Gesellschaft in Hamburg* **45**, 10-58.

Kinsella, T., 1970. *The Tain.* Oxford.

Lucas, A.T., 1960. *Furze, a survey and history of its uses in Ireland.*

Lynch, A., 1981. *Aspects of early man's environment in SW Ireland.* Brit Archaeol Rep **85**.

Mead, W.R., 1966. 'The study of field boundaries', *Geographische Zeitschrift* **54**, 101-17.

Mitchell, F., 1976. *The Irish landscape.* London.

Moore, N.W., Hooper, M.D. & Davis, B.N.K., 1967. 'Hedges. I. Introduction and reconnaissance studies', *J applied ecology* **4**, 201-20.

Müller-Wille, M., 1979. 'Flursysteme der Bronze- und Eisenzeit in den Nordseegebieten. Zum Stand der Forschung über celtic fields. *In* H. Beck, D. Denecke & H. Jankuhn (ed), *Untersuchungen zur eisenzeitlichen und frühmittelalterlichen Flur in Mitteleuropa und ihrer Nutzung* (Abhandlungen der Akademie der Wissenschaften in Göttingen, philologisch-historische Klasse, III. Folge **115**) 196-239. Göttingen.

Norman, E.R. & St. Joseph, J.K., 1969. *The early development of Irish society. The evidence of aerial photography* (Cambridge Air Surveys III).

Ó Riain, P., 1972. 'Boundary association in early Irish society', *Studia Celtica* **7**, 12-29.

Pilcher, J.R., 1969. 'Archaeology, palaeoecology, and C14 dating of the Beaghmore stone circle', *Ulster J Archaeol ser 3* **32**, 73-91.

Schweingruber, F., 1973. 'Der bandkeramische Siedlungsplatz Langweiler 2, Gemeinde Aldenhoven, Kreis Düren. Holzarten', *Rheinische Ausgrabungen* **13**, 152-56.

Thurneysen, R., 1912. *Zu irischen Handschriften und Litteraturdenkmälern.* (Abhandlungen der königlichen Gesellschaft der Wissenschaften zu Göttingen, philologisch-historische Klasse, NF **14**, 2).Berlin.

Troll, C., 1951. 'Heckenlandschaften im maritimem Grünlandgürtel und im Gäuland Mitteleuropas', *Erdkunde* **5**, 52-157.

Zeist, W. van & Casparie, W.A., 1974. 'Niederwil, a palaeobotanical study of a Swiss Neolithic lake shore settlement', *Geologie en mijnbouw* **53**. 415-28.

The Irish Element in Welsh Hagiographical Tradition

Pádraig Ó Riain

This paper is a revised English version of a Welsh public lecture held in May 1979, in Aberystwyth, at the invitation of the University College of Wales. Its concern with St Finnbarr is perhaps not inappropriate in a contribution honouring Professor M.J. O'Kelly since his very first piece of field-work was at Garranes, Co. Cork, where as an assistant to Professor S.P. Ó Ríordáin, he helped to excavate Ráith Raithleann, the reputed birthplace of Cork's version of the saint.

INTRODUCTION

The American scholar, C.H. Slover, suggested (1927, 89) in the course of his very valuable study of the literary contacts between Ireland and Wales that the two countries formed 'a community of hagiographical tradition'. The evidence he adduced however makes plain that, if such a community ever existed, its essence was very much more Irish than Welsh. Indeed, Irish dominance in the formation of this tradition could hardly be avoided, if for no other reason than that its early literary channels — martyrologies, catalogues of saints, lives of saints etc. — were exclusively of Irish provenance. One remarkable result of this is that the earliest part of the dossier of the three most important Welsh saints, David, Cadog and Beuno is to be found in Irish sources.

Other factors also contributed to the essentially Irish character of the tradition. Paradoxically, one of these was the relative remoteness of Ireland which led to the automatic inclusion of Wales in a medieval Irishman's itinerary, once his destination lay anywhere other than in northern Britain. Our earliest 'travel literature', the mostly eleventh- and twelfth-century lives of the saints, is a late reflection of this, with visits to Wales assigned in it to such saints as Ailbe, Máedóc, Colmán of Dromore and Molaca.

No doubt this type of intercourse had some effect on the spread of dedications to Irish saints. After all, cult is very much a question of (oral) transmission of legend. Furthermore, as recent studies have shown, particularly those of Professor E.G. Bowen (1934, 1956, 1969, 1972), the overland Welsh and Cornish routes tend to be signposted by traces of Irish (and in Cornwall, Welsh) *wanderkulte*. On the other hand, the single most important factor which accounts for the sizeable Irish element in Welsh and Cornish church dedications is, no doubt, the presence in early christian times in Wales, and perhaps in Cornwall, of Irish settlements.

Testifying to the comparative density and duration of the settlement in south Wales in particular are the many visible signs of a historical Irish presence there. These include the well-known Ogam and Latin memorial stones, the Irish element in the pedigree of the early Dyfed kings, placename materials and the traces of Irish influence on the local Welsh dialect. As this paper will show, however, one of the most eloquent reminders of the Irish settlement in South Wales is the manner in which the names of local saints commemorate it.

THE LOCAL SAINTS

Professor E.G. Bowen has suggested (1956, 96-7) that, while dedications to Irish saints in Wales are in his view fewer than might be expected, they are found 'for the most part in the south-western and the north-western regions of Wales', the two areas of Irish settlement. Even here, however, as has been shown (Fisher, 1906-7, 84), the number is in fact much larger than is immediately apparent, many originally Irish saints having assumed Welsh nationality. Among the examples cited are Caron, Cennech, Ffinan, Myllin, Saeran and Sannan, all of whose original Irishness shows through their names. Much less obviously Irish however are the many dedications throughout Wales to saints whose names, together with their affiliations, underwent cambricisation. Much of this paper, for instance, will be taken up with numerous and thoroughly Welsh-looking reflexes of the form *Finnia(n)*, hypocoristic of Finnbarr.

Another important measure of the widespread cambricisation which overtook originally Irish cults is the twelfth-century Welsh tract on the pedigrees of the saints, *Bonedd y Saint* (Bartrum, 1966, 51-67) which admits only three Irish saints, San Ffraid (Brigit), Brendan and Cwyfan (Kevin). Such originally Irish saints as Ailfyw (Ailbe), Madog (Máedóc) and Teyrnoc (Tigernach) are however left devoid of any trace of Irish ancestry.

It must be said, therefore, at the outset, *pace* Slover (1927, 89), Chadwick (1958, 141, 142) and Bowen (1956, 96), that the pattern of Irish settlement in Wales can have exercised little or no influence on the creation of the considerable Irish narrative element in the Welsh lives of saints. These begin to be written in the late eleventh century at a time when, manifestly, the originally Irish affiliations of local saints had with very few exceptions been forgotten. We must distinguish very carefully therefore between the two basic types of Irish saint in Welsh hagiographical tradition, the one local, the other literary. The most superficial of glances at Finnbarr's Welsh dossier suffices to bear this point out.

St Finnbarr figures in Rhigyfarch's Life of St David as *Barre*, a perfectly Irish, hence literary, hypocoristic form of the saint's name. The same Finnbarr however is given the local, Cambro-Latin name, *Barrucus*, in Lifris's *uita* of Cadog where there is no indication of his Irishness. On the other hand, considerable attention is paid in the same *uita* to another Irish saint, *Finian* (*Finianus*), the form of whose name again underlines his literary provenance. Locally however as I show below, this same saint appears to have been known *inter alia* as *Gwynog*, a Welsh reflex with diminutive ending of *Fin(n)ia(n)*. Thus, while the different types of Irish saints in Wales may be easily recognized, the manner in which each developed will give some idea of the form taken in reality by Slover's 'community of hagiographical tradition'.

BARRE AND RHIGYFARCH

The second and later of two Latin recensions of the *uita* of Finnbarr relates how Bairre returned from South Wales to Cork on a horse lent to him by St David (Plummer 1910, 69n). The story concludes:

He kept the said horse with him for the service of the brethren. But in memory of the miracle, his disciples made a brazen horse, which remains to this day in Cork.

It is very unlikely that the remains of a 'brazen horse' will ever be unearthed at Cork. Medieval hagiographers regularly invented images in token substantiation of their tales, pious forgery being very much its own justification (Delehaye, 1907, 91-106). On the strength of this episode however otherwise baseless aspersions have been cast on the character of the Cork saint, first by Plummer (1910, xxxi) who thought it showed that Bairre had 'annexed some of the attributes of a marine deity', then by Kenney (1929, 402) who added for good measure a reference to the maritime location of Bairre's church and, finally, by Bowen (1972, 40) who concluded that the saint was a 'christianized water-deity'.

In fact, however, the textual tradition of the famous story is anything but favourable to the view of these scholars, as indeed Plummer partly recognised (1910, xxxi) in deciding that its place in the late recension only of Finnbarr's *uita* meant that it was an interpolation rather than an omission from earlier versions *causa euitandi scandali*. However, if it is an interpolation, it follows that it came from the only other independent text in which it survives, Rhigyfarch's very much earlier Latin *uita* of St David (Wade-Evans, 1944, 161), of which, significantly, an Irish recension is preserved in the same manuscript (Rawlinson B. 485) as that which contains the earliest copy of Bairre's interpolated *uita* (James, 1967, xxvi).

Rhigyfarch's text is not only the earliest extant version of Finnbarr's ride across the Irish Sea. It is also by far the most substantial account, containing among other extras the detail of Finnbarr's encounter en route with St Brendan who was 'leading a wondrous life on a marine animal' (Wade-Evans, 1923, 20). The peculiar importance of this detail is that it helps to establish the source on which

Rhigyfarch was drawing as well as his *modus componendi*.

The *textgeschichte* which the late Kathleen Hughes (1958) painstakingly pieced together for the manuscript containing the earliest collection of Welsh lives of saints, Brit. Mus. Cotton Vespasian A. xiv, suggests that Rhigyfarch would have had access to a *uita* of St Brendan. In fact, however, as Slover has suggested (1927, 109), his more immediate source is likely to have been two notes added in succession to the text of the Calendar of Óengus for 2 January, the feast of St Scoithín.

The first of these notes explains Scoithín's name from the *scoth* 'flower' which he had cast to Bairre having met him while returning from Rome 'and he [i.e. Scoithín] walking on the sea and Bairre *in a vessel* '. The immediately following note draws attention to Scoithín's remarkable chasteness which as the test was to prove surpassed that of Brendan.

Following Slover, we may assume that Rhigyfarch modelled his story of Bairre on the first of these notes, replacing Scoithín by the better known Brendan, the companion saint in the second note. Certainly, this interpretation is very much in keeping with Rhigyfarch's otherwise observable use of his materials. Thus, having also found a place in his biography of David for Scoithín (Scutinus), Rhigyfarch made good his omission from the Bairre-episode by bringing him from Ferns in Wexford to St Davids, in a manner otherwise peculiar to Brendan, on the back of an 'aquatic monster' (Wade-Evans, 1944, 160).

Manifestly — and paradoxically this singles him out among Celtic hagiographers as a critical writer as well as a scholar — Rhigyfarch felt free to chop and change his sources. Thus, having brought Bairre to St Davids, a church which does not figure in the calendar note, he transformed his mode of travel from vessel to horse, no doubt because, as Mrs Chadwick has suggested (1958, 142-3), he was familiar with the *Vita Maedoci*, whose earliest recension, that in the *Vitae Sanctorum Wallensium* collection (Hughes, 1958; Plummer, 1910, lxxv) contains a similar passage. Máedóc, wishing to return quickly to Ferns is directed to the seashore by David with the words: *Vade ad mare et quodcumque animal uenerit tibi, super illud ascendens, et gradere per mare* (Rees, 1853, 243).

The first point to emerge from this discussion therefore is that Bairre's horse-ride across the Irish Sea, far from evoking an ancient pagan ancestry for the saint, seems to have been first composed towards the end of the eleventh century in the scriptorium of Llanbadarn Fawr by Rhigyfarch, a learned Welsh cleric, who was freely using and adapting Irish materials.

The second point is that Rhigyfarch is unlikely to have been using local materials in the construction of his tale. A.W. Wade-Evans has suggested (1923, 104) that the tenement-name, *Tir Barr*, near St Davids, may preserve Bairre's name, thus providing Rhigyfarch with a local stimulus to the inclusion of the saint in his *uita* of David. Against this however had Rhigyfarch been motivated by the place-name, he would have called the saint *Barr*, not *Barre*, and would almost certainly have treated him as a local saint. The form of name Rhigyfarch gave the saint, taken together with the type of source he was manifestly culling for his other detail, shows that Bairre of David's *uita* is a purely literary figure.

The third point concerns Rhigyfarch himself who, if he did use his materials as I have suggested, must have had ready access to copies of Irish calendars of saints and, more importantly, must have been able to cope with the Irish language of their notes. In fact, both requirements have already been independently established in part either for Rhigyfarch himself or for the community at Llanbadarn Fawr.

Thus, the editor of another of Rhigyfarch's works, his copy of the so-called Hieronymian Martyrology, J.H. Lawlor (1914), has explained its inclusion of some Irish saints by means of an Irish exemplar and, if there was one such Irish work in the scriptorium at Llanbadarn, then the possibility exists that there were more. Indeed, the presence there of a good deal of Irish manuscript material is all but assured by Michael Lapidge's recent study of the autograph works of Rhigyfarch and of his brother Ieuan, who are shown (1973-4, 76-7) to have observed not only Irish decorative techniques and construe marks but also Hiberno-Latin orthographical mannerisms.

Finally, while there is no other evidence to suggest that Rhigyfarch had a command of Irish, we do know that his father, Sulien, had spent a number of years studying in an Irish monastery (Lapidge, 1973, 84-6), a fact which is hardly unrelated to the prevalence of Irish influences at Llanbadarn Fawr as well as to the presence there of Irish manuscript materials. Also, Sulien had twice been elected bishop of St Davids and, while he died in 1091, a few years before Rhigyfarch's work appears to have been 'published', he could still have been at hand to assist his son in matters appertaining to the Irish language in the early stages of a composition which had probably been inspired in the first place by his tenure of the bishopric.

LIFRIS AND BARRUC

At much the same time as Rhigyfarch was writing his *uita* of St David, Lifris of Llancarfan was providing David's 'rival' in SE Wales, Cadog, with what is generally regarded as the most important Welsh *uita*. As yet the text of Cadog's *uita* (Wade-Evans, 1944, 24-141) has not been edited critically. A good deal of work has been done however on its *textgeschichte* and historical implications (Emanuel, 1951-2, 217-27; Brooke, 1964, 283-310; Davies, 1981). Also, its considerable Irish element has attracted the attention of such scholars as Slover (1927, 89-99) and Hughes (1954, 364-7).

The principal Irish saint in Cadog's *uita* is Finnian of Clonard whose own Irish and Latin *uitae* give similar prominence to his sojourn in Llancarfan. Indeed, Slover has suggested (1927, 97), very plausibly in my view, that Lifris drew his Irish material from a copy of Finnian's *uita*. Hughes and Brooke are more cautious however, preferring to hold that both *uitae* 'were drawing on common traditions, but that neither copied the other'. The difficulty I find with this suggestion is that it presupposes the presence both at Llancarfan and at Clonard of written materials which, while there seems to be no other evidence of their existence, were independently used by Lifris and the author of Finnian's *uita*. Whichever suggestion we may adopt, Lifris's source remains a written document. His Finnian, therefore, as indeed the form of his name (Finian, Finianus) shows, has a literary origin comparable to that of Bairre in the *uita* of St David.

There is no prior Welsh evidence of contacts between Llancarfan and Clonard. Consequently, if there is an authentic historical connection underlying the claims made for an association between Finnian and Cadog, this must be sought in Irish sources. In fact, the earlier recorded tradition of Finnian of Clonard, which Kathleen Hughes has carefully examined (1954a), has no place for Cadog or for Llancarfan. On the other hand, if we take Finnian's tradition further back to where, as I have argued recently (Ó Riain, 1977, 24-6), it unites with that of his namesake, Finnbarr *alias* Finnian, patron of Moville in Co. Down, the germ of an association between the saint and the Llancarfan area can be discerned.

Finbarr of Moville (ob.579), whose cult spread throughout Ireland and Scotland, taking in such important centres as Clonard and Cork, was by Adamnán's account (Anderson and Anderson, 1961, 196, 324, 470) tutor and intimate of Colum Cille. He was also one of the very few early Irish saints of whom we possess an almost contemporary authentication. Columbanus of Bobbio, who had been educated at Bangor near Moville, mentions a *Vennianus auctor* in a letter which he addressed to Pope Gregory the Great *c.* 600 A.D. (Walker, 1970, 8). The authorship he had in mind was no doubt that of the earliest extant Irish penitential which is ascribed to Finnian (Bieler, 1963, 3). Much more importantly for our purposes however, Columbanus informs Gregory that 'Finnian the writer questioned Gildas . . . and that he sent a most polished reply'.

Here we see the possible basis of the legendary association between Finnian and Cadog for Gildas, who is a prominent associate of Cadog in both Irish and Welsh sources, was 'patron' of the island of Echni, now Flatholm, where according to the *uita* of Oudoceus, he led an *anchoritala vita* (Evans and Rhys, 1893, 138-9). As I shall argue in a moment, Cadog, Gildas and Finnian, who form a threesome in Finnian's *uita*, are possibly brought together by Lifris in connection with this and a neighbouring island. Certainly Gildas and possibly Cadog, who is said to have usually spent Lent on Echni (Wade-Evans, 1944, 62), would seem to be implied by the 'holy men' *qui habitabant in insula que Echni vocatur* and who are visited by Finnian in the Llancarfan episode of his *uita ut consolationem de vita et doctrina eorum haberet* (Heist, 1965, 98).

To my knowledge, no other 'holy men' are associated with Echni although Lifris, who refers to Echni several times, mentions in one episode (Wade-Evans, 1944, 90-2) a disciple of Cadog called variously *Gualehes, Walees, Guales*, who was buried there. As the detail of the episode shows however (*pace* Williams, 1930,

214-5; Wade-Evans, 1934, 240-1) this form is likely to be a local Welsh reflex of the name Gildas which in its usual form is first put on record by Columbanus in his letter to Gregory.

Cadog, returning from Echni to Barry Island, is accompanied by two disciples, 'Barruc and Gualehes' who forgot to bring their teacher's book. Cadog angrily sends them back to retrieve it but their boat overturns; both are drowned and the book ends up in the belly of a salmon from which it is of course recovered. Lifris continues (Wade-Evans, 1944, 93):

The body of Barruc was found on the Barrensian shore and buried in the same island which is from his name called Barren to this day. The body of the other . . . Gualees was carried by the sea to the island of Echni and buried there.

There is a strong *dinnshenchus* flavour to this story which Lifris probably based on a local legend 'explaining' the presence on Barry and Echni of cults commemorating saints Barruc and 'Gualehes' respectively without adverting to the real origins of either saint. Thus, just as the association with Echni and the similarity of name point to the identity of Gildas and Gualehes, so also the proximity of Echni to Barry Island combines with other contextual evidence to help establish the identity of Barruc with Finnbarr of Moville.

With some notable exceptions (Wade-Evans in Doble, 1970, 156; Baring-Gould and Fisher, 1907, 194-6), commentators have tended to regard Barruc as an Irishman. Indeed he has been taken as the patron of Cork whose name, Bairre, resembles Barruc and whose feast, 25 September, precedes that of Barruc by a mere two days. A closer scrutiny reveals however that these two factors rather support the proposed identification with Finnbarr of Moville.

Thus, Finnbarr of Moville was also known as Bairrfhinn, the form from which the hypocoristic, Bairre, which presumably is at the base of Barruc, is derived. Furthermore, 27 September is set down as the feast of *Finniaui* (gen.) in the Irish Martyrology of Tallaght and the following day as that of *Finnio*, one of whose companions is named *Gildae* (gen.), the same form as is used to record Gildas's proper feast of 29 January.

Since *Gildae* in the list for 28 September no doubt represents Gildas, his inclusion on a day which is nowhere else assigned to him must stem from his historical association with Finnian. If so, Finnian of 28 September and by implication of the previous day can only be the *Vennianus auctor* whom we know to have been in correspondence with Gildas, an association which, as I have suggested, possibly led to the presence of Finnbarr's cult in the Llancarfan area. In this way then, the relationship between Gildas (Gualehes) and Finnbarr (Barruc) which Lifris depicts can be taken to reflect in local terms an association which appears to be corroborated and authenticated by Irish sources.

GENOCUS OF LLANCARFAN

Finnia(n) was by far the more common hypocoristic form of the Irish saint's name. It follows therefore that this too should have had a reflex in the Llancarfan tradition. Lifris, who might have been expected to use it as part of his local materials, is silent. It is something of an irony, therefore, that it may have survived in the source Lifris appears to have been using, Finnian's *uita*. According to this, Finnian, on the completion of his stay at Llancarfan, returned to Ireland *cum sancto Bitheo et sancto Genoco et cum aliis quibusdam religiosis Britonibus* (Heist, 1965, 99).

Bitheus, who elsewhere in the *uita* (Heist, 1965, 98), accompanies Cadog and Finnian to Rome, may represent the saint one would expect to have been the third companion on such an important pilgrimage, David whose name, if the *da* were taken as the prefix of endearment *da-(do-)*, could well yield a Hiberno-Latin form *Bitheus*. The Hiberno-Latin Genocus, on the other hand, reflects Welsh Gwynog (earlier *Guynnauc*), as has already been suggested by Baring-Gould and Fisher (1911, 242), the correspondence, Irish *-e-* Welsh *-wy-* being borne out by such forms as *gelt/gwyllt, fert/gwyrth*.

The likelihood is therefore that Welsh *Gwynog* represents Irish *Finn(i)o*, with the diminutive ending *-og* (*-auc*). In other words, Finnian's biographer who was possibly aware of a connection between his hero and *Gwynog*, but obviously unaware of its true nature, brought him back to Ireland in the saint's own, albeit cambricised, company. That the local form of Finnio is likely to have contained the element *gwyn* is further demonstrated by the context of an episode in the *uita* of Samson of Dol, a work which, traditionally regarded very early, has also been assigned a date in the early ninth century (Fawtier, 1912 (cf. Chadwick, 1969, 253-5); Poulin, 1977).

WINIAVUS OF DOCCO

Samson was a native Welsh saint, the greater part of whose life and missionary effort was devoted to Brittany. His Welsh background, as reflected by his *uita* (Plaine, 1887), is mainly associated with the monastery of Llanilltud Fawr, now Llantwit Major, some ten miles west of Barry Island and even nearer Llancarfan. He may be regarded, therefore, as having belonged to the greater Llancarfan area. This is important because the itinerary which his *uita* maps out for him across Cornwall (Bowen, 1934), beginning in the Padstow area and terminating on the Fowey Estuary, the point of departure for Brittany, follows a route laden with echoes of Llancarfan.

Thus Cadoc's chief church in Cornwall is Tregaddock, near St Kew which was formerly known as Landoho or Docco (Loth, 1914, 292-3; Doble, 1965, 105-6, 1970, 90), the monastery visited by Samson on his arrival in the Padstow area. Similarly, the saint commemorated in the church name *Landoho, Docco alias*

Dogwyn, figures in the names of two Welsh churches only, Llandochau Fawr and Llandochau Fach, both of which are situated in the general Llancarfan area. It is evidence such as the progress of Cadog's cult in Cornwall that led Doble (1965, 63-4) to regard 'Padstow, . . . being a key position on the ancient trade-route from Wales and Ireland . . . (as having) played a very important part' in the development of monasticism in Cornwall with its origins in south Wales, including the Llancarfan area. One piece of evidence for this which Doble did not use, however, is the manner in which the main stations of Samson's itinerary correspond to Welsh and Cornish manifestations of the Irish cult of St Finnbarr.

This is already the case in Wales. Thus in the *uita* of Padarn (Wade-Evans, 1944, 256-7), Samson and Guinnius (another Welsh form of Finnio) are together set down as 'leaders' of churches supposedly founded by Padarn in Cardiganshire, an association which at least bespeaks the proximity of their cults. It is in Cornwall however that their association becomes most apparent. Thus, on being brought by his biographer to Docco (Landoho), now St Kew near Padstow, Samson is met by 'the wisest of the brethren of the monastery, *Winniaus* by name, who was also named among them, in the British language, *Lux*'.

The form *Winnavius*, also written *Winniaus*, may be compared with Adamnan's *Vinniauo* (dat.), which is used to refer to Colum Cille's tutor, Finnian (Anderson and Anderson, 1961, 326; cf. Fleuriot, 1978, 612-3). The decisive evidence, however, is the reference to *lux* 'light', the British meaning of the name. This can only be Cornish *gwyn* (cf. Welsh *gwyn*, Ir. *finn*) normally meaning 'white, bright, lustrous' but including in its semantic range the notion of light (cf. Fleuriot, 1978, 613). We may infer, therefore, that Samson's 'host' at the monastery of Docco was locally known as **(G)wyn(y)ow* (Cornish) or **(G)wynyaw* (Welsh).

A dedication to a saint of this name does not now survive in the St Kew district, unless we take the saint to be represented by St Wenn of St Kew (Baring-Gould and Fisher, 1911, 167), following a change of sex not unusual in Celtic saints. The absence of a local saint **Gwyn(y)ow* is, however, probably best explained by reference to the rededication in the fifteenth century of the church at St Kew to the biblical Saint James the Apostle. Indeed, St James is very probably a surrogate of his Celtic predecessor because his feast of 25 July is that of **Gwyn(y)ow's* cognate, Finnbarr, in the Irish calendars. Similarly, in the list of Irish saints who are 'twinned' with saints of the universal church, Saint James's partner is Finnian of Moville.

It must seem likely, therefore, that *Winnavius alias *Gwyn(y)ow* of St Kew was a Cornish version of the Irish cult of St Finnian of Moville, whose presence in Cornwall is made all but certain by a group of dedications at the terminus of the transpeninsular route through Cornwall, the Fowey Estuary.

WINNOW AND BARRY OF FOWEY

The point of departure for the sea-journey from Cornwall to Brittany was the estuary of the Fowey and, as if to mark Samson's use of it, his church now stands on the Fowey at Lantyan. Across the river, opposite Lantyan and near Lostwithiel, is the church of St Winnow (earlier Winnuc, Winnoc), a name which replicates that of *Winnavius* at St Kew, despite Loth's objection (Loth, 1914, 295-6; Doble, 1970, 91, 152) that 'les deux noms sont . . . parfaitement distincts'. On the contrary as is shown by the evidence adduced in support of his view, the presence in a single sentence of a tenth-century charter of the forms *hraet Winiaw* and *Carn Winnioc*, the names only differ in the addition of a diminutive ending, *-oc* (Ir. *-ach*), to one of the forms.

Winnoc, whose main feast is 6 November represents in South Cornwall a cult which spread extensively on the Continent, its centres there being at Wormhout and Bergues-Saint-Winnoc in Flanders. A measure of the cult's popularity, which is borne out by the numerous *uitae* of the saint (*Acta Sanctorum*, 6 Nov.), is the fact that in the Irish Martyrology of Gorman the list for 6 November includes *Uinnocus*, a form which must derive from a 'foreign' source.

If Winnoc, whose *uitae* call him a Briton, does represent an originally Irish Finnbarr (alias Bairrfhinn) as his name suggests, then his feast had moved as the cult spread. This would only have occurred, however, within the limits of the feast's original octave, for both 8 November and 13 November are set down as feasts of Bairrfhinn in the Irish calendars.

The onomastic variation, Bairrfhinn/Winnoc (Finnbarr) which would then have accompanied the liturgical variation in feast days, is in fact characteristic of the cult as a whole (Ó Riain, 1977) and, as we have seen was also a feature of the saint's legend at Llancarfan. Its otherwise demonstrable presence in the traces of the saint's cult at Fowey is therefore of the greatest importance for the proposed identification of Winnoc with Finnbarr *alias* Bairrfhinn.

At Lantyan itself, which lies opposite St Winnows and near Samson's church, there stood formerly a cross called 'Barry's Crosse' (Doble, 1970, 155). While its original function is unclear, this cross may be taken as a signpost to the church of St Nicholas at Fowey, whose original patron, *Barrianus*, also *Fymbrianus*, was colloquially known as St Barry (Doble, 1970, 155).

The present dedication to St Nicholas is the result of a reconsecration performed by Bishop Grandisson in 1336. The choice of Nicholas is interesting in that he also replaced Barruc at Barry Island. The two Celtic saints have much more than this in common however. Barruc, as we have seen, was regarded by some as a cognate of Bairre of Cork. The same applies to Barry of Fowey whose feast fell on 26 September, the day after that of Finnbarr of Cork. There is one notable dissenting voice, however, that of A.W. Wade-Evans (Doble, 1970, 156), who took both the Cornish and Welsh saints to represent Berwyn son of Brychan whom the tract *De situ Brecheiniauc* places *apud Cornubiam*.

No doubt the allusion in this text is to Barry of Fowey but, as Wade-Evans notes, Berwyn is 'the exact, rule-right, Welsh equivalent of the Irish Barrfhind'. Consequently, in view of the cumulative evidence of this paper, it may be inferred that

Brychan's son also mediates the cult of St Finnbarr, thus providing the Moville saint with another local Welsh or Cornish reflex.

In sum, therefore, it would appear that Barry of Fowey if, as seems the case he is identical with Berwyn son of Brychan, also succumbed to the localising influences which turned his apparent cognate, Winnow, into a Briton and which affected practically all Irish cults in Wales and Cornwall.

CONCLUSIONS

By way of the progress of the cult of St Finnbarr, attention has been drawn here to the two essentially different types of Irish saint commemorated in Welsh and Cornish hagiographical tradition. The literary Irish saint is very much a latecomer whose introduction to Welsh hagiography in the late eleventh century resulted from the use made by Welsh hagiographers, such as Rhigyfarch of Llanbadarn Fawr and Lifris of Llancarfan, of Irish written materials as aids to the composition of their lives of David and Cadog respectively. From these sources, saints such as *Barre, Sgutinus, Modomnoc* and *Finian*, all of whose names betray their literary provenance, entered the realm of Welsh hagiography. Occasionally, one or other of these saints, *Finian* for example, had a local Welsh counterpart. In no case however can it be shown that the inclusion of a literary type of Irish saint in a Welsh *uita* was inspired by local traces of his cult.

The local type of Irish saint, on the other hand, has origins in Wales and Cornwall which take him back to the period of Irish settlement, that is to say, to the 'Age of Saints' itself. This is apparent not only from the correlation between the spread of dedications to originally Irish saints and the actual area of Irish settlement to which Bowen has drawn attention (1956, 96-7) but, more significantly perhaps, from the fluidity of name form which, to judge by the evidence presented here, characterized the progress of Irish cults and which at least presupposes the presence of an Irish-speaking population in the area to which the cult was introduced.

There can be no other explanation for the occurrence in the district of Llancarfan, for instance, of the variant hypocoristic forms *Barr(uc)* (Bairrfhinn) and *Gwynog (Finnbarr), both of which appear to have originally referred to Finnbarr *alias* Bairrfhinn *alias* Finnia(n), patron of Moville in Co. Down, the memory of whose scholarship and piety had inspired the rise and initial progress of the cult as a whole. Manifestly, as first recounted in the Llancarfan area, this saint's legend variously named him either Finnbarr or Bairrfhinn. Just as clearly, as is shown by Lifris's thoroughly local *Barrucus* and the ostensibly Welsh *Genocus* of Finnian's *uita*, Finnbarr's Irish affiliations cannot have survived for long the decline of the Irish settlement. In this regard also, he typifies the whole range of Irish cults in Wales.

More durable than mere national origins, however, are evidences of name and of feastday and it is basically these items which permit the 'recovery' of originally Irish cults in Wales and Cornwall. Of course, not all Irish saints enjoy the considerable advantage which Columbanus's association of *Vennianus* with Gildas gives to the study of the Welsh cult of Finnbarr. Here we have a glimpse of historical truth dating from *c.* 600 which can be used to 'explain' why Finnian of Clonard's eleventh-century biographer brought his hero to visit the 'holy men' in Echni and why Lifris, writing a little before 1100, brings the patron of the neighbouring island, Barruc, into contact with Gualehes (*alias* Gildas?). It is true, of course, that neither Finnian's biographer nor Lifris can have realised the true significance of their materials. The fact that they were still available to them, however, suggests that the usual gap of several centuries between the *floruit* of a saint and the beginning of his written record need not be quite as insurmountable as it seems.

The originally Irish character of Finnian's person has recently been called into question (Fleuriot, 1978). Here, however, it is the saint's cult rather than his person which has helped to establish the predominantly Irish character of Slover's Hiberno-Welsh 'community of hagiographical tradition'. Wherever Finnian's real place of origin may have been, Irish and, on examination, Welsh hagiographical tradition unquestionably saw the saint as *Hibernis ipsis Hibernior*.

REFERENCES

Acta Sanctorum. Société des Bollandistes, Brussels.
Anderson, A.O. and M.O., 1961. *Adomnan's Life of Columba*. Nelson, London.
Baring-Gould, S. and Fisher, J., 1907, 1908, 1911, 1913. *The Lives of the British Saints* I-IV. Hon. Society of Cymmrodorion, London.
Bartrum, P.C., 1966. *Early Welsh Genealogical Tracts*. University of Wales Press, Cardiff.
Bieler, L., 1963 (repr. 1975). *The Irish Penitentials*. Institute for Advanced Studies, Dublin.
Bowen, E.G., 1934. 'The travels of St Samson of Dol', *Aberystwyth Studies* 13.
Bowen, E.G., 1956. *The Settlements of the Celtic Saints in Wales*. University of Wales Press, Cardiff.
Bowen, E.G., 1969. 'The Irish Sea in the Age of Saints'. *Studia Celtica* 4, 56-71.
Bowen, E.G., 1972. 'The geography of early monasticism in Ireland', *Studia Celtica* 7, 30-44.
Brooke, C., 1964. 'St Peter of Gloucester and St Cadoc of Llancarfan'. *In* Chadwick *et al.* (ed), *Celt and Saxon*. University Press, Cambridge.
Chadwick, N.K., 1958. 'Intellectual life in west Wales in the last days of the Celtic Church'. *In* Chadwick *et al.* (ed), *Studies in the early British church*, 121-82. University Press, Cambridge.
Chadwick, N.K., 1969. *Early Brittany*. University of Wales Press, Cardiff.
Chadwick, N.K., 1970. 'Early literary contacts between Wales and Ireland'. In D.Moore (ed), *The Irish Sea Province in Archaeology and History*, 66-77. Cambrian Archaeol. Assoc., Cardiff.
Davies, W., 1981. 'Property rights and property claims in Welsh *Vitae* of the eleventh century'. *In* E. Patlagean, P. Riché, M. Sot (ed), *Hagiographie, Cultures et Sociétés IVe-XIIe siècles*, 515-33. Études Augustiniennes, Paris.

Delehaye, H., 1907. *The Legends of the Saints* (English trans. by V.M.Crawford of *Légendes Hagiographiques*). Longmans Green, London.

Doble, G.H., 1965, 1970. *The Saints of Cornwall* IV-V. (repr. from the 'Cornish Saints Series'). Holywell Press, Oxford.

Evans, J.G., and J.Rhys, 1893. *The Text of the Book of Llan Dav*. Old Welsh Texts IV, Oxford.

Fawtier, R., 1912. *La Vie de Saint Samson: essai de critique hagiographique*. Bibl Éc Hautes Études, Paris.

Fisher, J., 1906-7. 'Welsh church dedications', *Trans Hon Soc Cymmrod*, 76-108.

Fleuriot, L., 1978. 'Le "saint" Breton Winniau et le pénitentiel dit "de Finnian"?', *Études Celtiques* 15 , 607-17.

Heist, W.W., 1965. *Vitae Sanctorum Hiberniae*. Société des Bollandistes, Brussels.

Hughes, K., 1954a. 'The cult of St Finnian of Clonard from the eighth to the eleventh century', *Ir Hist Stud* 9, 13-27.

Hughes, K., 1954b. 'The historical value of the Lives of St Finnian of Clonard', *Engl Hist Rev* 69, 353-72.

Hughes, K., 1958 (repr. 1973). 'British Museum MS. Cotton Vespasian A. xiv ('Vitae Sanctorum Wallensium'), its purpose and provenance'. *In* N. Chadwick *et al.* (ed), *Studies in the Early British Church*, 183-200. University Press, Cambridge.

James, J.W., 1967. *Rhigyfarch's Life of St David*. University of Wales Press, Cardiff.

Kenney, J.F., 1929 (repr. 1966). *The Sources for the Early History of Ireland (Ecclesiastical)*. Columbia University Press, New York.

Lapidge, M. 1973-74. 'The Welsh-Latin poetry of Sulien's family', *Studia Celtica* 8-9, 68-106.

Lawlor, J.J., 1914. *The Psalter and Martyrology of Ricemarch*. Henry Bradshaw Society, London.

Loth, J., 1914. 'La vie la plus ancienne de Saint Samson de Dol', *Revue Celtique* 35, 269-300.

Ó Riain, P., 1977. 'St. Finnbarr: a study in a cult', *J Cork Hist Archaeol Soc* 82, 63-82.

Plaine, F., 1887. 'Vita Antiqua Sancti Samsonis', *Analecta Bollandiana* 6, 77-150.

Plummer, C. 1910 (repr. 1968). *Vitae Sanctorum Hiberniae*. University Press, Oxford.

Poulin, J.C., 1977. 'Hagiographie et politique. La première vie de Saint Samson de Dol', *Francia* 5, 1-26.

Rees, W.J., 1853. *Lives of the Cambro-British Saints*. Welsh MSS Society, Llandovery.

Slover, C.H., 1926, 1927. 'Early literary channels between Britain and Ireland', *University of Texas Studies in English* 6-7.

Wade-Evans, A.W., 1923. *Life of St. David*. Society for Promoting Christian Knowledge, London.

Wade-Evans, A.W., 1934. *Welsh Christian origins*. Alden Press, Oxford.

Wade-Evans, A.W., 1944. *Vitae Sanctorum Britanniae et Genealogiae*. University of Wales Press, Cardiff.

Walker, G.S.M., 1970. *Sancti Columbani Opera*. Institute for Advanced Studies, Dublin.

Williams, I., 1930. *Pedeir Keinc y Mabinogi*. University of Wales Press, Cardiff.

Notes on Monastic Archaeology and the Annals of Ulster, 650-1050

Aidan Macdonald

Archaeologists in Ireland and Celtic Britain as elsewhere are at a serious disadvantage when attempting to study the physical remains, and to reconstruct the physical appearance at any given stage, of the great monasteries of the period prior to the 12th century. Indeed, little has hitherto been done in this field, on a scale large enough to afford more than glimpses and partial answers. But many, perhaps most, such sites are not readily accessible to a detailed analysis by excavation of their groundplan, extent and the nature of their buildings, and the way in which all these developed and changed over the centuries: some are not so accessible at all. Most early ecclesiastical foundations of any local or regional importance continued in use in one way or another into later medieval, often into post-medieval times. They may well continue in use today. And even where from documentary sources or examination on the ground such later occupation cannot be shown to have occurred, or where it appears to be limited to a relatively small area within a larger early complex, successive building and rebuilding, alteration and expansion during the course of the pre-12th century occupation will only have served to obscure or destroy earlier phases of the sequence. In any case, continuing ritual activity at a given site whether in the form of a large monastic cathedral complex or of a small *cillín* graveyard, is likely to include, or fall within, the focal area of the earlier settlement — the area of the major early church or churches, burial ground and probably domestic buildings. Where furthermore such later occupation has stimulated the processes of urbanisation up to modern times, archaeologists may reasonably hope for no more than the scattered fragments of information occasionally afforded by redevelopment sites or other chance discovery. Possibly, we should more reasonably look for nothing at all. A large early ecclesiastical settlement that can be peeled layer by layer, each layer yielding itself intact, is most unlikely ever to be found.

In these circumstances recourse must be had to a systematic examination of those texts that can more or less safely be shown to reflect, more or less accurately, conditions obtaining prior to (or at least uninfluenced by) the introduction of the continental monastic orders during the 12th century. For the present limited exercise, the *Annals of Ulster* have been chosen for the following reasons. Though they are a composite compilation, drawing on various sources over a long timespan, under various editorial priorities and activities (and their attendant problems), they offer what purports to be basic historical information (unlike, say, most saints' lives, or explicitly religious documents), within a superficially coherent chronological framework. Thus, not only can individual items of archaeological significance be extracted from them and used but also overall developments, which might well not be recoverable by fieldwork or excavation alone, may be apparent that can be assumed to be genuinely historical with reasonable safety.

The edition used here is *Annals of Ulster*, ed. W.M. Hennessy and B. MacCarthy, 4 vols., Dublin 1887-1901: hereinafter referred to as AU. No account therefore has been taken of possible or actual problems of chronology or provenance posed by individual entries or groups of entries or associated with different MS hands — save only that verse passages have been ignored. Dates given are those of the above edition, uncorrected. Since any attempt at statistical analysis would almost certainly not be of any real use or meaning in the present context, the basic material is usually presented first and then discussed somewhat in the manner of a conventional excavation report. For the spelling of Irish words, except in quotations, the *Contributions to a Dictionary of the Irish Language*, published by the Royal Irish Academy, have normally been followed. They are cited hereinafter as *Contribb*, with references to the relevant fascicules. Latin words appear in classical rather than medieval guise, for purposes of discussion.

Certain areas of potential archaeological interest have not been dealt with at all here. Place-names have only been discussed where some notice of them seemed necessary to the development of the argument in another context. No attempt has been made to identify 'lost' sites: the present writer does not have the necessary background knowledge or linguistic and literary competence for Ireland and the few Scottish foundations mentioned are mostly sufficiently well known. No attention has been paid to the disappearance from the record of individual houses, whether of men or of women. The writer's concern is entirely with such evidence as may throw light on the physical nature and appearance of the larger monastic settlements, in terms of their buildings, groundplans and overall development, in the period 650-1050.

1. THE CHURCH AND THE MONASTIC BUILDINGS

THE CHURCH

Dairthech. 718 (*Drostan dairtaighe*: possibly of Ardbraccan); 761 (Kildare); 817 (transporting of the floor or foundation of a *dairthech: solaich daurthige:* Lat. *solum: Contribb* S, *sol*); 823 (Bangor); 824 (Magh-Bile burnt *cona derthigib*); 835 (Kildare: see further below); 839 (Armagh burnt *cona dertighibh 7 a doimliacc*); 844 (Clonmacnoise burnt *cona dertaigibh*); 849 (Trevet: see further below); 855 (Lusk); 868 (Armagh burnt *cona derthaigibh*); 873 (monasteries of Leinster burnt with their churches: *cealla cona derthaigibh*); 880 (*dertach Ciannain:* presumably Duleek: see further below); 891 (a great storm blows churches from their sites:

daurthaighi as a lathraigib); 963 (Kildare); 995 (Armagh burnt, including *dertach* and *damliac*); 1002 (Ferns); 1020 (Kildare); 1020 (Glendalough burnt *cona dairtighibh*); 1028 (the church of Slane fell down: *dertach Slane do thuitim*); 1031 (Comber, Co. Down); 1042 (Killeshin: see further below).

This is the commonest term for the church building. It means literally 'oak-house' — 'penitentiary, oratory, prayer-house (originally of wood), the smallest of the sacred edifices used in Ireland; generally fifteen feet long and ten feet broad': secondly, 'prayer-house in general, chapel' (*Contribb* D fasc. 1, *dairthech*). The possible range of size of the *dairthech* and of the church and monastic buildings generally will be discussed later. The belief that the building was originally and (probably) normally of wood, as its etymology indicates, is reinforced by its occasional juxtaposition with *do(i)mliacc* (infra). The *dairthech* may sometimes have had a wooden floor; but the *solaich daurthige* of 817 may equally well have been substantial sleeper-beams to be laid horizontally in a slot dug into the ground and into which the uprights of the frame of the building would be tenoned. Such a method of construction may have been employed in at least some of the churches destroyed in 891, rather than one of uprights sunk directly into post-holes. In a number of instances more than one *dairthech* existed at the same time at the same place. From the contexts, 'church' would seem to be the safest rendering of the term here. The *dairthech* was in use, and very likely being built also, throughout the period under review.

Oratorium. 788 (*lapideum,* at Armagh); 788 (Cluain-ferta-Mongain); 804 (*nouum*, at Killeigh); 808 (lightning killed a man *in oratorio Nodan*); 815 (Fore); 822 (Gallen); 850 (Clones); 903 (Kells: cf. *templum* (813); *domliac* (919), infra); 1008 (*oratorium Aird Macha . . . plumbo tegitur: damliac mor* in 1020, infra).

The meaning of *oratorium*, in medieval Irish and English usage, has been discussed recently by Radford (1977, 2): its normal meaning in this period is 'church' — a conclusion quite in accordance with the evidence afforded by AU. Radford, quoting Petrie, points out that *oratorium* in AU is sometimes *dairthech* elsewhere. But he further points out that *oratorium* is not necessarily *dairthech*, in AU or elsewhere, suggesting that the *oratorium lapideum* of 788 (AU) is probably the *doimliacc* referred to in 839 (AU). The *oratorium lapideum* of 788 is in fact the first explicit mention of a stone church in AU, apart from the rather problematical place-name Duleek (see further below). It is possible that the *oratorium* (903) and the *domliac* (919) at Kells are one and the same, if the stone building is not a replacement of a wooden structure in the meantime. But it would be reasonable to infer that the *oratorium* at Armagh (1008) was of stone, simply because of the nature of the (presumably) new roofing material, even if it were not explicitly said to be so in 1020. In the other instances cited above, the building material cannot certainly be inferred, for reasons that will be suggested when burnings are discussed later, though the roof of the *oratorium Nodan* (808) was presumably of thatch or shingles (assuming that lightning striking through the roof is what the entry implies). The term seems to have been in commonest use in the first half of the 9th century.

Do(i)mliacc, da(i)mliacc. 839 (Armagh burnt, *cona dertighibh 7 a doimliacc*); 919 (Kells); 919 (Dulane); 995 (Armagh burnt, including *dertach* and *damliac*); 1006 (Kells); 1019 (Durrow); 1020 (Armagh burnt, including *in damliac mor cona tuighi do luaidhe*, 'with its roof of lead'); 1031 (Ardbraccan: see further below); 1050 (Kildare).

Do(i)mliacc is the phrase *do(i)m, da(i)m liacc*, 'a stone house, stone church', formed from *dom, dam* 'house, home,' and *liacc*, usually printed as a compound. It is more frequent in the sense 'church'. (See *Contribb* dodénta-dúus, *dom, dam*). The *oratorium lapideum* of 788 apart, the term does not occur until well into the 9th century; and does not occur significantly until the end of the 10th. The nature of the buildings thus designated is (apart, of course, from the etymology) probably sufficiently attested by the two juxtapositions with *dairthech*, though in both cases the monastery in question is Armagh. Unlike *dairthech, do(i)mliacc* is never used in the plural explicitly; though the occasional use of the phrase *do(i)mliacc mór* (1006, Kells; 1020, Armagh) might conceivably imply more than one stone church within the monastic enclosure. (The phrase *dertach na damliac* etc., 995 (Armagh), is too vague to be pressed into service in this context).

Duleek, Co. Meath, is *do(i)mliacc (Contribb,* loc. cit. supra). It first occurs in AU at 724 (obit of Aldchu of *Doimliagg*): i.e., more than 60 years before the *oratorium lapideum*. The most straightforward explanation of the place-name and its appearance at this juncture is that it reflects the actual presence here of a stone church by the end of the first quarter of the 8th century — a time when such a building would be rare enough (at least in eastern and central Ireland) to be remarkable and therefore to be named as a feature of the local landscape. Duleek lies towards the E coast, SW of Drogheda and S of the Boyne Valley in an area probably easily accessible to Northumbrian influences, introduced perhaps by Irish *Romani*, during the second half of the 7th century or early in the 8th. However, the *dertach Ciannain* of 880, if it is to be given its literal meaning (and if in fact it refers to Duleek), poses a problem that does not admit of a ready solution.

Eclais, eclas. 890 (apparently the church of Cluain-fota: Clonfad, barony of Fartullagh, Co. Westmeath: Gwynn and Hadcock, 1970, 376); 1006 (Matadhan, King of Ulaid, killed *i n-ecluis Brigte for lar Duin dalethglas:* 'in (the middle of) Downpatrick').

This usage seems to be unusual generally. The meanings of *eclais, eclas* in early Irish are given as 1. 'the Christian church as an institution, whether regarded as a visible organization or a spiritual community of believers'; 2. 'a local church or community of believers; a unit of ecclesiastical organization, especially a monastery'; 3. 'clergy'; 4. 'a church, a building for worship' (*Contribb* E, *eclais, eclas*).

Templum is used once, of Kells: *Ceallach abbas Iae, finita constructione templi*

Cenindsa, reliquit principatum (813). The granting of Kells to Colum Cille (i.e., to his *paruchia*, more especially to Iona) is recorded at 803; and the building of the new monastery there at 806: *constructio nouae ciuitatis Columbae cille hi Ceninnus.* It may be both the *oratorium* of 903 and the *domliac* of 919: the unique use of *templum* could imply that the principal church of the monastery was a stone building from the outset (probably still a rarity in the early 9th century). On the other hand, it need be neither: a wooden church built in 813 might well have been replaced (perhaps more than once) by 903. It was presumably situated at or near the position occupied now by the Church of Ireland parish church, within the area of the present-day graveyard that also contains the round-tower and three of the high crosses. (Meath, 6 in., sheet 17 (revision of 1954-55)).

Reiclés likewise occurs once, at 1010: obit of Dunadhach *in reiclesa Coluim Cille i n-ard Macha.* Its etymology is doubtful: Stokes at one time suggested a formation from Lat. *reclusum* 'a recluse's cell'; later he proposed a derivation from *ro-eccles* (< *ecclesia*), 'a large church'. Its meanings are given as, originally, 'an oratory or small church built by an Irish saint for his own use; sometimes used to include the plot or enclosure about it', hence 'a monastic cell, the hut occupied by an Irish monk in a coenobitic settlement, and in general an anchorite's cell'. It is later used generally of a church connected with a monastery or of the monastery or abbey itself — the present instance is quoted in this context; then in the wider sense of a church or chapel in general. *Reiclésach* is 'a recluse or religious coenobite'. (See *Contribb* R, *reiclés, reiclésach*). Since the *reiclés* in question was apparently under the invocation of Colum Cille, it is likely that it contained a church, of whatever size. It is possible that what we are dealing with here is a small eremitical complex, having a chapel and quarters for one or more anchorites and perhaps its own enclosure, lying within the area of the monastic city that was early 11th century Armagh. A similar arrangement, also at Armagh, may underlie the reference at 1011 to the death in an epidemic there of Cennfaeladh of the *Saball* (infra), described as *anmchara toghaidhe*, 'a choice soul-friend (confessor, spiritual director)'. (Anchorites in AU are discussed in more detail later).

Two other churches at Armagh are mentioned: *Toi* and *Saball*, both apparently in the southern half of the settlement. They are mentioned together at 915 and 1020; the *Saball* alone at 1011. *Saball* (Lat. *stabulum*) means 'barn': *Saball Pátraic* is Saul, Co. Down (*Contribb* S, *saball*). The writer has not come across a suggested etymology for *Toi*.

Airdam occurs twice: in 995 Armagh was burned, including *dertach* and *damliac* and *erdamh* ('porch') and *fidnemedh;* in 1006 the great Gospel of Colum Cille was stolen in the night *as ind iardom iartharach in daimliacc moir Cenannsa,* 'out of the western *airdam* of the great stone-church of Kells' (translated 'sacristy' by both Hennessy and *Contribb* I, *iartharach*). *Airdam* is 'variously applied to any extraneous building attached to a larger one, vestibule, porch, etc.'; it seems to be composed of *ar* and *dom, dam* (*Contribb* A, fasc. 1, *airdam*). It is briefly discussed by Radford (1977, 4), who suggests that it may be the equivalent of the *porticus* of middle Saxon minster churches of the 7th to 9th or early 10th centuries: two annexes opening to N and S out of the E end of the nave. The western *airdam* of 1006 at Kells, however, was perhaps something more like a narthex (with a counterpart at the E end ?) — it was hardly an external W porch leading into the church proper, since it seems to have housed an important copy of the Gospels — or the western *airdam* of two or more lying on the same side of the main building, presumably N or S. The entry at 995 seems to suggest that there was more than one *airdam*, either in the same church, or more likely among all or some of the churches. But the wording is too vague to be sure what is meant.

Airnigde occurs in the phrase *na taigi aernaighi* (Armagh, 920), which is translated 'the houses of prayer' by Hennessy, though the genitive sg. and pl. should end in *-e* (*Contribb* A, fasc. 1, *airnigde*). The *taigi aernaighi* are associated with Céli Dé and with sick or lepers (*na taigi aernaighi . . . cona lucht de cheilibh de 7 di lobraibh*). *Tech n-urnaigthe* is translated 'oratory' (*Contribb* T-tnuthaigid, *tech, teg,* II (c)); the context here suggests that they are oratories connected with a leper house or infirmary complex, rather than the churches of the monastery at large.

ROUND-TOWERS

Clocthech, 'bell-house, belfry', occurs twice. In 949 the *clocthech* of Slane was burnt, including an important relic, a bell and a large number of people, the lector among them; and in 1020 Armagh was burnt, including *in cloicthech cona cloccaibh*. *Clocthech* is, of course, composed of *cloc* 'bell' and *tech* 'house' (*Contribb* C, fasc. 1, *cloc;* T-tnúthaigid, *tech, teg*), and must indicate the original or primary function of the round-tower. The bells were probably kept in the tower; and they may have been hung in some cases. The entry of 949, however, indicates other functions of the round-tower, which the design and appearance of surviving examples tend to confirm: it was also a repository of monastic valuables and a place of refuge in time of danger, not necessarily a safe one. Round-towers are briefly discussed by Radford (1977, 3-4): since, as he observes, the destruction of a *clocthech* is already in question at the middle of the 10th century, they very likely began to be built before 900, or at latest soon after. But, though the inspiration may well be Carolingian, it seems unnecessary to suggest a possible introduction of the idea to Ireland *via* 9th century England. Apart from two surviving examples in Scotland (Abernethy and Brechin) and one in the Isle of Man (St. Patrick's Isle, Peel) — all three within the early Irish cultural province — the freestanding round-tower is an architectural phenomenon peculiar to Ireland in this period. Wooden prototypes moreover, though possible, have yet to be demonstrated archaeologically — indeed, would be extremely difficult so to do, given the nature and proportions of most of the extant stone-built towers. And the writer is not aware that any known round-tower displays or displayed features that can reasonably be attributed to wood skeuomorphism, like the *antae* and 'butterfly' gable-finials of some of the early stone churches.

MONASTIC BUILDINGS

The abbot's house. Occisio Dunchon principis Telcha leiss . . . i tigh abaid Telcha liss (808: Tullylish, Co. Down); *tene di nim forsa foruth n-abbadh inardd Machae, conidroloiscc* (822); . . . *iar n-orcain in taighi abath i n-Druim inasclaind* (912: Dromiskin: referred to as the 'refectory', *proindtech,* at 911: see further below); 915 (*les:* Armagh burnt *cosind lius abbaid* etc.); 975 (erenagh of Nendrum burned *in sua domu*); 992 (king of Luighne killed *i taigh abbaid Domnaigh Patraic*: Donaghpatrick, Co. Meath). *Tech* is straightforward enough, as also is *domus*. *Forad,* translated 'mansion', by Hennessy, is defined as, primarily, 'a mound or platform, probably in most cases of earth, used as a seat or stand for spectators, but also as a post of outlook; it varied in size and shape, being often large enough to accommodate a number of persons, but sometimes apparently intended for only one; it may in some cases have been circular . . .' It was often associated with an *óenach* site or princely residence. It also seems to have been used to mean a part or the whole of a rampart. Then, by transference, it meant a fort, residence or place of meeting (common in this sense in poetry): the present instance is given here. (See *Contribb* fochratae-futhu, *forad*). It seems likely that what is implied by the use of the term in the present context is one or more buildings, forming the abbot's quarters, having its own enclosure (whether of earth or some other material) and situated (probably) within the main *vallum monasterii*. It is conceivable that the residential complex of a major abbot might have included a ceremonial mound but unlikely that defence was a consideration. The idea of enclosure is more explicit in the use of *les* at 915. *Les* is, primarily, 'the space about a dwelling-house or houses enclosed by a bank or rampart', including the enclosure around monastic buildings: the present instance is quoted here; then, it is sometimes 'the bank or rampart itself' (*Contribb* L, 2 *les*). Compare *Les oíged* (*infra*).

TECH MÓR

It is recorded, at 963, that most of the clerics of Kildare were ransomed after the monastery had been plundered by Norsemen: *.i. lan in taigi moir sanc(t) Brigti,* 7 *lan in derthaigi, issed do ruagell Níall diib dia argat fesin.* What seems pretty clear from the context is that the *tech mór* ('great house'; 'principal building': *Contribb* T-tnúthaigid, *tech, teg*) of Brigit, at least in this instance, is not a church, as Thomas thinks (1971, 39-40) in his discussion of a passage in the Tripartite Life of Patrick. Adamnán's *magna domus* etc. of a much earlier period is briefly discussed by the Andersons (Anderson and Anderson, 1961, 113): it is a domestic building, whatever its precise function or functions. We are very likely dealing here with a

large communal building of no highly specialized function, curvilinear or rectilinear in ground plan, which served a variety of purposes, regularly or on an *ad hoc*
basis, in the daily routine of the monastery. The term may indicate that it was
regarded as the principal domestic building of the monastic layout.

Proindtech. 911 (abbot of Dromiskin and the royal heir of the Conailli burnt to
death *i prainntigh Droma inasclainn*); 970 (man killed by Norsemen *i n-dorus in
proinntighi:* monastery not specified: Armagh?). *Proindtech* is made up of *proind*
(Lat. *prandium*), 'meal, refection' and *tech:* 'eating-house, dining-hall'; generally
'of the refectory of a monastery' (*Contribb* N-O-P, *proind, proindtech*). The refectory may often, or usually, have stood by itself. It was pointed out above, however,
that the killing said at 911 to have been *i prainntigh*, is referred to at 912 by the
phrase *iar n-orcain in taighi abath*. There may simply be confusion in one entry or
the other; but the interesting possibility remains that the apparent contradiction
actually reflects the fact that the abbot's quarters and the refectory formed one
building, or were adjacent to each other in a range of buildings under the one roof.

Cucann, 'kitchen', occurs once: at 915 (Armagh burnt *cusin chucin* etc.). The
word is a borrowing of Lat. *coquina* (*Contribb* C, fasc. 3, *cucann*). The context (.*i.*
*a leith deiscertach cosin toi 7 cosint saboll 7 cusin chucin 7 cosind lius abbaid
h-uile*) suggests that it was a separate building — a wise precaution if so where accidental fire was a serious hazard (see further below).

Les oiged. 1003 (obit of Eochaid Ua Flannacáin *airchinnech lis oeigedh 7 Cluana
Fiacna*, apparently *l.o.* of Armagh); 1016 (obit of Flannacán mac Conaing, *fosair-
chinnech arda Macha*, and of Muirghes *airchinnech Lis oeighedh*). This is the
'guest-house': *oigi* means 'stranger, esp. one receiving hospitality, a guest, visitor,'
compare *tech n-oiged* (*Contribb* N-O-P, *oigi*). The fact that its head is described as
airchinnech, 'erenagh', on both occasions and that the office is equal with, or
greater than the superiority of another monastery at 1003 (Clonfeacle, Co. Tyrone)
suggests a fairly large establishment, very likely having its own church or churches.
It may have lain outside the *vallum monasterii* proper. The significance of *les* as indicating enclosure has been discussed above: the combination of *les* and *airchinnech* here will be discussed further below.

'Houses' generally are mentioned at 911 (*taighi ili do loscadh irrait airdd Macha
per incuriam*); and at 920 (the Dublin Norse plunder Armagh, but spare the
monastic buildings and community, *nisi paucis in ea* (i.e., the monastery) *tectis ex-
austis per incuriam*). But these references are not detailed enough to say anything
more about the nature or function of the buildings than can be said about their
burning (infra).

SIZE OF BUILDINGS

The size and scale of individual churches and domestic buildings, in terms of
groundplan and elevation, probably varied greatly both within the same monastery
and as between houses of differing importance and wealth. A few entries, however,

show pretty clearly that these structures were sometimes fairly substantial. At 849 the church of Trevet was burned by the king of Cianachta with 260 men inside (. . . *7 corolscsad* (sic) *leis derthach Treoit 7 tri xxit dec di doinibh ann*). At 969 Monasterboice and Dunleer were plundered by the Uí Néill overking and 350 people burned in one house (*orcain Mainistrech 7 Lainne leire la Domnall, la righ nErend, ubi in una domu, .cccl. accensi sunt*). At 1031 Ardbraccan was plundered by the Dublin Norse, 200 men being burnt in the *do(i)mliacc* (*Ard mBrecain do argain do Gallaib Atha Cliath. Da cet duine do loscadh isin daimliac* . . .). At 1042, it is not entirely clear what the annalist had in mind. The text reads: *Glenn Uissen do loscadh do mac Mail na mbó, 7 in dairrtech do brisiudh, 7 cet duine do marbad, 7 .iiii. cet do breith eisti* . . . Hennessy translates: 'Glenn-Uissen was burned by the son of Mael-na-mbo, and the oratory was broken, and 100 men were slain, and 400 taken out of it . . .' At first reading, it might be thought that the 100 men were killed in, and the 400 taken from, the church. But *eisti* is *a* 'out of, from', with the 3 sg. feminine form of the suffixed pronoun; while *dairthech* is neuter, later masculine. While it is possible that it actually was the church which suffered in this way, it is safer to assume that the annalist was thinking of the monastery as a whole (Killeshin, Co. Laois) and, therefore, of a feminine noun like *cell*. The assumption would perhaps be strengthened by the fact that Killeshin was attacked in revenge for the burning of Ferns by Donnchad, son of Brian.

A few other entries, while not giving exact figures, point in the same direction. At 835 the abbot of Armagh and 'Patrick's congregation' were attacked and captured in the church of Kildare by Feidhlimidh, King of Cashel (*gabail in dairthige i Cill dara for Forindan abbaid n-aerdd Machae, co samadh Patraic olchena, la Feidlimidh co cath 7 indnu, 7 ro gabta i cact co n-anhumaloit friu*). At 880 the church of Duleek (*dertach Ciannain*) was plundered by Norsemen and 'its full of people taken out of it' (*a lan di dhoinibh do brith ass*). At 919 the church of Kells was attacked by Norsemen and great numbers martyred there (*domliac Cenannsa do brisiuth o Gentibh 7 sochaidhe martrai ann*). And at 963 the number of clerics ransomed after Kildare had been plundered by Norsemen is expressed as 'the full of the great house of St Bridget, and the full of the oratory' (*lan in taigi moir sanc(t) Brigti 7 lan in derthaigi:* Hennessy's translation). Neither the entries giving actual figures, however, nor those merely suggesting large numbers, indicate anything more precise than buildings significantly larger than the well-preserved therefore well-known, *clochāin* of the W coast and its islands.

BUILDING MATERIALS AND CONSTRUCTION

With due caution, something may be inferred about the nature of buildings and building materials from the frequent recording of (especially) natural or accidental disasters, particularly those caused by fire. Here, only those entries which seem to be clear and straightforward and which do not say that the damage was deliberately caused, are set out. 671 (burning of Armagh and Tihelly); 671 (burning of 'Bangor of the Britons' — *Bennchair Brittonum*); 672 (burning of Magh-luinge); 689 (burning of Armagh); 709 (burning of Kildare); 722 (burning of Clonmacnoise); 730 (burning of Coleraine); 748 (burning of Clonfert; and of Kilmore, Co. Monaghan, or ? Kilmore, Co. Armagh: Gwynn and Hadcock, 1970, 394, 39); 749 (burning of Fore; and of Donaghpatrick); 754 (burning of Clonmacnoise); 755 (burning of Bangor); 774 (burning of Armagh; of Kildare; of Glendalough); 774 (burning of Ennisboyne); 777 (burning of Clonmacnoise); 778 (burning of Kildare; of Clonmore, Co. Carlow; of Kildalkey); 779 (burning of Cloonburren; of Balla); 782 (burning of Armagh and of Mayo); 782 (wind destroyed Clonbroney: *uentus magnus 7 ualidissimus distruxit monasterium cluana Bronaigh*); 783 (burning of Trim); 787 (burning of Derry); 788 (burning of Clonard); 788 (burning of Inishkeen, Co. Monaghan); 789 (burning of Aughrim); 804 (burning of Killeigh, *cum oratorio nouo*); 805 (burning of Terryglass); 815 (burning of Clonmacnoise *de media ex maiore parte*); 815 (burning of the *oratorium* of Fore); 817 (burning of Clonmacnoise *tertia ex parte sui*); 822 ('fire from heaven fell on the Abbot's mansion in Ard-Macha, and burned it': *tene di nim forsa foruth n-abbadh i n-ardd Machae, conidroloiscc:* Hennessy's translation); 823 (burning of Roscommon *magna ex parte*); 833 (burning of Clonmacnoise *de media ex maiore parte*); 834 (burning of Clonmacnoise *tertia parte sui*); 839 (burning of Armagh *cona dertighibh 7 a doimliacc*); 891 (a great wind carried away churches and houses from their sites: *uentus magnus in feria Martini . . . 7 coruc na daurthaighi as a lathraigib, 7 na taighi olcena*); 911 (many houses burned in the *Rāth* of Armagh through carelessness: *taighi ili do loscadh irrait airdd Macha per incuriam*); 915 (the southern half of Armagh burnt by lightning, including the *Toi* and the *Saball*, the kitchen and the abbot's house: *Ard Macha do loscadh diait . . . .i. a leith deiscertach, cosin toi 7 cosint saboll 7 cusin chucin 7 cosind lius abbaid h-uile*); 919 (burning of the *do(i)mliacc* of Dulane, possibly by Norsemen); 977 (Cork destroyed by fire: *Corcach mor Muman do arcain la daigidh*); 995 (lightning struck Armagh, causing widespread fire: *tene diait do ghabail aird Macha, co na farcaibh dertach na damliac na h-erdamh na fidnemedh ann cen loscadh*); 997 (burning of Armagh *de media parte*); 1016 (burning of Downpatrick; and of Clonmacnoise, Clonfert and Kells); 1017 (burning of Glendalough *ex maiore parte*); 1019 (Kildare completely burned by lightning: *Ceall dara uile do loscadh do theinidh diaitt*); 1020 (Kildare burnt *cona dairtigh;* Glendalough all burnt *cona dairtighibh;* burning of Clonard, Clonmacnoise and Swords, *tertia parte*); 1020 (Armagh entirely burned, including the great *do(i)mliacc* with its lead roof, the belfry, the *Saball* and the *Toi* (*Ard Macha uile do leir do loscadh .i. in damliac mor cona tuighi do luaidhe, 7 in cloicthech cona cloccaibh, 7 in Saball 7 in Toai . . .*); 1027 (burning of Dunkeld); 1031 (burning of Kildare 'through the negligence of a wicked woman': *tria anfaitces drochmna*); 1040 (burning of Kildare; of Kells; of Downpatrick 'and many churches besides': *7 ilchealla archena*); 1050 (burning of Kildare, *co na daimliag*).

In some of the foregoing instances, perhaps especially in the earlier part of the period when entries provide less detail, the burnings may have been deliberately caused. A significant number, however, must have been accidental; and some are explicitly stated to have been so, or to have been the result of natural disasters. It seems reasonable to suppose therefore that many, if not most, of the buildings of a monastery were of wood. (Cf. the entries for Clonmacnoise 815 + 817, 833 + 834; for Armagh, 995 + 997; for Kildare, 1019 + 1020). Indeed, the entries of 782 (Clonbroney) and 891 suggest that they may sometimes have been of fairly light construction or at least so constructed that they could be uprooted given sufficient force (with sleeper-beam foundations?). The frequent references to the total or partial destruction of a monastery by fire suggest, too, that occupation may have been fairly, though perhaps not uniformly, dense at times. However, it should be borne in mind that buildings with stone walls, but having roofs of thatch or shingles and, it may be, some vertical timber framing, could as easily have been ruined or rendered useless by fire as wooden ones: the instances cited above contain a number of explicit references to stone buildings.

2.   THE MONASTIC COMMUNITY: SPECIALISED GROUPS

There are some indications of specialised groups within the larger monastic community, whose existence, if they had their own (especially enclosed) quarters, might be expected to have had a significant effect on the overall ground plan.

ANCHORITES

699 (obit of Aedh, anchorite *o Sleibtiu* (Sleaty)); 730 (obit of Echaid *anchoritae airdd Machae*); 732 (obit of Dochuma Bolggan *ancorita airdd Machae*); 735 (obit of Dublittir, *uir sapiens 7 anchorita Insole uaccae albae* (presumably Inchbofin, Co. Westmeath; or Inishbofin, Co. Galway)); 744 (obit of Conghus *anchorita Cluana tibrinne*); 747 (obit of Dodimóc *anchoritae, abbatis Cluana irairdd 7 Cille daro*); 747 (obit of Cúán *anchoirita o Lilcach* (Lully)); 751 (obit of Cilléne *anchoritae Iae*); 751 (obit of Osbran *anchorite 7 episcopi Cluana creamha* (Clooncraff)); 755 (obit of Ailgal *ancorita Cluana Cormaic*); 756 (obit of Fidhmuine *ancoritae Rathin* (Rahan)); 756 (*Cuidghal ancorita, Aildobur abbas Muccirt, mortui sunt*); 773 (obit of Imraithech *glinne Cloitighe, anchorita*); 775 (*quies Colmain fhinn ancoritae*); 779 (*congressio senodorum nepotum Neill Laginentiumque in opido Temro, ubi fuerunt ancoritae 7 scribe multi, quibus dux erat Dublitter*); 782 (obit of Suairlech *ancorita celibris Liss moer*); 786 (obit of Aldchú *ancorita Ratho oinbo*); 790 (obit of Dínertach, *ancorita*); 795 (*scribae 7 episcopi 7 ancoritae, dormierunt*); 795 (obit of Clothcú, *episcopus 7 ancorita Cluana iraird*); 800 (obit of Nindidh, *ancorita*); 806 (obit of Elarius, *ancorita et scriba Locha creae* (Monaincha)); 810 (obit of Dimmán of Araidh, *Muminensis ancorita*); 811 (obit of Flann *abbas Finnglaise*,

scriba et anchorita et episcopus; of Echaidh *episcopus et ancorita prinnceps Tamlachta;* of Nuadha *episcopus et ancorita, abbas airrd Machae*); 813 (obit of Feidilmidh *abbas Cille Moinni et moer Breg o phatraic ancorita precipuus scribaque optimus*); 814 (obit of Maelcanaigh *ancorita Lugmaidh*); 816 (*mors Dathail episcopi, scribae et ancoritae*); 820 (obit of Cennfaeladh, *scriba et episcopus et ancorita, abb Atho truim*); 821 (obit of Euchu *ancorita et episcopus, abbas Lugmaid*); 822 (obit of Sechnasach of Loch-Cendin *episcopus et ancorita*); 824 (obit of Diarmait *anchorita et religionis doctor totius Hiberniae*); 827 (*martre Temhnen anchorat*, probably at the hands of Norsemen, on the coast of Ard Cianachta); 835 (obit of Forbasach *episcopus et ancorita Luscan*); 836 (obit of Flaithroa *abbas monistrech Buti, episcopus et ancorita*); 837 (obit of Dochutu *sanctus episcopus et ancorita Slane*); 838 (obit of Maelgaimridh *scriba optimus et ancorita, abbas Benncair*); 839 (obit of Joseph, *episcopus et scriba optimus et ancorita, abbas Cluana auis et aliarum ciuitatum*); 842 (*Cumsudh mac Derero et Moinaigh mac Sothchadaigh, duo episcopi et duo ancorite, in una nocte mortui sunt i n-disirt Diarmata*); 842 (*Donnacan mac Maeletuile, scriba et ancorita, in Italia quieuit*); 842 (obit of Colgu *ancorita*); 844 (obit of Gormghal, *episcopus et ancorita Lainne leire* (Dunleer)); 846 (*Feidhlimidh (.i. mac Crimtain), rex Muman, optimus Scotorum, pausauit scriba et ancorita*); 847 (obit of Fínsnechta of Luibnech, *anchorita, et rex Connacht antea*); 848 (obit of Onchú *episcopus et ancorita Slane*); 851 (obit of Forindán, abbot of Armagh, *scriba et episcopus et anchorita*); 855 (obit of Suibhne, *scriba et anchorita, abbas Liss moer*); 857 (obit of Cumsuth, *episcopus et ancorita, princeps Cluana irairdd*); 861 (obit of Finan of Cluain Caín (Clonkeen, Co. Louth), *episcopus et anchorita*); 861 (obit of Muirghes *ancorita aird Macha*); 863 (obit of Áedgen Britt, *episcopus Cille daro, et scriba et anchorita*); 866 (obit of Coscrach of Tech Taille (Tihelly), *scriba et ancorita*); 866 (obit of Cormac, *scriba et episcopus et ancorita*); 869 (obit of Suairlech Indeidhnen (? Inan, p. of Killyon, Co. Meath: Gwynn and Hadcock, 1970, 37), *episcopus et ancorita et abbas Cluana irairdd, optimus doctor relegionis totius Hiberniae*); 869 (obit of Máelodhor, *ancorita abbas Daiminse*); 869 (obit of Comgan Fota *ancorita Tamhlactae daltae Maeleruain*); 869 (obit of Condla *ancorita Droma cara airde Ciannachta* (Drumcar)); 870 (obit of Colgu, *sacerdos et ancorita, abbas Cluana conaire Tommaen*); 871 (obit of Gnia, *princeps Doimliacc, ancorita et episcopus et scriba optimus*); 880 (obit of Crunnmáel of Cluain Caín, *episcopus et ancorita*); 890 (obit of Suibhne, *ancorita et scriba optimus Cluana macc U Nois*); 892 (obit of Mochta, *episcopus ancorita et scriba optimus aird Macha:* probably the Mochta captured by Norsemen at 878, there called *fer leghinn*); 902 (obit of Ceallach, *anchorita et episcopus aird Machae*); 907 (obit of Cormac, *ancorita princeps Droma moir* (Dromore, Co. Down)); 928 (obit of Céile, abbot of Bangor, *scriba et anchorita et apostolicus doctor totius Hibernie:* cf. 927); 929 (obit of Flann of Fore, *episcopus et ancorita*); 930 (obit of Maeleoin, *episcopus et ancorita Atho truim*); 935 (obit of Joseph, abbot of Armagh, *episcopus et sapiens et ancorita*); 951 (obit of Cele, *clam 7 ancorita*).

All the entries relating to anchorites in AU, 650-1050, have been presented here *in extenso* and (more or less) *verbatim* in the belief that the discussion will be easier to follow. All or any of the entries could refer to individuals living solitary lives of varying degrees of ascetic severity, within, at some remove, or quite apart from, a monastic community. Some read most naturally in that light: e.g., those of 773 (?), 775, 790, 800, 827, 842 (Colgu), 847 and 951. The number of entries, on the other hand, which describe an anchorite as 'of X', where X is usually an attested or well-known monastery, is sufficiently large to warrant the suggestion that the *anchorita* is frequently (for a period at least) a monastic official: e.g., 730, 732, 735, 744 (?), 751 (Iona), 755 (?), 756 (Rahan), 756 (*ancorita Muccirt?*), 782, 786 (?), 814, 861 (Armagh), 869 (Tallaght), 869 (Drumcar). In many cases, furthermore, a man seems to be anchorite of and abbot or (and) other official of a monastery: e.g., 747 (Clonard and Kildare: perhaps abbot only of both), 751 (Clooncraff), 795 (Clonard), 806, 835, 837, 844, 848, 869 (Clonard), 869 (Devenish), 890, 892, 902, 907, 930. If this be so, a significant number of other entries, in which the wording is ambiguous, may similarly indicate offices held in plurality: e.g., 811 (Finglas), 811 (Tallaght), 811 (Armagh), 813, 816, 820, 821, 822, 836, 838, 839, 851, 855, 857, 861 (Clonkeen), 863, 866 (Tihelly), 866 (Cormac), 870, 871, 880, 928, 929, 935. In no case is an entry informative enough or its construction explicit enough to permit firm conclusions to be drawn. It will be noticed, however, that the three rough categories proposed here show a chronological development from anchorites simply 'of X', through the suggested tenure of two offices only (as a rule) in plurality, to the more ambiguous situation where two, three or even more offices seem to be held by the same individual.

Anchorites must indeed have started as private individuals leading their own spiritual lives as hermits. The first notice of an anchorite in the period under review is at 699, where the dead man (Aedh) is merely described as *o Sleibtiu* (Sleaty): cf. 747 (Lully). It has been suggested above that there is evidence here for the continuation of this basic practice. It may well have outlasted the period of proposed 'institutional' eremitism (which seems to belong mainly to the 8th and 9th centuries); though, after the death of Cele, surely a solitary, in 951, there is no further notice of an anchorite in any capacity for a century anyway. Even allowing, however, for a loose honorific use of such terms as *anchorita, sapiens, scriba*, in some instances, the suspicion remains with the writer that, from the end of the first quarter of the 8th century until at least the end of the first quarter of the 10th, *anchorita* in AU usually means a monastic official having overall responsibility for those members of a community living a life of more advanced ascetic discipline, whether in groups or individually, whether within or outwith the main monastic enclosure. *Abbas* and *episcopus*, at least, can scarcely be used honorifically, even allowing for very loose usage. And the idiosyncratic character of the early Irish church notwithstanding, the overwhelming impression is gained that many, if not most, of these men enjoyed careers too public (and perhaps too lucrative) for hermits pure and simple. Conversely, they could not have exercised (other) high monastic office, or the functions of episcopal orders, efficiently or accessibly had they been pursuing the eremitic life continuously or even seasonally. Though it is beyond the period in question by over a century and probably does not represent a continuation of the phenomenon suggested here, it may not be irrelevant to draw attention at this point to the *dīsertach* at Iona, mentioned at 1164 in company with the *sacart mor*, the *fer léiginn*, the *cenn na Ceile nDe* and *maithi muinnteri Ia arcena*. A site called *Cladh* ('graveyard') *an Dìseirt* lies a short distance to NE of the N side of the surviving *vallum* at Iona, with *Port an Dìseirt* on the shore just to SE of it.

The entry relating to Castledermot at 842 (above) is interesting. The monastery was apparently founded in 812 (Gwynn and Hadcock, 1970, 31), during the period of the ascetic revival associated with the Céli Dé and St Maelruain of Tallaght. Its original name, moreover, has the element O Ir *dīsert* (*Contribb*, degra-dodelbtha) implying, surely, an eremitical bias. It may have been intended as an association of anchorites, whether living individually or severally. Both men referred to here were in episcopal orders and so it is possible that there were more than one organized group of anchorites within the community.

SRUITHI etc.

A number of other entries point, more or less definitely, to the existence in some monasteries of distinct groups, possibly the same as or similar to those postulated above, and having their own head. At 767 there occurs the obit of Ua Miannaigh, *abbas sruithi Cluana mic Nois*. This is translated by Hennessy 'most learned abbot of Clonmacnoise'. The word in question is *sruith*, as adjective, 'old, senior, venerable, to be revered, honoured, esteemed'; as substantive (masculine) 'elder, ancestor, reverend person, sage' etc. — an *i*-stem. The superlative is *sruithem* (see *Contribb* S). If therefore *sruithi* in this quotation were emended to *sruithe* (genitive pl.), Ua Miannaigh could be an abbot 'of seniors' in Clonmacnoise. And indeed we have, at 810, the obit of Tuathgal, *abbas sruithe Cluana* (i.e., Clonmacnoise) — similarly rendered by Hennessy 'a most wise abbot of Cluain'. It may be observed, though too much weight cannot be placed on the observation, that the obits of abbots of Clonmacnoise are also entered at 769 and 770; and at 813. But the suspicion that distinct sub-communities of *sruithi* are referred to in both instances is strengthened by the entry at 796 of the obit of Condal, *abatissa tighe sruithe Cille daro*, where Hennessy explains *tech sruithe* as 'house of seniors' (footnote). *Sruithi* are further mentioned at 985, when Iona was plundered by Danes, who killed the abbot and 15 seniors (*in apaidh 7 xu. uiros do sruithibb na cille*); and at 1014, when (after Clontarf) the abbot of Armagh went to Swords *co sruithibh 7 co minnaibh*, to take charge of the body of Brian Boru. In both these latter cases, however, the term may mean no more than older, therefore senior, members of the community at large.

It was noticed earlier that on two occasions, 1003 and 1016, the head of the guest establishment at Armagh — the *les oíged* — is called *airchinnech*. Here, at least, the complex seems to have had its own enclosure, or sub-enclosure; and such is very likely to have been the case elsewhere. Specialised groups had their own quarters within their own clearly defined boundaries, inside or outside the *vallum monasterii*. This was probably so in the case of the Céli Dé of Armagh (920), who appear to have run a leper house or infirmary at the time (see above). It may well have been the case also with students: Maelpetair, *fer leighinn 7 toisech macleighinn aird Macha*, was killed at 1042. In this last instance, however, it is worth noting that, although *scribae* are mentioned (frequently) between 696 and 1005, *fír léighinn* from 878, and *sapientes* etc. (fairly frequently) from 660, there is no mention of a school, scriptorium or library as a separate building or complex. (Cf. Hughes, 1966, 136: 'The high rank of the *scriba,* or *suí* (sage, *sapiens*), is indicated in the secular as well as in the ecclesiastical laws. His presence indicates a school of Latin learning . . .'). Craftsmen probably had their own quarters too, perhaps grouped according to occupation and outside the main monastic enclosure. They are mentioned only once explicitly, at 1029, where the obit is entered of Maelbrigte Ua Brolcháin, *primshaer Erenn*. (He is not actually said to be attached to a church, but, given his family name, he probably was).

A few other entries may point in the same general direction, though there is certainly nothing conclusive about their evidence and simple coincidence, later editing or politics may be the truth — alone or in combination. At 774, the obits of two abbots of Louth are entered together without comment (*Donngal . . . abbas Lugmaidh, 7 Fianchu abbas Lughmaidh*). Similarly, at 786, the obits are entered together of the abbot and two bishops of Kildare (*Muiredach . . . abbas Cille daro, Lomthuili episcopus Cille daro, Sneidbran episcopus chille daro*); at 874, the obits of two bishops of Kildare, who held individually the abbacy of another house (*Robartach . . . episcopus Cille daro, et scriba optimus, et princeps Cille achaidh, et Lachtnan . . . episcopus Cille daro et princeps Fernann*); at 876, the obits of two abbots of Clonmacnoise (*Eugan et Maeltuile . . . duo abbates Cluana macc U Nois, in pace dormierunt*); and at 964, the obits of two abbots of Terryglass (*Iosep 7 Dunchadh abbaid thire dha ghlas*). In no case is there any additional comment from the annalist(s).

Bede, describing the great Welsh monastery of Bangor-is-coed at the time of the battle of Chester (616), says: '*Erant autem plurimi eorum (sacerdotes) de monasterio Bancor, in quo tantus fertur fuisse numerus monachorum, ut, cum in VII portiones esset cum praepositis sibi rectoribus monasterium diuisum, nulla harum portio minus quam CCCtos homines haberet, qui omnes de labore manuum suarum uiuere solebant*' (Plummer, 1896 (1969), 1, 84 = *H.E.* ii, 2). The passage refers, admittedly, to an earlier period than that under discussion here, to a different country, and is reported by an English writer long afterwards. But the (probably diverse) origins of monasticism in the Celtic-speaking lands must have been substantially the same: would the organization described by Bede for Bangor-is-coed in the early 7th century have been that unfamiliar to St Pachomius and his successors, at Tabennisi, Canopus and elsewhere, in 4th-century Egypt?

ACKNOWLEDGEMENT

The writer wishes to express his thanks to Ms Máire Herbert, Dept of Old and Middle Irish, University College, Cork, for most useful and stimulating discussion during the preparation of this paper; and for reading and commenting on the MS. The writer is, however, entirely responsible for the final product.

REFERENCES

References have been used as sparingly as possible. It has been thought of more interest to let AU speak for themselves in the main, even to the extent that the information thus obtained is incomplete or misleading in the light of other sources.

Anderson, A.O. and M.O., 1961 (ed). *Adomnan's Life of Columba.* Nelson.
Gwynn, A. and Hadcock, R.N., 1970. *Medieval Religious Houses: Ireland.* London.
Hughes, K., 1966. *The Church in Early Irish Society.* London.
Plummer, C., 1896. *Venerabilis Baedae Historiam Ecclesiasticam Gentis Anglorum, Historiam Abbatum etc.* Oxford (reprinted 1946 . . . 1969).
Radford, C.A.R., 1977. 'The earliest Irish churches', *Ulster J Archaeol ser 3* **40**, 1-11.
Thomas, C., 1971. *The Early Christian Archaeology of North Britain.* Oxford University Press.

Surveys, Maps and the Study of Rural Settlement Development

Patrick O'Flanagan

It is clear that in spite of advances in various techniques of identification, analysis and interpretation, both in the field and in the laboratory, we are not any nearer in our efforts to solve some of the major problems of Irish settlement studies. The ring-fort has remained one of the hardest nuts to crack. A considerable array of questions touching ring-forts requires concise answers. Among these problems are the explanation of their distribution and diffusion, the identification and analysis of regional differences in their morphology, the economy of those responsible for their construction and occupation, the relationship (if any) between ring-forts and other contemporary 'forms' of settlement — and these other 'forms' of settlement have yet to be unmistakably recognised. There is also the question of establishing the processes which were responsible for the abandonment of the ring-fort and its replacement by other 'forms' of settlement. Finally, there are the problems of whether ring-forts can be regarded as an isolated or nucleated type of rural settlement and of significance can be attached to them as expressions of the prevailing socio-economic organisation of society.

This paper is not a direct attempt to solve any of these questions, many of which require considerable additional sustained research, but rather its purpose is to sound a note of caution concerning some of the basic premises upon which solutions to some of these problems have been sought in the past. To arrive at any deductions the evidence available must be as comprehensive and complete as possible; in the case of ring-forts the corollary is that date and distribution data should be considerable. Regrettably, this is seldom the case, as the traditional sources for building up such a 'total' picture are invariably seriously inadequate with the obvious repercussions for the findings of the research.

A combination of field survey and careful scrutiny of the 6 inch map (1:63,560), supplemented by information from air-photographs (where available), Ordnance Survey Letters and Name Books and any seminal local topographical accounts, constitutes the basis of any real survey of settlement. The intention of this paper is to demonstrate that reliance on these sources is simply not adequate, especially where extra vital information is available, particularly when the central direction of the research is to build up a picture of sequent occupation in any area.

The 6 inch map was basically designed to fulfil land-registry requirements. Such maps also selectively depict the disposition of a range of critical elements in the cultural landscape, particularly field-size and shape, townlands and their location in relation to settlements, roads, railways and canals and major physical elements such as hills, slopes and water masses. Demesnes, parklands, fox-coverts, woods, plantations and areas occupied by bog and wet ground are the leading biotic elements portrayed. Antiquities are also shown selectively since the early surveyors' categorisation of what exactly constitutes an antiquity is diffuse and not satisfactory. Their inclusion is not obviously related to the primary purpose of such maps and their depiction in some cases may be simply due to the fact that they serve as convenient points of reference.

There is also the question of map edition; the first edition generally shows more antiquities than later editions — particularly those of this century: there was after all no twentieth-century O'Donovan! The reduction in the number of antiquities shown is notably marked in those areas where landlord control on landscape modification was strong and in areas which notched up massive population increase during the nineteenth-century. Both resulted in the intensification of land use and the subsequent obliteration of field remains. The process of the dismemberment of one system of land-holding and its replacement by another later on in the same century brought about a similar outcome. Additional confusion is apparent when later editions show antiquities not included in earlier ones. This, however, is not a frequent occurrence. The surveyors responsible for later editions of the maps were more anxious to include the results of the processes mentioned above than to portray ploughed-out or even extant antiquities. On these grounds, as well as the selectivity element, the 6-inch map in whatever edition cannot be regarded as providing a secure basis for retrogressively reconstructing the pre-Ordnance Survey settlement pattern of any area. Furthermore, the same reservations also apply to other smaller scale maps, most especially to the 25 inch (1:2,500) maps the first editions of which appeared later than the 6 inch map and for certain parts of the country revisions were based on subsequent editions of the 6 inch map (Andrews, 1974).

Some of the leading questions concerning the evolution of rural settlement in Ireland centre upon the ring-fort and the farm clusters sometimes labelled *clachans* (Buchanan, 1970). The extensive literature on the subject is notorious for its dissension and disagreement (Barrett and Graham, 1976). Ring-forts were also constructed and in use for a very considerable length of time, at least for a thousand years, but the evidence is stridently elusive regarding when they were first built and when they ceased to be used. Some appear to have been occupied as late as the eighteenth century, most likely as secondary or much later occupation. Moreover, it appears that paradoxically some ring-forts were never occupied or inhabited and therefore must have performed more than domestic functions. The settlement pattern of rural Ireland as depicted upon the first edition of the Ordnance Survey maps, consisting, as it did, of a mosaic of farm clusters or a scattered habitat of isolated dwellings, has been regarded by some as the unilineal descendant of the

ring-fort. The relationship between these two forms of land occupation, symbolis-
ed by their respective settlement forms, has been based on flimsy evidence and is
not justifiable or sustainable except as a working hypothesis. These kinds of uncer-
tainties have deterred most geographers, amongst others in the past decade, from
attempting to pursue the reconstruction of the settlement geography in any area
from the medieval period to the present day. It is indeed curious that most of the
studies undertaken in this field have clung tenaciously to landscape evidence alone
in spite of there being rich and diverse archival material available. In this regard,
paradoxical as it may seem, we appear to have (with some exceptions) a clearer picture of early Christian and nineteenth-century settlement patterns than of those of
the extended intervening period.

Estate maps have been given far less attention than they merit in grappling with
some of the intricacies of the development of rural settlement in Ireland. There
are, of course, several obvious reasons for such neglect. Only certain areas of the
country were mapped in this way and the best endowed areas were mapped most
accurately and most frequently. The quality of such maps varies enormously in
regard to accuracy; early land surveyors, like those attached to the Ordnance Survey
were selective in what they included. For example, the surveyor often excluded
'. . . anything that was not of immediate interest to his customers' (Andrews,
1969). It is important to remember that only the surveyors who have a known and
proven reputation for accuracy to detail are worthy of our serious attention when
we attempt to reconstruct the minutiae of landscape change and formal landscape
design. It is curious to recall that some eighteenth-century land-surveyors should
include ring-forts in their townland surveys when as against cabins and other types
of settlement, ring-forts seem to have had no economic significance.

Only some large landowners in Ireland were able to afford the services of a major
land surveyor. The Duke of Devonshire was one of these and he commissioned
Bernard Scalé to make a survey of his Waterford and East Cork estates during the
years 1774-5 (National Library of Ireland, MSS 7216-7218). This survey on a
townland basis shows all the inhabited settlements, the field boundaries and roads
and depicts accurately all the 'Danish forts' — a contemporary term for ring-forts.
An accompanying memoir yields details of land-use, land-holding and field size.
The Danish forts are the only relict feature included apart from 'ruined' castles,
churches and lime-kilns. Rivers, streams, bogs, marshes, and woods are the only
topographic elements recorded.

A further dimension is added to this paper by also incorporating an earlier survey
of 1616-17 of part of the same estate, but concerned only with the lands south of
the Bride. This survey was expedited by Josias Bateman, a tenant of the estate, resident in the town of Tallow, (N.L.I. MSS 6148-49). Bateman's survey was executed
with the same objectives as that of Scalé. Once again there is a separate map for
each holding, covering usually an entire townland but sometimes several
townlands, as well as an additional memoir providing data on land tenure and

rent. It also shows 'Danes' forts'.

Scalé's survey clearly depicts the shape and size of each ring-fort whether square, round or otherwise. Bateman shows them only with a symbol and regrettably this symbol is similar to the one being used for lime-kilns. Scalé also shows several 'ancient fortifications', notably a bartizan in the townland of Garybrittas close to Lismore and several very early roads.

A tabular comparison on a townland basis of the incidence or non-occurrence of ring-forts in both of these surveys, as well as the first edition sheets of the Ordnance Survey maps and the early twentieth-century revisions of these maps will, it is hoped, indicate a salutary message concerning the dangers of relying slavishly upon the first edition of the Ordnance Survey to construct a 'total' picture of settlement development within an area.

The areas covered by the two surveys while not always coincident are quite

RINGFORTS NUMBER PER TOWNLAND

Area No.	No. of townlands	No. on Bateman	No. on Scalé	No. 1st Edition of O.S.	No. 2nd Edition of O.S. (1937)
1	17	2(2 townlands only)	4 on 2 townlands	1 on 1 townland	None
2	41	Not shown	6 on 3 townlands	6 on 2 townlands	None
3	78	5 on 3 townlands	Not shown	2 on 2 townlands	2 on 2 townlands
4	10	10 on 4 townlands	9 on 6 townlands	10 on 5 townlands	4 on 4 townlands
5	24	29 on 12 townlands	54 on 19 townlands	23 on 12 townlands	14 on 7 townlands
Total	170	46 on 21	73 on 30	42 on 22	20 on 13 townlands

Area 1 includes a handful of townlands on both sides of the River Bride focused upon the former medieval manors of Tallow and Lisfinny, Co. Waterford.

Area 2 covers the valley sides of the River Blackwater from Macollop to Cappoquin, Co. Waterford, and also comprises an area between the Blackwater and the Bride south of a line between Lismore and Cappoquin.

Area 3 is the largest area and comprises the modern parishes of Templemichael, Kilcoken and Kilwatermoy in south-west Co. Waterford.

Area 4 covers Curriglass and Mogeely and the lower lands on both sides of the River Bride in the barony of Kinatalloon.

Area 5 covers lands in the barony of Kinatalloon, Co. Cork, stretching as far as Clonmult to the south and Aghern to the east. The river Bride is the northern limit.

diverse. The leading topographic elements are reflected clearly in the selected area; these include the valley bottoms of the Bride and Blackwater and their adjacent lowlands, the middlelands from 30 to 300 feet south of the Bride and finally the remnants of the South Irish peneplain north of the Blackwater.

It is quite clear from the table that overall there is a considerable and sometimes very considerable disappearance in the representation of ring-forts from 1774 to 1841, that is, from Scalé's survey to the appearance of the first edition of the Ordnance Survey map. The disappearance is markedly more noticeable in some areas and less so in others over the same time period and even more so in the 1937 edition of the Ordnance Survey maps. In the areas where the incidence of ring-forts is light, notably in areas 1 to 4, the decrease is slight in area 1 while there is relatively little change in area 4. In area 2 there is a net gain of one fort but a loss of one townland recording incidence. As there are so few townlands with ring-forts in the first 4 zones, little by way of inference can be drawn from these facts.

In area 5, however, there is a net decrease of thirty-one ring-forts, more than half the total, but only a decrease of 7 townlands which record no ring-forts thus indicating that the general pattern seems to have remained static while significant variations in density occur. These are of extreme importance as far as any local or regional perspective is concerned. Extending the analysis to the 1937 edition, we find that there is a 75% loss of ring-forts and almost a 66% loss of townlands. This situation is most likely the result of farming intensification leading to destruction. The disappearances attributable to the earlier period i.e. 1840 cannot solely be due to the same process; it is more than likely that some ring-forts were not included by the surveyor. Overall, however, there is a total loss of some 50% of recorded sites between 1744 and 1841.

The earlier 1716-17 survey of Bateman is obviously less reliable than that of Scalé; nevertheless, it shows in area 5, six ring-forts more than the first edition of the Ordnance Survey maps and in the other zones the tally is the same although the comparison is not entirely valid as not all areas correspond. Thus, the Bateman survey, cruder, less accurate and less complete as it is, cannot be entirely disregarded.

The evidence from the 25 inch maps (1:2500) can be disregarded as these were only published for this area in the twentieth century, being drawn down from existing 6 inch maps.

On the basis of the above rudimentary analysis can general conclusions be drawn? The answer is clearly affirmative. Scalé's maps can be regarded as accurate in representing the distribution of ring-forts in 1774; this indeed is hardly the total picture and they demonstrate that in the lower Bride and Blackwater valleys of counties Cork and Waterford, the first edition 6 inch scale Ordnance Survey maps do not at all depict a clear pattern of total ring-fort settlement when as many as 50% of those shown by Scalé in one area are not shown on the Ordnance Survey maps. Quite apart from the question of the date of these kinds of 'settlements', the implications of the above argument are clear: many local and regional studies of ring-fort incidence based on O.S. map evidence alone are not valid.

How representative is Lismore in this aspect? These river valleys and adjacent lowlands were deeply affected by the Munster plantations and witnessed the early emergence in the area of one of the great estates in Ireland. From the sixteenth to the early nineteenth centuries, estate management varied considerably. From early on the townland was the basic landholding unit and most attention was directed towards improvement and this may have indeed led to the destruction of even more ring-forts. Most of the improvements were however directed towards reclaiming the valley bottoms, hillsides and uplands, areas where ring-forts are conspicuously absent, thus strengthening the view that Scalé's representation is generally authentic. It could be argued, therefore, that the picture for the Lismore area is broadly comparable with that in other parts of Ireland where great estates developed early and only more research into such zones can confirm the thrust of this essay.

Given these facts, can anything be stated concerning the chronology of settlement in this zone in the last 1000 years? The answer to this question must be tentative. If the ring-forts are accepted as early, then it seems that middlelands particularly on the south of the Bride were first occupied and settled, with one exception, namely, the entire area between Youghal and the confluence of the Bride with the Blackwater which is shown by Bateman and the first edition of the Ordnance Survey as being empty of ring-fort settlement. The early church sites and the Anglo-Norman and Geraldine castles and tower-houses were generally built in the valley bottoms or the not extensive upland areas, for example, Lismore and Tallow, or in the middleland generally south of the Bride. Ballyknock, a townland in area no. 5 shows a cabin in the middle of a ring-fort which appears to have been occupied in 1774. The apparent absence of ring-forts on the middlelands south and east of Lismore is a strange anomaly not easily explained, while the lands north of the Blackwater were not opened up for permanent settlement until the population explosion beginning towards the end of the eighteenth century. The increase in population south of the Blackwater is marked by reclaiming the lowlands and the uplands, a process which still remains to be completed satisfactorily.

One last question also requires attention. Do the ring-forts clearly represent relict features in the eighteenth-century landscape as depicted on the two surveys? One method of confirming this is to establish how incongruous ring-forts were to other functional elements in the landscape, such as townland and field boundaries and the organisation of settlements and roads in the area. This is no easy task. The Bateman survey can be disregarded here as it does not depict field boundaries.

Generally, the majority of the ring-forts are isolated from roads though a half-dozen of them are linked to main roads by smaller paths or trackways. The majority of ring-forts are sited in areas where large fields predominate, areas which were not fully enclosed by 1774. They are rarely located adjacent to small plots or fields

indicating a strong continuity between this kind of settlement and the development of townland-based farm clusters. The evidence is confusing regarding
settlements: ring-forts are not always beside clusters or large farmhouses. Finally,
ring-forts only in a few instances are bisected by field boundaries, are often parts of
townland boundaries or act as boundaries between different fields, thus indicating
that they may have retained a symbolic function at least.

ACKNOWLEDGMENT

The author wishes to acknowledge the permission granted by the Trustees of the National
Library of Ireland, Dublin, to examine and quote from manuscripts held in their care.

REFERENCES

Andrews, J.A., 1970. Changes in the rural landscape of late eighteenth-century and early
    nineteenth-century Ireland: an example from Co. Waterford. Unpublished paper
    delivered at the Conference of the Institute of British Geographers, Belfast.
Andrews, J.A., 1974. *History in the Ordnance Map*. Dublin.
Barrett, G. and Graham, J., 1975. 'Some considerations concerning the dating and
    distribution of ring-forts in Ireland.' *Ulster J Archaeol ser 3* **39**, 33-45.
Buchanan, R.A., 1970. 'Rural Settlement in Ireland'. *In* M. Stephens and R.E. Glasscock
    (ed), *Irish Geographical Studies*. Belfast.
N.L.I. MSS 6148-49. Survey of Lands south of the Bride, 1716-1717, by Josias Bateman.
N.L.I. MSS 7216-18. Survey of the Manors of Lismore, Lisfinny, Mogeely and Curriglas by
    B. Scalé 1773-4.

The Early Irish Churches:
Some Aspects of Organisation

Donnchadh Ó Corráin

Professor O'Kelly's exemplary excavations at Beginish and Church Island are of central importance to the historian as well as to the archaeologist (O'Kelly, 1956; 1958). Here he has laid bare with the techniques of the archaeologist the historical growth and development of an early Irish church and, if I am not mistaken, he has thrown a great deal of light on the economy of what is very probably its associated out-farm on Beginish. It is, therefore, with great pleasure that I offer him this attempt at a general survey of the typology and development of the early Irish church and, as we shall see, his discoveries fit neatly into one of the categories recorded in the early literature.

The church establishment of the eighth and ninth centuries and before was rich, comfortable and powerful. By now, clerical and lay society had become so intermeshed that any attempt to distinguish the traditional categories of church and state does some violence to the evidence. The self-confidence, not to say arrogance, of the churches is evident from a number of documents. The prologue to the Félire of Óengus, written about 800, far from being revolutionary or reformist, gives full voice to the Christian triumphalism of the establishment — an attitude perhaps already foreshadowed in Muirchú's work on St Patrick. Significantly, Óengus's basic metaphor is the kingship of the christian saints, seen here of course as the representatives of their earthly foundations, the great churches and monastic federations (*paruchiae*) of his contemporaries. His is the exultant voice of a powerful and influential church rather than the expression of simple joy at the passing of heathenism (Stokes, 1905, 23-7). It is notable that Óengus refers not to what historians have considered to be the spiritual power-houses of the *céili Dé* (or culdees) to whom he had traditionally been supposed to belong, but to the church in general and to the older, richer and more powerful establishments. Nor is Óengus alone in his attitudes.

When we turn to examine the role of the church in society at large and especially in its upper echelons, we see good reason for the triumphalism of Óengus and his peers. Already, Armagh and the Uí Néill kings were working in tandem, each it would seem content to boost the pretensions of the other. In Leinster, the monastic town of Kildare can quite properly be regarded as a dynastic capital in the ninth century, though of course its connections with the Uí Dúnlainge dynasty which was to dominate Leinster — if we can trust the record — were intimate even in the seventh century, when Cogitosus, the biographer of the foundress, describes

Kildare as a great and metropolitan *civitas* where the treasures of the kings were kept. In fact, it is quite likely that he was writing when a member of the Uí Dúnlainge dynasty held office as abbot. In the case of Emly, its first explicit documented connection with the kingship of Munster was the simultaneous proclamation of the 'law' of its founder and the ordination of the king of Munster (793) and two, if not three of its abbots, held the kingship of Munster in the ninth century. A Munster king-list, edited at Emly, stresses the participation in the kingship of Munster of the dynastic stock which dominated its area and supplied many of its abbots (Meyer, 1913, 478-9, 482).

A general principle can be stated in regard to abbatial succession though as we shall see some modifications will be required: the great hereditary clerical families were usually discard segments of royal lineages, pushed out of the political struggle and forced to reprise themselves in the church. Once established there, they proved extremely tenacious and were displaced by later royal segments or by new and expansive dynasties only with the greatest difficulty (Ó Corráin, 1973, 52-63). And here of course lay good grounds for conflict which might more conventionally be interpreted as conflict between church and state. It may be useful to cite some examples. Lann Léire was ruled from the eighth to the tenth centuries by a segment of the locally ruling Fir Rois. Another lineage of the same dynasty later held the office of hereditary priest at Armagh (Ó Fiaich, 1969, 75-127; Lec. 79va-c = BB. 114b-115c).[1] Some branches of the Éoganacht Áine held power in Emly and from them derived the hereditary abbatial family, Uí Laígenán (Lec. 214ra = BB. 178d). Uí Meicc Brócc, an early discard segment of the Éoganacht, held abbatial office in Cork in the second half of the seventh century while the genealogy of their kinsmen, Uí Meicc Iair, a similar lineage, is full of clerical names. The later hereditary abbots of Cork, Uí Selbaig, claimed descent from Uí Meicc Iair (however true that descent may be) and were ousted from office only in the twelfth century (O'Brien, 1962, 213-5). The tenacity of ecclesiastical families was remarkable. A branch of the Cianachta, settled about Portrane and Lusk, dominated the monastery of Lusk from the late seventh to the early ninth century while their secular kinsmen succumbed to Uí Néill power in the early eighth century (O'Brien, 1962; 168: Hughes, 1966, 162; Walsh, 1940, 517-9; Byrne, 1968, 396-7). Another branch of the Cianachta, who apparently went under to Uí Néill attack in the early ninth century, held out as abbots and clergy at Monasterboice until the twelfth century and produced many scholars amongst whom the historian, Flann Mainistrech († 1056), is the best-known (O'Brien, 1962, 168-9; Dobbs, 1923, 149-53; Hughes, 1966, 162). Despite the collapse of Uí Fiachrach power in the seventh century, clerical lineages of the dynasty supplied some eight of the fourteen abbots of Tuaim Gréne between 752 and 1100 in the teeth of the expanding power of Dál Cais (Ó Corráin, 1973, 55). Most remarkable of all, despite the power of the great Leinster royal families, the splintered and declining Fotharta, who claimed Brigit herself as their own and whose archaic poem states that they would hold Leinster as long as they were loyal to her, continued to supply leading clergy to Kildare. To Uí Chúlduib, one of their branches, belonged the two abbesses, Muirenn († 918) and Eithne († 1016), to the obscure Fothairt Airbrech belonged the earlier abbess, Sebdann († 732) and her nephew (or cousin), aue Cuirc († 750), while two further abbesses, Coblaith († 916) and Muirenn († 964) belonged to an ecclesiastical branch of Fothairt Fea. And it is highly probable that many other Kildare clerics whose origins cannot be established with certainty belonged to the Fotharta (O'Brien, 1962, 80-86).

The monastery of Trim, on which we have more information than most, may be taken as an example of hereditary succession though how typical it was is difficult to judge. It was ruled from the early eighth century to the middle of the ninth by the descendants of Colmán mac Duib Dúin, a discard segment, on its own admission, of the ruling dynasty of the kingdom of Lóegaire in which Trim lay. According to a claim which goes back at least to the seventh century, Trim was founded by St Lommán, a disciple of Patrick, and by St Fortchern, son of one Feidlimid, a leading early prince of the dynasty. This claim was well known to the abbots of Trim in the ninth century who, if we may judge from the genealogies of the saints and from an entry in the Martyrology of Tallaght, apparently taken from the records of Trim itself, looked upon themselves as the heirs of St Lommán and his disciples. The same genealogies list a formidable group of some thirty-seven saints of Lóegaire, a number of whom like the eighth- and ninth-century abbots are represented as married men and themselves ancestors of other saints. The hereditary clergy of Trim clearly saw the past in terms of their own present and their own institutions and they seem to have acted quite unselfconsciously as an ecclesiastical dynasty. In a matter-of-fact way, they record in the genealogies of Lóegaire (which were kept at Trim) their own marriages to the daughters of aristocratic and royal families though they preserve no such details for the kings of Lóegaire. These marriages are highly informative for they used marriage not only to establish contacts with leading aristocratic families but also to extend their connections with neighbouring monasteries. For instance, Báethchellach, abbot of Trim († 756), was married to the daughter of Feradach, king of Lóegaire († 704) — a fact which passed into the genealogies and into the traditions of the later martyrologies which account Báethchellach a saint. Others of the family were married to the daughters of the local aristocracy. Still other members established a marital alliance with the ecclesiastical family of Cell Duma Glind (now Kilglyn), a few miles to the south-east of Trim. This church is said to have been founded by St Mugenóc, brother of St Lommán, founder of Trim and, an interesting parallel, the abbots of Trim considered themselves to be dynastically related to the monastic family of Cell Duma Glind, Uí Chuanna, who lived there and also held Telach Ard, a minor ecclesiastical foundation about two miles to the north of Trim. At any rate this relationship was cemented by two marriage alliances. Colmán, the family founder, married Fínnechta, daughter of Máel Fithrig of Cell Duma Glind. His great-grandson, Móenach chose one of his wives from the same family, Nathí, his third

and fourth cousin. The family of Trim attempted to expand into the great·
monastery of Clonard, some fifteen miles to the south-west. Two abbots of Trim,
Suibhne († 796) and Cenn Fáelad († 821) held office there as *tánaise abbad* and
though Suibhne's son, Cormac, died as abbot of Clonard in 830, they did not succeed despite a great deal of effort in bringing it under their control.

The Uí Chrítáin, hereditary clergy at Druim Inesclainn, who were claimed as
remote collaterals of Lóegaire, shared some of the characteristics of their better-
known cousins. Here the patron was St Rónán mac Beraig who died in the great
plague of 665 and whose relics were enshrined in 801. Uí Chrítáin ruled Druim
Inesclainn without an apparent break from the mid-ninth century to 978. Like
other families, they created a suitable background for themselves: they claimed to
be descendants of Lóegaire and quite impossibly identified their eponym, Crítán,
with the grandfather of St Rónán. Further, they claimed five saints of their lineage,
one being St Colum Cúile, their direct ancestor. Such legend-building was
widespread and I suspect that the genealogies of the saints, most of which were put
together in the eighth century, primarily served the needs of such clerical dynasties
(BB. 86al-88e46; Lec. 61vba1 - 62vd51; Walsh, 1918, 49-53).

There were of course factors which ran counter to the general relationship of
church and dynasty. Some monasteries kept up close contact with the homeland of
the founder, often from a different part of Ireland. Monasteries on the borders of
powerful kingdoms were pushed and pulled between rival dynasties and no doubt
got a great deal of their own way as a result. Uí Maine and Múscraige, for example,
provided clergy on different occasions to Terryglass and when Dál Cais rose to
power they in turn intruded their own clerical lineages. The building up of
monastic federations or *paruchiae*, which was advanced to the point of confronta-
tion by the late seventh century, if we may judge by Tírechán's embittered comments, also tended to cut across dynastic lines (Bieler, 1979, 130, 136, 138, 140,
142). Great monastic families at the head of their federations, generated an ambition and momentum of their own and this is frequently expressed as grand
pluralism in the eighth century and in even less edifying inter-monastic warfare,
even though the lesser churches, as we shall see, made a stand for their
independence.

Nonetheless, the dynastic and hereditary factor lay at the heart of Irish church
life. And perhaps the most telling point in favour of this view is the fact that the
greater part of the surviving genealogical corpus, far from being the work of secular
men of learning, is the product of the dynastically-minded clergy. For example, the
core of the Airgialla genealogies derives from Armagh where it was preserved by
the clerical lineages of the dynasty (Meyer, 1912, 317-24; Mac Neill, 1912, 411-8).
The terminal names in the Cianachta genealogies are those of the early twelfth-
century hereditary abbots of Monasterboice and it is probably they, themselves
men with a reputation for learning, who preserved the record. The Múscraige
genealogies were kept at the monastery of Lothra. These explicitly quote from

Lebor Sochair Lothra (which must date from the period 750 to 800), list the Múscraige families associated with some dozen ecclesiastical foundations and record the genealogy of the *fer léigind* (head of the monastic school), perhaps the compiler of the text itself. It is interesting to note that the Múscraige genealogies have come under the influence of the greatest of ecclesiastical legends, the Patrician story, and quote extensively from the Vita Tripartita of St Patrick (Lec. 104rb, 110rd; BB. 141b13). To the monastery of Glenn Uissen we no doubt owe the Uí Bairrche genealogies with their detailed listing of churches and church families (O'Brien, 1962, 46-54). Other books cited in the genealogical tracts — Saltair Caisil, Lebor Inse Dúine and Lebor Dromma Sailech — also point to clerical compilation and the author of such a dynastic origin-legend as *Do bunad imthechta Éoganachta*, which models itself directly on the scriptural story of Joseph, can only have come from a monastic environment (Lec. 111vb7, 15; 113ra32; Meyer, 1912, 312-3). In some aspects the genealogies are none other than the files of an aristocratically-minded hereditary clergy, documents which justify their offices and possessions by right of descent and the proper exploitation of these sources may yet throw a great deal of light on the organisation of the early Irish churches.

The churches and the churchmen had early found an honoured place for themselves in native Irish law. How early is difficult to determine but they had certainly achieved it by the seventh century when the secular law tracts were being given their shape. The impression one gets from the law tracts (though of course not from all) is that the churches were deeply concerned with law and had a large part in moulding it. This is especially so of the seventh-century texts emanating from the southern *Nemed* school of law which laid particular stress on the dignity and importance of the ecclesiastical scholar, the *saí litre* who practises *ecne*, here largely understood as canon law and the law of scripture, no doubt the mish-mash of scriptural, canon and secular law best represented in the *Collectio canonum hibernensis*, the material of which was certainly in existence at the beginning of the eighth century (Binchy, 1955, 4-6; Binchy, 1958, 44-54; Wasserschleben, 1885). In another text of the *Nemed* school, Uraicecht Becc, the seven ecclesiastical orders are listed and are said to correspond to the secular grades of society. However, most of the orders are subsequently ignored and the text chiefly concerns itself with important bishops, abbots and monastic literati. The highest grade of bishop and the abbots of great monastic cities, such as Emly and Cork are equated in dignity with the king of Munster. In the case of the *brithem*, the highest status is accorded only to those who can handle canon law as well as customary law and the law of the poets. The drift of the text, from its initial arguments on the foundations of law to the status awarded the clergy argues for clerical compilation at Cork or Emly by an ecclesiastical scholar (Binchy, 1978, 1590-1618, 634-55, 2318-2335, 2255-7, 2261-82; Mac Neill, 1923, 265-81). The prefatory matter to the legal collections, early and late, draws heavily on a legend that Irish law was revised in the light of christian revelation and drew its inspiration from it — in reality, an argument not only in defence of certain unorthodox teachings of Irish law but of the practice of secular law or rather an admixture of secular and canon law by the clerical scholars (Binchy, 1975-6, 15-28). These indications, together with the presence of Irish legal technical terms (in Latin translation or adaptation) in the earliest canon law — and increasingly in the later — must lead us to believe that churchmen had a large part in the shaping of Irish law and practised as secular as well as canon lawyers. There is solid annalistic evidence for this from the ninth to the twelfth centuries and equally good evidence for the study of Irish law in Slane, Cork, Cloyne, Glendalough and other monastic towns in the same period (Ó Corráin, 1978, 13-16). There was of course no central ecclesiastical authority, practice differed no doubt from place to place, and differing customs and standards were tolerated amongst the churches. Nonetheless, we can take it that the Irish law tracts taken as a whole, fairly represent in a general way the church establishment of the seventh and eighth centuries, its attitudes and place in society.

In the tracts of all the schools, early and late, the principal ecclesiastics are equated in status with the local king and the masters of the privileged professions and the lesser orders with the appropriate secular grades and, though there are differences in detail and in interpretation in the various tracts, the broad classification is universal. All the privileges of the *fili* and *brithem* are extended to the clergy. For example, a bishop, like a king or *fili*, is not responsible for the liabilities of his son (Binchy, 1978, 905, 1045, 1841). The familial element is equally if less explicitly present in canon law. The church is not liable for the delicts of others — fugitive monks, wicked pilgrims or those whom it has expelled — in the same way, the canonist argues, as God and his angels are not responsible for the delicts of the devil. Much more important, the church (read churchmen) is not responsible for the liabilities of its lay kindred, a rule which takes on a great deal more significance when we understand how close was the relationship — in blood and politics — between the lay aristocracy and the clerical families. On the other hand, canon law lays great stress on the kindred responsibility of laymen in offences against the church and, borrowing almost verbatim from secular law, it lists the widening circle of persons responsible for another's crime and finally, a significant addition, if a person has offended the church and none can be found to bear liability recourse is to be had to the king of the province (*rex maximus provinciae*) in which the church is situated (Wasserschleben, 1885, 170; Binchy, 1978, 2011-2). Here we find the churches making an appeal to the larger kingships which had arisen and giving them their blessing and, as the annals show, over-kings of the eighth and ninth centuries did avenge attacks on churches within their provinces.

The churches enjoyed the protection of the law, the patronage of the rich and powerful (and of the not so rich) and fitted cosily into the society in which they found themselves. In their own canon law, the churchmen largely unconsciously took over many of the fundamental concepts of secular law and many of its rules in matters of detail. For example, those excluded from the right to contract independently are essentially identical in both legal systems and secular law explicitly recognised that the *manach* (earlier 'monk', later 'monastic tenant') may not contract independently of his abbot (Wasserschleben, 1885, 122; Binchy, 1978, 522). In the matter of the law of succession to property, canon law is a mirror image of secular custom and, while teaching the usual christian norms, tacitly recognises secular polygamic marriage (Wasserschleben, 1885, 110, 111, 113). As in native law, the father is bound to divide his property equally between sons while a certain extra portion is reserved for the son on whom devolves the duty of maintaining his parents in their old age, the *macslabra gaire* of the secular texts. The custom of assignment by lot is supported by scriptural citation while the rules governing the disposition of estates in the absence of sons are exactly those of secular law. Indeed, canon law concerns itself in detail with the problems of heiresses in a patrilineal society and adopts the rulings of secular law almost *in toto*. They must give sureties that they will not alienate family estates; they have a life interest in them, but the estates must eventually revert to their father's nearest male relatives. They may make bequests from the estate to the church provided such bequests are not contested by the ultimate heirs. It is envisaged that they should marry men of their paternal *fine* ('kindred') and thus pass the property to their agnates while giving their children an interest in the estate, a provision supported by scriptural citation (Num. xxxvi 8) and one which runs quite counter to the earlier romanising ruling which forbids marriage between those related within four degrees of consanguinity (Wassserschleben, 1885, 116; Dillon, 1936, 129-79; Bieler, 1963, 197). More remarkable still, the relationship of the abbot with his church and his *manaig* is explicitly modelled on secular institutions, on that of a lord with his clients and on the contractual relationship of a man and his wife in secular marriage. And when an abbot parts with his church, willingly or unwillingly, the arrangements for the disposition of property and the categories of property involved are strikingly similar in concept and terminology to those in use in the secular law of divorce (Wasserschleben, 1885, 173, 179n). The rules vary in detail but the principles are clear. What property the abbot brought with him to the office, he takes in full; what was given him as part of the office he leaves intact, except that the necessary expenses of office may be deducted from it; the offerings of the faithful during tenure and the ordinary increase and profits of the monastic herds are divided in two between the abbot and the church. This is remarkably close to the secular rules governing divorce by mutual consent. If however the abbot were a priest, the rules are different and identify his interests more closely with those of the church.

The churches then, at their lowest as well as at their highest levels, in canon law as well as in personnel, were fully integrated with Irish society as a whole and deeply imbued with the values of that society. This was certainly the case by the late seventh and early eighth centuries: there is no reason to believe that the relationship changed significantly in the following centuries.

The bond of church and people was conceived in terms of a legal contract involving mutual obligations (*folud* and *frithfolud*), a basic concept in Irish law. The church provides religious rites and services — baptism, communion, requiems, mass on Sundays and on the chief festival days — in return for which the people pay the church its dues for the maintenance of the clergy. In this regard, we know most about the class called *manaig*, a class occupying an intermediate position between clergy and laity. Usually they were tenantry of church lands or at least bound to render certain services to their church. They lived in lawful wedlock (I take this to mean canonical marriage with all that it entails) and, ideally at least, observed a remarkably strict sexual regime. There is early evidence that they attended church regularly and were entitled to spiritual guidance and a monastic education for at least some of their sons. According to a text of *c*. 750, an abbot forfeited his right to rule over his *manaig* and the church was not entitled to its income from them — tithes, heriots, labour services and bequests — unless an ordained cleric was provided to carry out religious services for them. The priest who ministered was entitled to take certain legal steps to ensure proper payment for his service — proof, if any were needed, that dues were hard to collect — and the *manaig* in turn maintained him with their labour (O'Keeffe, 1904, 216-24). The secular law tract (insofar as one can call it such), Córus Béscna, deals similiarly with the relationships of the church and the laity in general and here again relationships are contractual. In return for preaching and the usual religious services, the church is entitled to tithes, firstlings, first fruits and burial payments. Firstlings include animals as well as humans. The first-born child of lawful wedlock is to be given to the church but he is not cut off from his family. He receives his share in his inheritance in the same way as other sons and lives on his own farm but he is educated by the church and is under certain obligations of service to it as a *manach*. First fruits are defined as the first of every crop big and small, and each first lamb and first calf born in the year (Binchy, 1978, 520-36).

I doubt very much if these provisions applied to the population at large. They are a cleric's ideal and if they applied to anyone they applied to the church's *manaig*. Ministry to the people seems to have been haphazard and occasionally non-existent, and if we may judge from the lives of the saints the ordinary layman was regarded as a sinner at best, beyond redemption at worst. And the shrill insistence of Ríaguil Phátraic (*c*. 750) on the need for priests, for the administration of baptism and communion and for the provision of altar-furnishings in the churches indicates that the level of religious practice was low, even among the *manaig*.

In the seventh century, monastic federations or *paruchiae* came into being, led by powerful monastic foundations such as Clonmacnoise. Their extensive lands and services from their *manaig*, the offerings of the faithful, bequests, burial dues and income from relic circuits made the churches rich and prosperous. In the seventh century monasteries were becoming towns. The early life of St Munnu represents his monastery (*civitas*) as containing seven places marked with crosses where the principal buildings were erected (Heist, 1965, 203). In drawing up the regulations concerning the precincts of monastic towns the canonists of the seventh century quote the extensive measurements for holy places from Ezechiel xlv and speak of large areas of sanctuary, surrounded by their suburbs, and no doubt identify the Irish clergy (very appropriately) with the well-endowed Levites of the scriptural text. Again, in describing the divisions of the monastery into areas which are holy, holier and holiest they speak of the second as an area 'into the streets of which we allow to enter the crowds of rustics not much given to wickedness'. And beyond this again is an area of the monastery not forbidden to sinners (Wasserschleben, 1885, 175).

Power and riches led to ambition and to the burgeoning of monastic *paruchiae* and there seems to have been a steady build-up of paruchial organisation in the seventh and eighth centuries. The sense of property in dependent churches was highly developed among the federations of the late seventh century. So much we know from Tírechán who reports adversely on the expansionism of Clonmacnoise and other churches (Bieler, 1979, 130, 136, 138, 140, 142). It is equally reflected in the hagiography, early and late. The great Patrician federation at Armagh stretched its tentacles southwards into Munster. In the tenth century, it was strong enough to negotiate with the king of Munster and, using a change of dynasty to its advantage, cut into the territory of the powerful monastery of Emly. Cork claimed most of the churches in its hinterland and soon came into conflict with Cloyne in the east and Ross on the west and even did battle with more distant Clonfert. Clonard claimed an extensive *paruchia* in the midlands but also held properties in Connacht and Munster.

The patchwork quilt political map of Ireland is simplicity itself compared with the complicated network of ecclesiastical ownership, loyalties, conflicts, claims and counter-claims which extended throughout the entire country and even overseas. Involvements in secular politics and dynastic loyalties — and disloyalties — served to make the ecclesiastical situation even more complex. The records are preserved in many sources, especially in those dossiers of monastic claims, the lives of the saints but historians have yet only begun to unravel the tangled skein.

Growing wealth and increasing ambition led to deep rivalry and the invective of Tírechán in the seventh century becomes the armed conflict of the eighth. In 760 Clonmacnoise and Birr were at war, a hostility reflected in the life of St Ciarán. Four years later, there was a major battle between Clonmacnoise and Durrow and Bressal mac Murchada, who led Clonmacnoise to victory on that occasion was murdered shortly afterwards. In 807 there was a battle between Cork and Clonfert in which there was 'a countless slaughter of the ecclesiastics and of the noblest of the community of Cork'. Kildare plundered the *céle Dé* monastery of Tallaght in 824 and in 842 Kinnitty and Clonmacnoise were at war. We can take it that the annals note only the major conflicts and countless local scuffles and skirmishes between rival monastic interests have escaped the record for ever. These struggles bear witness to the rapid consolidation of the *paruchiae* and when they die out, as they seem to do, in the late ninth century, we should perhaps consider that the *paruchiae* had reached the limits of expansion and that a relatively stable situation had come about rather than attribute the change to any feeling of solidarity in the face of the threat from the Vikings.

Wealth, power, and close dynastic connections brought violence and warfare in their train. The three battles at Ferns between 769 and 817, for example, were part of a segmentary struggle for supremacy between two branches of Uí Chennselaig, the dominant dynasty in the area, in which the monasteries were participants as well as victims. According to the annals Ferns lost 400 men, lay and cleric, at the hands of Cathal mac Dúnlainge, king of Uí Chennselaig, and his ally, the monastery of Taghmon. Similarly, the killings at Kilclonfert in 789 were really part of a dynastic struggle between two leaders of Uí Failge. The kings attempted to gain control of the monastic towns and draw on their resources in their own struggles. And we need be in no doubt about the extent of these resources. Bodbgal, abbot of Mungret, had sufficient forces to engage the king of Uí Fidgente in battle in 752 and the Uí Néill drew heavily and successfully on the military support of Durrow in 776. No attacker could afford to ignore the monastic town of his enemy, frequently his ally, bound to him by dynastic ties and on occasion the place of his principal residence. And so the churches quite apart from being victims in times of famine were drawn into the general pattern of secular warfare. The Viking raiders fell on no innocent monkdom but on populous centres and towns with a long history of violence. One is not surprised then that Taghmon should join forces with the king of Uí Chennselaig to drive off Viking raiders in 828, that forces from Armagh should be the aggressors in doing battle with the Vikings as far afield as Carlingford Lough in 831 or that the abbot of Terryglass and Clonenagh and the vice-abbot of Kildare should fall fighting the Vikings at the head of their monastic contingents at Dunamase.

If the heads of great monastic towns such as Cork and Emly could be equated in dignity with the king of the province at least in clerical eyes and if the rulers of Armagh, Kildare, Clonard, Clonmacnoise and other towns could be ranked among the great political figures of the land, the abbots or bishops and clergy of the hundreds of tiny churches scattered throughout the countryside could have no such pretensions and rarely if ever appear in the records of the great and powerful, the annals. These small churches and monastic establishments, which were much more plentiful than parish churches now are and which served the local people (if they served them at all) must have been altogether different from busy and bustling towns like Lismore or Trim or Clonmacnoise which, after all, were as distant from most men's lives as cities were from the average medieval countryman. And archaeologists and historians who regard the great monastic towns as the churches of a man's everyday experience and who see church life in early christian Ireland from their angle alone are a good deal wide of the mark.

Very many of these small churches were private or proprietary churches owned by an ecclesiastical branch of the local aristocratic families. Hundreds of entries in the genealogies record their existence and that of the families who owned them. The following is an example of such records chosen at random from the genealogies of the Lóichsi.

Lugna mac Éogain had seven sons: Ruadán, Garbán, Nisse, Laignech, Ercc, Columb, Comgall. Ruadán, Garbán and Columb: their land is Ráith Ruadán and Caílle Coluimb and Cell Meithne and Ard mBruchas. Nisse: his inheritance is Bile Methes and Cluain meic Nisse. Laignech son of Lugna, from whom descend Uí Báeth and Uí Bróccáin: his inheritance is Loch Laignich and Cluain Connaid. Ercc son of Lugna, from whom descend Uí Diamráin and De-Deccae and Uí Forandla and Uí Cormaic: his land is Tech Décláin and Domnach Findchon and Cóelbóthur and Cluain Dá Fiach and Cluain Dartada and the inheritance which Uí Forandla occupy

In this aetiological piece, at least three churches and very likely more (another text adds a fourth, Cell Garbán) occur in the ordinary inheritance of a group of families and the descent group is seen as the owner of both secular and ecclesiastical property (O'Brien, 1962, 89-90). A similar entry in the genealogies of the Uí Bairrche may be cited.

These are the portions of the Uí Bairrche amongst the Laigin: Cluain Conaire and Cell Auxilli and that Cróebán who first founded the church is of them and they have kindred at the church i.e. Uí Laigéni in Caisse and Uí Duib Cillíne (O'Brien, 1962, 54).

Families of quite different origins could have proprietary rights in the same church though, one must add, it is not clear whether they were simultaneous owners or whether one family was being displaced by the other. For example, a branch of the Fothairt also owned property at Cell Auxilli: 'Nad Fróech from whom descend Síl nAnmerech i.e. Uí Máili Tólae and Uí Mael Odráin of Domnach Mór and Cell Auxilli and Uí Máele Rubae' (O'Brien, 1962, 82). Amongst the Múscraige the aristocratic family, Uí Raibne owned Cell Cére (Kilkeary), allegedly founded by Ciar, a saint of their own lineage, while their cousins held the nearby churches of Druim Inbir (Dromineer), Tóm in Baird (Toomyvara) and Cell Ua Máel Lachtna (Kilaughnane). Other aristocratic branches of the same family held other and smaller foundations and some of them were settled at the great monastery of Birr. Uí Daigre, another branch of the Múscraige, held the church of Letracha Odráin (Latteragh) and claimed that Odrán, its founder, was one of them (O'Brien, 1962, 368; Lec. 104rd; BB. 141c).

These churches were of different origins and no doubt underwent changes of ownership and of function with the passage of time. The question of origins gives rise to serious and wide-ranging problems since we know little of the organisation of the Irish churches in the missionary period. Canon law however gives some indication of the different kinds of church founders. It is clear from the *Collectio canonum hibernensis* that there were bishops with recognised territories or spheres of influence amongst whom there were conflicts over jurisdiction and property and that if anybody (including a bishop) built a church within a bishop's territory the consecration and rule of the church belonged to the bishop in whose territory it lay. It is laid down that a monk should not presume to erect a church without the permission of his abbot whilst other decrees state that when a priest builds a church and holds it for a year it is his *hereditas* forever. Lastly, it is decreed that churches should be founded by clerics, not by laymen or *infideles* (Wasserschleben, 1885, 12, 73, 171-2). These canons are evidence for the problems of the Irish church in the seventh century and indicate a wide diversity of practice. In Ireland, as elsewhere in Europe in this period and later, private ownership of churches was the norm. In addition, there was a profound consciousness of family right (*finechas*) and the churches were transmitted from generation to generation as family property by a non-celibate clergy. Some churches were early episcopal foundations and many such are mentioned in the genealogies. Domnach Findchon of the Loíchsi, cited above, may well be one. Mag nAirthir of Ciarraige Luachra, the eighth-century genealogists tell us, was the foundation of one bishop Fáelán of the local ruling family: it reappears as the parish church of Murher in the later middle ages (Ó Corráin, 1969, 29, 34). Others were the tribal churches of small communities some of which disappeared or were overrun at a very early period — Cell Lámraige, Domnach Saírigi, Cell Tídill, Cell Cnámraige are examples to point. Cell Cnámraige must have been the tribal church of the Cnámraige, a tribe which barely leaves a trace in the records. It and another parcel of land are described in a text of the early tenth century as the *hereditas* (family estate) of one Cendlachán mac Muindig of the ruling family among the Múscraige (Ó Corráin, 1979, 179-80). Others may, in origin at least, have been anchorites' cells. Whatever their ultimate origin, the vast bulk of them appear to be proprietary churches owned, as ordinary estates were owned, by noble or at least land-owning families but claiming of course the freedom from secular imposts and other privileges usually claimed by churches. Indeed, some were so closely associated with such families that the families themselves took their name from the church: Aicme Cille Cúile of the Déisi were named from their church of Cell Cúile (Kilcooley), Uí Briúin Cille Cruimthir of Cenél Fiachach from their church, Cell Cruimthir Fiachrach (Kilcumreragh), and there are other examples of this practice (O'Brien, 1962, 162; Lec. 61vaa).

Such churches appear to be mentioned in ecclesiastical documents. Ríaguil Phátraic speaks of a lord who does not impose the duty of providing religious services on his own church (*a eclais saindíles*) and one provision of canon law in regard to bequests to the church by female heirs may also refer to family-owned churches (O'Keeffe, 1904, 219 Wasserschleben, 1885, 116). Indeed, one may suspect that some churches were merely family estates which were turned into church establishments by their owners with little change either in function or appearance apart from a little church and graveyard and the ministrations of a priest if he were available. Others may have been early foundations, the ecclesiastically privileged lands of which were farmed as a secular holding except that a minimal religious function was maintained.

It is difficult to judge if many of these were churches or monasteries in any real sense of the word and it may well be incorrect to describe them as such. Some no doubt were but the difficulties under which they laboured must have been very great. In the first place, there seems to have been a chronic shortage of ordained clergy. Early synods laid down that a fallen cleric should depart his cure and serve under an abbot elsewhere but the ruling *c.* 700 allowed a rehabilitated cleric to minister explicitly because of the shortage of priests (Wasserschleben, 1885, 30; Bieler, 1963, 263). Ríaguil Phátraic allows one priest to minister to three or four churches when ordained clergy are scarce. It also refers explicitly to 'the little churches of the community (*túath*)' and lays down that when there is a priest serving in one of them he is entitled to the reward of his order — a house and enclosure and his rations, a milch cow every quarter, a sack of grain with its condiment, and food on festival days (O'Keeffe, 1904, 220). Very often, the abbot was not in major orders in the eighth century and earlier (Wasserschleben, 1885, 173, 179; Hughes, 1966, 158-60) and it is likely that there were churches and monasteries which had no ordained clergy at all and rarely saw a priest. The law tracts speak of the church which has lost its right to ecclesiastical privilege — the church which has become a den of thieves or a place of sin, the church ruled by a layman or by a backslider who has failed to honour his vow of chastity, the church from which bell and psalm have departed and the derelict church — and echo faithfully the strictures of ecclesiastical documents as such (Binchy, 1978, 1-3). These are called unlawful churches and are excluded from privilege though in fairness it must be said that some of the greater monasteries should have lost their status if these rules had been enforced or enforceable. One can only conclude that there were many churches of this kind in the eighth and ninth centuries and that ecclesiastical discipline had grown extremely slack. And, given their remoteness and often isolation, the shortage of ordained clergy, the pressure from greater houses which used them for their own purposes, the vicissitudes of the rise and fall of the aristocratic families which owned them and the probability that these families subordinated religious matters to the interests of property, it is likely that their survival as churches in any real sense was a matter of chance.

From the foregoing it could I think be argued that Church Island may have been a proprietary church which began as a remote hermit's cell. Phase I, with its small wooden church, circular wooden hut and burials, may belong at least in its earliest period to eremitic times. The community even during Phase I was not however necessarily monastic and the circular hut 'sufficient to house three or four monks' was equally suited to house a small church family, perhaps that of the founder or the donor (real or pretended). The early burials may be those of the church family together with those of the devout laity brought to the island to be interred (for a substantial consideration) in the holy ground and the female burial discussed by Professor O'Kelly may belong to either group. Phase II with its larger stone oratory, round stone house and later rectangular stone house and cashel represents a period of very considerable investment and development and indicates an ecclesiastical territory much wider than Church Island and Beginish, as indeed do the materials used in building. The finds — querns, the stone axe, bronze pins, sheet and strip bronze, nails, knives, the mattock, the cutting hook and extensive remains of iron-working together with the bell fragments, the cross-inscribed slab and small slate cross — can be taken to be the normal (and modest) equipment of a farming church settlement. Beginish may well have been the outfarm of the church, farmed on its behalf by church tenantry (*manaig*) although it is unlikely that the church settlement, almost certainly in Phase II, was limited to such meagre resources. If this interpretation is correct, and it is by no means the one proposed by historians at the time of the excavation, we have in the reports on Church Island and Beginish a fascinating account of the culture and economy of one of the more 'normal' types of Irish proprietary churches in the mixed farming and fishing environment of the west coast.

NOTE

1 Special abbreviations: BB. = Robert Atkinson (ed), *The Book of Ballymote*, Facsimile, Royal Irish Academy, Dublin 1887; Lec. = Kathleen Mulchrone (ed), *The Book of Lecan*. Facsimiles in Collotype of Irish Manuscripts II, Irish Manuscripts Commission, Dublin 1937. Reference is in all cases to the pagination and foliation respectively of these facsimiles.

An extended version of this paper is to appear in *A New History of Ireland* i (forthcoming).

REFERENCES

Bieler, Ludwig, 1963. *The Irish Penitentials*, Scriptores Latini Hiberniae V. Dublin.

Bieler, Ludwig, 1979. *The Patrician Texts in the Book of Armagh*. Scriptores Latini Hiberniae X. Dublin.

Binchy, D.A., 1955. 'Bretha Nemed', *Ériu* 17, 4-6.

Binchy, D.A., 1958. 'The date and provenance of Uraicecht Becc', *Ériu* 18, 44-54.

Binchy, D.A., 1975-6. 'The pseudo-historical prologue to the Senchas Már', *Studia Celtica* 10-11, 15-28.

Binchy, D.A., 1978. *Corpus Iuris Hibernici*. Institute for Advanced Studies, Dublin.

Dillon, Myles, 1936. 'The relationship of mother and son, father and daughter, and the law of inheritance with regard to women'. *In* D.A. Binchy (ed), *Studies in Early Irish Law*. Royal Irish Academy, Dublin.

Byrne, F.J., 1968. 'Historical note on Cnogba (Knowth)'. *In* George Eogan, 'Excavations at Knowth, Co. Meath, 1962-1965', *Proc Roy Ir Acad C* 66, 383-400.

Dobbs, M.E., 1923. 'The pedigree and family of Flann Mainistrech', *J Louth Archaeol Soc* 5, 149-53.

Heist, W.W., 1965. *Vitae Sanctorum Hiberniae*, Subsidia Hagiographica, No. 28. Brussels.

Hughes, Kathleen, 1966. *The Church in Early Irish Society*. Methuen, London.

Mac Neill, John [= Eoin], 1912, 'Notes on the Laud genealogies', *Z Celt Philol* 8, 411-8.

Mac Neill, Eoin, 1923. 'Ancient Irish law. The law of status or franchise', *Proc Roy Ir Acad* C 36, 265-316.

Meyer, Kuno, 1912. 'The Laud genealogies and tribal histories', *Z Celt Philol* 8, 291-338.

Meyer, Kuno, 1913. 'The Laud synchronisms', *Z Celt Philol* 9, 478-9, 482.

O'Brien, M.A., 1962. *Corpus Genealogiarum Hiberniae*. Institute for Advanced Studies, Dublin.

Ó Corráin, D., 1968. 'Alltraighe', *J Kerry Archaeol Hist Soc* 2, 27-37.

Ó Corráin, D., 1973. 'Dál Cais — church and dynasty', *Ériu* 24, 52-63.

Ó Corráin, D., 1978. 'Nationality and kingship in pre-Norman Ireland'. *In* T.W. Moody (ed), *Nationality and the Pursuit of National Independence*. Belfast.

Ó Corráin, D., 1979. 'Onomata', *Ériu* 30,165-80.

Ó Fiaich, Tomás, 1969. 'The church of Armagh under lay control', *Seanchas Ardmhacha* 5, 75-127.

O'Keeffe, J.G., 1904. 'The Rule of Patrick', *Ériu* 1, 216-24.

O'Kelly, M.J., 1956. 'An island settlement at Beginish', *Proc Roy Ir Acad* C 57, 159-94.

O'Kelly, M.J., 1958. 'Church Island near Valencia, Co. Kerry', *Proc Roy Ir Acad* C 59, 57-136.

Stokes, Whitley, 1905. *Félire Óengusso Céli Dé*, 23-7. Henry Bradshaw Society, London.

Walsh, Paul, 1918. *Genealogiae Regum et Sanctorum Hiberniae*. Maynooth.

Walsh, Paul, 1940. 'Meath in the Book of Rights'. *In* John Ryan (ed), *Féilsgríbhinn Eoin Mhic Néill*, 508-21. Dublin.

Wasserschleben, Hermann, 1885. *Die Irische Kanonensammlung*. Leipzig.

Published Work of
Professor O'Kelly

Helen Moloney Davis

1940

(With Seán P. Ó Ríordáin) 'Old house types near Lough Gur, Co. Limerick'. *In* John Ryan (ed), *Féilsgríbhinn Eóin Mhic Néill*, 227-36. Three Candles, Dublin.

1942

'A survey of the antiquities of the barony of Small Countie, Co. Limerick', *N Munster Antiq J* 3, 75-97, 169-84, 224-26.

1943

(With P. Ó Móghráin) 'Some Mayo traditions of the *buaile*', *Béaloideas* 13, 161-71.

1944

'Cork's new public museum', *J Roy Soc Antiq Ir* 74, 228-29.
'Excavation of a cist grave at Bealick, Macroom, Co. Cork', *J Roy Soc Antiq Ir* 74, 229.
'Excavation of a cist grave at Bealick, Macroom, Co. Cork', *J Cork Hist Archaeol Soc* 49, 116-21.
'A new museum for Cork', *University College Cork Rec*, 34-35.
Review: Seán P. Ó Ríordáin, *Antiquities of the Irish Countryside*, 2nd ed., Cork University Press, Cork, 1943. In *J Cork Hist Archaeol Soc* 49, 139.
Review: Robert Herbert, *Worthies of Thomond*, Herbert, Limerick, 1944. In *J Cork Hist Archaeol Soc* 49, 70-71.

1944-45

'A survey of the antiquities in the barony of Small Countie', *N Munster Antiq J* 4, 16-53.

1945

'Some prehistoric monuments of Imokilly', *J Cork Hist Archaeol Soc* 50, 10-25, 158.
Contributions in P.J. Hartnett (ed), *Cork Public Museum Guide*, 21-23; 41-42; 61-76. Cork University Press, Cork.
Guide to the Thomas Davis Commemortive Exhibition. Cork Public Museum, Cork.
Review: R.A.S. Macalister, *Corpus inscriptionum insularum celticarum* I, Irish Manuscripts Commission, Dublin, 1945. In *J Cork Hist Archaeol Soc* 50, 152-53.
Review: *J Louth Archaeol Soc* 10 (1944). In *J Cork Hist Archaeol Soc* 50, 156.
Review: *N Munster Antiq J* 4 (1944-45). In *J Cork Hist Archaeol Soc* 50, 157.

1946

The Collegiate Chapel, Cork. Cork University Press, Cork.

Guide to the Easter Week Commemorative Exhibition. Cork Public Museum, Cork.

'Excavation of a cist-grave at Ballynahow, Fermoy, Co. Cork', *J Cork Hist Archaeol Soc* **51**, 78-84.

'Reopening of Cork Public Museum, Ireland', *Mus J* **46**, 37-39.

'Excavation of a ring fort at Garryduff, Co. Cork', *Antiquity* **20**, 122-26 (reprinted: *J Cork Hist Archaeol Soc* **51**, 164-69.)

'Recent southern archaeological finds', *J Cork Hist Archaeol Soc* **52**, 61-68.

1947

'A cinerary urn from Oatencake, Midleton', *J Cork Hist Archaeol Soc* **52**, 126-27.

Catalogue of Cork prints and drawings. Cork Public Museum, Cork.

'Cork public museum', *University College Cork Rec*, 22-23.

'Excavation of a long cist grave at Coolnacranagh, Macroom', *J Cork Hist Archaeol Soc* **52**, 36-40.

Review: R.J.C. Atkinson, *Field archaeology*, Methuen, London, 1946. In *J Cork Hist Archaeol Soc* **52**, 97.

Review: R.A.S. Macalister, *Monasterboice*, Tempest, Dundalk, 1946. In *J Cork Hist Archaeol Soc* **52**, 195.

Review: R.L.S. Bruce Mitford, *The Sutton Hoo Ship Burial: a provisional guide*, Trustees of the British Museum, London, 1947. In *J Cork Hist Archaeol Soc* **52**, 184.

1948

Review: Andreas Oldeberg, *Metallteknik under forhistorisk tid*, Lund, 1942-43. In *J Cork Hist Archaeol Soc* **53**, 72.

1949

'An example of a passage grave from Co. Cork', *J Cork Hist Archaeol Soc* **54**, 8-10.

Review: G.W. Beard and A.R. Billington, *English Abbeys*, Worcester Press, Worcester, 1949. In *J Cork Hist Archaeol Soc* **54**, 103-04.

'Two burials at Labbamolaga, Co. Cork', *J Cork Hist Archaeol Soc* **55**, 15-20.

'An amber necklace from Co. Cork', *J Cork Hist Archaeol Soc* **55**, 96-97.

'The Honan Chapel Cork', *The Furrow* **I**, 290-96.

'Ringforts and housetypes in the South of Ireland' *Actes III Congrès Internat Sci Prehist Protohist*, 317-21, Zürich.

'Obituary: P.J. O'Shea, Fermoy', *J Cork Hist Archaeol Soc* **55**, 127-28.

Review: R.A.S. Macalister, *Archaeology of Ireland*, 2nd ed., Methuen, London, 1949. In *J Cork Hist Archaeol Soc* **55**, 68.

Review: Ferdinand Windels, *The Lascaux cave paintings,* Faber and Faber, London, 1950.

In *J Cork Hist Archaeol Soc* 55, 69-70.

Review: J.C. Coleman, *Journeys into Muskerry*, Tempest, Dundalk, 1950. In *J Cork Hist Archaeol Soc* 55, 129.

1951

'Some soil problems in archaeological excavation' [with notes by S. Graham Brade-Birks, and F.J. North], *J Cork Hist Archaeol Soc* 56, 29-44.

'An early Bronze Age ringfort at Carrigillihy, Co. Cork', *J Cork Hist Archaeol Soc* 56, 69-86.

'Our ancient monuments', *The Furrow* 2, 596-602.

1952

'Excavation of a cairn at Moneen, Co. Cork' [with notes by M.A. MacConaill and P. O'Connor], *Proc Roy Ir Acad C* 54, 121-59. .

'St Gobnet's House, Ballyvourney, Co. Cork', *J Cork Hist Archaeol Soc* 57, 18-40 (reprinted: O'Kelly, M.J., Henry, Françoise, Ó hEaluighthe, D., *Gobnait Naomhtha Bhaile Mhuirne — St Gobnet of Ballyvourney,* Ballyvourney, 1978).

'Three promontory forts in Co. Cork' [with notes by P. O'Connor, W.A. Stelfox, G. Roche, G.A. Hayes-McCoy and J.T. Collins], *Proc Roy Ir Acad C* 55, 25-59.

1953

Review: S.P. Ó Ríordáin, *Antiquities of the Irish Countryside*, 3rd ed., Methuen, London. In *J Cork Hist Archaeol Soc* 58, 99.

'Cashel — ruined or restored?', *The Furrow* 4, 17-21.

1954

'Ancient Irish method of cooking meat', *Actes IV Congrès Internat Sci Prehist Protohist,* 615-18. Madrid.

'Excavations and experiments in ancient Irish cooking places', *J Roy Soc Antiq Ir* 84, 105-55.

(With Séamus Kavanagh) 'A new Ogham stone from Co. Kerry', *J Cork Hist Archaeol Soc* 59, 50-53.

(With Séamus Kavanagh) 'An Ogham inscribed cross slab from Co. Kerry', *J Cork Hist Archaeol Soc* 59, 101-10.

1955

'A shell midden at Carrigtohill, Co. Cork', *J Cork Hist Archaeol Soc* 60, 28-32.

'A long cist grave at Hoddersfield, Co. Cork' [with a note by M.A. MacConaill], *J Cork Hist Archaeol Soc* 60, 95-96.

Review: H.G. Leask, *Irish churches and monastic buildings* I, Tempest, Dundalk, 1955. In *J Cork Hist Archaeol Soc* 60, 135-36.

1956

'An island settlement at Beginish, Co. Kerry' [with notes by Séamus Kavanagh, M.A. MacConaill, J.P. Scannell and G. Roche], *Proc Roy Ir Acad C* 57, 159-94.

1957

'Obituary: Seán P. Ó Ríordáin', *J Roy Soc Antiq Ir* 87, 89-90.

Review: H.H. Coghlan, *Notes on prehistoric and early iron in the Old World,* Oxford University Press, London, 1956. In *J Cork Hist Archaeol Soc* 62, 59.

1958

'Church Island near Valencia, Co. Kerry' [with notes by M.A. MacConaill, G. Roche, J.P. Scannell, A.S. Henshall, British Leather Manufacturers' Research Association], *Proc Roy Ir Acad C* 59, 57-136.

'A new group of rock scribings in Co. Kerry', *J Cork Hist Archaeol Soc* 63, 1-4.

'A horned cairn at Shanballyedmond, Co. Tipperary', *J Cork Hist Archaeol Soc* 63, 37-72.

'A court cairn at Shanballyedmond, Co. Tipperary', *N Munster Antiq J* 8, 34-37.

'The ancient method of smelting iron', *Bericht V Internat Kongress Vor- u. Frühgeschichte,* 459-61. Hamburg.

'A wedge-shaped gallery grave at Island, Co. Cork' [with notes by M.A. MacConaill], *J Roy Soc Antiq Ir* 88, 1-23.

Review: Helen M. Roe, *The High Crosses of Western Ossory,* Kilkenny Archaeol Soc, Kilkenny, 1958. In *J Cork Hist Archaeol Soc* 63, 131.

Review: H.G. Leask, *Irish churches and monastic buildings* II, Tempest, Dundalk, 1958. In *J Cork Hist Archaeol Soc* 63, 132-33.

Review: S.J. de Laet, *Archaeology and its problems,* Phoenix, London, 1957. In *J Cork Hist Archaeol Soc* 63, 133.

1959

'A wedge gallery grave at Baurnadomeeny, Co. Tipperary', *N Munster Antiq J* 8, 62-63.

Review: Helen M. Roe, *High Crosses of Kells,* Meath Archaeol Hist Soc, 1959. In *J Cork Hist Archaeol Soc* 64, 137-38.

1960

'A wedge-shaped gallery grave at Baurnadomeeny, Co. Tipperary' [with a note by M.A. MacConaill], *J Cork Hist Archaeol Soc* 65, 85-115.

1961

'The Cork horns, the Petrie crown and the Bann disk: the technique of their ornamentation' [with a note by E.M. Jope], *J Cork Hist Archaeol Soc* 66, 1-12.

'A stone bowl of Viking type from Beginish Island, Co. Kerry', *J Roy Soc Antiq Ir* 91, 64-68.

'An urn burial at Ballagharea, Co. Cork' [with notes by T.F. Murphy and M.A. MacConaill], *J Cork Hist Archaeol Soc* 66, 130-35.

'A wooden bridge over the Cashen river, Co. Kerry', *J Roy Soc Antiq Ir* 91, 135-52.

'Introduction' to: Conchubhar Ó Cuilleanáin and T.F. Murphy, 'A ring fort at Old Court, Co. Cork', *J Cork Hist Archaeol Soc* 66, 79.

Review: H.G. Leask, *Irish churches and monastic buildings* III, Tempest, Dundalk, 1960. In *J Cork Hist Archaeol Soc* 66, 78.

1962

'Béal Boru, Co. Clare' [with notes by Geraldine Roche and R.H.M. Dolley], *Proc Roy Ir Acad C* 63, 17-125.

'Two ring-forts at Garryduff, Co. Cork' [with a note by A.W. Stelfox], *Proc Roy Ir Acad C* 63, 17-125.

1964

'Newgrange, Co. Meath', *Antiquity* 38, 288-90.

Review: P.A. Jewel (ed), *The experimental earthwork on Overton Down*, British Association for the Advancement of Science, London, 1963. In *Antiquity* 38, 150-51.

Review: Alena Rybora and Bohumil Soudsky, *Libence: a Celtic sanctuary in Central Bohemia*, Czechoslovak Academy of Sciences, Prague, 1962. In *J Cork Hist Archaeol Soc* 69, 65-67.

Review: Máire Mac Néill, *The festival of Lughnasa*, Oxford University Press, London, 1962. In *J Cork Hist Archaeol Soc* 69, 67.

1965

'The belt shrine from Moylough, Sligo' [with a note by J.S. Jackson], *J Roy Soc Antiq Ir* 95, 149-88.

Review: Seán P. Ó Ríordáin and Glyn Daniel, *Newgrange and the Bend of the Boyne* (Ancient Peoples and Places 40), Thames and Hudson, London, 1964. In *Antiquity* 35, 147-48.

1966

'New discoveries at Newgrange passage-grave in Ireland', *Acta Musei Nationalis Pragae* 20, 95-98.

'Newgrange excavations, Co. Meath', *Oibre* 4, 7-9.

(With Elizabeth Shee) 'A clothed burial from Emlagh, near Dingle, Co. Kerry' [with notes from British Leather Manufacturers' Association, J.S. Jackson, M.A. MacConaill, P. O'Connor and M.L. Ryder], *J Cork Hist Archaeol Soc* 71, 81-91.

The Honan Chapel Cork, 3rd ed., Cork University Press, Cork.

'Obituary: P.J. Hartnett', *J Cork Hist Archaeol Soc* 71, 164.

(With Frances Lynch) 'Newgrange, Site C and Site L: interim report', *Royal Irish Academy Annual Report 1965-66*, 38-40.

Review: R. De Valera and S. Ó Nualláin, *Survey of the megalithic tombs of Ireland* II, Co. Mayo, Stationery Office, Dublin, 1964. In *J Cork Hist Archaeol Soc* 71, 166-67.

Review: Isobel Smith (ed), *Windmill Hill and Avebury: excavations by Alexander Keiller, 1925-1939,* Clarendon Press, Oxford, 1965. In *Antiquity* 40, 72-73.

1967

'Knockea, Co. Limerick' [with notes by G.F. Mitchell, G. Roche, and J.P. Scannell]. *In* Etienne Rynne (ed), *North Munster Studies: essays in commemoration of Monsignor Michael Moloney,* 72-101. Thomond Archaeol Soc, Limerick.

'Two examples of megalithic art from Newgrange', *J Roy Soc Antiq Ir* 97, 45-46.

(With Frances Lynch) 'Newgrange and Site L: interim report', *Royal Irish Academy Annual Report, 1966-1967,* 24-25.

1968

'Excavations at Newgrange, Co. Meath, Ireland', *Antiquity* 42, 40-42.

'Newgrange and Site K: interim report', *Royal Irish Academy Annual Report, 1967-1968,* 23-25.

'Surface-collected flints from two sites in the Boyne Valley, Co. Meath', *J Cork Hist Archaeol Soc* 73, 114-19.

'The Bronze Age'. *In* Victor Mealy *et al* (ed), *Encyclopaedia of Ireland,* 69-72. Allen Figgis, Dublin.

(With Elizabeth Shee) 'Three souterrains in Co. Cork, one with Ogham stones at Underhill, another at Carrignagroghers and part of a souterrain at Lyre', *J Cork Hist Archaeol Soc* 73, 40-47.

(With Ailve O'Connell) 'An urn burial at Castlerichard, Co. Cork' [with a note by M.A. MacConaill], *J Cork Hist Archaeol Soc* 73, 48-51.

'Earliest Irish art', *Irish Independent,* 7 May.

1969

'Radiocarbon dates for the Newgrange passage-grave, Co. Meath', *Antiquity* 43, 140-41.

'Newgrange: an interim report', *Royal Irish Academy Annual Report, 1968-1969,* 20-21.

'A stone mould for axeheads from Doonour, Bantry, Co. Cork', *J Roy Soc Antiq Ir* 99, 117-24.

1970

'Newgrange passage-grave, Ireland: the mural art', *Actes VII Congrès Internat Sci Prehist Protohist,* 534-36. Prague.

'Problems of Irish ringforts'. *In* Donald Moore (ed), *The Irish Sea province in archaeology and history,* 50-54. Cambrian Archaeol Soc, Cardiff.

'Wooden water mains at South Terrace, Cork', *J Cork Hist Archaeol Soc* 75, 125-28.

'Newgrange excavations: interim report', *Royal Irish Academy Annual Report, 1969-1970,* 23-25.

Review: E.R. Norman and J.K. St Jospeh, *The early development of Irish society: the evidence of aerial photography,* Cambridge University Press, Cambridge, 1969. In *Antiquity* **45**, 159-60.

Review: L.N.W. Flanagan, *Ulster,* Heinemann, London, 1970. In *J Cork Hist Archaeol Soc* **75**, 165-66.

1971

'Newgrange excavations: interim report', *Royal Irish Academy Annual Report, 1970-1971,* 37-40.

(With Elizabeth Shee) 'The Derrynablaha "shield" again', *J Cork Hist Archaeol Soc* **76**, 72-76.

1972

'Excavations of two ringforts at Lisduggan North, Co. Cork', *J Cork Hist Archaeol Soc* **77**, 105-07.

'Further radio-carbon dates from Newgrange, Co. Meath, Ireland', *Antiquity* **46**, 226-27.

1973

'Current excavations at Newgrange'. *In* Glyn Daniel and P. Kjaetum (ed), *Megalithic graves and ritual,* 137-46. Moesgård (= Jutland Archaeol Soc Publ 11).

'Monastic sites in the west of Ireland', *Scot Archaeol Forum* **5**, 1-16.

(With Elizabeth Shee) 'A Gallego Atlantic rock-art motif', *Cuadernos de Estudios Gallegos* **28**, 103-10.

Review: Charles Thomas (ed), *The Iron Age in the Irish Sea province* (Counc Brit Archaeol Res Rep 9), 1972. In *J Cork Hist Archaeol Soc* **78**, 160-62.

1974

(With Elizabeth Shee) 'Bronze Age burials at Coolnahane and Ballinvoher, Co. Cork', *J Cork Hist Archaeol Soc* **79**, 71-85.

Review: Philip Rahtz (ed), *Rescue archaeology,* Penguin, Harmondsworth, 1974. In *J Cork Hist Archaeol Soc* **80**, 138.

Review: Mary Carbery, *The farm by Lough Gur,* Mercier, Cork (reprint of 1937 ed.). In *J Cork Hist Archaeol Soc* **80**, 140.

1975

Archaeological field guide to Lough Gur, Co. Limerick. Hickey, Kimallock, Co. Limerick.

(With Ann Lynch and Mary Cahill) *Archaeological survey and excavations of St Vogue's church, enclosure and other monuments at Carnsore, Co. Wexford.* Electricity Supply Board Publications, Dublin.

'Obituary: Dr E.F. Fahy', *J Cork Hist Archaeol Soc* **81**, 44.

'Plough pebbles from the Boyne'. *In* Caoimhín Ó Danachair (ed), *Folk and farm: essays in honour of A.T. Lucas,* 165-75. Roy Soc Antiq Ir, Dublin.

'Some thoughts on the megalithic tombs of Ireland'. *In* J.V.S. Megaw (ed), *To illustrate the monuments: essays on archaeology presented to Stuart Piggott*, 126-33. Thames and Hudson, London.

'Newgrange excavations, Co. Meath', *Oibre* 12, 9-11.

Review: Peter Harbison, *The archaeology of Ireland,* Bodley Head, London, 1978. In *J Cork Hist Archaeol Soc* 81, 136.

1977

'The excavation of St Vogue's well and dolmen at Carnsore, Co. Wexford', *J Old Wexford Soc* 6, 55-60.

Review: Frank Mitchell, *The Irish landscape*, Collins, London, 1976. In *J Cork Hist Archaeol Soc* 82, 52-54.

1978

[Introduction to] 'Dunboy Castle, Co. Cork. Excavated by the late Dr E.M. Fahy' (Report compiled by Margaret Gowen), *J Cork Hist Archaeol Soc* 83, 1.

Review: D.W. Harding, *Hillforts: later prehistoric earthworks in Great Britain and Ireland,* Academic Press, London, 1976. In *J Cork Hist Archaeol Soc* 83, 85.

(With Frances Lynch and Claire O'Kelly) 'Three passage graves at Newgrange, Co. Meath', *Proc Roy Ir Acad C* 78, 249-352.

1979

(With C.A. Shell) 'Stone objects and a bronze axe from Newgrange, Co. Meath'. In M.F. Ryan (ed), *The origins of metallurgy in Atlantic Europe: proceedings of the Fifth Atlantic Colloquium, Dublin, 1978*, 127-44. National Museum, Dublin.

(With Claire O'Kelly) *Illustrated guide to Lough Gur.* O'Kelly, Blackrock, Cork.

'The restoration of Newgrange', *Antiquity* 53, 205-10.

1981

'Irish megalithic tombs'. *In* Colin Renfrew (ed), *Antiquity and man: essays in honour of Glyn Daniel.* London.

(In the press) *Newgrange, Co. Meath.* Thames and Hudson, London.

Professor O'Kelly was honorary editor of the *Journal of the Cork Historical and Archaeological Society* from 1947 to 1967 and again in 1980.

ACKNOWLEDGMENTS

I gratefully acknowledge the assistance I have received from the following: National Library of Wales, Aberystwyth; Mr D.G. Grogan, Department of Bibliographical Studies, College of Librarianship Wales, Aberystwyth; the Editor; Cathryn Power, Department of Archaeology, University College Cork; Marjory Sliney and Frank Davis.

The Contributors

E. Estyn Evans	Emeritus Professor of Geography, Queen's University, Belfast.
M.G.L. Baillie	Lecturer in Archaeology, Queen's University, Belfast.
Ann Lynch	Albert Egges Van Giffen Instituut voor Prae- en Protohistorie, University of Amsterdam.
B.G. Scott	Senior Conservation Officer, Joint Conservation Laboratory, Ulster Museum/Queen's University, Belfast.
P.J. Francis	Conservation Officer, Joint Conservation Laboratory, Ulster Museum/Queen's University, Belfast.
Laurence N.W. Flanagan	Keeper of Antiquities, Ulster Museum, Belfast.
Richard Warner	Assistant Keeper of Antiquities, Ulster Museum, Belfast.
I.G. Meighan	Lecturer in Geochemistry, Queen's University, Belfast.
Eamonn P. Kelly	Assistant Keeper of Irish Antiquities, National Museum, Dublin.
Louise H. van Wijngaarden-Bakker	Albert Egges Van Giffen Instituut voor Prae- en Protohistorie, University of Amsterdam.
Joseph Raftery	Former Director of the National Museum, Dublin.
Peter C. Woodman	Assistant Keeper, Dept. of Antiquities, Ulster Museum, Belfast.
A.E.P. Collins	Formerly of Historic Monuments and Buildings Branch, Dept of the Environment, Northern Ireland.
Michael Ryan	Keeper of Irish Antiquities, National Museum, Dublin.
George Eogan	Professor of Archaeology, University College, Dublin.
John Waddell	Lecturer in Archaeology, University College, Galway.
Barry Raftery	Lecturer in Archaeology, University College, Dublin.
Séamus Caulfield	Lecturer in Archaeology, University College, Dublin.
M.A. Monk	Lecturer in Archaeology, University College, Cork.
Peter Harbison	Archaeologist, Bórd Fáilte, Dublin.
Thomas Fanning	Lecturer in Archaeology, University College, Galway.
Patrick F. Wallace	Assistant Keeper, National Museum, Dublin.
Raghnall Ó Floinn	Assistant, National Museum, Dublin.
Mary Cahill	Assistant, National Museum, Dublin.
W. Groenman-van Waateringe	Albert Egges Van Giffen Instituut voor Prae- en Protohistorie, University of Amsterdam.
Pádraig Ó Riain	Professor of Old and Middle Irish, University College, Cork.
Aidan Macdonald	Lecturer in Archaeology, University College, Cork.
Patrick O'Flanagan	Lecturer in Geography, University College, Cork.
Donnchadh Ó Corráin	Associate Professor of Irish History, University College, Cork.
Helen Moloney-Davis	Library Assistant, University College, Cork.

PLATES

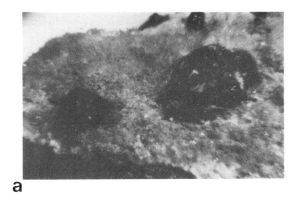

Pl I: X-radiographs of native copper specimens in their zeolite matrices (actual size): (A) massive copper — sample (1); (B) crystalline aggregate.

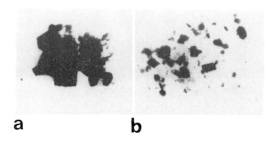

Pl II: Crystalline native copper: (A) natural; (B) after cleaning (x3).

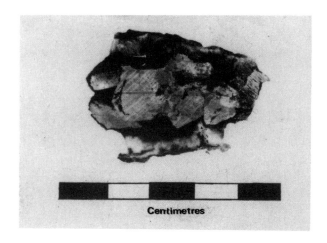

Pl III: Polished section through sample (1): note regular crystal faces.

Pl IV: Flint arrowheads from the 'clay-with-flints' horizon showing characteristic stainings: the small
arrowhead in the centre is the modern native copper example (all x1).

Pl V: View of inner ditch (zone 1) showing distribution of buttercups.

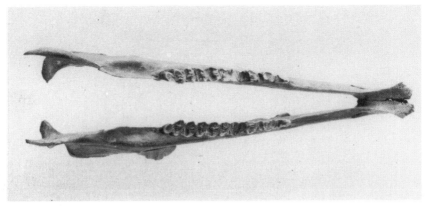

a

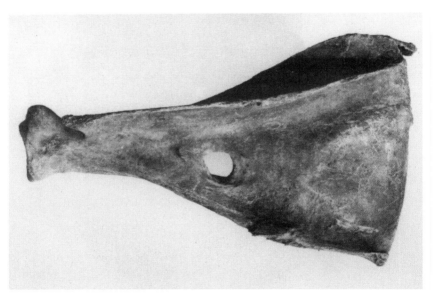

b

Pl VI: a Mandibula, scale 1:3
b Left scapula with healed injury, scale 2:5

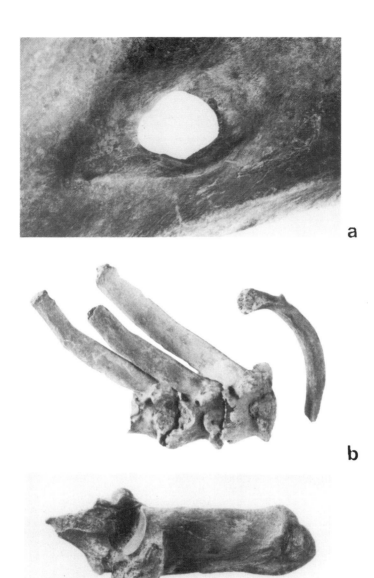

a

b

c

Pl VII: a Detail of healed injury, scale 1:1
b Spondylosis in thoracic vertebrae, scale 2:5
c Left calcaneum, scale 2:3

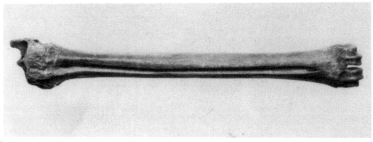

a

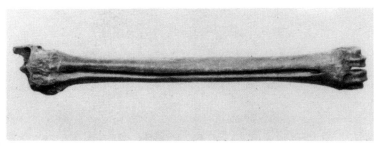

b

Pl VIII: a Left metatarsal (dorsal view) with ankylosis of the tarsal joint. Scale 1:3
         b Left metatarsal (planter view) with ankylosis of the tarsal joint. Scale 1:3

Pl IX: Disc no. 1, Enniscorthy. Diameter 117 mm. Front (top) and back (bottom) views.
(Photo. M.M.A., New York.)

Pl X: Disc no. 2, Enniscorthy. Diameter 121-24 mm. Front (top) and back (bottom) views.
(Photo. N.M.I.)

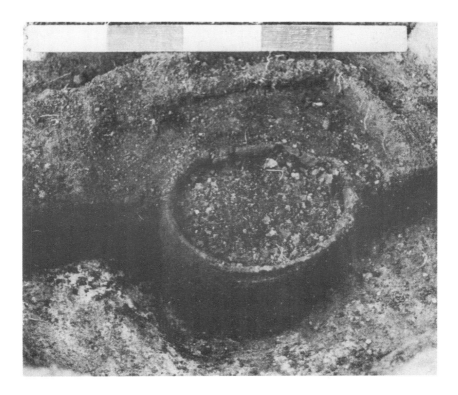

Pl XI.

Pl XII: The Moylough Belt Shrine, one side of the buckle.
(Photograph: Bórd Fáilte).

Pl XIII: The Moylough Belt Shrine, the other side of the buckle.
(Photograph: Bórd Fáilte).

Pl XIV: *Top.* The Moylough Belt Shrine, one of the cross-shaped medallions. (Photograph: National Museum of Ireland).
Bottom left. The Dagulf Psalter, fo. 67ᵛᵒ, written between 783 and 795, Austrian National Library, Codex 1861 (reproduced by permission of the pictorial archive of the Austrian National Library).
Bottom right. The Ekerö Erozier (Photograph: Swedish National Museum, Stockholm).

Pl XV: *Top.* Two D-shaped objects in the Museum of National Antiquities, St Germain-en-Leye. (Photograph: National Museum of Ireland).
Bottom. The Adelhausen portable altar, detail of one of the ends. (Photograph: Bildverlag, Freiburg, reproduced by kind permission of the Augustiner Museum, Freiburg).

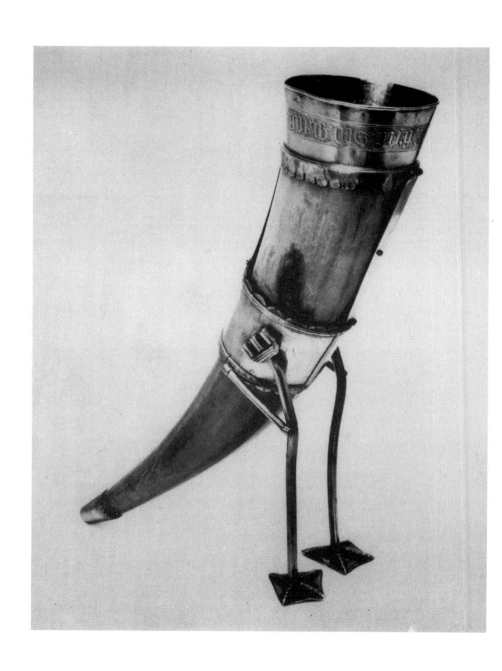

Pl XVI: The Kavanagh 'Charter' Horn.

Pl XVII: The rim mount showing the decorative scalloped band and hinged strap.

Pl XVIII: Pietà. Cloran Old, Co. Tipperary.